Fodor's

NINTH
New
EDITION

Singapore

"When it comes to information on regional history, what to see and do, and shopping, these guides are exhaustive."

—*USAir Magazine*

"Usable, sophisticated restaurant coverage, with an emphasis on good value."

—Andy Birsh, *Gourmet Magazine* columnist

"Valuable because of their comprehensiveness."

—*Minneapolis Star-Tribune*

"Fodor's always delivers high quality...thoughtfully presented...thorough."

—*Houston Post*

"An excellent choice for those who want everything under one cover."

—*Washington Post*

Fodor's Travel Publications, Inc.
New York • Toronto • London • Sydney • Auckland
http://www.fodors.com/

Fodor's Singapore

Editor: Deborah Field Washburn

Editorial Contributors: Audra Epstein, Nigel Fisher, Christine Hill, Wendy Hutton, Tracy Patruno, Caragh Rockwood, Ilsa Sharp

Gold Guide Contributors: Steven Amsterdam, Robert Andrews, David Brown, Audra Epstein, Heidi Sarna, Helayne Schiff, Mary Ellen Schultz, M. T. Schwartzman (editor), Dinah Spritzer

Creative Director: Fabrizio La Rocca

Associate Art Director: Guido Caroti

Photo Researcher: Jolie Novak

Cartographer: David Lindroth

Cover Photograph: Bob Krist

Text Design: Between the Covers

Copyright

Ninth Edition

ISBN 0–679–03283–5

"A Nation of Contradictions" is excerpted from *The Lands of Charm and Cruelty* by Stan Sesser. Copyright © 1993 by Stan Sesser. Reprinted by permission of Alfred A. Knopf, Inc.

Special Sales

Fodor's Travel Publications are available at special discounts for bulk purchases for sales promotions or premiums. Special editions, including personalized covers, excerpts of existing guides, and corporate imprints, can be created in large quantities for special needs. For more information contact your local bookseller or write to Special Markets, Fodor's Travel Publications, 201 East 50th Street, New York, NY 10022. Inquiries from Canada should be directed to your local Canadian bookseller or sent to Random House of Canada, Ltd., Marketing Department, 1265 Aerowood Drive, Mississauga, Ontario L4W 1B9. Inquiries from the United Kingdom should be sent to Fodor's Travel Publications, 20 Vauxhall Bridge Road, London SW1V 2SA, England.

PRINTED IN THE UNITED STATES OF AMERICA

10 9 8 7 6 5 4 3 2 1

III

CONTENTS

ON THE ROAD WITH FODOR'S

WE'RE ALWAYS THRILLED to get letters from readers, especially one like this:

It took us an hour to decide what book to buy and we now know we picked the best one. Your book was wonderful, easy to follow, very accurate, and good on pointing out eating places, informal as well as formal. When we saw other people using your book, we would look at each other and smile.

Our editors and writers are deeply committed to making every Fodor's guide "the best one"—not only accurate but always charming, brimming with sound recommendations and solid ideas, right on the mark in describing restaurants and hotels, and full of fascinating facts that make you view what you've traveled to see in a rich new light.

About Our Writers

Our success in achieving our goals—and in helping to make your trip the best of all possible vacations—is a credit to the hard work of our extraordinary writers.

Christine Hill grew up in the United States and has lived in Asia for seven years. She writes for *Institutional Investor* and *Business Week,* among other publications. Currently based in Singapore, she is our resident expert on exploring the city-state and enjoying its opportunities for nightlife, shopping, and sports.

Nigel Fisher, who wrote and updated portions of this and earlier editions, is a British subject who has lived in Singapore and traveled every inch of Southeast Asia. Publisher of *Voyager International,* a newsletter that covers the globe, Fisher is usually on the road, trying out all variety of lodgings, finding wonderful food, and discovering what's new and notable.

Wendy Hutton, a New Zealander by birth, has worked in Southeast Asia as a writer since 1967, specializing in travel and cuisine. She has written and edited many books on Asian food, including what many people believe to be the definitive work on Singapore's culinary culture and cuisine, *Singapore Food.*

Ilsa Sharp, who wrote the new introduction to this ninth edition of *Fodor's Singapore,* is a British-born Chinese studies graduate and professional writer who has lived in Singapore since 1968. She is married to a Tamil-Indian Singaporean writer and entertainer. The author of more than half a dozen books on the history, culture, and wildlife of Singapore and the Asia-Pacific region, she freelances out of Singapore and her alternate home in Perth, Western Australia.

New This Year

This year we've reformatted our guides to make them easier to use. *Fodor's Singapore* has brand-new walking tours and a timing section that tells you exactly how long to allot for each tour. You may also notice our fresh graphics, new in 1996. More readable and more helpful than ever? We think so—and we hope you do, too.

On the Web

Also check out Fodor's Web site (http://www.fodors.com/), where you'll find travel information on major destinations around the world and an ever-changing array of travel-savvy interactive features.

How to Use This Book

Organization

Up front is the **Gold Guide.** Its first section, **Important Contacts A to Z,** gives addresses and telephone numbers of organizations and companies that offer destination-related services and detailed information and publications. **Smart Travel Tips A to Z,** the Gold Guide's second section, gives specific information on how to accomplish what you need to in Singapore as well as tips on savvy traveling. Both sections are in alphabetical order by topic.

Chapter 1 starts with a **new introduction** that conveys the dynamism of Singapore today. In constant flux but retaining its green core, the Garden Isle is a patchwork of high-rise developments, ethnic neighborhoods, and parkland. **What's Where** offers thumbnail sketches that will orient you to the diverse areas explored in Chapter 2. Favorite activities are described under the heading

Pleasures and Pastimes. Recommendations to help you use your time in Singapore to best advantage are included as **Great Itineraries.**

Chapter 2, **Exploring Singapore,** is subdivided by neighborhood; each subsection recommends a walking or driving tour and lists neighborhood sights alphabetically. Off the Beaten Path sights appear after the places from which they are most easily accessible. The remaining chapters are arranged in alphabetical order by subject: dining, lodging, nightlife and the arts, outdoor activities and sports, shopping, and side trips.

In Chapter 9, **Portraits of Singapore,** you'll find illuminating pieces on the history and peoples of Singapore, along with a wonderful essay by Stan Sesser, excerpted from his book *The Lands of Charm and Cruelty.* Suggestions for pretrip reading, both fiction and nonfiction, follow.

Icons and Symbols

★ Our special recommendations
✕ Restaurant
🏨 Lodging establishment
🐤 Good for kids (rubber duckie)
☞ Sends you to another section of the guide for more information
✉ Address
☎ Telephone number
🕐 Opening and closing times
💰 Admission prices (those we give apply only to adults; substantially reduced fees are almost always available for children, students, and senior citizens)

Numbers in white and black circles that appear on the maps, in the margins, and within the tours correspond to one another.

Credit Cards

The following abbreviations are used: **AE,** American Express; **DC,** Diners Club; **MC,** MasterCard; and **V,** Visa.

Please Write to Us

You can use this book in the confidence that all prices and opening times are based on information supplied to us at press time; Fodor's cannot accept responsibility for any errors. Time inevitably brings changes, so always confirm information when it matters—especially if you're making a detour to visit a specific place. In addition, when making reservations be sure to mention if you have a disability or are traveling with children, if you prefer a private bath or a certain type of bed, or if you have specific dietary needs or any other concerns.

Were the restaurants we recommended as described? Did our hotel picks exceed your expectations? Did you find a museum we recommended a waste of time? If you have complaints, we'll look into them and revise our entries when the facts warrant it. If you've discovered a special place that we haven't included, we'll pass the information along to our correspondents and have them check it out. So send your feedback, positive *and* negative, to the Singapore editor at Fodor's, 201 East 50th Street, New York, New York 10022—and have a wonderful trip!

Karen Cure
Editorial Director

Southeast Asia

CHINA

Guangzhou

Macao HONG
KONG

Mandalay

Hanoi

Luang
Prabang

Haiphong

HAINAN

UNION OF
MYANMAR
(BURMA)

LAOS

Vientiane

Pegu

Chiang
Mai

Yangon
(Rangoon)

Hue

Danang

THAILAND

Bangkok

VIETNAM

Andaman
Sea

Angkor Wat

CAMBODIA
(KAMPUCHEA)

Isthmus of
Kra

Phnom Penh

Ho Chi Minh City
(Saigon)

Gulf of
Thailand

South China
Sea

Songkhla

Georgetown

PENINSULAR
MALAYSIA

MALAYSIA

Bandar Seri
Begawan

BRUNEI

Medan

Kuala Lumpur

SARAWAK

Strait of Malacca

Kuching

Johore Bahru

SINGAPORE

BORNEO

KALIMANTAN

INDIAN OCEAN

SUMATRA

Jambi

Karimata Strait

KEPULAUAN

INDONESIA

Palembang

Banjarmasin

GREATER SUNDA ISLANDS

Jakarta

Java Sea

0   500 miles

Bandung

Surabaya

0   750 km

Yogyakarta

JAVA

Malang

BALI

N

Singapore Island

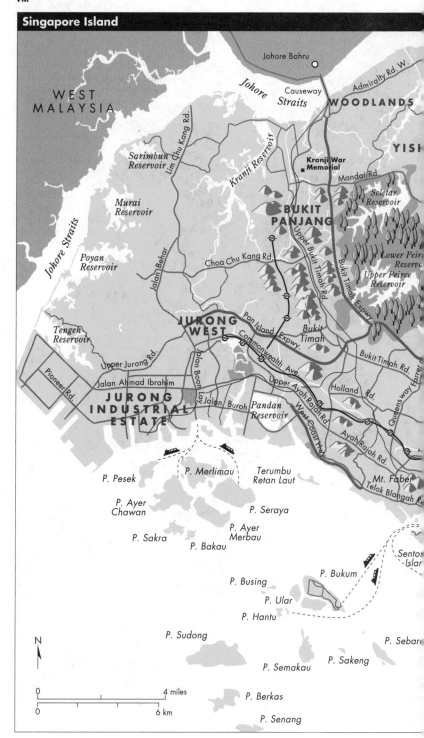

WEST
MALAYSIA

Johore Bahru

Johore Causeway
Straits

WOODLANDS

Admiralty Rd. W.

YISH

*Sarimbun
Reservoir*

Kranji War
Memorial

Mandai Rd.

*Murai
Reservoir*

Kranji Reservoir

Lim Chu Kang Rd.

BUKIT
PANJANG

*Seletar
Reservoir*

Johore Straits

*Poyan
Reservoir*

Jalan Behar

Choa Chu Kang Rd.

Upper Bukit Timah Rd.

Bukit Timah Expwy

*Lower Peirce
Reservoir*
*Upper Peirce
Reservoir*

*Tengeh
Reservoir*

JURONG
WEST

Pan Island Expwy

*Bukit
Timah*

Bukit Timah Rd.

Upper Jurong Rd.

Commonwealth Ave.

Jalan Boon Lay

Jalan Ahmad Ibrahim

Pioneer Rd.

JURONG
INDUSTRIAL
ESTATE

Jalan Buroh

*Pandan
Reservoir*

Upper Ayah Rajah Rd.

West Coast Hwy

Holland Rd.

Queensway Farrer

Ayah Rajah Rd.

Mt. Faber
Telok Blangah R

P. Pesek

P. Merlimau

Terumbu
Retan Laut

P. Ayer
Chawan

P. Seraya

P. Sakra

P. Ayer
Merbau

P. Bakau

P. Busing

P. Bukum

Sento
Islar

P. Ular

P. Hantu

N

P. Sudong

P. Sebare

P. Sakeng

P. Semakau

0   4 miles

0   6 km

P. Berkas

P. Senang

WEST
MALAYSIA

TO DESARU,
MALAYSIA

P. Seletar

Johore *Straits*

Yishun Ave. 2

S. Seletar

P. Serangoon

P. Ubin

P. Ketam

TO P.
TEKONG

Yio Chu Kang Rd.

PUNGGOL

Punggol Rd.

S. Serangoon

Serangoon Harbour

CHANGI

SERANGOON

Upper Thomson Rd.

Central Expwy

Upper Serangoon Rd.

Tampines Rd.

Loyang Ave.

U. Changi Rd.

Changi Airport

Ritchie eservoir

Paya Lebar Rd.

Pan Island Expressway

BEDOK

New Upper Changi Rd.

Airport Blvd

Changi Coast Rd.

Serangoon Rd.

Sims Ave.

Geylang Rd.

East Coast Rd.

Kallang Rd.

KATONG

Mountbatten Rd.

Orchard Rd.

Nicoll Hwy.

National Stadium

East Coast Parkway

ld Trade re Ferry inal

P. Brani

Buran Darat

P. Tekukor

P. Renggit

Kusu Island

Lazarus Island

ister's lands

St. John's Island

Strait of Singapore

Subway & Rail Lines

- - - - North-South MRT line
───── East-West MRT line
───── Railroad lines
⊖ Subway stop

x

World Time Zones

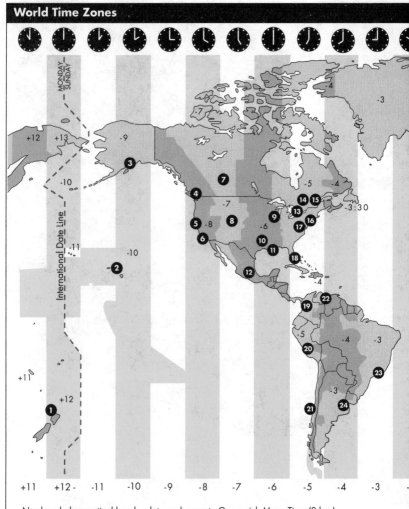

Numbers below vertical bands relate each zone to Greenwich Mean Time (0 hrs.).
Local times frequently differ from these general indications,
as indicated by light-face numbers on map.

Algiers, **29**
Anchorage, **3**
Athens, **41**
Auckland, **1**
Baghdad, **46**
Bangkok, **50**
Beijing, **54**

Berlin, **34**
Bogotá, **19**
Budapest, **37**
Buenos Aires, **24**
Caracas, **22**
Chicago, **9**
Copenhagen, **33**
Dallas, **10**

Delhi, **48**
Denver, **8**
Djakarta, **53**
Dublin, **26**
Edmonton, **7**
Hong Kong, **56**
Honolulu, **2**

Istanbul, **40**
Jerusalem, **42**
Johannesburg, **44**
Lima, **20**
Lisbon, **28**
London (Greenwich), **27**
Los Angeles, **6**
Madrid, **38**
Manila, **57**

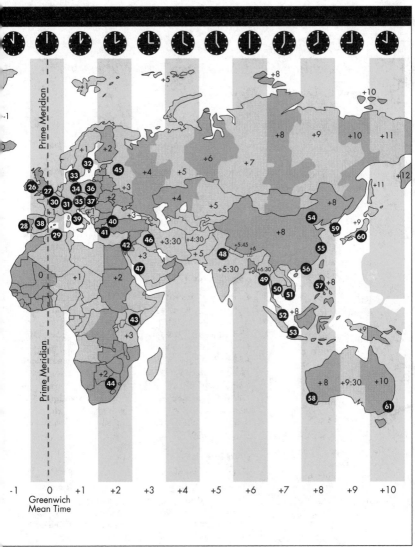

-1
0 Greenwich Mean Time
+1
+2
+3
+4
+5
+6
+7
+8
+9
+10

Mecca, **47**
Mexico City, **12**
Miami, **18**
Montréal, **15**
Moscow, **45**
Nairobi, **43**
New Orleans, **11**
New York City, **16**

Ottawa, **14**
Paris, **30**
Perth, **58**
Reykjavík, **25**
Rio de Janeiro, **23**
Rome, **39**
Saigon (Ho Chi Minh City), **51**

San Francisco, **5**
Santiago, **21**
Seoul, **59**
Shanghai, **55**
Singapore, **52**
Stockholm, **32**
Sydney, **61**
Tokyo, **60**

Toronto, **13**
Vancouver, **4**
Vienna, **35**
Warsaw, **36**
Washington, D.C., **17**
Yangon, **49**
Zürich, **31**

IMPORTANT CONTACTS A TO Z

An Alphabetical Listing of Publications, Organizations, & Companies That Will Help You Before, During, & After Your Trip

A

AIR TRAVEL

The major gateway to Singapore is **Changi International Airport** (☎ 541–9828).

FLYING TIMES

Singapore is 18 hours from Los Angeles and San Francisco, 20 hours from Chicago, and 22 hours from New York. East-coast travelers departing from New York should consider using **Finnair** via Helsinki for flights to Bangkok and Singapore, as the flying time, respectively, is 17 hours and 18 hours.

CARRIERS

Carriers serving Singapore include **Singapore Airlines** (☎ 800/742–3333), **China Airlines** (☎ 800/227–5118), **Japan Airlines** (☎ 800/525–3663), **Korean Air** (☎ 800/438–5000), **Cathay Pacific Airways** (☎ 800/233–2742 in the U.S.; 800/663–1338 in Canada), and **United Airlines** (☎ 800/241–6522).

WITHIN THE REGION

Aside from the major regional carriers (Garuda Indonesia, Malaysian Airline System, Singapore Airlines, Thai International) flying to destinations in Southeast Asia, there are smaller airlines such as **Silk Air** (✉ 6 Shenton Way, 0107 DBS Building, Tower 2, ☎ 221–2221)—a Singapore Airlines affiliate with flights from Singapore to smaller cities in China, Malaysia, Indonesia, and Thailand. Silk Air has an excellent reputation for safety, but you might want to be careful on some of the other smaller carriers.

FROM THE U.K.

Daily departures from London's Heathrow airport are scheduled aboard **British Airways** (☎ 0181/897–4000 or 0345/222–111 outside London), **Qantas** (☎ 0800/747–767 or 0345/747–767), **Singapore Airlines** (☎ 0171/439–8111), and **Thai Airways** (☎ 0171/499–9113).

COMPLAINTS

To register complaints about charter and scheduled airlines, contact the U.S. Department of Transportation's **Aviation Consumer Protection Division** (✉ C-75, Washington, DC 20590, ☎ 202/366–2220). Complaints about lost baggage or ticketing problems and safety concerns may also be logged with the **Federal Aviation Administration (FAA) Consumer Hotline** (☎ 800/322–7873).

CONSOLIDATORS

For the names of reputable air-ticket consolidators, contact the **United States Air Consolidators Association** (✉ 925 L St., Suite 220, Sacramento, CA 95814, ☎ 916/441–4166, FAX 916/441–3520). For discount air-ticketing agencies, *see* Discounts & Deals, *below.*

PUBLICATIONS

For general information about charter carriers, ask for the Department of Transportation's free brochure **"Plane Talk: Public Charter Flights"** (✉ Aviation Consumer Protection Division, C-75, Washington, DC 20590, ☎ 202/366–2220). The Department of Transportation also publishes a 58-page booklet, **"Fly Rights,"** available from the Consumer Information Center (✉ Supt. of Documents, Dept. 136C, Pueblo, CO 81009; $1.75). For other tips and hints, consult the Consumers Union's monthly **"Consumer Reports Travel Letter"** (✉ Box 53629, Boulder, CO 80322, ☎ 800/234–1970; $39 1st year).

B

BETTER BUSINESS BUREAU

For local contacts in the hometown of a tour operator you may be considering, consult the **Council of Better Business Bureaus** (✉ 4200 Wilson Blvd., Suite 800, Arlington, VA 22203, ☎ 703/276–0100, FAX 703/525–8277).

BUS TRAVEL

For all information on bus travel within Singapore, contact the **Singapore Bus Service Passenger Relations Center** (☎ 287–2727). For buses to Malaysia, contact **Singapore-Johore Bahru Express** (☎ 292–8149).

C

CAR RENTAL

The major car-rental companies represented in Singapore are **Avis** (☎ 800/331–1084; in Canada, 800/879–2847), **Budget** (☎ 800/527–0700; in the U.K., 0800/181181), **Hertz** (☎ 800/654–3001; in Canada, 800/263–0600; in the U.K., 0345/555888), and **National InterRent** (sometimes known as Europcar InterRent outside North America; ☎ 800/227–3876; in the U.K., 01345/222–525). Rates in Singapore begin at US$91 a day and US$548 a week for an economy car with unlimited mileage. This does not include tax on car rentals, which is 3%.

LOCAL AGENCIES

Should you want to look up firms in the Singapore Yellow Pages, check under "Motorcar Renting and Leasing." The following are some local branches of international agencies: **Avis** (✉ Changi Airport, ☎ 542–8833; ✉ Boulevard Hotel, ☎ 737–1668), **Hertz** (✉ Changi Airport, ☎ 542–5300; ✉ Tanglin Shopping Centre, Tanglin Rd., ☎ 734–4646; ✉ 280 Kampong Arang Rd., 447–3388), **National**

(✉ 73 Bukit Timah Rd., ☎ 338–8444), **Sintat** (✉ Changi Airport, ☎ 542–7288).

For reservations in Malaysia from Singapore, call the following Singaporean numbers: **Avis** (International Reservations ☎ 800/737–9477); **Hertz** (International Reservations ☎ 800/839–3388); and **National** (International Booking, ☎ 800/223–0144).

CHILDREN & TRAVEL

FLYING

Look into **"Flying with Baby"** (✉ Third Street Press, Box 261250, Littleton, CO 80163, ☎ 303/595–5959; $4.95 includes shipping), cowritten by a flight attendant. **"Kids and Teens in Flight,"** free from the U.S. Department of Transportation's Aviation Consumer Protection Division (✉ C-75, Washington, DC 20590, ☎ 202/366–2220), offers tips on children flying alone. Every two years the February issue of *Family Travel Times* (☞ Know-How, *below*) details children's services on three dozen airlines. **"Flying Alone, Handy Advice for Kids Traveling Solo"** is available free from the American Automobile Association (AAA; send SASE: ✉ Flying Alone, Mail Stop 800, 1000 AAA Dr., Heathrow, FL 32746).

KNOW-HOW

Family Travel Times, published quarterly by Travel with Your Children (✉ TWYCH, 40 5th Ave., New York,

NY 10011, ☎ 212/477–5524; $40 per year), covers destinations, types of vacations, and modes of travel.

CRUISES

For information on cruise ships to the island, phone Chan Brother Travel (✉ 150 South Bridge Rd., Fook Hai Building #01-09, ☎ 535–5333) or Centre Wind Travel (✉ People's Park Complex #03-28, ☎ 538–8082).

CUSTOMS

IN THE U.S.

The **U.S. Customs Service** (✉ Box 7407, Washington, DC 20044, ☎ 202/927–6724) can answer questions on duty-free limits and publishes a helpful brochure, "Know Before You Go." For information on registering foreign-made articles, call 202/927–0540 or write U.S. Customs Service (✉ Resource Management, 1301 Constitution Ave. NW, Washington DC, 20229).

COMPLAINTS➤ Note the inspector's badge number and write to the commissioner's office (✉ 1301 Constitution Ave. NW, Washington, DC 20229).

CANADIANS

Contact **Revenue Canada** (✉ 2265 St. Laurent Blvd. S, Ottawa, Ontario K1G 4K3, ☎ 613/993–0534) for a copy of the free brochure **"I Declare/ Je Déclare"** and for details on duty-free limits. For recorded information (within Canada only), call 800/461–9999.

U.K. CITIZENS

HM Customs and Excise (⊠ Dorset House, Stamford St., London SE1 9NG, ☎ 0171/ 202–4227) can answer questions about U.K. customs regulations and publishes a free pamphlet, **"A Guide for Travellers,"** detailing standard procedures and import rules.

D
DISABILITIES & ACCESSIBILITY

COMPLAINTS

To register complaints under the provisions of the Americans with Disabilities Act, contact the U.S. Department of Justice's **Disability Rights Section** (⊠ Box 66738, Washington, DC 20035, ☎ 202/514–0301 or 800/514–0301, FAX 202/ 307–1198, TTY 202/ 514–0383 or 800/514– 0383). For airline-related problems, contact the U.S. Department of Transportation's **Aviation Consumer Protection Division** (☞ Air Travel, *above*). For complaints about surface transportation, contact the Department of Transportation's **Civil Rights Office** (⊠ 400 7th St., SW, Room 10215, Washington, DC 20590 ☎ 202/366–4648).

LOCAL INFORMATION

For more information, contact the **Singapore Council of Social Services** for a copy of **"Access Singapore"** (⊠ 11 Penang Lane, ☎ 336– 1544 or 331–5417).

ORGANIZATIONS

TRAVELERS WITH HEAR-ING IMPAIRMENTS➤ The **American Academy of**

Otolaryngology (⊠ 1 Prince St., Alexandria, VA 22314, ☎ 703/ 836–4444, FAX 703/ 683–5100, TTY 703/519–1585) publishes a brochure, "Travel Tips for Hearing Impaired People."

TRAVELERS WITH MOBIL-ITY PROBLEMS➤ Contact **Mobility International USA** (⊠ Box 10767, Eugene, OR 97440, ☎ and TTY 541/343– 1284, FAX 541/343– 6812), the U.S. branch of a Belgium-based organization (☞ *below*) with affiliates in 30 countries; **MossRehab Hospital Travel Information Service** (☎ 215/ 456–9600, TTY 215/ 456–9602), a telephone information resource for travelers with physical disabilities; the **Society for the Advancement of Travel for the Handicapped** (⊠ 347 5th Ave., Suite 610, New York, NY 10016, ☎ 212/447–7284, FAX 212/725–8253; membership $45); and **Travelin' Talk** (⊠ Box 3534, Clarksville, TN 37043, ☎ 615/552– 6670, FAX 615/552– 1182), which provides local contacts worldwide for travelers with disabilities.

TRAVELERS WITH VISION IMPAIRMENTS➤ Contact the **American Council of the Blind** (⊠ 1155 15th St. NW, Suite 720, Washington, DC 20005, ☎ 202/467– 5081, FAX 202/467– 5085) for a list of travelers' resources or the **American Foundation for the Blind** (⊠ 11 Penn Plaza, Suite 300, New York, NY 10001, ☎ 212/502–7600 or 800/232–5463, TTY

212/502–7662), which provides general advice and publishes "Access to Art" ($19.95), a directory of museums that accommodate travelers with vision impairments.

IN THE U.K.

Contact the **Royal Association for Disability and Rehabilitation** (RADAR; ⊠ 12 City Forum, 250 City Rd., London EC1V 8AF, ☎ 0171/250–3222) or **Mobility International** (⊠ rue de Manchester 25, B-1080 Brussels, Belgium, ☎ 00–322– 410–6297, FAX 00– 322–410–6874), an international travel-information clearinghouse for people with disabilities.

PUBLICATIONS

Several publications for travelers with disabilities are available from the **Consumer Information Center** (⊠ Box 100, Pueblo, CO 81009, ☎ 719/948–3334). Call or write for its free catalog of current titles. The Society for the Advancement of Travel for the Handicapped (☞ Organizations, *above*) publishes the quarterly magazine **"Access to Travel"** ($13 for 1-year subscription).

The 500-page **Travelin' Talk Directory** (⊠ Box 3534, Clarksville, TN 37043, ☎ 615/552– 6670, FAX 615/552– 1182; $35) lists people and organizations who help travelers with disabilities. For travel agents worldwide, consult the **Directory of Travel Agencies for the Disabled** (⊠ Twin Peaks Press, Box 129, Vancouver, WA 98666, ☎

360/694–2462 or 800/637–2256, FAX 360/696–3210; $19.95 plus $3 shipping).

TRAVEL AGENCIES, TOUR OPERATORS

The Americans with Disabilities Act requires that all travel firms serve the needs of all travelers. That said, you should note that some agencies and operators specialize in making travel arrangements for individuals and groups with disabilities, among them **Access Adventures** (⊠ 206 Chestnut Ridge Rd., Rochester, NY 14624, ☎ 716/889–9096), run by a former physical-rehab counselor.

TRAVELERS WITH MOBILITY PROBLEMS➤ Contact **Hinsdale Travel Service** (⊠ 201 E. Ogden Ave., Suite 100, Hinsdale, IL 60521, ☎ 630/325–1335), a travel agency that benefits from the advice of wheelchair traveler Janice Perkins, and **Wheelchair Journeys** (⊠ 16979 Redmond Way, Redmond, WA 98052, ☎ 206/885–2210 or 800/313–4751), which can handle arrangements worldwide.

TRAVELERS WITH DEVELOPMENTAL DISABILITIES➤ Contact the nonprofit **New Directions** (⊠ 5276 Hollister Ave., Suite 207, Santa Barbara, CA 93111, ☎ 805/967–2841).

TRAVEL GEAR

The **Magellan's** catalog (☎ 800/962–4943, FAX 805/568–5406) includes a section devoted to products designed for travelers with disabilities.

AIRFARES

For the lowest airfares to Singapore, call 800/FLY–4–LESS.

CLUBS

Contact **Entertainment Travel Editions** (⊠ Box 1068, Trumbull, CT 06611, ☎ 800/445–4137; $28–$53, depending on destination), **Great American Traveler** (⊠ Box 27965, Salt Lake City, UT 84127, ☎ 800/548–2812; $49.95 per year), **Moment's Notice Discount Travel Club** (⊠ 7301 New Utrecht Ave., Brooklyn, NY 11204, ☎ 718/234–6295; $25 per year, single or family), **Privilege Card International** (⊠ 3391 Peachtree Rd. NE, Suite 110, Atlanta, GA 30326, ☎ 404/262–0222 or 800/236–9732; $74.95 per year), **Travelers Advantage** (⊠ CUC Travel Service, 49 Music Sq. W, Nashville, TN 37203, ☎ 800/548–1116 or 800/648–4037; $49 per year, single or family), or **Worldwide Discount Travel Club** (⊠ 1674 Meridian Ave., Miami Beach, FL 33139, ☎ 305/534–2082; $50 per year for family, $40 single).

PASSES

☞ Bus Travel, *below.*

STUDENTS

Members of Hostelling International–American Youth Hostels (☞ Students, *below*) are eligible for discounts on car rentals, admissions to attractions, and other selected travel expenses.

PUBLICATIONS

Consult **The Frugal Globetrotter,** by Bruce Northam (⊠ Fulcrum Publishing, 350 Indiana St., Suite 350, Golden, CO 80401, ☎ 800/992–2908; $16.95 plus $4 shipping). For publications that tell how to find the lowest prices on plane tickets, *see* Air Travel, *above.*

E
EMBASSIES & DIPLOMATIC MISSIONS

Most countries maintain embassies, consulates, or high commissions in Singapore. Phone ahead to confirm their hours. If you decide to travel to other countries in the area but did not obtain the appropriate visas before leaving home, be aware that the visa-application process at one of these Singapore consular offices may take several days.

Australia High Commission (⊠ 25 Napier Rd., ☎ 737–9311), open weekdays 8:30–noon and 2–4.

British High Commission (⊠ Tanglin Rd., ☎ 473–9333), open weekdays 9–noon and 2–4.

Brunei Darussalem High Commission (⊠ 325 Tanglin Rd., ☎ 733–9055), open weekdays 8:30–12:30 and 1:30–4:30.

Canadian High Commission (⊠ 80 Anson Rd., ☎ 325–3200), open weekdays 8–12:30 and 1:30–4:30.

India (✉ 31 Grange Rd., ☎ 737–6777), open weekdays 9–5.

Indonesia (✉ 7 Chatsworth Rd., ☎ 737–7422), open weekdays 8:30–12:30 and 2–4:30.

Japan (✉ 16 Nassim Rd., ☎ 235–8855), open Mon.–Tues. and Thurs.–Fri. 8:30–12:30 and 2–4:30, Wed. and Sat. 8:30–12:30.

Malaysia (✉ 301 Jervois Rd., ☎ 235–0111), open weekdays 8:30–3:15.

New Zealand (✉ 13 Nassim Rd., ☎ 235–9966), open weekdays 9–noon and 2–4.

Philippines (✉ 20B Nassim Rd., ☎ 737–3977), open weekdays 9–noon and 2–4:30.

Sri Lanka (✉ #13-07 Goldhill Plaza, 51 Newton Rd., ☎ 254–4595), open weekdays 8:45–1 and 2–5.

Thailand (✉ 370 Orchard Rd., ☎ 235–4175 or 737–2644), open weekdays 9–12:30 and 2–5.

Union of Myanmar (✉ 15 St. Martin Dr., ☎ 737–8566), open weekdays 9:30–1 and 2–5.

United States of America (✉ 30 Hill St., ☎ 338–0251), open weekdays 8:30–noon and 2–3:30.

EMERGENCIES

Police (☎ 999); **ambulance and fire** (☎ 995).

DOCTORS & HOSPITALS

Singapore's medical facilities are among the best in the world, and most hotels have their own doctors on 24-hour call. **Paul's Clinic**

(✉ #11–01 Wisma Atria, 435 Orchard Rd., ☎ 235–2511), a centrally located clinic with several doctors, is open weekdays 9–5. The following are government hospitals accustomed to treating overseas visitors: **Alexandra Hospital** (✉ Alexandra Rd., ☎ 473–5222), **Kadang Kerbau Hospital** (✉ Maternity–Hampshire Rd., ☎ 293–4044), and **Singapore General Hospital** (✉ Outram Rd., ☎ 222–3322).

F

FERRY TRAVEL

Ferries from the Marine Terminal at the World Trade Centre connect Singapore with the surrounding islands.

TIOMAN ISLAND➤ **Kaplin Tours** (☎ 271–4866).

MALAYSIA➤ **Ferrylink** (☎ 545–3600 or 733–6744).

BATAAM AND BINTAN➤ **Kaplin Tours** (☎ 271–4866); **Channel Holidays** (☎ 270–2228); or **Bintan Resort Ferries** (☎ 345–1210).

G

GAY & LESBIAN TRAVEL

ORGANIZATIONS

The **International Gay Travel Association** (✉ Box 4974, Key West, FL 33041, ☎ 800/448–8550, FAX 305/296–6633), a consortium of more than 1,000 travel companies, can supply names of gay-friendly travel agents, tour operators, and accommodations.

PUBLICATIONS

The 16-page monthly newsletter **"Out & About"** (✉ 8 W. 19th St., Suite 401, New York, NY 10011, ☎ 212/645–6922 or 800/929–2268, FAX 800/929–2215; $49 for 10 issues and quarterly calendar) covers gay-friendly resorts, hotels, cruise lines, and airlines.

TOUR OPERATORS

Toto Tours (✉ 1326 W. Albion Ave., Suite 3W, Chicago, IL 60626, ☎ 773/274–8686 or 800/565–1241, FAX 773/274–8695) offers group tours to worldwide destinations.

TRAVEL AGENCIES

The largest agencies serving gay travelers are **Advance Travel** (✉ 10700 Northwest Fwy., Suite 160, Houston, TX 77092, ☎ 713/682–2002 or 800/292–0500), **Club Travel** (✉ 8739 Santa Monica Blvd., W. Hollywood, CA 90069, ☎ 310/358–2200 or 800/429–8747), **Islanders/ Kennedy Travel** (✉ 183 W. 10th St., New York, NY 10014, ☎ 212/242–3222 or 800/988–1181), **Now Voyager** (✉ 4406 18th St., San Francisco, CA 94114, ☎ 415/626–1169 or 800/255–6951), and **Yellowbrick Road** (✉ 1500 W. Balmoral Ave., Chicago, IL 60640, ☎ 773/561–1800 or 800/642–2488). **Skylink Women's Travel** (✉ 2460 W. 3rd St., Suite 215, Santa Rosa, CA 95401, ☎ 707/570–0105 or 800/225–5759) serves lesbian travelers.

H

HEALTH

FINDING A DOCTOR

For its members, the **International Association for Medical Assistance to Travellers** (IAMAT; membership free; ⊠ 417 Center St., Lewiston, NY 14092, ☎ 716/754–4883; ⊠ 40 Regal Rd., Guelph, Ontario N1K 1B5, ☎ 519/836–0102; ⊠ 1287 St. Clair Ave. W., Toronto, Ontario M6E 1B8, ☎ 416/652–0137; ⊠ 57 Voirets, 1212 Grand-Lancy, Geneva, Switzerland, no phone) publishes a worldwide directory of English-speaking physicians meeting IAMAT standards.

MEDICAL ASSISTANCE COMPANIES

The following companies are concerned primarily with emergency medical assistance, although they may provide some insurance as part of their coverage. For a list of full-service travel insurance companies, see Insurance, below.

Contact **International SOS Assistance** (⊠ Box 11568, Philadelphia, PA 19116, ☎ 215/244–1500 or 800/523–8930; ⊠ Box 466, Pl. Bonaventure, Montréal, Québec H5A 1C1, ☎ 514/874–7674 or 800/363–0263; ⊠ 7 Old Lodge Pl., St. Margarets, Twickenham TW1 1RQ, England, ☎ 0181/744–0033), **Medex Assistance Corporation** (⊠ Box 5375, Timonium, MD 21094, ☎ 410/453–6300 or 800/537–

2029), **Near Travel Services** (⊠ Box 1339, Calumet City, IL 60409, ☎ 708/868–6700 or 800/654–6700), **Traveler's Emergency Network** (⊠ 1133 15th St. NW, Suite 400, Washington DC 20005, ☎ 202/828–5894 or 800/275–4836, FAX 202/828–5896), **TravMed** (⊠ Box 5375, Timonium, MD 21094, ☎ 410/453–6380 or 800/732–5309), or **Worldwide Assistance Services** (⊠ 1133 15th St. NW, Suite 400, Washington, DC 20005, ☎ 202/331–1609 or 800/821–2828, FAX 202/828–5896).

I

INSURANCE

IN CANADA

Contact **Mutual of Omaha** (⊠ Travel Division, 500 University Ave., Toronto, Ontario M5G 1V8, ☎ 800/465–0267 (in Canada) or 416/598–4083).

IN THE U.S.

Travel insurance covering baggage, health, and trip cancellation or interruptions is available from **Access America** (⊠ 6600 W. Broad St., Richmond, VA 23230, ☎ 804/285–3300 or 800/334–7525), **Carefree Travel Insurance** (⊠ Box 9366, 100 Garden City Plaza, Garden City, NY 11530, ☎ 516/294–0220 or 800/323–3149), **Tele-Trip** (⊠ Mutual of Omaha Plaza, Box 31716, Omaha, NE 68131, ☎ 800/228–9792), **Travel Guard International** (⊠ 1145 Clark St., Stevens Point, WI 54481, ☎ 715/345–0505 or 800/

826–1300), **Travel Insured International** (⊠ Box 280568, East Hartford, CT 06128, ☎ 203/528–7663 or 800/243–3174), and **Wallach & Company** (⊠ 107 W. Federal St., Box 480, Middleburg, VA 22117, ☎ 540/687–3166 or 800/237–6615).

IN THE U.K.

The **Association of British Insurers** (⊠ 51 Gresham St., London EC2V 7HQ, ☎ 0171/600–3333) gives advice by phone and publishes the free pamphlet **"Holiday Insurance and Motoring Abroad,"** which sets out typical policy provisions and costs.

M

MAIL

For postal information, contact the **General Post Office (GPO)** in Fullerton Square, off Collyer Quay (☎ 533–6234).

American Express cardholders or traveler's-check users can have mail sent c/o American Express International, 3 Killeney Road, Winsland House #01-04/05, Singapore 239519. Envelopes should be marked "Client Mail."

MONEY MATTERS

ATMS

For specific foreign **Cirrus** locations, call 800/424–7787; for foreign **Plus** locations, consult the Plus directory at your local bank.

CURRENCY EXCHANGE

If your bank doesn't exchange currency, contact **Thomas Cook**

Currency Services (☎ 800/287–7362 for locations). **Ruesch International** (☎ 800/424–2923 for locations) can also provide you with foreign banknotes before you leave home and publishes a number of useful brochures, including a "Foreign Currency Guide" and "Foreign Exchange Tips." For exchange rates, *see* Money *in* Smart Travel Tips A to Z, *below.*

WIRING FUNDS

Funds can be wired via **MoneyGram℠** (for locations and information in the U.S. and Canada, ☎ 800/926–9400) or **Western Union** (for agent locations or to send money using MasterCard or Visa, ☎ 800/325–6000; in Canada, 800/321–2923; in the U.K., 0800/833833; or visit the Western Union office at the nearest major post office).

P

PACKING

For strategies on packing light, get a copy of *The Packing Book,* by Judith Gilford (✉ Ten Speed Press, Box 7123, Berkeley, CA 94707, ☎ 510/559–1600 or 800/841–2665, FAX 510/524–4588; $7.95 plus $3.50 shipping).

PASSPORTS & VISAS

IN THE U.S.

For fees, documentation requirements, and other information, call the State Department's **Office of Passport Services** information line (☎ 202/647–0518).

CANADIANS

For fees, documentation requirements, and other information, call the Ministry of Foreign Affairs and International Trade's **Passport Office** (☎ 819/994–3500 or 800/567–6868).

U.K. CITIZENS

For fees, documentation requirements, and to request an emergency passport, call the **London Passport Office** (☎ 0990/210410).

PHOTO HELP

The **Kodak Information Center** (☎ 800/242–2424) answers consumer questions about film and photography. The *Kodak Guide to Shooting Great Travel Pictures* (available in bookstores; or contact Fodor's Travel Publications, ☎ 800/533–6478; $16.50 plus $4 shipping) explains how to take expert travel photographs.

S

SAFETY

"Trouble-Free Travel," from the AAA, is a booklet of tips for protecting yourself and your belongings when away from home. Send a stamped, self-addressed, legal-size envelope to Trouble-Free Travel (✉ Mail Stop 75, 1000 AAA Dr., Heathrow, FL 32746).

SENIOR CITIZENS

CLUBS

Sears's **Mature Outlook** (✉ Box 10448, Des Moines, IA 50306, ☎ 800/336–6330; annual membership $14.95) includes a lifestyle/travel magazine and membership in ITC-50 travel club, which offers discounts of up to 50% at participating hotels and restaurants.

ORGANIZATIONS

Contact the **American Association of Retired Persons** (✉ AARP, 601 E St. NW, Washington, DC 20049, ☎ 202/434–2277; annual dues $8 per person or couple). Its Purchase Privilege Program secures discounts for members on lodging, car rentals, and sightseeing.

SIGHTSEEING

A wide range of sightseeing tours covers the highlights of Singapore. They are a good introduction to the island and are especially convenient for business travelers or others on a tight schedule. Tours can take two hours or the whole day, and prices range from S$20 to S$109. Most are operated in comfortable, air-conditioned coaches with guides and include pickup and return. Tour agencies can also arrange private-car tours with guides; these are considerably more expensive.

There is no need to book tours in advance of your visit; they can be easily arranged through the tour desks in hotels. The following are a few of the tour operators providing services through major hotels, but there are many others as well. **RMG Tours** (✉ 25 Hoot Kiam Rd., ☎ 738–7776) organizes nightlife and food tours. **Siakson Coach Tours** (✉ Siakson Bldg., 3 Miller St., ☎ 336–

0288) has daily tours to the zoo and Mandai Gardens, plus excursions to Malaysia.

Water Tours (✉ #01–31, 70 Clifford Pier, ☎ 533–9811) operates motorized junks for cruises in the harbor and to Kusu Island. **Elpin Tours and Limousine Services** (✉ 317 Outram Rd., #02–23 Glass Hotel, ☎ 235–3111) arranges tours of Sentosa Island, Night Safari, Jurong Bird Park, the east coast, and Malacca. **Singapore River Cruises & Leisure** (✉ 24 Peck St., #05–08/10 Nehsons Building, ☎ 336–6119) offers tours of the Singapore River, leaving at regular intervals from the Parliament House Landing Steps, near the statue of Sir Thomas Stamford Raffles; adults $7, children, S$3.

HOSTELING

In the United States, contact **Hostelling International–American Youth Hostels** (✉ 733 15th St. NW, Suite 840, Washington, DC 20005, ☎ 202/783–6161, FAX 202/783–6171); in Canada, **Hostelling International–Canada** (✉ 205 Catherine St., Suite 400, Ottawa, Ontario K2P 1C3, ☎ 613/237–7884); and in the United Kingdom, the **Youth Hostel Association of England and Wales** (✉ Trevelyan House, 8 St. Stephen's Hill, St. Albans, Hertfordshire AL1 2DY, ☎ 01727/855215 or 01727/845047). Membership (in the U.S., $25; in Canada, C$26.75; in the U.K.,

£9.30) gives you access to 5,000 hostels in 77 countries that charge $5–$40 per person per night.

ORGANIZATIONS

A major contact is the **Council on International Educational Exchange** (mail orders only: ✉ CIEE, 205 E. 42nd St., 16th floor, New York, NY 10017, ☎ 212/822–2600, FAX 212/822–2699). The **Educational Travel Centre** (✉ 438 N. Frances St., Madison, WI 53703, ☎ 608/256–5551 or 800/747–5551, FAX 608/256–2042) offers rail passes and low-cost airline tickets, mostly for flights that depart from Chicago.

In Canada, also contact **Travel Cuts** (✉ 187 College St., Toronto, Ontario M5T 1P7, ☎ 416/979–2406 or 800/667–2887).

For information on subway routes and schedules, call the **Singapore Tourist Promotion Board** (STPB; ☎ 736–6622) or inquire at your hotel.

T

The country code for Singapore is 65. For local access numbers abroad, contact **AT&T** USADirect (☎ 800/874–4000), **MCI** Call USA (☎ 800/444–4444), or **Sprint** Express (☎ 800/793–1153).

Among the companies that sell tours and packages to Singapore, the following are nationally known, have a

proven reputation, and offer plenty of options.

GROUP TOURS

SUPER-DELUXE➤ **Abercrombie & Kent** (✉ 1520 Kensington Rd., Oak Brook, IL 60521-2141, ☎ 708/954–2944 or 800/323–7308, FAX 708/954–3324) and **Travcoa** (✉ Box 2630, 2350 S.E. Bristol St., Newport Beach, CA 92660, ☎ 714/476–2800 or 800/992–2003, FAX 714/476–2538).

DELUXE➤ **Globus** (✉ 5301 S. Federal Circle, Littleton, CO 80123, ☎ 303/797–2800 or 800/221–0090, FAX 303/795–0962), **Maupintour** (✉ Box 807, 1515 St. Andrews Drive, Lawrence, KS 66047, ☎ 913/843–1211 or 800/255–4266, FAX 913/843–8351), and **Tauck Tours** (✉ Box 5027, 276 Post Rd. West, Westport, CT 06881, ☎ 203/226–6911 or 800/468–2825, FAX 203/221–6828).

FIRST-CLASS➤ **Brendan Tours** (✉ 15137 Califa St., Van Nuys, CA 91411, ☎ 818/785–9696 or 800/421–8446, FAX 818/902–9876), **Collette Tours** (✉ 162 Middle St., Pawtucket, RI 02860, ☎ 401/728–3805 or 800/832–4656, FAX 401/728–1380), **DER Tours** (✉ 11933 Wilshire Blvd., Los Angeles, CA 90025, ☎ 310/479–4411 or 800/937–1235), **General Tours** (✉ 53 Summer St., Keene, NH 03431, ☎ 603/357–5033 or 800/221–2216, FAX 603/357–4548), **Orient Flexi-Pax Tours** (✉ 630 3rd Ave., New York, NY 10017, ☎ 212/692–9550 or 800/

545–5540), **Pacific Bestour** (⊠ 228 Rivervale Rd., River Vale, NJ 07675, ☎ 201/664–8778 or 800/688–3288), and **Pacific Delight Tours** (⊠ 132 Madison Ave., New York, NY 10016, ☎ 212/684–7707 or 800/221–7179).

BUDGET➤ **Cosmos** (☞ Globus, *above*).

PACKAGES

Independent vacation packages are available from major airlines and tour operators. Contact **United Vacations** (☎ 800/328–6877). Many of the operators listed under group tours, above, also sell independent tours. Try **DER Tours, Orient Flexi-Pax Tours, Pacific Bestour,** and **Pacific Delight Tours.**

FROM THE U.K.

Tour operators offering packages to Thailand include **British Airways Holidays** (⊠ Astral Towers, Betts Way, London Rd., Crawley, West Sussex RH10 2XA, ☎ 01293/723–350), **Kuoni Travel** (⊠ Kuoni House, Dorking, Surrey RH5 4AZ, ☎ 01306/740–500), **Bales Tours** (⊠ Bales House, Junction Rd., Dorking, Surrey RH4 3HB, ☎ 01306/876–881 or 01306/885–991), and **Hayes and Jarvis** (⊠ Hayes House, 152 King St., London W6 0QU, ☎ 0181/748–5050).

Travel agencies that offer cheap fares to Singapore include **Trailfinders** (⊠ 42–50 Earl's Court Rd., London W8 6FT, ☎ 0171/937–5400), **Travel Cuts** (⊠ 295 Regent St., London W1R 7YA, ☎

0171/637–3161), and **Flightfile** (⊠ 49 Tottenham Court Rd., London W1P 9RE, ☎ 0171/700–2722).

THEME TRIPS

Customized, deluxe tours of Singapore, tailored to individual interests, are available from **Pacific Experience** (⊠ 366 Madison Ave., #1203, New York, NY 10017, ☎ 212/661–2604 or 800/279–3639, FAX 212/661–2587).

ORGANIZATIONS

The **National Tour Association** (NTA; ⊠ 546 E. Main St., Lexington, KY 40508, ☎ 606/226–4444 or 800/755–8687) and the **United States Tour Operators Association** (USTOA; ⊠ 211 E. 51st St., Suite 12B, New York, NY 10022, ☎ 212/750–7371) can provide lists of members and information on booking tours.

PUBLICATIONS

Contact the USTOA (☞ Organizations, *above*) for its **"Smart Traveler's Planning Kit."** Pamphlets in the kit include the "Worldwide Tour and Vacation Package Finder," "How to Select a Tour or Vacation Package," and information on the organization's consumer protection plan. Also get a copy of the Better Business Bureau's **"Tips on Travel Packages"** (⊠ Publication 24-195, 4200 Wilson Blvd., Arlington, VA 22203; $2).

For information in the United States, call 800/524–2420.

FROM MALAYSIA

Eight trains a day operated by Malay Railways arrive from Kuala Lumpur and points north, such as Ipoh and Butterworth (Penang), at Singapore's **Keppel Road station** (☎ 222–5165).

For names of reputable agencies in your area, contact the **American Society of Travel Agents** (ASTA; ⊠ 1101 King St., Suite 200, Alexandria, VA 22314, ☎ 703/739–2782), the **Association of Canadian Travel Agents** (⊠ 1729 Bank St., Suite 201, Ottawa, Ontario K1V 7Z5, ☎ 613/521–0474, FAX 613/521–0805), or the **Association of British Travel Agents** (⊠ 55–57 Newman St., London W1P 4AH, ☎ 0171/637–2444, FAX 0171/637–0713).

For travel apparel, appliances, personal-care items, and other travel necessities, get a free catalog from **Magellan's** (☎ 800/962–4943, FAX 805/568–5406), **Orvis Travel** (☎ 800/541–3541, FAX 540/343–7053), or **TravelSmith** (☎ 800/950–1600, FAX 415/455–0554).

ELECTRICAL CONVERTERS

Send a self-addressed, stamped envelope to the **Franzus Company** (⊠ Customer Service, Dept. B50, Murtha Industrial Park, Box 142, Beacon Falls, CT 06403, ☎ 203/723–6664) for a copy of the free brochure "Foreign Electricity Is No Deep, Dark Secret."

U

U.S. GOVERNMENT TRAVEL BRIEFINGS

The U.S. Department of State's American Citizens Services office (✉ Room 4811, Washington, DC 20520; enclose SASE) issues **Consular Information Sheets** on all foreign countries. These cover issues such as crime, security, political climate, and health risks as well as listing embassy locations, entry requirements, currency regulations, and providing other useful information. For the latest information, stop in at any U.S. passport office, consulate, or embassy; call the interactive hot line (☎ 202/647–5225, FAX 202/647–3000); or, with your PC's modem, tap into the department's computer bulletin board (☎ 202/647–9225).

V

VISITOR INFORMATION

Contact the **Singapore Tourist Promotion Board.**

IN THE U.S.

✉ 590 5th Ave., 12th floor, New York, NY 10036, ☎ 212/302–4861, FAX 212/302–4801; ✉ Two Prudential Plaza, 180 North Stetson Ave., Suite 1450, Chicago, IL 60601, ☎ 312/938–1888, FAX 312/938–0086; ✉ 8484 Wilshire Blvd., Suite 510, Beverly Hills, CA 90211, ☎ 213/852–1901, FAX 213/852–0129.

IN CANADA

✉ The Standard Life Centre, 121 King St. West, Suite 1000, Toronto, Ontario, M5H 3T9, ☎ 416/363–8898, FAX 416/363–5752.

IN THE U.K.

✉ Carrington House, 126–130 Regent St., London W1R 5FA, ☎ 0171/437–0033.

IN SINGAPORE

✉ Tourism Court, 1 Orchard Spring La., Singapore 247729, ☎ 736–6622, 800/738–3778, or 800/738–3779; ✉ 328 North Bridge Rd., #02–34 Raffles Hotel Arcade, ☎ 800/334–1335 or 800/334–1336. The staff here will answer any questions you may have on Singapore and will attend to legitimate complaints.

The STPB's 24-hour "Tourist Line" provides tourist information in English, Japanese, German, and Mandarin. The toll-free number (in Singapore) is 800/831–3311.

W

WEATHER

For current conditions and forecasts, plus the local time and helpful travel tips, call the **Weather Channel Connection** (☎ 900/932–8437; 95¢ per minute) from a Touch-Tone phone.

The *International Traveler's Weather Guide* (✉ Weather Press, Box 660606, Sacramento, CA 95866, ☎ 916/974–0201 or 800/972–0201; $10.95 includes shipping), written by two meteorologists, provides month-by-month information on temperature, humidity, and precipitation in more than 175 cities worldwide.

THE GOLD GUIDE / IMPORTANT CONTACTS

SMART TRAVEL TIPS A TO Z

Basic Information on Traveling in Singapore &
Savvy Tips to Make Your Trip a Breeze

A

AIR TRAVEL

Singapore is the transport hub of Asia. Fifty-two airlines link the republic with 111 cities in 54 countries. The distance between Singapore and North America is too great for planes to fly without refueling and changing crews. There are, however, "direct" flights with no change of airplane, but one or two stops in major cities. If possible, **avoid connecting flights,** which stop at least once and can involve a change of plane, although the flight number remains the same; if the first leg is late, the second waits.

For better service, **fly smaller or regional carriers,** which often have higher passenger satisfaction ratings. Sometimes they have such in-flight amenities as leather seats or greater legroom, and they often have better food.

CUTTING COSTS

The Sunday travel section of most newspapers is a good place to look for deals.

MAJOR AIRLINES➤ The least-expensive airfares from the major airlines are priced for round-trip travel and are subject to restrictions. Usually, you must **book in advance and buy the ticket within 24 hours** to get cheaper fares, and you may have to **stay over a Saturday night.** The lowest fare is subject to availability, and only a small percentage of the plane's total seats is sold at that price. It's smart to **call a number of airlines, and when you are quoted a good price, book it on the spot**—the same fare may not be available on the same flight the next day. Airlines generally allow you to change your return date for a $25 to $50 fee. If you don't use your ticket, you can apply the cost toward the purchase of a new ticket, again for a small charge. However, most low-fare tickets are nonrefundable. To get the lowest airfare, **check different routings.** If your destination has more than one gateway, **compare prices to different airports.**

FROM THE U.K.➤ To save money on flights, **look into an APEX or Super-Pex ticket.** APEX tickets must be booked in advance and have certain restrictions. Super-PEX tickets can be purchased right at the airport.

CONSOLIDATORS➤ Consolidators buy tickets for scheduled flights at reduced rates from the airlines, then sell them at prices below the lowest available from the airlines directly—usually without advance restrictions. Sometimes you can even get your money back if you need to return the ticket.

Carefully **read the fine print** detailing penalties for changes and cancellations. If you doubt the reliability of a consolidator, **confirm your reservation with the airline.**

ALOFT

AIRLINE FOOD➤ If you hate airline food, **ask for special meals when booking.** These can be vegetarian, low-cholesterol, or kosher, for example; commonly prepared to order in smaller quantities than standard fare, they can be tastier. Singapore Airlines offers two particularly tasty alternatives: Indian vegetarian and Oriental vegetarian. Not only are the meals better, you get served before everyone else.

JET LAG➤ To avoid this syndrome, which occurs when travel disrupts your body's natural cycles, try to maintain a normal routine. At night, **get some sleep.** By day, move about the cabin to **stretch your legs, eat light meals, and drink water—not alcohol.**

SMOKING➤ Smoking is not allowed on flights of six hours or less within the continental United States. Smoking is also prohibited on flights within Canada. For U.S. flights longer than six hours or international flights, **contact your carrier regarding its smoking policy.** Some carriers have prohibited smoking throughout their system; others allow smoking only on certain routes or even certain departures of that route.

AIRPORT TRANSFERS

BY TAXI

Under normal traffic conditions, the trip by taxi takes 20 to 30 minutes, depending on the location of your hotel. The fare ranges from S$13 to S$20, plus a S$3 airport surcharge (not applicable for trips *to* the airport, but be wary of taxi drivers who try imposing this charge anyway). Other surcharges apply when baggage is stored in the trunk or when more than two adults travel in the same cab.

BY BUS

Public buses leave at frequent intervals from the basement level of both terminals. The fare is S$1.80 to Orchard Road, where, if necessary, you can catch a taxi or change buses to get to your hotel. Bus 390 returns to the airport from downtown Singapore via Orchard Road.

BY CAR

Should you wish to rent a car, major agencies are represented at the airport's car-rental counter (☞ Car Rental *in* Important Contacts A to Z, *above*).

B

BOOKS ON SINGAPORE

A great book to take home with you is *Singapore,* with wonderful photographs by Ian Lloyd and text by Betty Rabb Schafer (Times Editions, 1988). It is available in most Singapore bookstores. Other books on Singapore include the following: *A History of Singapore, 1819–1975,* by Constance M. Turnbull (Oxford University Press, 1977); *The Worst Disaster: The Fall of Singapore,* by Raymond A. Callahan (University of Delaware Press, 1977); *Raffles of the Eastern Isles,* by Charles Wurtzburg (Oxford University Press, 1984); and *Saint Jack,* a novel set in Singapore, by Paul Theroux (Houghton Mifflin, 1984). *See also* English-Language Bookstores, *below.*

BUMBOATS

Bumboats are motorized launches that serve as water taxis. Sailors use these to shuttle between Singapore and their ships. You can hire bumboats to the islands from Clifford Pier or Jardine Steps. The charge is approximately S$30 an hour for a boat that can comfortably accommodate six passengers.

BUS TRAVEL

Buses are much cheaper than taxis and—with a little practice—easy to use. During rush hours, they can be quicker than cabs, since there are special bus lanes along the main roads. Some buses are air-conditioned, and service is frequent—usually every five to 10 minutes on most routes. Even without the excellent *Bus Guide,* available for S$1.20 at any bookstore, finding your way around is relatively easy. Bus stops close to sightseeing attractions have signs pointing out the attractions.

The minimum fare is S$.50, the maximum S$1.10 for non-air-conditioned buses, S$.60–S$1.70 for air-conditioned ones. **Deposit exact change** in the box as you enter the bus (conductors cannot give change), and **remember to collect your ticket.** Bus numbers are clearly marked, and most stops have a list of destinations with the numbers of the buses that service them. Most buses run from 5:30 or 6 AM until around 11:30 PM, while some run all night.

The new Singapore Trolley bus service starts at the Botanic Gardens and continues to Orchard Road, Tanjong Pagar, and the World Trade Centre. It's not very convenient, and it's expensive (S$9 adults, S$7 children), but it does make 22 stops and your ticket is good all day for unlimited journeys. You can buy the ticket (you'll need exact change) when you board. A one-ticket point-to-point fare is S$3.

DISCOUNT PASSES

You can **purchase a Singapore Explorer Bus Ticket** at most major hotels; it lets you travel anywhere on the island on any bus operated by Singapore Bus Service (SBS, the red-and-white buses) or Trans Island Bus Service (TIBS, the orange-and-yellow buses). You may embark and disembark as frequently as you like, flashing your pass as you board. A one-day pass costs S$5 and a three-day pass costs S$12. With this ticket you also receive an Explorer Bus Map with color-coded routes showing bus stops and all major points of interest. Most major hotels and tour agents sell Explorer tickets; they are also available at the SBS Travelcentres at bus interchanges.

Use the recently introduced Transitlink fare-card, a prepaid mass-transit ticket. You can purchase one for S$12 to S$52 (including a S$2 deposit), from Transitlink sales offices at MRT stations and at bus interchanges. The card lets you travel on the trains and on many buses; the fare for each trip is deducted from the balance on the card. Any unused fare and the deposit can be refunded at Transitlink offices.

FROM MALAYSIA

Getting the bus from Johore Bahru, the Malaysian city right next to Singapore, is complicated. Unless you have a Singapore Transit Card, you have to ride all the way out to the Johore bus station (20 minutes out of town), pay S$.80 for your ticket, and then journey back to the Causeway. You get off the bus on the other side of the Causeway at the Singapore checkpoint, then reboard the bus for the ride into the city's center. Since you may not be reboarding the same bus—depending on the line at immi-

gration—do not leave your belongings behind when you get off. Take a taxi or the train whenever possible.

BUSINESS HOURS

Businesses are generally open weekdays 9 or 9:30 to 5 or 5:30; some, not many, are also open on Saturday morning.

BANKS

Banking hours are weekdays 10–3, Saturday 9:30–11:30 AM. Branches of the Development Bank of Singapore stay open until 3 PM on Saturdays. The bank at Changi Airport is open whenever there are flights. Money changers operate whenever there are customers in the shopping centers they serve.

MUSEUMS

Many museums close on Monday; otherwise, they are generally open 9–5.

PHARMACIES

Pharmaceuticals are available at supermarkets, department stores, hotels, and shopping centers. Registered pharmacists work 9–6. Some pharmacies in the major shopping centers stay open until 10 PM. Prescriptions must be written by locally registered doctors (hospitals can fill prescriptions 24 hours a day).

POST OFFICES

There are 87 post offices on the island, most of them open weekdays 8:30–5 and Saturday 8:30–1. The airport post office and the Takashimaya post office are open daily 8–8.

SHOPS

Shop opening times vary. Department stores and many shops in big shopping centers are generally open seven days a week from about 10 AM to 9 PM (later some evenings). Smaller shops tend to close on Sunday, although there is no firm rule now that competition is so intense.

C

CAMERAS, CAMCORDERS, & COMPUTERS

IN TRANSIT

Always **keep your film, tape, or disks out of the sun;** never put these on the dashboard of a car. Carry an extra supply of batteries, and **be prepared to turn on your camera, camcorder, or laptop computer for security personnel** to prove that it's real.

X RAYS

Always **ask for hand inspection at security.** Such requests are virtually always honored at U.S. airports and are usually accommodated abroad. Photographic film becomes clouded after successive exposure to airport X-ray machines. Videotape and computer disks are not harmed by X rays, but **keep your tapes and disks away from metal detectors.**

CUSTOMS

Before departing, **register your foreign-made camera or laptop with U.S. Customs.** If your equipment is U.S.-made, call the consulate of the country you'll be visiting to find out whether it should be registered with local customs upon arrival.

CUTTING COSTS

To get the best deal, **book through a travel agent who is willing to shop around.** Ask your agent to **look for fly-drive packages,** which also save you money, and **ask if local taxes are included** in the rental or fly-drive price. These can be as high as 20% in some destinations. Don't forget to find out about required deposits, cancellation penalties, drop-off charges, and the cost of any required insurance coverage.

Also **ask your travel agent about a company's customer-service record.** How has it responded to late plane arrivals and vehicle mishaps? Are there often lines at the rental counter, and—if you're traveling during a holiday period—does a confirmed reservation guarantee you a car?

Always **find out what equipment is standard** at your destination before specifying what you want; automatic transmission and air-conditioning are usually optional—and very expensive.

Be sure to **look into wholesalers**—companies that do not own their own fleets but rent in bulk from those that do and often offer better rates than traditional car-rental operations. Prices are best during off-peak periods; rentals booked through wholesalers must be paid for before you leave the United States.

RENTING IN MALAYSIA➣
If you plan to do an overland drive through Malaysia, you can rent a car from a Singapore agency, but **to save money, rent in Malaysia.** Take the bus for S$.80 to Johore Bahru and you can save approximately S$50 a day on your car rental. Furthermore, you can make reservations with a rental agency in Johore from Singapore, and even be picked up from your Singapore hotel by private car at no extra charge. For a small fee, Avis lets you drop off the car back in Singapore.

Once you are on the Malaysian side of the Causeway (☞ Bus Travel in Important Contacts A to Z), take the underpass to the taxi stand, and take a taxi to the rental car office. For car rental contacts, *see* Car Rental *in* Important Contacts A to Z.

INSURANCE

When driving a rented car, you are generally responsible for any damage to or loss of the rental vehicle, as well as any property damage or personal injury that you cause. Before you rent, **see what coverage you already have** under the terms of your personal auto insurance policy and credit cards.

If you do not have auto insurance or an umbrella insurance policy that covers damage to third parties, purchasing CDW or LDW is highly recommended.

LICENSE REQUIREMENTS

In Singapore, your own driver's license is ac-

ceptable. An International Driver's Permit is a good idea; it's available from the American or Canadian automobile associations or, in the United Kingdom, from the AA or RAC.

SURCHARGES

Before you pick up a car in one city and leave it in another, **ask about drop-off charges or one-way service fees,** which can be substantial. Note, too, that some rental agencies charge extra if you return the car before the time specified on your contract. To avoid a hefty refueling fee, **fill the tank just before you turn in the car**—but be aware that gas stations near the rental outlet may overcharge.

When traveling with children, **plan ahead** and **involve your youngsters** as you outline your trip. When packing, **include a supply of things to keep them busy** en route. On sightseeing days, try to **schedule activities of special interest to your children,** like a trip to a zoo or a playground. If you **plan your itinerary around seasonal festivals,** you'll never lack for things to do. In addition, **check local newspapers for special events** mounted by public libraries, museums, and parks.

BABY-SITTING

For recommended local sitters, **check with your hotel desk.**

DRIVING

If you are renting a car, don't forget to **arrange**

THE GOLD GUIDE / SMART TRAVEL TIPS

for a car seat when you reserve. Sometimes they're free.

FLYING

As a general rule, infants under two not occupying a seat fly at greatly reduced fares and occasionally for free. If your children are two or older ask about special children's fares. Age limits for these fares vary among carriers. Rules also vary regarding unaccompanied minors, so again, check with your airline.

BAGGAGE➤ In general, the adult baggage allowance applies to children paying half or more of the adult fare. If you are traveling with an infant, ask about carry-on allowances before departure. In general, for infants charged 10% of the adult fare you are allowed one carry-on bag and a collapsible stroller, which may have to be checked; you may be limited to less if the flight is full.

SAFETY SEATS➤ According to the FAA, it's a good idea to use safety seats aloft for children weighing less than 40 pounds. Airline policies vary. U.S. carriers allow FAA-approved models but usually require that you buy a ticket, even if your child would otherwise ride free, since the seats must be strapped into regular seats. However, some U.S. and foreign-flag airlines may require you to hold your baby during takeoff and landing—defeating the seat's purpose. Other foreign carriers may not allow infant seats at all, or may charge a child

rather than an infant fare for their use.

FACILITIES➤ When making your reservation, request children's meals or freestanding bassinets if you need them; the latter are available only to those seated at the bulkhead, where there's enough legroom. If you don't need a bassinet, think twice before requesting bulkhead seats—the only storage space for in-flight necessities is in inconveniently distant overhead bins.

GAMES

Look for travel versions of popular games such as Yahtzee, Trouble, Sorry, and Monopoly ($5–$8) in your local toy store.

LODGING

Most hotels allow children under a certain age to stay in their parents' room at no extra charge; others charge them as extra adults. Be sure to ask about the cutoff age.

CRUISES

Singapore is trying to attract more cruise ships to the island. Right now, you can take one- to three-day cruises to nowhere, or to destinations in Malaysia, Singapore, or Indonesia. Trips start at around S$279 on the city-state's two main ships, the *Star Aquarius* and the *Superstar Gemini*. The *Star Aquarius* has karaoke, swimming, discos, and restaurants on board and travels to Malaysia and to nowhere. The smaller *Superstar Gemini* has similar facilities, but bigger rooms. It takes longer trips up

Malaysia's west coast and on to Sumatra and Thailand. To get the best deal on a cruise, consult a cruise-only travel agency.

CUSTOMS & DUTIES

To speed your clearance through customs, keep receipts for all your purchases abroad and be ready to show the inspector what you've bought. If you feel that you've been incorrectly or unfairly charged a duty, you can appeal assessments in dispute. First ask to see a supervisor. If you are still unsatisfied, write to the port director at your point of entry, sending your customs receipt and any other appropriate documentation. The address will be listed on your receipt. If you still don't get satisfaction, you can take your case to customs headquarters in Washington.

IN SINGAPORE

Duty-free customs allowances in Singapore are in line with those of other countries in the region: Visitors over 18 are allowed to bring in up to 1 liter of spirits, wine, or beer. Singapore does not permit importing any duty-free cigarettes. Chewing gum is not banned in Singapore. You can usually get away with bringing in a few packs. Most Singaporeans are embarrassed by the chewing gum law and will be glad to see you chewing yours. Special import permits are required for animals, live plants, meats, arms, and controlled drugs. Penalties for drug abuse are very severe in Singapore and rigidly enforced. Customs also restricts any form of pornography, which in the past has been interpreted to include *Playboy* magazine. Customs is also extremely strict regarding the import of any form of arms, including such items as ceremonial daggers purchased as souvenirs in other countries. These are held in bond and returned to you on your departure.

There are no restrictions or limitations on the amount of cash, foreign currencies, checks, and drafts imported or exported by visitors.

IN THE U.S.

You may bring home $400 worth of foreign goods duty-free if you've been out of the country for at least 48 hours and haven't already used the $400 allowance, or any part of it, in the past 30 days.

Travelers 21 or older may bring back 1 liter of alcohol duty-free, provided the beverage laws of the state through which they reenter the United States allow it. In addition, regardless of their age, they are allowed 100 non-Cuban cigars and 200 cigarettes. Antiques, which the U.S. Customs Service defines as objects more than 100 years old, are duty-free. Original works of art done entirely by hand are also duty-free. These include, but are not limited to, paintings, drawings, and sculptures.

Duty-free, travelers may mail packages valued at up to $200 to themselves and up to $100 to others, with a limit of one parcel per addressee per day (and no alcohol or tobacco products or perfume valued at more than $5); on the outside, the package must be labeled as being either for personal use or an unsolicited gift, and a list of its contents and their retail value must be attached. Mailed items do not affect your duty-free allowance on your return.

IN CANADA

If you've been out of Canada for at least seven days, you may bring in C$500 worth of goods duty-free. If you've been away for fewer than seven days but for more than 48 hours, the duty-free allowance drops to C$200; if your trip lasts between 24 and 48 hours, the allowance is C$50. You cannot pool allowances with family members. Goods claimed under the C$500 exemption may follow you by mail; those claimed under the lesser exemptions must accompany you.

Alcohol and tobacco products may be included in the seven-day and 48-hour exemptions but not in the 24-hour exemption. If you meet the age requirements of the province or territory through which you reenter Canada, you may bring in, duty-free, 1.14 liters (40 imperial ounces) of wine or liquor *or* 24 12-ounce cans or bottles of beer or ale. If you are 16 or older, you may bring in, duty-free, 200 cigarettes, 50 cigars or cigarillos,

and 400 tobacco sticks or 400 grams of manufactured tobacco. Alcohol and tobacco must accompany you on your return.

An unlimited number of gifts with a value of up to C$60 each may be mailed to Canada duty-free. These do not affect your duty-free allowance on your return. Label the package "Unsolicited Gift—Value Under $60." Alcohol and tobacco are excluded.

IN THE U.K.

From countries outside the EU, including Singapore, you may import, duty-free, 200 cigarettes, 100 cigarillos, 50 cigars, or 250 grams of tobacco; 1 liter of spirits or 2 liters of fortified or sparkling wine or liqueurs; 2 liters of still table wine; 60 milliliters of perfume; 250 milliliters of toilet water; plus £136 worth of other goods, including gifts and souvenirs.

CYCLE-RICKSHAWS

Once the major method of getting around the city, rickshaws are now driven mostly by elderly Chinese, and there are only a few dozen left. The best place to get a rickshaw is in the square before the National Museum. **Bargain for the fare**; you should not pay more than S$15 for a 45-minute ride. The best time to take a rickshaw ride is early evening, after rush hour.

D

DISABILITIES & ACCESSIBILITY

Singapore is the easiest place in Southeast Asia

for people with disabilities to visit. Most new major hotels, office buildings, and tourist attractions have wheelchair access and grab bars in the public toilets. Traffic lights make a chirping sound when the signal turns to WALK.

When discussing accessibility with an operator or reservationist, **ask hard questions.** Are there any stairs, inside *or* out? Are there grab bars next to the toilet *and* in the shower/tub? How wide is the doorway to the room? To the bathroom? For the most extensive facilities, meeting the latest legal specifications, **opt for newer accommodations,** which more often have been designed with access in mind. Older properties or ships must usually be retrofitted and may offer more limited facilities as a result. Be sure to **discuss your needs before booking.**

DISCOUNTS & DEALS

You shouldn't have to pay for a discount. In fact, you may already be eligible for all kinds of savings. Here are some time-honored strategies for getting the best deal.

LOOK IN YOUR WALLET

When you **use your credit card to make travel purchases,** you may get free travel-accident insurance, collision damage insurance, or medical or legal assistance, depending on the card and the bank that issued it. American Express, Visa,

and MasterCard provide one or more of these services, so **get a copy of your card's travel benefits.** If you are a member of the AAA or an oil-company-sponsored road-assistance plan, always **ask hotel or car-rental reservationists for auto-club discounts.** Some clubs offer additional discounts on tours, cruises, or admission to attractions. And don't forget that auto-club membership entitles you to free maps and trip-planning services.

SENIOR CITIZENS & STUDENTS

As a senior-citizen traveler, you may be eligible for special rates, but you should mention your senior-citizen status up front. If you're a student or under 26 you can also get discounts, especially if you have an official ID card (☞ Senior-Citizen Discounts *and* Students on the Road, *below*).

DIAL FOR DOLLARS

To save money, **look into "1-800" discount reservations services,** which often have lower rates. These services use their buying power to get a better price on hotels, airline tickets, and sometimes even car rentals. When booking a room, always **call the hotel's local toll-free number** (if one is available) rather than the central reservations number—you'll often get a better price. Ask the reservationist about special packages or corporate rates, which are usually available even if you're not traveling on business.

JOIN A CLUB?

Discount clubs can be a legitimate source of savings, but you must use the participating hotels and visit the participating attractions in order to realize any benefits. Remember, too, that you have to pay a fee to join, so **determine if you'll save enough to warrant your membership fee.** Before booking with a club, **make sure the hotel or other supplier isn't offering a better deal.**

GET A GUARANTEE

When shopping for the best deal on hotels and car rentals, **look for guaranteed exchange rates,** which protect you against a falling dollar. With your rate locked in, you won't pay more even if the price goes up in the local currency.

DRIVING

It is unneccessary to rent a car or hire a chauffeur to get around in Singapore. Distances are short, besides which, parking is very expensive, especially in the central business district. Taxis and public transportation are far more convenient and less expensive. And almost everything worth seeing is accessible by tour bus.

Singapore's speed limits are 80 kph (50 mph) on expressways unless otherwise posted, and 50 kph (31 mph) on other roads. One rule to keep in mind: **Yield right of way at rotaries. Drive on the left-hand side of the road** in both Malaysia and Singapore. Unleaded gas starts at S$1.08 per liter in Singapore, significantly less in Malaysia. A government ruling requires any car passing the Causeway out of Singapore to **drive with at least half a tank of gas or be fined**; the republic's huge losses in revenue as a result of Singaporeans' driving to Malaysia to gas up cheaply led to the understandably unpopular ruling.

FROM MALAYSIA

Kuala Lumpur is approximately 400 kilometers (250 miles) from Singapore and only a three- to four-hour drive on the new four-lane North-South highway, Southeast Asia's longest highway and a shining achievement for Malaysia. You drive all the way from Singapore to the Thai border in only eight hours. The only way into Singapore by car is over the Causeway from Johore Bahru, the city at the southern tip of the Malay Peninsula. Malay and Singapore checkpoints are on either side of the Causeway. During rush hours there can be lines, but the formalities are as straightforward as those required at the airport. **Make sure that your car has the necessary insurance to be driven into Singapore.** Once in Singapore, pick up the expressway, which will lead you into the center of the city. If you are heading from Singapore to Kuala Lumpur, make sure that once you are in Johore Bahru, you follow the big green and white signs to the North–South highway. Otherwise, you may find yourself on the old two-lane road, an eight-hour journey.

E ENGLISH-LANGUAGE BOOKSTORES

Since English is the lingua franca, all regular bookstores carry English-language books, and there are bookstores in most of the larger shopping centers. Most major hotels also have a bookstore/newsstand, though selections are often limited. The Shangri-La and the Hyatt have good collections of magazines and newspapers from around the world. The three-story MPH Bookstore at the corner of Stamford Road and Armenian Street is one of the best English-language bookshops in Asia. Other MPH outlets are scattered over the island.

Should you have trouble finding a book, try the Times Bookstore head office (☎ 284–8844), which will tell you whether any of its branches carries the title. Its main shops are at the Centrepoint, Plaza Singapura, Lucky Plaza, Specialists Centre, Raffles City, and Marina Square shopping complexes.

Be aware that Singapore has a policy of censorship. Certain books and magazines are banned from being sold or even owned. Only one serious English-language newspaper, the *Straits Times,* is published in Singapore. It concentrates on local news but has international coverage as well. Editorially, it speaks for the ruling People's Action Party, and its reporting is highly biased.

The same company, Singapore Press Holdings, owns all the major newspapers and magazines on the island, most of which give similar fawning coverage to the government, but in different languages. The same publisher prints the *Business Times.* A popular newcomer, *The New Paper,* is a daily tabloid with a focus on local news and sports. For more international news coverage, seek out the *International Herald Tribune* or the *Asian Wall Street Journal.* Usually, both are available at the newsstands of leading hotels, though it is wise to reserve your copy ahead of time. Occasionally, in a fit of pique over an article, the government will ban a foreign publication, but the favored mode of censorship these days is lawsuits.

F FERRY TRAVEL

Hop a ferry to Bataam or Bintan and connect with an airline inside Indonesia; it's less expensive than flying directly from Singapore, although some people prefer the service and safety of Singapore Airlines.

H HEALTH

There are no serious health risks associated with travel to Singapore. Proof of vaccination

THE GOLD GUIDE / SMART TRAVEL TIPS

against yellow fever is required if you are entering from an infected area (e.g., often, Africa or South America). Occasionally though, there are reports of outbreaks of malaria or dengue fever, both spread by mosquitoes. If you are out exploring Singapore's wilder parks, **use insect repellent.**

Tap water is safe to drink, and every eating establishment—from the most elegant hotel dining room to the smallest sidewalk stall—is regularly inspected by the very strict health authorities.

HOLIDAYS

Singapore has 10 public holidays: New Year's Day (January 1), Hari Raya Puasa, Chinese New Year, Good Friday, Hari Raya Haji, Labor Day (May 1), Vesak Day, National Day (August 9), Deepvali, and Christmas Day (December 25). Many dates vary year by year.

I

INSURANCE

Travel insurance can protect your monetary investment, replace your luggage and its contents, or provide for medical coverage should you fall ill during your trip. Most tour operators, travel agents, and insurance agents sell specialized health-and-accident, flight, trip-cancellation, and luggage insurance as well as comprehensive policies with some or all of these coverages. Comprehensive policies may also reimburse you for delays

due to weather—an important consideration if you're traveling during the winter months. Some health-insurance policies do not cover preexisting conditions, but waivers may be available in specific cases. Coverage is sold by the companies listed in Important Contacts A to Z; these companies act as the policy's administrators. The actual insurance is usually underwritten by a well-known name, such as The Travelers or Continental Insurance.

Before you make any purchase, **review your existing health and homeowner's policies** to find out whether they cover expenses incurred while traveling.

BAGGAGE

Airline liability for baggage is limited to $1,250 per person on domestic flights. On international flights, it amounts to $9.07 per pound or $20 per kilogram for checked baggage (roughly $640 per 70-pound bag) and $400 per passenger for unchecked baggage. Insurance for losses exceeding the terms of your airline ticket can be bought directly from the airline at check-in for about $10 per $1,000 of coverage; note that it excludes a rather extensive list of items, shown on your airline ticket.

COMPREHENSIVE

Comprehensive insurance policies include all the coverages described above plus some that may not be available in more specific policies. If you have purchased an expensive vacation,

especially one that involves travel abroad, comprehensive insurance is a must; **look for policies that include trip delay insurance,** which will protect you in the event that weather problems cause you to miss your flight, tour, or cruise. A few insurers will also sell you a waiver for preexisting medical conditions. Some of the companies that offer both these features are Access America, Carefree Travel, Travel Insured International, and Travel Guard International (☞ Insurance *in* Important Contacts A to Z).

FLIGHT

You should **think twice before buying flight insurance.** Often purchased as a last-minute impulse at the airport, it pays a lump sum when a plane crashes, either to a beneficiary if the insured dies or sometimes to a surviving passenger who loses his or her eyesight or a limb. Supplementing the airlines' coverage described in the limits-of-liability paragraphs on your ticket, it's expensive and basically unnecessary. Charging an airline ticket to a major credit card often automatically provides you with coverage that may also extend to travel by bus, train, and ship.

HEALTH

Medicare generally does not cover health care costs outside the United States; nor do many privately issued policies. If your own health insurance policy does not cover you outside the United States, **consider buying supple-**

mental medical cover-
age. It can reimburse
you for $1,000–
$150,000 worth of
medical and/or dental
expenses incurred as a
result of an accident or
illness during a trip.
These policies also may
include a personal-
accident, or death-and-
dismemberment,
provision, which pays a
lump sum ranging from
$15,000 to $500,000 to
your beneficiaries if you
die or to you if you lose
one or more limbs or
your eyesight, and a
medical-assistance
provision, which may
either reimburse you for
the cost of referrals,
evacuation, or repatria-
tion and other services
or automatically enroll
you as a member of a
particular medical-
assistance company. (☞
Health *in* Important
Contacts A to Z.)

U.K. TRAVELERS

You can buy an annual
travel insurance policy
valid for most vacations
during the year in which
it's purchased. If you
are pregnant or have a
preexisting medical
condition make sure
you're covered before
buying such a policy.

TRIP

Without insurance, you
will lose all or most of
your money if you
cancel your trip, regard-
less of the reason.
Especially if your airline
ticket, cruise, or pack-
age tour is nonrefund-
able and cannot be
changed, it's essential
that you **buy trip-
cancellation-and-inter-
ruption insurance.**
When considering how
much coverage you
need, look for a policy
that will cover the cost

of your trip plus the
nondiscounted price of
a one-way airline ticket
should you need to
return home early. Read
the fine print carefully,
especially sections that
define "family member"
and "preexisting medi-
cal conditions." Also
**consider default or
bankruptcy insurance,**
which protects you
against a supplier's
failure to deliver. Be
aware, however, that if
you buy such a policy
from a travel agency,
tour operator, airline,
or cruise line, it may
not cover default by the
firm in question.

L

LANGUAGE

Singapore is a multira-
cial society with four
official languages:
Malay, Mandarin,
Tamil, and English.
The national language
is Malay; the lingua
franca is English.
English is also the
language of administra-
tion, is a required
course for every
schoolchild, and is
used in the entrance
examinations for uni-
versities. Hence, **virtually all Singaporeans
speak English** with
varying degrees of
fluency. Mandarin is
increasingly replacing
the other Chinese
dialects. However,
many older Chinese do
not speak Mandarin
and communicate in
"Singlish", a Singa-
porean version of
English that has its
own grammar.

M

MAIL

Most hotels sell stamps
and mail guests' letters.

Postage on local letters
up to 20 grams (0.8
ounces) is S$.22. Air-
mail takes about seven
business days to reach
North America and
Great Britain. An air-
mail postcard costs
S$.30 to most overseas
destinations; for over-
size postcards, the cost
is S$.70. A letter up to
20 grams is S$.35 to
Malaysia or Brunei,
S$.40 to other foreign
countries. Printed
aerogram letters (avail-
able at most post of-
fices) are S$.45.

Shops are normally
trustworthy in shipping
major purchases, but if
you prefer to make
arrangements yourself,
you will find post office
staff helpful and effi-
cient. All branches sell
"Postpac" packing
cartons, which come in
different sizes.

RECEIVING MAIL

If you know which
hotel you'll be staying
at, have mail sent there
marked "Hold for
Arrival." If you are not
sure where you will be
staying, you can pick
up mail addressed to
you c/o General Deliv-
ery, General Post Of-
fice, Fullerton Square,
Singapore.

MEDICAL
ASSISTANCE

No one plans to get sick
while traveling, but it
happens, so **consider
signing up with a medi-
cal assistance company.**
These outfits provide
referrals, emergency
evacuation or repatria-
tion, 24-hour telephone
hot lines for medical
consultation, cash for
emergencies, and other
personal and legal
assistance. They also

dispatch medical personnel and arrange for the relay of medical records. Coverage varies by plan, so **read the fine print carefully.**

MONEY & EXPENSES

The local currency is the Singapore dollar (S$), which is divided into 100 cents. At press time, the following exchange rates applied: US$1 = S$1.40, UK£1 = S$2.16, A$1 = S$1.09, C$1 = S$1.02, NZ$1 = S$.95. Notes in circulation are S$1, S$2, S$5, S$10, S$20, S$50, S$100, S$500, S$1,000, and S$10,000. Coins: S$.01, S$.05, S$.20, S$.50, and S$1.

ATMS

CASH ADVANCES➤ Before leaving home, **make sure that your credit cards have been programmed for ATM use in Singapore.** Note that Discover is accepted mostly in the United States. Local bank cards often do not work overseas either; **ask your bank about a Visa debit card,** which works like a bank card but can be used at any ATM displaying a Visa logo.

TRANSACTION FEES➤ Although fees charged for ATM transactions may be higher abroad than at home, Cirrus and Plus exchange rates are excellent, because they are based on wholesale rates offered only by major banks.

COSTS

Singapore ranks up there with other world capitals as far as expenses go. Prices have risen consistently over

the last 10 years, while the currency has also appreciated against the US dollar and other major currencies. While a gastronomical delight is still a little less than you would pay in Paris, hotel rooms are in the New York range. You can **keep costs down by eating at the inexpensive but hygienic hawker food centers,** especially those in the major shopping malls, and using the efficient, clean public transportation system, which provides easy access around the city of Singapore and the island very inexpensively.

EXCHANGING CURRENCY

For the most favorable rates, **change money at banks.** You won't do as well at exchange booths in airports or rail and bus stations, in hotels, in restaurants, or in stores, although you may find their hours more convenient. To avoid lines at airport exchange booths, **get a small amount of the local currency before you leave home.**

TAXES

There is a 3% sales tax in Singapore, called the GST. You can get refunds for purchases over S$500 at the airport on your way out of the country. This government tax is added to restaurant and hotel bills; sometimes a 10% service charge is added as well.

AIRPORT➤ There is a S$15 airport departure tax (for travelers to Malaysia, the tax is S$5). It is payable at the airport. To save time and avoid standing in

line, buy a tax voucher at your hotel or any airline office.

TRAVELER'S CHECKS

Whether or not to buy traveler's checks depends on where you are headed; **take cash to rural areas and small towns, traveler's checks to cities.** The most widely recognized checks are issued by American Express, Citicorp, Thomas Cook, and Visa. These are sold by major commercial banks for 1%–3% of the checks' face value—it pays to **shop around.** Both American Express and Thomas Cook issue checks that can be countersigned and used by either you or your traveling companion. So you won't be left with excess foreign currency, **buy a few checks in small denominations** to cash toward the end of your trip. Before leaving home, **contact your issuer for information on where to cash your checks** without a incurring a transaction fee. Record the numbers of all your checks, and keep this listing in a separate place, crossing off the numbers of checks you have cashed.

WIRING MONEY

For a fee of 3%–10%, depending on the amount of the transaction, you can have money sent to you from home through MoneyGram℠ or Western Union (☞ Money Matters *in* Important Contacts A to Z). The transferred funds and the service fee can be charged to a MasterCard or Visa account.

P

PACKING FOR SINGAPORE

Take casual, loose-fitting clothes made of natural fabrics to see you through days of heat and high humidity (you'll have to wash them often). Walking shorts, T-shirts, slacks, and sundresses are acceptable everywhere. Immodest clothing is frowned upon. You'll need a sweater or jacket to cope with air-conditioning in hotels and restaurants that sometimes borders on the glacial. Evening wear is casual; few restaurants require jacket and tie. The standard businessman's outfit in Singapore is trousers, a dress shirt, and a tie. Businesswomen wear lightweight suits. Same-day laundry service is available at most hotels, but it can be expensive.

It's advisable to **wear a hat, sunglasses, sunblock, and—of course—comfortable shoes while sightseeing.** You'll need an umbrella all year long; you can pick up inexpensive ones locally. Leave the plastic or nylon raincoats at home—the high humidity makes them extremely uncomfortable. Bring an extra pair of eyeglasses or contact lenses in your carry-on luggage, and if you have a health problem, **pack enough medication** to last the trip or have your doctor write you a prescription using the drug's generic name, because brand names vary from country to country (you'll then need a duplicate prescription from a local

doctor). It's important that you **don't put prescription drugs or valuables in luggage to be checked,** for it could go astray. To avoid problems with customs officials, carry medications in the original packaging. Also, don't forget the addresses of offices that handle refunds of lost traveler's checks.

ELECTRICITY

To use your U.S.-purchased electric-powered equipment, **bring a converter and an adapter.** The electrical current in Singapore 220 volts, 50 cycles alternating current (AC); wall outlets take plugs with two round oversize prongs or plugs with three prongs.

If your appliances are dual-voltage, you'll need only an adapter. Hotels sometimes have 110-volt outlets for low-wattage appliances near the sink, marked FOR SHAVERS ONLY; don't use them for high-wattage appliances like blow-dryers. If your laptop computer is older, carry a converter; new laptops operate equally well on 110 and 220 volts, so you need only an adapter.

LUGGAGE

Airline baggage allowances depend on the airline, the route, and the class of your ticket; **ask in advance.** In general, on domestic flights and on international flights between the United States and foreign destinations, you are entitled to check two bags. A third piece may be brought on board, but it must fit easily under the seat in

front of you or in the overhead compartment. In the United States, the FAA gives airlines broad latitude regarding carry-on allowances, and they tend to tailor them to different aircraft and operational conditions. Charges for excess, oversize, or overweight pieces vary.

If you are flying between two foreign destinations, note that baggage allowances may be determined not by piece but by weight—generally 88 pounds (40 kilograms) in first class, 66 pounds (30 kilograms) in business class, and 44 pounds (20 kilograms) in economy. If your flight between two cities abroad *connects* with your transatlantic or transpacific flight, the piece method still applies.

SAFEGUARDING YOUR LUGGAGE➤ Before leaving home, **itemize your bags' contents** and their worth, and label them with your name, address, and phone number. (If you use your home address, cover it so that potential thieves can't see it readily.) Inside each bag, **pack a copy of your itinerary.** At check-in, **make sure that each bag is correctly tagged** with the destination airport's three-letter code. If your bags arrive damaged—or fail to arrive at all—file a written report with the airline before leaving the airport.

PASSPORTS & VISAS

If you don't already have one, **get a passport.** It is advisable that you **leave one photo-copy of your passport's data page** with some-one at home and keep another with you, separated from your passport, while travel-ing. If you lose your passport, promptly call the nearest embassy or consulate and the local police; having the data page information can speed replacement.

IN THE U.S.

All U.S. citizens, even infants, need only a valid passport to enter Singapore for stays of up to 14 days. Applica-tion forms for both first-time and renewal passports are available at any of the 13 U.S. Passport Agency offices and at some post offices and courthouses. Pass-ports are usually mailed within four weeks; allow five weeks or more in spring and summer.

CANADIANS

You need only a valid passport to enter Singa-pore for stays of up to 14 days. Passport appli-cation forms are avail-able at 28 regional passport offices, as well as at post offices and travel agencies. Whether for a first or a renewal passport, you must apply in person. Chil-dren under 16 may be included on a parent's passport but must have their own to travel alone. Passports are valid for five years and are usually mailed within two to three weeks of application.

U.K. CITIZENS

Citizens of the United Kingdom need only a valid passport to enter Singapore for stays of up to 14 days. Applica-tions for new and renewal passports are available from main post offices and at the passport offices in Belfast, Glasgow, Liver-pool, London, New-port, and Peterborough. You may apply in person at all passport offices, or by mail to all except the London office. Children under 16 may travel on an accompanying parent's passport. All passports are valid for 10 years. Allow a month for processing.

S

SENIOR-CITIZEN DISCOUNTS

To qualify for age-related discounts, **men-tion your senior-citizen status up front** when booking hotel reserva-tions, not when check-ing out, and before you're seated in restau-rants, not when paying the bill. Note that discounts may be lim-ited to certain menus, days, or hours. When renting a car, **ask about promotional car-rental discounts**—they can net even lower costs than your senior-citizen discount.

STUDENTS ON THE ROAD

To save money, **look into deals available through student-oriented travel agencies.** To qualify, you'll need to have a bona fide student ID card. Members of international student groups are also eligible (☞ Students *in* Impor-tant Contacts A to Z).

SUBWAY TRAVEL

The most recent addi-tion to Singapore's public transport system is a superb subway, known as the MRT, consisting of two lines that run north–south and east–west and cross at the City Hall and Raffles Place inter-changes. The system includes a total of 42 stations along 67 kilo-meters (42 miles). All cars and underground stations are air-condi-tioned, and the trains operate between 5:45 AM and midnight daily.

Tickets may be pur-chased in the stations from vending machines (which give change) or at a booth. Large maps showing the station locations and the fares between them hang above each vending machine. There's a S$2 fine for underpaying, so **make sure you buy the right ticket for your destination.** The mag-netic tickets are inserted in turnstiles to let you on and off the platform. Fares start at S$.60 for about two stations; the maximum fare is S$1.60. The fare be-tween Orchard Road Station and Raffles Place Station (in the business district) is S$.60.

T

TAXIS

There are more than 10,000 taxis in Singa-pore, strictly regulated and metered. Many are air-conditioned. The starting fare is S$2.40 for the first 1.5 kilome-ters (0.9 miles) and S$.10 for each subse-quent 240 meters (787 feet). After 10 kilome-ters (6 miles) the rate increases to S$.10 for every 225 meters (820 feet). Every 30 seconds of waiting time carries a S$.10 charge. Drivers do not expect tips.

Be aware of several surcharges that may apply. A S$2.20 surcharge is charged for taxis booked by phone, and there is an additional S$1 surcharge for every booking half an hour or more in advance. Trips made between midnight and 6 AM have a 50% surcharge; rides from, *not to,* the airport carry a S$3 surcharge; and there are "entrance and exit fees" on taxis and private cars going into and out of the central business district, or CBD.

Unless a taxi displays a yellow permit, a S$1 surcharge is added to fares from the CBD between 4 and 7 PM on weekdays and noon and 3 PM on Saturday. To the CBD, there's a S$3 surcharge for the purchase of an Area License, which is needed to enter the Restricted Zone between 7:30 AM and 6:30 PM Monday–Friday and between 7:30 AM and 2 PM Saturday and on the eve of five major public holidays. Passengers do not pay the fee if the taxi already has the sticker. A $1 surcharge is added for all trips in London cabs and a Station Wagon taxi; an extra 10% of the fare is charged for payment by credit card.

Find taxis at stands or hail them from any curb not marked with a double yellow line. Radio cab services are available 24 hours (☎ 552–1111); a S$2.20

surcharge is imposed, and the meter should not be switched on until after you have entered the taxi. A driver showing a red disk in the window is returning to his garage and may pick up passengers going only in his direction. Often, it's almost impossible to get through to reserve a cab, so it's better to just hail one or take the bus.

Drivers carry tariff cards, which you may see if you want clarification of your tab. Register complaints with the STPB (☎ 736–6622); just threatening to complain usually resolves any difficulty, since drivers can lose their licenses if they break the law.

TELEPHONES

TELEPHONES

From a pay phone, the cost is S$.10; insert a coin and dial the seven-digit number. (Actually, most public phone booths take only phone cards; ☞ *below.*) Hotels charge anywhere from S$.10 to S$.50 a call. There are free public phones at Changi Airport, just past Immigration.

LONG-DISTANCE

The long-distance services of AT&T, MCI, and Sprint make calling home relatively convenient, but in many hotels you may find it impossible to dial the access number. The hotel operator may also refuse to make the connection. Instead, the hotel will charge you a premium rate—as much as 400% more than a calling card—for calls placed from your hotel room. To avoid such

price gouging, **travel with more than one company's long-distance calling card**—a hotel may block Sprint but not MCI. If the hotel operator claims that you cannot use any phone card, ask to be connected to an international operator, who will help you to access your phone card. You can also dial the international operator yourself. If none of this works, try calling your phone company collect in the United States. If collect calls are also blocked, call from a pay phone in the hotel lobby. Before you go, **find out the local access codes** for your destinations.

Direct dialing is available to most overseas countries. The top hotels provide direct-dial phones in guest rooms; smaller hotels have switchboards that will place your calls. In either case, check the service charge: It can be substantial. You can avoid the hotel charge by making international calls from the General Post Office (☞ Mail *in* Important Contacts A to Z), by using the international telephone services at Changi Airport, or by using your Singapore Telecoms phone card (☞ *below*) from a public phone. (Phone cards offer considerable savings over the use of hotel telephones, which add an 80% markup on overseas calls.) International cables may also be sent from the GPO or the airport. (☞ Operators & Information, *below.*)

The direct-dial prefix for Malaysia is 106. For

other international calls, dial 104 and the country code.

OPERATORS & INFORMATION

For directory assistance, dial 100. An economical way to call North America or the United Kingdom is to use international Home Countries Direct phones—USA Direct or UK Direct—which put you immediately in touch with either an American or a British telephone operator. The operator will place your call, either charging your telephone credit card or making the call collect. These phones may be found at the GPO and at many of the post offices around the city center, such as the one in the Raffles City shopping complex. You can also use pay phones by first depositing S$.10 and then dialing 8000–111–11 to reach the U.S. operator or 8000–440–440 for the British operator.

PHONE CARDS

Use the Telecoms phone card if you'll be making several long-distance calls during your stay in Singapore. The cards, similar to the Foncards used in Great Britain, can be purchased in denominations of S$2, S$5, S$10, S$20, and S$50 and permit you to make local and overseas calls. The price of each call is deducted from the card total, and your balance is roughly indicated by the punched hole in the card. Phone cards are available from post offices, Telecoms Customer Services outlets, and many drugstores.

Telephones that accept the phone card are most frequently found in shopping centers, post offices, subway stations, and the airport. Several public phones at the airport and many at city post offices accept Diners Club, Master-Card, and Visa.

TIPPING

Tipping is not customary in Singapore, and the government actively discourages it. It is prohibited at the airport and not encouraged in hotels that levy a 10% service charge or in restaurants. After experiencing some Singapore service, you may soon wish that they did allow tipping. Hotel bellboys are usually tipped S$1 per bag for handling luggage. Taxi drivers are not tipped by Singaporeans, who become upset when they see tourists tip; of course, the drivers don't mind!

TOUR OPERATORS

A package or tour to Singapore can make your vacation less expensive and more hassle-free. Firms that sell tours and packages reserve airline seats, hotel rooms, and rental cars in bulk and pass some of the savings on to you. In addition, the best operators have local representatives available to help you at your destination.

A GOOD DEAL?

The more your package or tour includes, the better you can predict the ultimate cost of your vacation. Make sure you know exactly what is covered, and **beware of hidden costs.**

Are taxes, tips, and service charges included? Transfers and baggage handling? Entertainment and excursions? These can add up.

Most packages and tours are rated deluxe, first-class superior, first class, tourist, or budget. The key difference is usually accommodations. If the package or tour you are considering is priced lower than in your wildest dreams, **be skeptical.** Also, **make sure your travel agent knows the accommodations** and other services. Ask about the hotel's location, room size, beds, and whether it has a pool, room service, or programs for children, if you care about these. Has your agent been there in person or sent others you can contact?

BUYER BEWARE

Each year a number of consumers are stranded or lose their money when operators—even very large ones with excellent reputations—go out of business. To avoid becoming one of them, take the time to **check out the operator**—find out how long the company has been in business and ask several agents about its reputation. Next, **don't book unless the firm has a consumer-protection program.** Members of the USTOA and the NTA are required to set aside funds for the sole purpose of covering your payments and travel arrangements in case of default. Nonmember operators may instead carry insurance; look for the details in the operator's brochure—and for the name of an underwriter with a solid reputation. Note: When it comes to tour operators, **don't trust escrow accounts.** Although there are laws governing those of charter-flight operators, no governmental body prevents tour operators from raiding the till.

Next, **contact your local Better Business Bureau and the attorney general's offices** in both your own state and the operator's; have any complaints been filed? Finally, **pay with a major credit card.** Then you can cancel payment, provided that you can document your complaint. Always **consider trip-cancellation insurance** (☞ Insurance, *above*).

BIG VS. SMALL➤ Operators that handle several hundred thousand travelers per year can use their purchasing power to give you a good price. Their high volume may also indicate financial stability. But some small companies provide more personalized service; because they tend to specialize, they may also be more knowledgeable about a given area.

USING AN AGENT

Travel agents are excellent resources. In fact, large operators accept bookings made only through travel agents. But it's good to **collect brochures from several agencies** because some agents' suggestions may be skewed by promotional relationships with tour and package

firms that reward them for volume sales. If you have a special interest, **find an agent with expertise in that area**; ASTA can provide leads in the United States. (Don't rely solely on your agent, though; agents may be unaware of small-niche operators, and some special-interest travel companies only sell direct.)

SINGLE TRAVELERS

Prices are usually quoted per person, based on two sharing a room. If traveling solo, you may be required to pay the full double-occupancy rate. Some operators eliminate this surcharge if you agree to be matched up with a roommate of the same sex, even if one is not found by departure time.

TRAIN TRAVEL

The same company that operates the Venice Simplon–Orient Express now runs the Eastern & Oriental Express deluxe train once a week between Singapore and Bangkok, with a stop in Butterworth (Malaysia) permitting an excursion to Penang. The 1,943-kilometer (1,200-mile) journey takes 41 hours and includes two nights and one full day on board. The cabin decor is modeled on the Josef von Sternberg–Marlene Dietrich movie *Shanghai Express*. Fares, which vary according to cabin type and include meals, start at US$860 per person one-way.

FROM MALAYSIA

Malay Railways serves Singapore from Kuala Lumpur and points

north. There are immigration and customs offices at Singapore's Keppel Road station. Keppel Road is at the southern end of the city's business district, a good 15 to 20 minutes by taxi from Orchard Road. But there is an MRT subway station at Tanjong Pagar, six minutes away by foot, that will whisk you to Orchard Road in about 10 minutes for S$1.

TRAVEL GEAR

Travel catalogs specialize in useful items that can **save space when packing** and make life on the road more convenient. Compact alarm clocks, travel irons, travel wallets, and personal-care kits are among the most common items you'll find. They also carry dual-voltage appliances, currency converters, and foreign-language phrase books. Some catalogs even carry miniature coffeemakers and water purifiers.

U

U.S.

GOVERNMENT

The U.S. government can be an excellent source of travel information. Some of this is free and some is available for a nominal charge. When planning your trip, **find out what government materials are available.** For just a couple of dollars, you can get a variety of publications from the Consumer Information Center in Pueblo, Colorado. Free consumer information also is available from individual government agencies, such as the

Department of Transportation or the U.S. Customs Service. For specific titles, see the appropriate publications entry under topics in Important Contacts A to Z.

W

WHEN TO GO

Singapore has neither peak nor off-peak tourist seasons. Hotel prices remain the same throughout the year, though during quiet spells many properties will discount room rates upon request (either in person or by mail). The busiest tourist months are December and July.

CLIMATE

With the equator only 129 kilometers (80 miles) to the south, Singapore is usually either hot or very hot. The average daily temperature is 80°F (or 26.6°C); it usually reaches 87°F (30.7°C) in the afternoon and drops to a cool 75°F (23.8°C) just before dawn. The months from November through January, during the northeast monsoon, are generally the coolest. The average daily relative humidity is 84.5%, though it drops to 65%–70% on dry afternoons.

Rain falls year-round, but the wettest months are November through January. February is usually the sunniest month; December, the most inclement. Though Singapore has been known to have as much as 20 inches (512.2 millimeters) of rainfall in one 24-hour period, brief, frequent rainstorms are the norm, and the washed streets soon dry in the sun that follows.

The climate may sound daunting, but don't let it put you off. All the hotels, except those in the budget range, are centrally air-conditioned. So are the shopping malls and restaurants and most sightseeing coaches and taxis. **Try to do most of your walking in the morning or late afternoon.** The heat grows really sticky in the early afternoon—that's the time to seek out air-conditioning or a cool sea breeze.

The following are average daily maximum and minimum temperatures for Singapore.

Climate In Singapore

Jan.	86F	30C	May	89F	32C	Sept.	88F	31C
	74	23		75	24		75	24
Feb.	88F	31C	June	88F	31C	Oct.	88F	31C
	74	23		75	24		74	23
Mar.	88F	31C	July	88F	31C	Nov.	88F	31C
	75	24		75	24		74	23
Apr.	88F	31C	Aug.	88F	31C	Dec.	88F	31C
	75	24		75	24		74	23

1 Destination: Singapore

INTRODUCTION

EVER SINCE SINGAPORE BECAME an independent nation in 1965, it has been a standing joke among Singaporeans that if you turn your back for a second, you won't be able to find your way home, the streetscape will have changed so much.

Demolition, development, and renewal rotate in endless cycles on the 646-square-kilometer tropical island, contributing to the underlying nervous tension of the place. Singapore's history, pocked with the turbulence of the World War II Japanese Occupation and postwar communist insurgency, has left a residue of anxiety. The vulnerability many feel is heightened by the former British colony's geographical situation as a predominantly Chinese island surrounded by the more traditional and conservative Malayo-Islamic cultures of Malaysia and Indonesia. Hypersensitive to perceived danger and to criticism from without and within, Singapore's government has waged feisty battles with both the foreign press and local liberals.

A real dependence on the global economy and trading system exacerbates this strung-out feeling as the nation darts hither and thither like a nimble shrimp, deftly changing course in response to international currents. But Singapore has always insisted it is a shrimp with a sting in its tail, thanks to a well-equipped army and action-ready citizenry, schooled by military National Service and regular Civil Service drills.

Singapore has a relentless urge to develop and capitalize its limited land resources; the economy has often been primed by massive infrastructural projects, such as the construction of the world's best, most comfortable airport at Changi and also one of the world's most efficient subway systems, the MRT (Mass Rapid Transit System). In addition the government has built blocks of high-rise housing in which more than 80 percent of Singapore's 2.9 million citizens live as homeowners, thanks in part to a government-run compulsory savings fund. Both government and people are economic-growth junkies, working hard and long hours together for an average annual fix of about 7% growth—down from the double-digit rates of recent years but still extraordinary even by East Asian standards.

Another local joke (yes, Singaporeans do know how to laugh at themselves, notwithstanding the seeming earnest formality of their public and official personae) has it that all the Singapore girl cares about in Mr. Right is the Five C's—Car, Condo, Cash, Credit Card, and Country Club. That's sexist—those badges of material success are pretty high on the agenda for all Singaporeans, male and female. In a country where you have to bid for the right to own a car before you even begin to buy one—the Certificate of Entitlement was S$42,000–S$66,000 at last bidding—and where private landed property sells for about S$5 million and high-rise government-built apartments for half a million, such acquisitions imply serious wealth.

But wealth is one thing many Singaporeans have, in a resource-poor nation that has used chiefly its formidable wits to win ranking as the third-richest country in Asia, after Japan and Brunei (which latter has oil); per capita gross domestic product is S$34,000 a year, while the nation's official foreign reserves stand at a staggering S$85 billion, testimony to a thrifty, conservative, and sometimes ruthlessly business-minded government. Singapore's politicians, civil servants, and private-sector executives are among the highest-paid in the world (well over S$1 million a year apiece for the prime minister, deputy prime minister, and senior minister).

Singapore always has been a social laboratory. Singaporeans have taken pride in doing it their way, making up their own rules. Western concepts of liberal democracy, freedoms of the press, speech, and assembly, privacy of information, and the like have often been brushed aside as bothersome brakes on action by a People's Action Party (PAP) government repeatedly re-elected to overwhelming majority power since 1959. (The party's first secretary-general and longtime leader, Lee Kuan Yew, stepped down as prime minister in 1990 but retains major influence in his current post as senior minister.) Detention without trial for both criminal elements and those deemed political internal security risks is a weapon of state inherited from the British colonial administration and still occasionally used.

There being little real prospect of electoral defeat for the PAP, a certain stability permitting efficient long-term planning has resulted. The populace is largely compliant, give or take a few intellectuals, in return for the government's guarantee of a "full rice bowl": it's an ancient, essentially Confucian, social contract.

Stability should not be confused with complacency, however. When faced with an election, the PAP campaigns hard to increase its share of the vote. Likewise, the government is concerned about the declining economic growth rate and strives to recapture the higher rates of the late 1980s and early 1990s.

SINGAPORE IS INDEED its own nation. When in the late 1970s the government set up an official matchmaking unit, the SDU (Social Development Unit), dedicated initially to getting reluctant or unsuccessful female graduates married off, yet another Singaporean joke scoffed at it as standing for "Single, Desperate, and Ugly." But today it has melted into the mainstream.

That Singapore favors tough laws—hanging for drug trafficking or mere association with firearms carried for a criminal purpose, and caning for various offenses, including immigration visa overstay and vandalism—is well known. Yet it has to be said that the streets of Singapore are among the safest in the world for a woman, or man, to walk alone by night, besides being clean and drug-free.

There is an old saw that Singapore is "a fine city"—S$1,000 fine for littering, S$500 for smoking indoors, S$500 for not flushing the toilet; it's all part of the Singaporean penchant for order, orderliness, and Victorian-style propriety (and sometimes, hypocrisy to match).

In pursuit of order and decorum, there are now laws banning the importation, sale, purchase, or manufacture (but not the possession or consumption) of chewing gum, backed up by a S$1,000 fine (kids were jamming up the MRT sliding doors with the stuff), and not only nudity in public places but also nudity in private places visible to the public (e.g., your own highrise apartment, as seen from your neighbor's facing window), with a fine of S$2,000, or three months' jail. Another new law holds parents liable for their minor children's delinquency, and yet another allows parents to sue grown children for financial support.

But beneath the orderly surface, tremendous social change is under way. Confronted with its limits to growth, Singapore is externalizing its economy, intentionally creating mini-Singapores abroad, notably in China and India. It is also networking with extensive expatriate and emigrant Singaporean communities in Australia, Canada, and the United States, among other locations. A general broadening of the national mind has been the inevitable result.

With the Five C's becoming ever less affordable, many young Singaporeans are reassessing their culture's fabled work ethic (Saturday morning is still all hands to the deck), wondering if it is worth striving so hard. That's a big change from their parents' attitude.

Barring occasional incidents of censor backlash, the arts scene is becoming more liberal. Reasonably adult films are at last standard cinema fare, in the R(A) or "Restricted (Artistic)" classification category; both local theater and local literature are blooming. Independent voices are more often heard than in the past; among these are fairly vocal green and feminist lobby groups.

In a sense, Singapore wears a reversible costume—Western-suit/Mandarin jacket—and swaps Chinese opera masks at will to reflect whatever character it wants to play at any given moment. That makes it a uniquely deceptive place, difficult to know beyond the Western gloss and, in a way, treacherous for the unwary.

Behind the computer terminals sit people who set superstitious store in the power of numbers (unlucky 4 brings death, while lucky 8 wins prosperity) and position their homes and business premises according to the precepts of feng shui, or geomancy; in their leisure hours, some of them may be temple spirit mediums or fire-walkers. But then, in the "surprising Singapore" of the recent Singapore Tourist Promotion Board slogan, they could just as easily turn out to be cricket aces or Scots bagpipers, too.

Careful background reading, particularly of the country's history, will help you to understand these contradictions, as would study of Singapore's various languages, including that vibrant street-jive creole "Singlish," a potpourri of English, Chinese, and Malay impenetrable to the native English-speaker. (Fortunately, Singaporeans switch easily to "Queen's English.") And don't forget to talk to taxi drivers.

Most foreigners in Singapore (including about 300,000 "guest workers," mostly construction laborers and maids, who do the dirtier work most Singaporeans will not do anymore) are mere birds of passage, but some have found reasons to linger. They find it hard to put their finger on what it is that has made them stay: "It's just a certain something." But when pressed, many point to an underlying gentleness bordering on innocence, or a childlike enjoyment of simple, often material, pleasures that together typify the Singaporean. Others relish the vibrant multicultural street life of a tropical city. Still others cite the energy of the place, the constant sense of being busy and purposeful, of going somewhere.

As in a traditional arranged marriage, you have to *learn* to love Singapore —it's not a love-at-first-sight place. And as the old song goes, to know it is to love it. It only takes time.

—Ilsa Sharp

WHAT'S WHERE

The diamond-shaped island of the Republic of Singapore, lying offshore but connected by a causeway to peninsular Malaysia, is only 622 square kilometers (646 square kilometers if you include the satellite islands), and yet it has nature reserves, a thriving metropolis, ethnic enclaves, industrial parks, beaches, and entertainment parks. Slightly under 3 million people now live in Singapore, and the majority of their ancestors arrived from all points of the compass within the past 200 years. They brought cultural diversity, which shaped Singapore's evolution into today's vibrant ethnic mix.

Sir Thomas Raffles chose to develop Singapore as a trading center for the East India Company because of the island's commanding position on the Straits of Malacca and the safe anchorage in the southwestern harbor at the mouth of Singapore River. This was to be the cauldron of sweat and toil that produced Raffles's commercial emporium. Paramount to maintaining a smooth trading operation was the prevention of racial strife, and so Raffles applied his knowledge of 19th-century urban planning. In his perspective, racial harmony was best achieved by geographical segregation: the Chinese, Indians, Malays, and, of course, the Europeans were allotted their separate domains. The vestiges of these racial divisions are still apparent.

Since the most desirable land lay to the east of the river and overlooking the waterfront, Raffles designated it as the domain of the British and their administration. Here, in what has been termed **Colonial Singapore,** is what's left of the work of the Irish architect George Coleman, who with Raffles created one of the major entrepôts in Asia. Coleman's Palladian-style buildings, modified to confront the steaming tropical heat, are impressive monuments to his era and now serve as a buffer zone between the high-tech glitz of Orchard Road and Chinatown. Here, too, is the famous **Raffles Hotel,** now renovated, standing alongside the tallest hotel in the world, the **Westin.**

The Chinese, on whose backs Singapore's trade depended, were allotted the area south of the Singapore River. Even within **Chinatown,** different ethnic clusters formed. Arriving from China often with no money and in debt to the boat captains who brought them, these immigrants sought shelter with those who came from the same region of China. Crowding was horrendous, with one or more families living in a single room. The only escape was to smoke a pipe in one of the many opium dens, seek company at the corner brothel, or pay tribute to the gods in the hope they'd assist lady luck in the gambling dens. Although Singapore's quest to be a futuristic metropolis caused much of old

Chinatown to be bulldozed, there still remain signs of the past. Rows of shophouses (two-story buildings with a store or a factory at ground level and living space upstairs); streets specializing in such particularities as herbal medicines or death houses; elaborate temples to the gods of the old country; wet markets; and other structures built by the original immigrants maintain the flavor of Raffles's day.

Land to the east and north of Colonial Singapore beginning at Sungei Road was allotted to the Indian community, whose main street is Serangoon Road. While many Indians came as convict labor and later taught crafts, others came to work as traders, clerks, teachers, and moneylenders. And though they came from all over ethnically diverse India, they melded into their own Singaporean Indian culture. Many of them shared the Hindu religion, and here, in what is known as **Little India,** are the ornate temples of **Sri Srinivasa Perumal,** dedicated to Vishnu the Preserver, and **Sri Veeramakaliamman,** dedicated to Kali the Courageous. The whole area, especially the streets branching off Serangoon Road, is perfumed with smells of spices and curries, colored by women wearing saris, and crammed with stores brimming with goods brought from the Indian subcontinent.

Slightly to the east of Little India, bordered by Beach and North Bridge roads, is the **Arab District,** sometime known as **Little Araby.** Though Malays lived in *kampongs* (small communities) throughout the island, this area was assigned to Malays who wanted to be close to the action. Not only Malays but also other Muslims, especially traders from Indonesia, congregate here. Binding this community is the great **Sultan Mosque.** Here too in the Arab District is the former palace of the sultan, **Istana Kampong Glam.** Streets named Bussorak and Kandahar not only evoke images of the Muslim world, but also provide, along with Arab Street, excellent shopping for imported batiks and Indonesian crafts.

Modern, fashion-conscious Singapore is north and slightly west of Colonial Singapore, the administrative center. **Orchard Road,** its main street, is like New York's Fifth Avenue or London's Regent Street. Here are countless glittering shopping plazas and hotels. At the junction of Orchard and Scotts roads, a central hub,

you will see every person who comes to Singapore.

Out of the central city, the **East Coast Parkway** runs towards Changi Airport and the infamous **Changi Prison,** where the Japanese incarcerated the Europeans captured at the fall of Singapore in 1941. Along this coast are the best, albeit limited, beach areas with facilities for water sports. In the opposite direction, down past the World Trade center and running along the southwest coast, is the **West Coast Highway,** leading to the industrial area of Jurong. Along this route are theme parks **Haw Par Villa** and **Tang Dynasty Village;** the **Jurong Bird Park,** with a 5-acre walk-in aviary; and the **Chinese and Japanese gardens.**

Less than 5% of the island remains forested. However, there is more to Singapore than its concrete buildings and glass skyscrapers. It is not too much of a stretch to call at least the interior of Singapore the **Garden Isle.** Going north and inland from downtown Singapore, you come upon the beautiful **Botanic Gardens,** said to be second only to those in Bogor on Java for the display of tropical plants. Farther north and slightly to the west is the **Bukit Timah Nature Reserve,** where trails wind their way through thick forest. To the north of that is the superb **Singapore Zoo** and the equally fascinating **Night Safari** park, where nocturnal animals roam in "natural" surrounds. Farther north, ten miles before the causeway to the Malay Peninsula, you come to the **Mandai Orchid Gardens,** which have more than 2,000 varieties of orchids. So despite the island's poor soil, the government has made a strenuous effort to re-create—and sanitize—nature for its citizens and tourists.

Some 60 small islands lie off the southern coast of the main island of Singapore. The largest is **Sentosa,** now linked by a causeway and a cable car, which has become a full-blown entertainment island with two hotels, museums, aquariums, nature parks, and restaurants. **Kusu Island** and **St. John's Island,** lying south of Sentosa, are reached by a scheduled boat service and make popular picnic spots for Singaporeans escaping the city. Other islands are rarely visited except by fishermen and those desperate to do a little scuba diving.

Bintan, an Indonesian island in the Singapore Strait, is just 45 minutes from Singapore's World Trade Centre by hydrofoil ferry.

Over the causeway at the northern apex of Singapore's diamond island is **Johore Bahru,** the southernmost town on the Malay Peninsula. Approximately halfway up the Malay Peninsula from Johore Bahru is **Kuala Lumpur,** Malaysia's capital. **Malacca,** where the colonial influence of the Portuguese and Dutch is still evident, is on the west coast of Malaysia and can be visited on the return trip from Kuala Lumpur to Singapore.

PLEASURES AND PASTIMES

Dining

Eating is an all-consuming passion among Singaporeans, and the visitor soon discovers why. There is a stunning array of delicious cuisine from all around the world, particularly from the three major cultures that make up the island nation: Chinese, Malay, and Indian. Singaporeans eat out frequently, and they are particular. No restaurant can stay in business longer than a month if it fails to meet their high standards. And though the cost of living in Singapore has escalated over the last decade, competition among the restaurants has kept dining inexpensive. The cleanliness of Singapore also makes dining a pleasure. You can eat with the same confidence at a roadside stand as in a gourmet five-star hotel dining room.

Food is a route to cultural empathy for the visitor, especially if it's consumed at a hawker's stall in one of Singapore's food centers, preferably of the old-style open-air variety. Here the multicultural, East-West crossroads flavors of Singapore achieve their full piquancy. It may be noisy, hot, and somewhat odiferous, but here you can experience the essence of Singapore.

Gardens and Parks

You can escape from the concrete and glass that is modern downtown Singapore to wonderfully kept gardens, such as the Botanic Gardens, or visit orchid farms.

The more energetic can hike the trails of Bukit Timah Nature Reserve—the tigers have long gone, but the sounds and smells of the jungle are still there. If you want to see a tiger or two, as well as animals from as far away as the North Pole, Singapore has one the world's most pleasant zoos, designed on the open-moat concept. And because many animals are nocturnal, there is another zoo, the Night Safari, where tigers and rhinoceroses wake up at dusk to feed.

Lodging

Less than 10 years ago, travelers in Asia would periodically return to Singapore for creature comforts and top-notch accommodations. Hotels were not just the best in Asia, but better than many of the top hotels in Europe. And they were very affordable. Hotel prices have escalated since then, and other Asian destinations have built their own grand and luxurious hotels. Yet, though Singapore is not the same indulgent retreat it once was, it is hard to match the standard of comfort, efficiency of staff, and level of ancillary services that the Singapore hotel offers. The luxury hotels cater to every whim—and so they should at $300 a night—but good service, freshly decorated rooms, cleanliness, and modern facilities can be found for around $200. For less money, there are simple, clean hotels (often more personal than the larger ones), with rooms for about $90. If you are on a tight budget, the youth hostels are spotless, cosmopolitan, and cheap. With Singapore hotels you get what you pay for, and perhaps a bit more.

Shopping

Once upon a time Singapore, a duty free republic, was a haven for shoppers. And though shopping is still the major pastime for Singaporeans, nowadays they are rich and sassy. The strong Singaporean dollar and expensive real estate have caused prices to shoot up, and except for a lucky find in an antique store, bargains no longer exist. Still, nowhere else will you find so many shops carrying the latest fashions and electronic equipment, so browsing rather than shopping becomes the pleasurable pastime. Look here, decide what you want, then purchase it when you reach another Asian capital—perhaps Kuala Lumpur or Bangkok.

Theme Parks

No other country of Singapore's size has put so much effort into creating attractions for both its citizens and tourists. Singapore may have spent millions destroying its heritage buildings, but private enterprise has also spent a fortune re-creating the old at theme parks, usually designed to educate and entertain. Haw Par Villa emphasizes Chinese mythology, and the Tang Dynasty Village displays life in ancient China.

NEW AND NOTEWORTHY

Singapore is always adding **new and sparkling hotels** to its huge inventory of rooms—in excess of 30,000. Three of the new ones, the Ritz-Carlton, the Inter-Continental and the Four Seasons, are in the luxury category, with the Ritz-Carlton being the most dramatic. The Shangri-La group has opened the more economical Traders Hotel, designed for the traveler who wants convenience, comfort, and efficiency, but not the high tariff. The **new convention center** at Suntec City (it, too, has a new 1,000-room hotel, the Marina Pontiac) is expected to increase the number and size of conventions held in Singapore.

The **Singapore Art Museum,** which opened in 1996 on Bras Basah Road, was a decade in the making. Its permanent collection encompasses some 3,000 works from Singapore, Indonesia, Malaysia, Brunei, the Philippines, Thailand, and Vietnam. Thematic exhibitions are drawn from this vast resource. The entire collection is accessible through the museum's Electronic Gallery, called E-mage, where visitors can call up digitized images of artworks on computer monitors. The goal of the museum is to study and present the region's modern art, although there are some pre-20th-century works as well.

FODOR'S CHOICE

Special Moments

★**Cricket on the Padang** is a nostalgic reminder of bygone days.

★**Street wayangs** (Chinese opera) provide a rare taste of traditional Chinese entertainment.

★**Breakfast at the Jurong Bird Park** is a musical feast.

★**Breakfast at the zoo** with the irresistible Ah Meng, the star orangutan, is unforgettable.

★**A boat trip to Pulau Sakeng** is a rare opportunity to visit a traditional Malay village.

Taste Treats

★**Fiery-hot chili crab** can be sampled at the UDMC Seafood Centre.

★**Fish-head curry** is the dish to order at Banana Leaf Apollo.

★*Dosai* **pancakes** are the highlight of Samporna dinner at Annalakshmi.

★**Durian fruit** tastes better than it smells at Clarke Quay's Durian House.

★**Hairy crab** is available for a very brief season in autumn.

★**High tea** at the Goodwood Park offers a taste of British tradition.

★*Kaiseki* **dinner** at Nadaman epitomizes the refinement of Japan.

Festivals and Seasonal Events

★Seeing is not believing at **Thaipusam** (mid-January–early February).

★You will not lose your appetite at the **Festival of the Hungry Ghosts** (August–September).

Sights and Museums

★The **Botanic Gardens** is both an escape from the brick and mortar and a chance to appreciate tropical flora.

★**Empress Place** has absolutely top-notch exhibitions, most of which display antiquities from mainland China.

★The different deities and overpowering aura of the otherworld at the **Fuk Tak Chi Temple** make all of us believers.

★The **Pioneers of Singapore Museum** gives a three-dimensional recounting of Singapore's early days.

★The open plan of Singapore's **Zoological Gardens** and **Night Safari** zoo places you in the animals' habitat rather than making you watch nature's creations behind bars.

★**Sri Mariamman Temple** brings Hinduism down to earth.

★The **Sultan Mosque** is the focus of the Malay community.

Restaurants

★**Chang Jiang**'s sophisticated presentation is matched by exquisite Shanghainese cuisine. Gold-plated chopsticks set the style. $$$$

★**Latour** offers arguably the best Continental cuisine in town, served in an elegant setting. $$$$

★**Li Bai**'s superior surroundings set the tone for "nouvelle Chinoise," the best of creative Cantonese cuisine. $$$–$$$$

★**Bastiani's** serves today's food, inspired by the Mediterranean and California. $$$

★**Cherry Garden** offers unusual cuisine from China's Hunan Province, in surroundings reminiscent of a Chinese pavilion. $$$

★**Nadaman** serves the ultimate in refined Japanese cuisine, with the Singapore skyline as a backdrop. $$$

★**Tandoor** gives the impression of dining in a maharaja's palace. The North Indian dishes are first-rate. $$$

★**Dragon City** is rated by many Singaporeans as the best place to enjoy the emphatic cuisine of Szechuan. $$–$$$

★**La Brasserie** is in the style of a typical Parisian brasserie, with consistently good food. $$–$$$

★**Thanying** serves refined Thai palace cuisine, produced by Thai chefs under the supervision of a noble Thai family. $$–$$$

★**Banana Leaf Apollo** produces robust South Indian curries, including the famous Singaporean fish-head curry. $

★**Madras New Woodlands Restaurant** serves the world's most creative vegetarian cuisine in unpretentious surroundings. $

Hotels

★**The Goodwood Park** is Singapore's bastion of tradition and gentility. $$$$

★**The Ritz-Carlton,** where you can see Singapore Harbor from your bathtub, pampers you with modern comfort. $$$$

★**The Shangri-La** wins our top recommendation for its excellent service. $$$$

★**The Duxton** is the best of Singapore's boutique hotels. $$$

★**Traders Hotel** does not offer fancy frills, but instead gives very comfortable accommodation and efficient service at a reasonable price. $$

★**Ladyhill Hotel** is a pleasant retreat from high-rise and high-tech Singapore. $

★**RELC International House** offers the best value in inexpensive lodgings. $

Nightlife

★**Brannigans** pub is a friendly waterhole, good for meeting old and new friends.

★**Xanadu**'s stage gadgetry creates changing scenes and different moods during the dancing evening.

★**Saxophone** is hard to beat for good jazz.

★**Boat Quay,** with its many indoor and outdoor bars and restaurants, is the best place for easy refreshment, people-watching, and partying.

Shopping

★**Ngen An City** has a collection of high-fashion shops anchored by the Takashimaya department store.

★Antiques are becoming hard to find, but sometimes you get lucky in **Holland Village.**

★The stores and shops along **Arab Street** spill out onto the sidewalk with an array of Malay and Indonesian wares.

★Nothing beats **Chinatown Centre**'s wet market for mouthwatering exotic foods.

★**P. Govindasamy Pillai** has the best-quality Indian silks.

★**China Silk House** has a deservedly high reputation for Chinese silks.

GREAT ITINERARIES

You can do as much or as little as you like in Singapore. If you took in all of the regions explored in this guide without stopping for breath, you would see virtually all of Singapore in five days—and not even have begun to shop! There's plenty to see and do if you have the time.

One way to experience Singapore is to use it as a hub for travel throughout Southeast Asia. From the city-state's airport, Changi, planes travel in all directions, and many flights between countries connect through Singapore. So you may want to see Singapore in installments. After a couple of days spent exploring the city-state, go to another Southeast Asian country, then return to Singapore before continuing to yet another destination. Singapore permits you to catch your breath: it's safe, clean, and everything works efficiently.

If You Have 2 Days

On the first morning, you might visit the **Colonial** and **Chinatown** districts, then spend the afternoon shopping and exploring on **Orchard Street.** In the evening, dine at one of the city's many excellent restaurants. The next day have breakfast at the zoo, then return to the city to explore **Little India** and the **Arab District.** In the afternoon, you may want to take the ferry or cable car to **Sentosa Island** to see the **Pioneers of Singapore Museum.** In the evening, try dining at a food center, such as **Newton Circus.**

If You Have 4 Days

In the first two, get to know the city by covering the **Colonial, Chinatown, Little India,** and **Arab districts.** You'll surely spend some time on **Orchard Street** shopping, browsing, and people-watching.

One evening soon after dusk, visit the **Night Safari** park, then have dinner at a hawker food center. On the third day, take a trip out to **Kusu** or one of the other islands and spend a few hours exploring. For the afternoon, try one of Singapore's theme parks, perhaps **Haw Par Villa.** In the evening, stroll first around **Clarke Quay** before moving on to **Boat Quay** for drinks, people-watching, and perhaps something to eat. On the fourth day, visit some museums and parks on **Sentosa Island;** try not to miss the **Pioneers of Singapore Museum,** since that gives a good idea of what Singapore was like in the early 1800s. In the evening treat yourself at one of Singapore gourmet havens. Alternatively, on your last day you could visit the Indonesian island of **Bintan,** boarding a ferry from the World Trade Centre at about 10 AM for the 90-minute run to Tanjung Pinang. Browse the market for good buys, then head out to the beaches. Ferries return to Singapore in the late afternoon.

If You Have 7 or More Days

Use the first three or four to explore Singapore, then cross the causeway to **Malaysia.** To see as much as possible, start from **Johore Bahru** and drive up the east coast. You will not have time to go out to Tioman Island unless that is all you want to do. So, plan on **Kuantan** being your first night's stop. You will have enough time on the following day to test the sea waters, go up to **Cherating,** and visit the **Pancing Caves** before crossing the peninsula to the Malaysian capital, **Kuala Lumpur.** In the late afternoon on the next day, drive down to **Malacca,** the trading seaport used by the Portuguese, then the Dutch, and then the British, until it was eclipsed by Singapore. Stay the night in Malacca and return to Johore Bahru the next morning. You may want to tarry here awhile before crossing back onto Singapore Island.

FESTIVALS AND SEASONAL EVENTS

Singapore is a city of festivals, from the truly exotic (Thaipusam, Festival of the Nine Emperor Gods) to the strictly-for-tourists (International Shopping Festival, Miss Tourism Pageant). Timing your visit to coincide with one of the more colorful celebrations can greatly increase the pleasure of your stay; with so many different cultural and religious groups, you'll find festivals going on almost all the time. There are numerous national holidays and celebrations as well.

Except for the family-oriented festivals and the monthlong fast of Ramadan, these events are as much fun for visitors as they are for the native celebrants. The following is a chronological listing of the major festivals. The dates and seasons of many of them vary from year to year according to the lunar calendar. For a complete listing with current dates, contact the Singapore Tourist Promotion Board.

WINTER

LATE DEC.–LATE JAN.➤ **Ramadan** is the month of daytime fasting among the city's Muslim population. Its date is set by the Islamic calendar. Special stalls in Bussorah Street and around the Sultan Mosque sell a variety of dishes, including Malay rice cakes wrapped in banana leaves, fragrant puddings flavored with pandanus and coated in coconut syrup, and mutton cubes topped with sweet roasted coconut. The best time to

visit the food stalls is between 5 and 7:30 PM, when the Muslim community emerges from the day's fast for a binge of snacking.

The end of Ramadan is marked with a celebration, **Hari Raya Puasa.** A major feast is undertaken as celebrating Muslims, dressed in traditional garb, visit friends and relatives.

MID-JAN.➤ During **Pongal,** the four-day harvest festival, Tamil Indians from South India offer rice, curries, vegetables, sugarcane, and spices in thanksgiving to the Hindu gods. The Perumal Temple on Serangoon Road is the best place to view these rites. During this holiday, the Tamils give presents and send greeting cards. The cards are sold in most Indian shops and stalls along Serangoon Road.

MID-JAN.–FEB.➤ **Thaipusam** celebrates the victory of the Hindu god Subramaniam over the demon Idumban, who, according to legend, tried to run off with two sacred mountains.

After nightlong ritual purification and chanting, penitents enter a trance and pierce their flesh—including their tongues and cheeks—with knives, steel rods, and fishhooks, which they wear during the festival's spectacular procession. Mysteriously, the wounds do not bleed or leave scars. The devotees carry *kavadi* (half hoops adorned with peacock feathers) to symbolize the mountains that caused the epic

battle. The 8-kilometer (5-mile) procession begins at the Perumal Temple on Serangoon Road, passes the Sri Mariamman Temple on South Bridge Road, and ends at the Chettiar Temple, where women pour pots of milk over the image of Lord Subramaniam.

Thaipusam is not for the squeamish, but it is an extraordinary demonstration of faith.

Chinese New Year is the only time the Chinese stop working. The lunar New Year celebration lasts for 15 days, and most shops and businesses close for about a week. (In 1998 the New Year begins on January 27.) Employees and children are given *hong bao* (small red envelopes containing money), and hawkers and vendors do brisk business selling such delicacies as flattened waxed ducks, white mushrooms, red sausages, melon seeds, and other treats. Mandarin oranges, which symbolize gold and the wish for prosperity, are given in even numbers (odd numbers bring bad luck) to friends, relatives, and business associates.

The end of the Chinese New Year is marked by the **Chingay Procession.** Chinese, Malays, and Indians all get into the act for this event. Accompanied by clashing gongs and beating drums, lion dancers lead a procession of Chinese stilt-walkers, swordsmen, warriors, acrobats, and characters from Chinese myth and legend. A giant dragon weaves through the dancers in its eternal pursuit of a flaming pearl. The parade route varies from year to year, but all the details are described in local newspapers. This procession is not to be missed if you are in town.

FEB. OR MAR.➤ **The Birthday of the Monkey God** celebrates this character greatly loved by the Chinese (many ask him to be godfather to their children). Among other things, he is believed to cure the sick and absolve sins. Chinese street operas and puppet shows are usually performed in temple courtyards, and processions are held at the temples along Eng Hoon and Cumming streets. Visitors are welcome to take photographs, but stand back: When the medium dressed as the Monkey God leaps from the throne, burning incense flies in all directions.

SPRING

MAR. OR APR.➤ On the **Birthday of the Saint of the Poor,** the image of Guang Ze Zun Wang is carried from the White Cloud Temple on Ganges Avenue around the neighborhood and back to the temple through streets thronged with devotees. Spirit mediums—their cheeks, arms, and tongues pierced with metal skewers—join the procession.

Hari Raya Haji is a holy day for Muslims, commemorating the Haj, or pilgrimage, to Mecca. Prayers are said in the mornings at the mosques. Later in the day, in remembrance of the prophet Ibrahim's willingness to sacrifice his son, animals are ritually slaughtered

and their meat distributed among the poor. (The date of this holiday is set by the Islamic calendar.)

During the **Qing Ming Festival,** families honor their ancestors by visiting their graves, cleaning the cemeteries, and making offerings of food and incense. This is not a sad event; it is a celebration. The cemeteries where the festival is most often celebrated are along Upper Thomson Road, Lim Chu Kang, and Lornie Road. However, photographers and spectators are not welcome—the Chinese consider Qing Ming a private affair.

Good Friday is a national holiday in Singapore, and Christians celebrate it by attending church services and observing family ceremonies. There is a candlelight procession on the grounds of St. Joseph's Catholic Church on Victoria Street, during which a wax figure of Christ is carried among the congregation.

Songkran (April 18) is a traditional Thai water festival that marks the beginning of the year's solar cycle. In Singapore's Thai Buddhist temples, images of Buddha are bathed with perfumed holy water, caged birds are set free, and blessings of water are splashed on worshipers and visitors. The liveliest (and wettest) celebrations are at the Ananda Metyrama Thai temple on Silat Road and the Sapthapuchaniyaram Temple on Holland Road. Visitors are welcome. Keep your camera in a waterproof bag—everyone tries to throw as much water as possible on everyone else.

MAY➤ **The Birthday of the Third Prince** celebrates this child god, who carries a magic bracelet in one hand, a spear in the other, and rides on the wheels of wind and fire. The Chinese worship him as a hero and a miracle-worker. A temple in his honor is located at the junction of Clarke Street and North Boat Quay, near Chinatown; on his birthday, it is crowded with noisy worshipers who come to watch the flashy Chinese operas, which begin around noon. Offerings of paper cars and houses and imitation money are burned, and in the evening there is a colorful procession.

Vesak Day commemorates the Buddha's birth, Enlightenment, and death. It is the most sacred annual festival in the Buddhist calendar. Throughout the day, starting before dawn, saffron-robed monks chant holy sutras in all the major Buddhist temples. Captive birds are set free. Many temples offer vegetarian feasts, conduct special exhibitions, and offer lectures on the Buddha's teachings. Visitors are permitted at any temple; particularly recommended are the Kong Meng San Phor Kark See temple complex on Bright Hill Drive and the Temple of 1,000 Lights on Race Course Road. Candlelight processions are held around some of the temples in the evening.

SUMMER

JUNE➤ **The Arts Festival** is a new biannual international event that features both Asian and Western attractions—musical recitals, concerts, plays,

Chinese opera—with local and visiting performers. Performances take place throughout the city; the STPB will have the schedule.

The Dragon Boat Festival commemorates the martyrdom of Qu Yuan, a Chinese poet and minister of state during the Chou Dynasty (4th century BC). Exiled by the court for his protests against injustice and corruption, he wandered from place to place writing poems about his love for his country. Persecuted by the officials wherever he went, he finally threw himself into the river. Today, the anniversary of his death is celebrated with a regatta of boats decorated with dragon heads and painted in brilliant colors. The 11.6-meter-long (38-foot-long) boats—each manned by up to 24 rowers and a drummer—compete in the sea off East Coast Park. In recent years, the race has attracted crews from Australia, Europe, New Zealand, and the United States.

JULY➣ During the **Birdsong Festival,** owners of tuneful birds hold competitions to see whose chirps best. This is serious business for the bird owners and interesting entertainment for visitors. Places and times vary; contact the STPB.

AUG. 9➣ **National Day,** the anniversary of the nation's independence, is a day of processions, fireworks, folk and dragon dances, and national pride. The finest view is from the Padang, where the main participants put on their best show. Tickets for special

seating areas are available through the STPB.

AUG.–SEPT.➣ For a month each year, during the **Chinese Festival of the Hungry Ghosts,** the Gates of Hell are opened and ghosts are free to wander the earth. It's a busy time. The happy ghosts visit their families, where they are entertained with sumptuous feasts. The unhappy ghosts, those who died without descendants, may cause trouble and must therefore be placated with offerings. Imitation money ("Hell money") and joss sticks are burned, and prayers are said at all Chinese temples and in front of Chinese shops and homes. Noisy auctions are also held, to raise money for the next year's festivities. Street-opera performances begin in the late afternoon and continue until late evening. The STPB has details.

AUTUMN

SEPT.➣ **The Mooncake Festival,** a traditional Chinese celebration, is named for special cakes—found for the most part only during this festival—that are the subject of legend. One tells of a cruel king of the Hsia Dynasty who discovered an elixir for immortality. Desperate to stop him from drinking it and tyrannizing his subjects eternally, his good-hearted wife swallowed every drop and escaped by leaping to the moon, where she has lived ever since.

The festival is held on the night of the year when the full moon is thought to be at its brightest. There are lantern-making

competitions and special entertainments, including lion and dragon dances. (Locations are published in local newspapers.) Mooncakes—sweet pastries filled with red-bean paste, lotus seeds, nuts, and egg yolks—are eaten in abundance.

SEPT.–OCT.➣ During the nine-day **Navarathri Festival,** Hindus pay homage to three goddesses. The first three days are devoted to Parvati, consort of Shiva the Destroyer. The next three are for Lakshmi, goddess of wealth and consort of Vishnu the Protector. The final three are for Sarawathi, goddess of education and consort of Brahma the Creator. On all nights, at the Chettiar Temple on Tank Road, there are performances of classical Indian music, drama, and dancing from 7 to 10 PM. On the last evening the image of a silver horse is taken from its home in the Chettiar Temple and paraded around the streets. Thousands take part in the procession, including women in glittering saris, and the air is heavy with perfumes and incense. The festival is best seen at the Sri Mariamman Temple.

OCT.➣ The Chinese believe that the deities celebrated in the **Festival of the Nine Emperor Gods** can cure illness, bring good luck and wealth, and encourage longevity. Understandably, these deities are very popular! They are honored in most Chinese temples on the ninth day of the ninth lunar month; the celebrations are at their most spectacular in the temples on Upper Serangoon Road (8 kilometers, or 5 miles, from the city) and at Lorong Tai Seng.

OCT.–NOV.➤ During the **Pilgrimage to Kusu Island,** more than 100,000 Taoist believers travel to the temple of Da Bo Gong, the god of prosperity. They bring offerings of exotic foods, flowers, joss sticks, and candles and pray for good health, prosperity, and obedient children. If you want to join in, take one of the many ferries that leave from Clifford Pier. Be prepared to deal with immense crowds.

In the **Thimithi Festival,** Indian Hindus honor the goddess Duropadai by walking on fire. According to myth, Duropadai proved her chastity by walking over flaming coals. Today worshipers walk barefoot over a bed of red-hot embers. Only the "pure of heart and

soul" are said to be able to accomplish this feat— some do walk more quickly than others! See the spectacle at the Sri Mariamman Temple on South Bridge Road. The fire-walking ceremony begins at 4 PM.

Deepavali celebrates the triumph of Krishna over the demon king Nasaka- sura. All Indian homes and temples are decorated with oil lamps and gar- lands for the Hindu festival, which marks a time for cleaning house and wearing new clothes. Little India is where the festival is best seen. The streets are brilliantly illuminated, and Indians throng the markets, which do a roaring business selling special greeting cards, gifts, clothes, and food.

NOV.➤ **Merlion Week** is Singapore's version of

Carnival, with food fairs, fashion shows, masquer- ade balls, and fireworks displays. The events start with the crowning of Miss Tourism Singapore and end with the international Singapore Powerboat Grand Prix. Brochures of the activities are available in every hotel.

NOV.–DEC.➤ Being a multicultural society, Singapore has taken **Christmas** to heart—and a very commercial heart it is. All the shops are deep in artificial snow, and a Chinese Santa Claus appears every so often to encourage every- one to buy and give presents, which they do with enthusiasm. A lighting ceremony takes place on Orchard Road, the fashionable shopping street, sometime during the last 10 days of November.

2 Exploring Singapore

Worlds away from the glittering hotels of Orchard Road, Singapore's older ethnic neighborhoods offer unexpected backstreet delights. The colonial central business district around the downtown cricket ground, or Padang, and the legendary 110-year-old Raffles Hotel evoke the era of Joseph Conrad. And Singapore's bosky interior contains close to 7,000 acres of nature-reserve wilderness. "Clean and green" Singapore still surprises those who look beneath its surface gloss.

Updated by
Christine Hill

THE MAIN ISLAND OF SINGAPORE is shaped like a flattened diamond, 42 kilometers (26 miles) east to west and 23 kilometers (14 miles) north to south. Near the peak is the causeway leading to peninsular Malaysia—Kuala Lumpur is less than four hours away by car. At the foot is Singapore city, with its gleaming office towers and working docks. Offshore are Sentosa and some 59 smaller islands—most of them uninhabited—that serve as bases for oil refining or as playground or beach escape from the city. To the east is Changi International Airport, connected to the city by a parkway lined for miles with amusement centers of one sort or another. To the west are the industrial city of Jurong and several decidedly unindustrial attractions, including gardens and a bird park. At the center of the diamond is Singapore island's "clean and green" heart, with a splendid zoo, an orchid garden, and reservoirs surrounded by luxuriant tropical forest. Of the island's total land area, less than half is built up, with the balance made up of farmland, plantations, swamp areas, and forest. Besides the cities of Singapore and Jurong, there are several suburbs, such as Kallang, an old colonial residential district; Katong, a stronghold of Peranakan culture, with pastel terrace houses and Nonya restaurants; Bedok, once an area of Malay kampongs and now a modern suburb of high-rises; and Ponggal, a fishing village on the northeast shore that is a popular destination with seekers of water sports and seafood restaurants. Well-paved roads connect all parts of the island, and Singapore city has an excellent public transportation system.

No other capital city in Southeast Asia is as easy to explore independently as Singapore. The best way is by foot, wandering the streets to discover small shops, a special house, or a temple, or just to observe the daily scene. When leaving the city to explore the rest of the island, you might consider taking an organized tour, since they are relatively inexpensive and transport is provided, but with public transportation so cheap and easy to use, such tours are not at all necessary.

It is very difficult for a new visitor to get lost in Singapore. Visitors can orient themselves in a general way by such landmarks as the financial district's skyscrapers, the new buildings of the Marina Square complex, and Fort Canning Rise, a small hill in the center of town. Also, every street is signposted in English, and most Singaporeans speak English. Getting around is easy, thanks to the efficient and convenient bus and subway service and the numerous (except in heavy rain) taxis waiting to be flagged.

A return visitor to Singapore might be surprised at how much the city has changed in a relatively short time. Singapore has been Southeast Asia's most modern city for over a century for a reason. Successive governments have kept it that way through constant change, still in progress. Just since 1994, whole blocks in Singapore's old ethnic neighborhoods have disappeared. Little India's last dhobi-wallah (laundryman) house has been converted into office space; an old silver merchant in the Arab District cleared out to make way for a mall; a Chinese shophouse that used to sell traditional engraved ivory chopsticks has been torn down and replaced by a brand new pink-trimmed "refurbished" version of the original. At least some of the older buildings are being preserved, but lots of the character is missing. Little India becomes just another mall when crumbling shophouses selling flower garlands and silver charms are renovated and rented out to the Body Shop.

To get a feel for the vanished Singapore, you'll have to look at old photographs or paintings and read some books. One of the best places

16

Singapore City *(Boxes Refer to Detail Maps)*

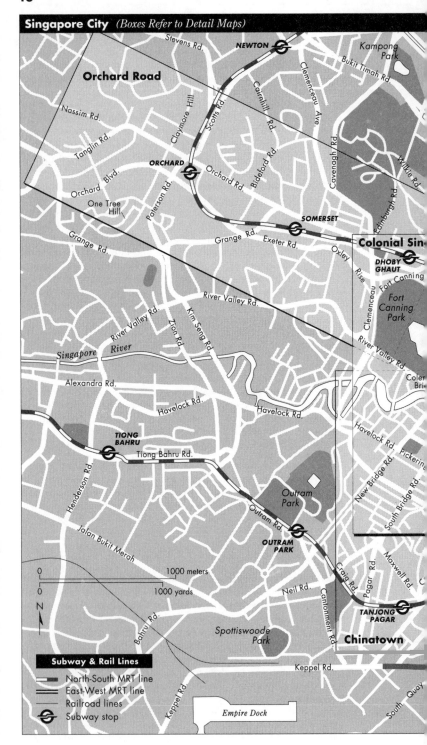

Stevens Rd.

NEWTON

Kampong Park

Bukit Timah Rd.

Orchard Road

Clemenceau Ave.

Cairnhill Rd.

Scotts Rd.

Nassim Rd.

Claymore Hill

Cavenagh Rd.

Wilkie Rd.

Tanglin Rd.

ORCHARD

Orchard Rd.

Bideford Rd.

Edinburgh Rd.

Orchard Blvd.

Paterson Rd.

One Tree Hill

SOMERSET

Colonial Sin

Grange Rd.

Grange Rd.

Exeter Rd.

Oxley Rise

DHOBY GHAUT

Clemenceau

Fort Canning

Fort Canning Park

River Valley Rd.

River Valley Rd.

Zion Rd.

Kim Seng Rd.

River Valley Rd.

Singapore River

Coler Bri

Alexandra Rd.

Havelock Rd.

Havelock Rd.

Havelock Rd.

Pickerin

TIONG BAHRU

Tiong Bahru Rd.

New Bridge Rd.

South Bridge Rd.

Henderson Rd.

Outram Park

Jalan Bukit Merah

Outram Rd.

0 ————————— 1000 meters

0 ————————— 1000 yards

OUTRAM PARK

Craig Rd.

Pagar Rd.

Maxwell Rd.

N

Neil Rd.

Cantonment Rd.

TANJONG PAGAR

Bahru Rd.

Spottiswoode Park

Chinatown

Subway & Rail Lines

━━━ North-South MRT line

≡≡≡ East-West MRT line

--- Railroad lines

⊖ Subway stop

Keppel Rd.

Keppel Rd.

Empire Dock

South Quay

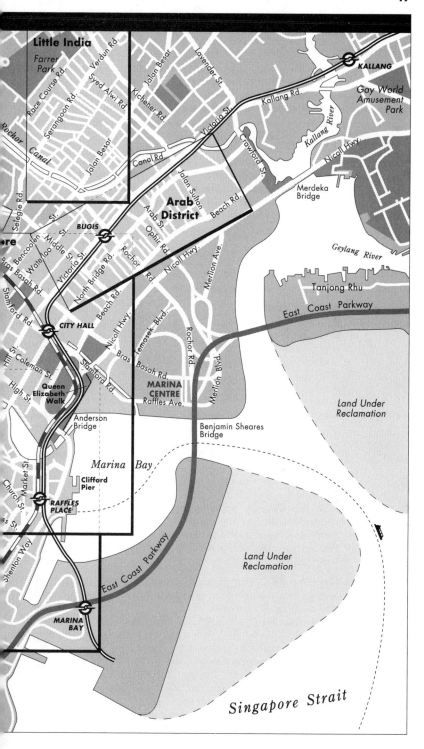

to do this is in Antiques of the Orient, an old map and print shop on the second floor of the Tanglin Shopping Centre, where Orchard Road meets Tanglin Road. The shop's owner, Laurence Chua, has an extensive collection of photos and prints of 19th- and early-20th-century Singapore. You can also view the many photo exhibits on the second floor of the shopping malls in Clarke Quay. Comparing the old Singapore with the new makes one question the value of the city's all-too-extensive redevelopment.

COLONIAL SINGAPORE

You'll find the heart of Singapore's history and its modern wealth in Colonial Singapore. The area stretches from the skyscrapers in Singapore's financial district to the Raffles Hotel, and from the super-modern convention centers of Marina Sqaure to the National Museum and 19th-century Fort Canning. Although most of old Singapore has been knocked down to make way for the modern city, in Colonial Singapore most of the major landmarks have been preserved, including early-19th-century buildings designed by the Irishman George Coleman.

Numbers in the text and in the margin correspond to points of interest on the Colonial Singapore map.

A Good Walk

A convenient place to start exploring Colonial Singapore is at **Collyer Quay** ① (quay is pronounced "key") and Clifford Pier, where most Europeans alighted from their ships to set foot on the island. Leaving Clifford Pier, walk up Collyer Quay toward the Singapore River; Change Alley—once the site of a popular old bazaar and row of money changers—would have been on your left. In 1989 the area was closed down to make way for a modern business complex. Beyond what was Change Alley is the old **General Post Office** ②, a proud Victorian building of gray stone. This also is slated for a new use. To the left as you face the GPO is Fullerton Square, where cycle-rickshaw drivers snooze peacefully in their vehicles. Walk down the short, narrow, tree-lined street alongside the GPO to cross the gracious old iron-link **Cavenagh Bridge** ③. If you walk along the south bank of the river before crossing the bridge, you'll find a wide towpath, now a paved pedestrian street, called **Boat Quay** ④—a popular area for restaurants and bars. The second building on your left is home to Harry's Bar, which gained international attention in 1995 as a favorite haunt of derivatives trader Nick Leeson, the young whippersnapper who brought down the venerable Barings Bank.

Once over the Cavenagh Bridge, take a left onto North Boat Quay. Slightly back from the river is **Empress Place** ⑤, a huge white Victorian building. A bit farther along the quay is a **statue of Sir Thomas Stamford Raffles** ⑥, who is believed to have landed on this spot in 1819. Turn right onto St. Andrew's Road until you come to **Parliament House** ⑦ on your left, the oldest government building in Singapore, and on your right, **Victoria Memorial Hall** ⑧, built in 1905 as a tribute to Queen Victoria, and the Victoria Theatre, built in 1862 as the town hall. Across the road from the theater is the old **Singapore Cricket Club** ⑨. Just past the Cricket Club on your right as you continue up St. Andrews Road is the **Padang** ⑩, or playing field. To your left are the **Supreme Court** ⑪ and **City Hall** ⑫, two splendidly pretentious, imperial-looking gray-white buildings.Continuing east on St. Andrew's Road, which runs along the Padang, cross Coleman Street toward the green lawns that surround the Anglican **St. Andrew's Cathedral** ⑬.

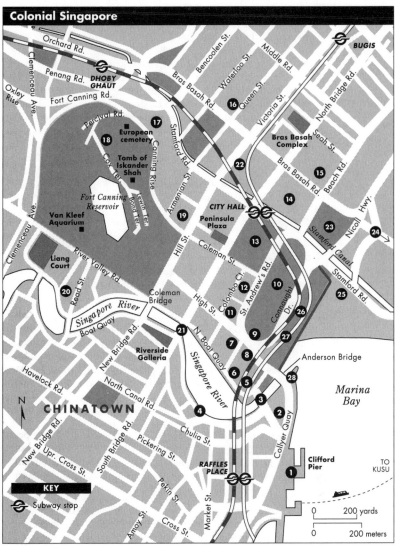

Colonial Singapore

Armenian Church, **19**
Boat Quay, **4**
Cavenagh Bridge, **3**
Cenotaph War Memorial, **26**
City Hall, **12**
Clarke Quay, **20**
Collyer Quay, **1**
Convent of the Holy Infant Jesus, **22**
Elgin Bridge, **21**
Empress Place, **5**

Fort Canning Park, **18**
General Post Office, **2**
Marina Square, **24**
Memorial to Major Gen. Lim Bo Seng, **27**
Merlion Park, **28**
National Museum and Art Gallery, **17**
Padang, **10**
Parliament House, **7**
Queen Elizabeth Walk, **25**
Raffles City, **14**
Raffles Hotel, **15**

St. Andrew's Cathedral, **13**
Singapore Art Museum, **16**
Singapore Cricket Club, **9**
Statue of Sir Thomas Stamford Raffles, **6**
Supreme Court, **11**
Victoria Memorial Hall, **8**
War Memorial, **23**

To the northeast of the cathedral, within easy walking distance, is the huge **Raffles City** ⑭ complex, easily recognized by the towers of the two Westin hotels. Take the MRT underpass north across Stamford Road, and walk through Raffles City to Bras Basah Road. Across the street is the venerable **Raffles Hotel** ⑮. After touring the hotel, turn right onto Bras Basah Road until you cross Queen Street and come to the **Singapore Art Museum** ⑯, housed in the former St. Joseph's Institution, a Catholic boys' school, built in 1852. After touring the exhibits, cross Bras Basah Road, and walk up Armenian Street. Turn right onto Stamford Road, and the **National Museum and Art Gallery** ⑰, a grand colonial building topped by a giant silver dome, will be on your left. You may wish to conclude the tour with a stroll through **Fort Canning Park** ⑱, pausing at the European Cemetery and the Tomb of Iskander Shah. Or, walk back to the **Armenian Church** ⑲ and admire the work of architect George Coleman.

TIMING

This walking tour, with time factored in to wander through the Raffles Hotel and view the exhibits at the Singapore Art Museum and the National Gallery, will take five to six hours. Allow an hour for the Raffles, including time out for a Singapore sling in the Long Bar. Allow one to two hours to view the exhibits in the two museums.

Sights to See

⑲ **Armenian Church.** More correctly, the **Church of St. Gregory the Illuminator,** this is one of the most endearing buildings in Singapore. It was built in 1835, which makes it the oldest surviving church in the republic, and it is still used for regular services. The Armenians were but one of many minority groups that came to Singapore in search of fortune. A dozen wealthy Armenian families supplied the funds for the ubiquitous architect George Coleman to design this church. It is, perhaps, his finest work. The main internal circular structure is imposed on a square plan with four projecting porticoes. In the churchyard is the weathered tombstone of Agnes Joaquim, who bred the parent plants of Singapore's national flower. The orchid, with a purplish pink center, was discovered in her garden in the 1890s and still carries her name.

❹ **Boat Quay.** Right next to the financial district, along the Singapore River, is this popular new area for restaurants with both indoor and outdoor dining. It is one of the few places that has not been masterminded by the Singapore Tourist Promotion Board or by a quasi-government real estate developer; instead, local restaurant and café entrepreneurs have created a mélange of eateries and nightclubs to satisfy diverse tastes. Between 7 PM and midnight, the place swells with both locals and tourists, who stroll along the pleasant quay, stopping to take a meal or refreshment.

❸ **Cavenagh Bridge.** This gracious old iron-link bridge is named after Major General Orfeur Cavenagh, governor of the Straits Settlements from 1859 to 1867. The bridge, built in 1868 from iron girders imported from Scotland, once carried the principal road across the river; now the **Anderson Bridge** bears the main burden of traffic.

㉖ **Cenotaph War Memorial.** This imposing structure honors the dead of the two world wars.

⑫ **City Hall.** Completed in 1929, this building now houses a number of government ministries, including the Ministry of Foreign Affairs. It was here that the British surrender took place in 1942, followed by the surrender of the Japanese in 1945. Each year on August 9, the building's steps serve as a reviewing stand for the National Day Parade, celebrating

Singapore's independence from Great Britain and the birth of the republic.

🐚 ② **Clarke Quay.** Named in remembrance of Sir Andrew Clarke, the second governor of Singapore, this quay functions as a festival village combining entertainment, food, and shopping. Several scenarios are played throughout the day: A tinsmith demonstrates his skill; a band performs in a small gazebo at the central square; stilt-walkers wobble down the pedestrians-only streets. Be aware that prices in the shops and restaurants are inflated. The river here is close to being the sleepy waterway it was when Raffles first arrived; cargo vessels are banned from entering. You can board one of the bumboats (small launches) that offer daily 30-minute **cruises** along the river and into Marina Bay; it's a pleasant ride, and a respite for tired feet.

❶ **Collyer Quay.** Land reclamation in 1933 pushed the seafront back, and Collyer Quay, which now fronts Telok Ayer Street, is three blocks from its original site. In the 19th century, the view from the quay would have included a virtual wall of ships lying at anchor. Today, one looks out upon a graceful bridge carrying the East Coast Parkway from one landfill headland to another, enclosing what is now called Marina Bay. **Clifford Pier**, a covered jetty with high vaulted ceilings, still reveals some of the excitement of the days when European traders arrived by steamship and Chinese immigrants by wind-dependent junks. Now Indonesian sailors sit around smoking clove-scented cigarettes, and seamen from every seafaring nation come ashore to stock up on liquor and duty-free electronics. The atmosphere here is seedy, and this is one of the few places in Singapore where women might feel uncomfortable by themselves. Passengers from the ocean liners no longer come ashore here—those whose trade the jet aircraft have not stolen now arrive at the new cruise terminal at the World Trade Centre—but tourists set sail from Collyer Quay for day cruises around Singapore's harbor and to the outlying islands. Bumboats wallow in the bay, waiting to take sailors back to their ships or carry tourists wherever they want to go for about S$30 an hour.

㉒ **Convent of the Holy Infant Jesus.** One of Singapore's most charming Victorian buildings, the convent church has been slated for renovations, but a financial commitment has yet to be made. The arcaded buildings around the church, with their lovely old tiled roofs and thick pillars, are also sorely in need of repair.

㉑ **Elgin Bridge.** At the end of Boat Quay and named after Lord Elgin, a governor-general of India, this bridge was built to link Chinatown to the colonial quarter. The original rickety wooden bridge was replaced in 1863 with an iron bridge imported from Calcutta; the current ferroconcrete structure was installed in 1926.

❺ **Empress Place.** A huge white Victorian building that was meticulously restored as an exhibition hall, the neoclassical building is now closed and crumbling again. Constructed in the 1860s as the new courthouse, it has had four major additions and housed nearly every government body, including the Registry of Births and Deaths and the Immigration Department. Virtually every adult Singaporean has been inside this building at one time or another.

🐚 ⑱ **Fort Canning Park.** Until recently Fort Canning was hallowed ground, a green sanctuary from the surrounding city's mass of concrete commercialism. Alas, like everything else in Singapore, the park is undergoing extensive renovations. The government has recently added a 19th-century walk, with guideposts pointing you to all the 19th-century sites at the park. There are designated picnic areas. Like many of

Singapore's so-called improvements, the changes to Fort Canning are turning one of the island's few partly natural rest areas into a controlled environment. The government is even building a country club at the park's edge.

What still remains, though, are the tombstones of the **European cemetery.** Once divided into areas for Protestants and for Catholics, the tombstones have been moved to form a wall around an open field. The plaques are weathered, and it is difficult to read the inscriptions, but their brevity suggests the loneliness of the expatriates who had sought fortune far from home.

Seven centuries ago **Fort Canning Rise** (now Fort Canning Park) was home to the royal palaces of the Majapahit rulers, who no doubt chose it for the cool breezes and commanding view of the river. The last five kings of Singa Pura, including the legendary Iskandar Shah, are said to be buried on the hill. Some dispute this, claiming that Iskandar Shah escaped from Singa Pura before its destruction in 1391.

For several hundred years the site was abandoned to the jungle. It was referred to by the Malays as Bukit Larangan, the Forbidden Hill, a place where the spirits of bygone kings roamed on sacred ground. Then Raffles came and, defying the legends, established government house (headquarters for the colonial governor) on the Rise. Later, in 1859, a fort was constructed; its guns were fired to mark dawn, noon, and night for the colony.

❷ General Post Office. The GPO recently moved out of this proud Victorian building of gray stone with huge pillars. It's hopelessly outdated, an anachronism in an area of glass-and-steel high-rises. The government has promised not to knock it down, but has not made a decision on how to use this beautiful old building. To the left as you face the old GPO is **Fullerton Square,** a rest stop for cycle-rickshaw drivers who don't seem eager to find passengers.

㉔ Marina Square. A minicity of its own, the square has two malls and four smart atrium hotels—the **Pan Pacific,** the **Marina Mandarin,** the estimable **Oriental,** and the spanking new **Ritz-Carlton,** which opened in January 1996. The whole area is built on reclaimed land. A mammoth convention center and shopping mall, **Suntec City,** opened in 1995. An even bigger new shopping mall, the **Millenia Walk,** which includes a three-story Duty Free Shop, had its official opening in the third quarter of 1996. The complex symbolizes much of what Singapore has become: a modern convention city built on landfills, and clusters of theme parks designed to entertain the delegates and their spouses. In a few years, an arts center will be added to the complex.

㉗ Memorial to Major General Lim Bo Seng. Lim was a well-loved freedom fighter of World War II who was tortured and died in a Japanese prison camp in 1944.

㉘ Merlion Park. Here stands a statue of Singapore's tourism symbol, the Merlion—half lion, half fish, all white and plastic-looking. In the evening, the statue—on a point of land looking out over the harbor—is floodlit, its eyes are lighted, and its mouth spews water. You can see an even bigger one on Sentosa.

⑰ National Museum and Art Gallery. Housed in a grand colonial building topped by a giant silver dome, the museum originally opened as the Raffles Museum in 1887. Included in its collection are 20 dioramas depicting the republic's past; the **Revere Bell,** donated to the original St. Andrew's Church in 1843 by the daughter of American patriot Paul Revere; the 380-piece **Haw Par Jade Collection,** one of the largest of its kind; ethnographic collections from Southeast Asia; and many historical documents. ⊠ *Stamford Rd.,* ☎ *330–9562.* ⬚ *S$3.* ☉ *Tues.–Sun. 9–5:30.*

⑩ Padang. Padang is Malay for "field" or "plain." It used to be only half its present size; it was extended through land reclamation in the 1890s. From the beginning, the Padang has been a center for Singapore's political and social events. Once called the Esplanade, it was where the colonial gentry strolled, exchanging pleasantries and gossip. It was also where, in World War II, 2,000 British civilians gathered, a ragged bunch of prisoners, to be marched off by the Japanese to Changi Prison and, in many cases, to their deaths. It is now used primarily as a playing field.

❼ Parliament House. George Coleman designed the Parliament House building in 1827 for a wealthy merchant, but it went unoccupied until the government purchased it for S$15,600 in 1841 as a courthouse. It is considered the oldest government building in Singapore. Additions were built, and in the 1870s it became the meeting place for Parliament. The bronze statue of an elephant in front of the building was a gift from King Chulalongkorn of Siam during his state visit in 1871.

㉕ Queen Elizabeth Walk. Running alongside Marina Bay, this promenade was opened in 1953 to mark the queen's coronation and remains a popular place to take the evening air.

⑭ Raffles City. The Raffles City complex of offices and shops contains Asia's tallest hotel, the **Westin Stamford,** not to be confused with the **Westin Plaza,** which is in the same building and operates as a semiseparate hotel (☞ Chapter 4). You'll get a beautiful view of downtown Singapore and the harbor from the **Compass Rose** restaurant at the top of the Westin Stamford.

⑮ Raffles Hotel. Once a "tiffin house," or tearoom, the Raffles Hotel started life as the home of a British sea captain. In 1887 the Armenian Sarkies brothers took over the building and greatly expanded it, making it into one of the grandest hotels in Asia. The Raffles has had many ups and downs, especially during World War II, when it was first a center for British refugees, then quarters for Japanese officers, then a center for released Allied prisoners of war. There is a certain delicious irony to the Raffles: Viewed as a bastion of colonialism, it was not only the creation of Armenians, but in its 130 years of hosting expatriates, it only once had a British manager. Even so, service by the hotel's staff has been unfailingly loyal to the colonial heritage. In the nick of time before the Japanese arrived, the Chinese waiters took the silverware from the dining rooms and buried it in the Palm Court garden, where it remained safely hidden until the occupiers departed.

After the war the hotel deteriorated. It survived mostly as a tourist site, trading on its heritage rather than its facilities. However, in late 1991, after two years of renovating and rebuilding some of the original structures and adding new buildings, the Raffles reopened as the republic's most expensive hotel. The casual tourist is no longer welcome to roam around, but instead is channeled through new colonial-style buildings to visit the museum of Raffles memorabilia (⬚ Free; ☉ Daily 10–9); attend the multimedia show on the history of the hotel at the Victorian-style Jubilee Hall playhouse (☉ Shows at 10, 11, 12:30, and 1); and take refreshment in a reproduction of the **Long Bar,** where the famous Singapore sling was created in 1903 by the bartender Ngiam Tong Boon. The sling here is still regarded as the best in Singapore, slightly drier than the one, for example, at the Westin Stamford's Compass Rose lounge. The S$17.15 tab includes service and tax, but not the glass—

that's another S$8. Be forewarned that some veterans consider the new Long Bar a travesty of the old one, with such ridiculous substitutes as *punkahs*—the manually operated colonial fans—that are electrically powered. If you're hungry there's the new **Empress Café;** if you want to browse, there are 60 shops in the new arcade. However, if you are persistent and walk to the end of the constructed tourist attractions and then turn left, you can reach the original **Tiffin Room** and the **Bar and Billiard Room,** much better bets than the Long Bar if you are looking for authenticity. Casual visitors are discouraged from entering the original part of the hotel, but you may want to brazen it out just to see how unlikely it would be to find a Conrad at the tiny and stiff new **Writers Bar.**

⓭ **St. Andrew's Cathedral.** This Anglican church, surrounded by a green lawn, is the second built on this site. The first church was built in 1834; after being struck twice by lightning, it was demolished in 1852. (Locals took the bolts from the heavens as a sure sign that the site was bedeviled.) It was suggested that before another place of worship be built here, the spirits should be appeased with the blood from 30 heads; fortunately, the suggestion was ignored. Indian convicts were brought in to construct a new cathedral in the 12th-century English Gothic style. The structure, completed in 1862, with bells cast by the firm that made Big Ben's, resembles Netley Abbey in Hampshire, England. So impressed by the cathedral were the British overlords that freedom was granted to the Indian convict who supplied the working drawings. The cathedral's lofty interior is white and simple, with stained-glass windows coloring the sunlight as it enters. Around the walls are marble and brass memorial plaques, including one remembering the British who died in the 1915 Mutiny of Native Light Infantry and another in memory of 41 Australian army nurses killed in the 1942 Japanese invasion of Singapore.

⓰ **Singapore Art Museum.** A restored schoolhouse, the all-boys Catholic St. Joseph's Institution, built in 1852, closed in 1987 and reopened as a museum in 1995. Names of school donors still adorn the porch at the entranceway to the building. When Prime Minister Goh Chok Tung opened the museum in 1996, he described a vision of Singapore "reliving, through its museums, its historic role as an entrepôt for art, culture, civilization, and ideas." Judge for yourself.

NEED A BREAK?   On the porch at the back of the Singapore Art Museum, you'll find one of Singapore's most pleasant casual lunch spots, **Olio Dome** (☎ 298–5054). While serving a Western menu of soups, salads, and sandwiches on toasted focaccia bread, the Dome, one of several in Singapore, specializes in coffee. A latte goes for S$4.90. You can eat outside on the curving neoclassical porch or inside in a 1920s-style bistro.

⑨ **Singapore Cricket Club.** Founded during the 1850s, it became the main center for the social and sporting life of the British community. It now has a multiracial membership of more than 4,000 and offers facilities for various sports, in addition to bars and restaurants. If you are going to be in Singapore for more than a couple of weeks, you may apply, with the support of a member, for a visiting membership. The club is not open to passing sightseers, but you can sneak a quick look at the deep, shaded verandas around back, from which members still watch cricket, rugby, and tennis matches.

⑥ **Statue of Sir Thomas Stamford Raffles.** This statue near the Empress Place on North Boat Quay is on the spot where Raffles first landed in

Singapore early on the morning of January 29, 1819. Pause here a moment to observe the contrast between the old and the new. Once this river was the organ of bustling commercial life, packed with barges and lighters that ferried goods from the cargo ships to the docks. There were no cranes—the unloading was done by teams of coolies. Swarms of them would totter under heavy loads, back and forth from the lighters to the riverside godowns, amid yells and screams from the compradores (factotums).

⑪ **Supreme Court.** In the neoclassical style so beloved by Victorian colonials, the Supreme Court boasts Corinthian pillars and the look of arrogant certainty. However, it is not as old as it seems. The Supreme Court was completed in 1939, replacing the famous Hôtel de l'Europe, where Conrad used to prop up the bar eavesdropping on sailors' tales that he would later use in his novels. The pedimental sculptures of the Greek-temple-like facade portray Justice and other allegorical figures. Inside, the echoing hall and staircase are on a grand scale and, high above, the vast paneled ceiling is an exercise in showmanship. All of this was completed just in time for the Japanese to use the building as their headquarters.

⑧ **Victoria Memorial Hall.** The Memorial Hall was built in 1905 as a tribute to Queen Victoria. Along with the adjacent **Victoria Theatre**, built in 1862 as the town hall, it is the city's main cultural center, offering regular exhibitions, concerts, and theatrical performances of all types (☞ Chapter 5).

㉓ **War Memorial.** The four 70-meter (230-foot) tapering white columns (known locally as "The Four Chopsticks") commemorate the thousands of civilians from the four main ethnic groups (Chinese, Malay, Indian, and European) who lost their lives during the Japanese occupation of Singapore during World War II. The highest of the "chopsticks" represents the Chinese, who were the most persecuted—some 25,000 were immediately executed for being too Western, and others were sent to help build the bridge over the River Kwai.

CHINATOWN

In a country where 76% of the people are Chinese, it may seem strange to name a small urban area Chinatown. But Chinatown was born some 170 years ago, when the Chinese were a minority (if only for half a century) in the newly formed British settlement. In the belief that it would minimize racial tension, Raffles allotted sections of the settlement to different ethnic groups. The Chinese immigrants were given the area to the south of the Singapore River. Today, the river is still the northern boundary of old Chinatown, while Maxwell Road marks its southern perimeter and New Bridge Road its western one. Before the 1933 land reclamation, the western perimeter was the sea. The reclaimed area between Telok Ayer Street and Collyer Quay–Shenton Way has become the business district, often referred to as Singapore's Wall Street. Despite all the talk about preservation, the business district needs more space, so most of the Chinese shophouses are being knocked down all the way to Cross Street.

Inside the confines of the relatively small rectangle apportioned to the Chinese, immigrants from mainland China—many of them penniless and half-starved—were crammed. Within three years of the formation of the Straits Settlement, 3,000 Chinese had moved in; this number increased tenfold over the next decade. The most numerous of these immigrants were the Hokkien people, traders from Fukien Province. They made up about a quarter of Chinatown's immigrant community.

Other leading groups were the Teochews, from the Swatow region of Guangdong Province, and their mainland neighbors, the Cantonese. In smaller groups, the Hainanese, the nomadic Hakkas, and peoples from Guangxi arrived in tightly packed junks, riding on the northeast monsoon winds.

Most immigrants arrived with the sole intention of exchanging their rags for riches, then returning to China. They had no allegiance to Singapore or to Chinatown, which was no melting pot but, rather, consisted of separate pockets of ethnically diverse groups, each with a different dialect, a different cuisine, and different cultural, social, and religious attitudes.

In the shophouses—two-story buildings with shops or small factories on the ground floor and living quarters upstairs—as many as 30 lodgers would live together in a single room. Life was a fight for space and survival. Crime was rampant. What order existed was maintained not by the colonial powers but by Chinese guilds, clan associations, and secret societies, which fought—sometimes savagely—for control of various lucrative aspects of community life.

Until recently, all of Chinatown was slated for the bulldozer, to be wiped clean of its past and replaced by uniform concrete structures. The traditional ways of the individual Chinese groups were to melt away into the modern Singaporean lifestyle. In the name of "progressive social engineering," much of the original community was disassembled and entire blocks were cleared of shophouses. However, the government finally recognized not only the people's desire to maintain Chinese customs and strong family ties, but also the important role these play in modern society. Chinatown received a stay of execution, and an ambitious plan to restore a large area of shophouses is partially completed. Fortunately, enough of the old remains to permit the imaginative visitor to experience a traditional Chinese community.

Numbers in the text and in the margin correspond to points of interest on the Chinatown map.

A Good Walk
Begin at the Elgin Bridge, built to link Chinatown with the colonial administration center. At the south end of the bridge, logically enough, South Bridge Road begins. Off to the right is Upper Circular Road, on the left-hand side of which is **Yeo Swee Huat** ① at No. 13, which sells paper replicas of houses, cars, and other worldly goods intended to be burned at Chinese funerals. Circular Road was the cloth wholesalers' street, but now is also being redeveloped into bars and restaurants. Walk down **Lopong Telok Street** ②, with its architecturally interesting shops and clan houses, and take a right onto **North Canal Road.** Here are stores selling Chinese delicacies—dried foods, turtles for soup, sea cucumbers, sharks' fins, and birds' nests.

Continue to New Bridge Road, turn left, and walk past the Furama Singapore Hotel and the People's Park Centre, now home to the Singapore Handicrafts Centre. Cross Upper Cross Street and take a left onto **Mosque Street.** The old shophouses here—now being redeveloped into offices—were originally built as stables. Turn right onto South Bridge Road. The **Jamae Mosque** ③ will be on your right. On the next block is the **Sri Mariamman Temple** ④, the oldest Hindu temple in Singapore.

If you take the next right, onto **Temple Street,** you may be fortunate enough to see one of the few remaining scribes in Singapore. At the junction of Trengganu Street, notice the old building on the corner. Reliable sources say this was a famous **brothel** ⑤ in its time. You are now

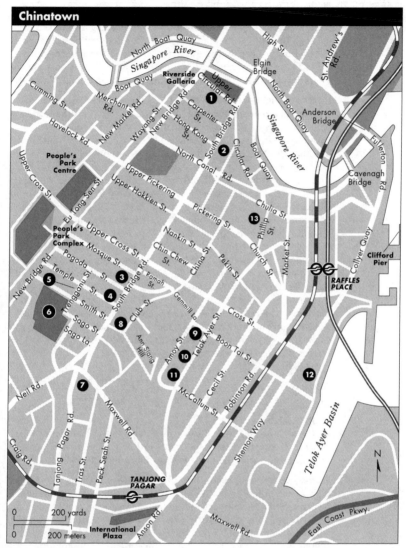

Chinatown

Al Abrar Mosque, **11**

Brothel, **5**

Chinatown Centre, **6**

Guild for amahs, **8**

Jamae Mosque, **3**

Jinriksha Station, **7**

Lopong Telok
Street, **2**

Nagore Durghe
Shrine, **9**

Sri Mariamman
Temple, **4**

Telok Ayer
Market, **12**

Thian Hock Keng
Temple, **10**

Wak Hai Cheng Bio
Temple, **13**

Yeo Swee Huat, **1**

in the core of Chinatown, an area known as **Kreta Ayer.** Trengganu Street leads to the new **Chinatown Centre** ⑥. Leaving the market, walk up **Sago Street** to see more family factories that make paper models to be burned for good fortune at funerals. Parallel to Sago Street is Sago Lane. There's nothing to see here now, but the street was once known for its death houses, where Chinese would go to wait out their last days.

If you turn right onto South Bridge Road, you'll come to the intersection of **Tanjong Pagar Road** and Neil Road. The old **Jinriksha Station** ⑦ here was once a rickshaw depot, but now it's a food court. After strolling down Tanjong Pagar Road to see the restored shophouses, head back to South Bridge Road. **Smith Street,** on the left, has stores selling everything from chilis to ground rhinoceros horn. Ann Siang Road, on the other side of South Bridge Road, is full of old shops and site of the **Guild for amahs** ⑧. From Ann Siang Road, turn left onto Club Street, and then right at Gemmill Lane. When you get to Telok Ayer Street, turn right, and you will find the **Nagore Durghe Shrine** ⑨, an odd mix of minarets and Greek columns, decorated with Christmas lights, and built by South Indian Muslims from 1828 to 1830. Keep going down the road to the **Thian Hock Keng Temple** ⑩, the most interesting temple in Chinatown. Go a little farther down the street, and you'll see the **Al Abrar Mosque** ⑪, built in 1827. Walk east along McCallum Street toward the bay and take a left up Shenton Way. At Boon Tat Street, you'll see the **Telok Ayer Market** ⑫, the largest Victorian cast-iron structure in Southeast Asia. It looks like a chicken coop. Here you can refresh yourself at the food court, then take the subway back to Raffles Place on Collyer Quay.

TIMING

Allow two to three hours for this walk, and factor in a half an hour each for the Thian Hock Keng and Sri Mariamman temples.

Sights to See

⑪ **Al Abrar Mosque.** Also known as **Kuchu Palli** (Tamil for "small mosque"), this structure dates from 1850. The original mosque, built in 1827, was one of the first for Singapore's Indian Muslims.

⑤ **Brothel.** Reliable sources say this was a famous brothel in its time. Opium dens and brothels played important roles in the lives of Chinese immigrants, who usually arrived alone, leaving their families behind, and worked long days, with little time for relaxation or pleasure. Many immigrants took to soothing their aching minds and bodies at opium dens; as only 12% of the Chinese émigré community were women, men often sought female comfort from professionals.

Gambling was another popular pastime. Except for the state lottery and the official horse-race-betting system, gambling is now outlawed by the government. But you can be sure that when you hear the slap of mah-jongg in a coffeehouse, a wager or two has been made. Raffles tried to ban gambling, but to no avail—the habit was too firmly entrenched. One legendary figure, Tan Che Seng, who had amassed a fortune by subsidizing junks bringing immigrants to work in his warehouses, resolved to give up gambling and, as a reminder, amputated the first joint of his little finger. Still, he continued to gamble!

⑥ **Chinatown Centre.** This market is mobbed inside and out with jostling shoppers. At the open-air vegetable and fruit stands, women—toothless and wrinkled with age—sell their wares. Inside, on the first floor, hawker stalls sell a variety of cooked foods, but it is the basement floor that fascinates: Here you'll find a wet market (so called because water is continually sloshed over the floors), where an amazing array of meats, fowl, and fish are bought and sold. Some of the sights are enough to quiet any appetite you may have had. At the far left corner, for example, live pigeons, furry white rabbits, and sleepy turtles are crammed into cages, awaiting hungry buyers.

❽ Guild for amahs. Club Street is full of old buildings that continue to house clan associations, including the professional guild for amahs. Though their numbers are few today, these female servants were once an integral part of European households in Singapore. Like the *samsui* (women who vowed never to marry)—a few of whom can still be observed in their traditional red headdresses passing bricks or carrying buckets at construction sites—the amahs choose to earn an independent living, however hard the work, rather than submit to the servitude of marriage. (In traditional Chinese society, a daughter-in-law is considered the lowest-ranking member of the family.) In the past, when a woman decided to become an amah or samsui, she would go through a ritual that was a sort of substitute marriage. Family and friends would gather—even bring her gifts—and she would tie up her hair to indicate that she was not available for marriage. She would then move to a *gongxi,* or communal house, where she would share expenses and household duties and care for her sisters.

❸ Jamae Mosque. Popularly called **Masjid Chulia,** the simple, almost austere mosque was built in the 1830s by Chulia Muslims from India's Coromandel Coast. So long as it is not prayer time and the doors are open, you are welcome to step inside for a look (you must be dressed conservatively and take your shoes off before entering).

❼ Jinriksha Station. This station was once the bustling central depot for Singapore's rickshaws, which numbered more than 9,000 in 1919. Now there is nary a one. The station has been converted into a food market on one side and an office block on the other. This is a good place to sit down with a cool drink.

Kreta Ayer. Named after the bullock carts that carried water for cleaning the streets, this is the core of Chinatown.

❷ Lopong Telok Street. Nos. 27, 28, and 29 on this architecturally interesting street have intricately carved panels above the shop doorways. Across the street are old clan houses whose stonework facades appear to have a Portuguese influence—possibly by way of Malacca, a Portuguese trading post in the 17th century until the Dutch, and then the British, took possession of it.

Mosque Street. The old shophouses here—mercifully spared by the demolition squad—were originally built as stables. Now they house Hakka families selling second- or, more likely, thirdhand wares, from clothes to old medicine bottles. Keep an eye out for No. 20, **Fong Moon Kee,** which sells the best tikar mats, used by the older Chinese instead of soft mattresses. They are easy to carry and are excellent for picnics or for the beach.

❾ Nagore Durghe Shrine. This odd mix of minarets and Greek columns was built by South Indian Muslims between 1828 and 1830. Inside it is now decorated with Christmas tree lights.

Sago Street. A cake shop at **No. 36** is extremely popular for fresh baked goods, especially during the Mooncake Festival. Two doors up, at **No. 32,** is a store selling dry snakes and lizards, for increasing fertility, and powdered antelope horn, for curing headaches and cooling the body.

Smith Street. Stores sell chilis, teas, and soybeans, and a medicine hall offers ground rhinoceros horn to help overcome impotency and pearl dust to help ladies' complexions.

❹ Sri Mariamman Temple. The oldest Hindu temple in Singapore, the building has a pagoda-like entrance topped by one of the most ornate *gopurams* (pyramidal gateway towers) you are ever likely to see. Hundreds of brightly colored statues of deities and mythical animals line the tiers of this towering porch; glazed cement cows sit, seemingly in great contentment, atop the surrounding walls. The story of this Hindu temple smack in the heart of Chinatown begins with Naraina Pillay, who came to Singapore on the same ship as Raffles in 1819 and started work as a clerk. Within a short time, he had set up his own construction business, often using convicts sent over to Singapore from India, and quickly made a fortune. He obtained this site to build a temple on, so that devotees could pray on the way to and from work at the harbor. This first temple, built in 1827 of wood and *atap* (wattle and daub), was replaced in 1843 by the current brick structure. The gopuram was added in 1936. Inside are some spectacular paintings that have been recently restored by Tamil craftsmen brought over from South India.

Tanjong Pagar Road. The center of an area of redevelopment in Chinatown, the road has a number of shophouses restored to their 19th-century appearance—or rather a sanitized, dollhouse-like version of it. It now contains teahouses, calligraphers, mah-jongg makers, and other shops. More shophouses are presently being restored and at current rents, will probably be occupied by upmarket boutiques and restaurants.

OFF THE
BEATEN PATH

A special Sunday-morning treat is to take breakfast with the birds at a **bird-singing café.** Bird fanciers bring their prize specimens, in intricately made bamboo cages, to coffee shops and hang the cages outside for training sessions: By listening to their feathered friends, the birds learn how to warble. Bird-singing enthusiasts take their hobby very seriously and, incidentally, pay handsomely for it. For you, it costs only the price of a coffee to sit at a table and listen to the birds. One place to try is the coffee shop on the corner of Tiong Bahru and Seng Poh roads, west of Tanjong Pagar—get there around 9 AM on Sunday.

⓬ Telok Ayer Market. The market is the largest Victorian cast-iron structure left in Southeast Asia. Already a thriving fishmarket in 1822, it was redesigned as an octagonal structure by George Coleman in 1894. Now it has reopened as a planned food court, with hawker stalls offering the gamut of Asian fare. By day it's busy with office workers. After 7 PM Boon Tat Street closes to traffic and the mood turns festive: The hawkers wheel out their carts, and musicians give street performances until midnight. The market opened in 1992, backed by an investment of S$8.3 million for marketing and development.

Temple Street. Here you may be fortunate enough to see one of the few remaining practitioners of a dying profession. Often found sitting on a stool here is a scribe, an old man to whom other elderly Chinese who have not perfected the art of writing come to have their letters written. Today all Singaporean children are required to complete 10 years of schooling, so the scribes will soon be out of work.

⓾ Thian Hock Keng Temple. This Temple of Heavenly Happiness was completed in 1841 to replace a simple shrine built 20 years earlier. It is one of Singapore's oldest and largest Chinese temples, built on the spot where, prior to land reclamation, immigrants stepped ashore from their hazardous journey across the China Sea. In gratitude for their safe passage, the Hokkien people dedicated the temple to Ma Chu P'oh, the goddess of the sea. Thian Hock Keng is richly decorated with gilded carvings, sculptures, tiled roofs topped with dragons, and fine carved stone pillars. The pillars and sculptures were brought over from China, the cast-iron railings outside were made in Glasgow, and the blue porcelain tiles on an outer building came from Holland. Outside, on either side of the entrance, are two stone lions. The one on the left is female and holds a cup, symbolizing fertility; the other, a male, holds a ball, a symbol of wealth. As you enter the temple you must step over a high threshold board. This serves a dual function. First, it forces devotees to look downward, as they should, when entering the temple. Second, it keeps out wandering ghosts—ghosts tend to shuffle their feet, so if they try to enter, the threshold board will trip them.

Inside, a statue of a maternal Ma Chu P'oh, surrounded by masses of burning incense and candles, dominates the room. On either side of her are the deities of health (on the left if your back is to the entrance) and of wealth. The two tall figures you'll notice are her sentinels: One can see for 1,000 miles, the other can hear for 1,000 miles. The gluey black substance on their lips—placed there by devotees in days past— is opium, to heighten their senses. While the main temple is Taoist, the temple at the back is Buddhist and dedicated to Kuan Yin, the goddess of mercy. Her many arms represent how she reaches out to all those who suffer on earth. This is a good place to learn your fortune. Choose a number out of the box, then pick up two small, stenciled pieces of wood at the back of the altar and let them fall to the ground. If they land showing opposite faces, then the number you have picked is valid. If they land same-side up, try again. From a valid number, the person in the nearby booth will tell you your fate, and whether you like it or not, you pay for the information. Leave the grounds by the alley that runs alongside the main temple. The two statues to the left are the gambling brothers. They will help you choose a lucky number for your next betting session; if you win, you must return and place lighted cigarettes in their hands.

⑬ Wak Hai Cheng Bio Temple. Built between 1852 and 1855 by Teochew Chinese from Guangdong Province and dedicated to the goddess of the sea, this temple is currently undergoing renovations. Its wonderfully ornate roof is covered with decorations—including miniature pagodas and human figures—depicting ancient Chinese villages and scenes from opera. Chinese temples, incidentally, are invariably dusty, thick with incense, and packed with offerings and statuary—evidence of devotees asking for favors and offering thanks for favors granted. To a Chinese, a sparkling clean, spartan temple would suggest unsympathetic deities with few followers. Where burning joss sticks have left a layer of dust and continue to fill the air with smoky scent, the gods are willing to hear requests and grant wishes. If word spreads that many wishes have been realized by people visiting a particular temple, it can, virtually overnight, become the most popular temple in town.

❶ Yeo Swee Huat. At No. 13 Upper Circular Road (☎ 533–4288), you'll see a cottage industry designed to help Chinese take care of one obligation to their ancestors: making sure they have everything they need in the afterlife. Here, paper models of the paraphernalia of life— horses, cars, boats, planes, even fake money—are made, to be purchased by relatives of the deceased (you can buy them, too) and ritually burned so that their essence passes through to the spirit world in flames and smoke.

LITTLE INDIA

Indians have been part of Singapore's development from the beginning. While Singapore was administered by the East India Company, headquartered in Calcutta, Indian convicts were sent here to serve their time. These convicts left an indelible mark on Singapore, reclaiming land from swampy marshes and constructing a great deal of the city's infrastructure, including public buildings, St. Andrew's Cathedral, and many Hindu temples. The enlightened penal program permitted convicts to study a trade of their choice in the evenings. Many, on gaining their freedom, chose to stay in Singapore.

Other Indians came freely to seek their fortunes as clerks, traders, teachers, and moneylenders. The vast majority came from the south of India—both Hindu Tamils and Muslims from the Coromandel and Malabar coasts—but there were also Gujaratis, Sindhis, Sikhs, Parsis, and Bengalis. Each group brought its own language, cuisine, religion, and social customs, and these divisions remain evident today. The Indians also brought their love of colorful festivals, which they now celebrate more frequently and more spectacularly than is done in India itself. The gory Thaipusam and the festival of lights, Deepavali, are among the most fascinating (☞ Festivals and Seasonal Events *in* Chapter 1).

The area Raffles allotted to the Indian immigrants was north of the British colonial district. The heart of this area—known today as Little India—is Serangoon Road and the streets east and west of it between Bukit Timah and Sungei roads to the south and Perumal Road to the north. Although new buildings have replaced many of the old, the sights, sounds, and smells will make you believe you are in an Indian town. After spending so much money refurbishing Chinatown, the Singapore Tourist Promotion Board has set its sights on Little India, and the color is fading.

Numbers in the text and in the margin correspond to points of interest on the Little India map.

A Good Walk

A good starting point for a tour of Little India is the junction of Serangoon and Sungei roads. As you walk along Serangoon, your senses will be sharpened by the fragrances of curry powders and perfumes, by tapes of high-pitched Indian music, by jewelry shops selling gold and stands selling garlands of flowers. (Indian women delight in wearing flowers and glittering arm bangles, but once their husbands die, they never do so again.) Other shops supply the colorful dyes used to mark the *tilak*—the dot seen on the forehead of Indian women. Traditionally, a Tamil woman wears a red dot to signify that she is married; a North Indian woman conveys the same message with a red streak down the part of her hair. However, the modern trend is for an Indian girl or woman to choose a dye color to match her sari or Western dress. Occasionally you will see an unmarried woman with a black dot on her forehead: This is intended to counter the effects of the evil eye.

The first block on the left is **Zhu Jiao Centre** ①, one of the largest wet markets in the city. The streets to the right off Serangoon Road—Hastings Road, **Campbell Lane,** and Dunlop Street—are also filled with shops, many of them open-fronted, selling such utilitarian items as pots and pans, plus rice, spices, brown cakes of palm sugar, and every other type of Indian grocery imaginable. You'll see open-air barbershops and tailors working old-fashioned treadle sewing machines, and everywhere you go you'll hear sugar-sweet love songs from Indian movies. Along **Buffalo Road,** to the left off Serangoon, are shops specializing in saris, flower garlands, and electronic equipment. Above the doorways are strings of dried mango leaves, a customary Indian sign of blessing and good fortune. (If you detour down Dunlop Street, to the right off Serangoon Road, you'll pass **P. Govindasamy Pillai** ⑩, a shop famous

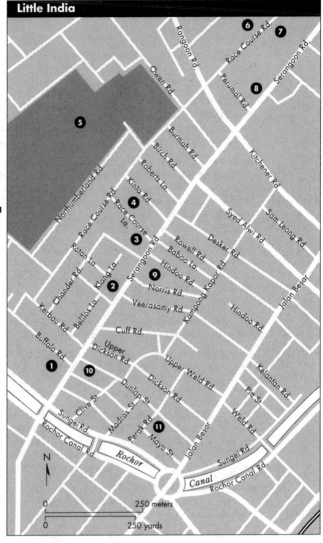

for its beautiful silk saris, and come to the **Abdul Gaffoor Mosque** ⑪, with its detailed facade of green and gold.)

A little farther down Serangoon Road on the left (opposite Veerasamy Road), you'll notice the elaborate gopuram—adorned with newly re-painted sculptures—of the **Sri Veeramakaliamman Temple** ②, built in 1881 by indentured Bengali laborers working the lime pits nearby. At the corner of Race Course Lane, you'll see the **Mahatma Gandhi Memorial Hall** ③. Take Kinta Road to the **Burmese Buddhist Temple** ④ with its 3.3-meter-tall (11-foot-tall) white marble Buddha. Turn right on Race Course Road to **Farrer Park** ⑤, site of Singapore's original racecourse. Farther along Race Course Road is the charming **Leong San See Temple** ⑥, dedicated to Kuan Yin. Across the road is Sakya Muni Buddha Gaya Temple, more commonly referred to as the **Temple of 1,000 Lights** ⑦. Backtrack on Race Course Road to Perumal Road; to the left is the **Sri Srinivasa Perumal Temple** ⑧. Dedicated to Vishnu the Pre-server, the temple is easy to recognize by the 18-meter-high (59-foot-high) monumental gopuram, depicting Vishnu in nine forms. If you continue along Race Course Road, you'll come to the Banana Leaf Apollo, an excellent place for a drink and a curry (☞ Chapter 3).

Allow two to three hours for this walk, and factor in a half an hour each for the temples.

Sights to See

⑪ **Abdul Gaffoor Mosque.** This small and personable temple has none of the exotic, multicolor statuary of the Hindu temples but woos you with an intricately detailed facade in the Muslim colors of green and gold.

Buffalo Road. Shops here specialize in saris, flower garlands, and electronic equipment. Also along this short street are a number of moneylenders from the Chettiar caste—the only caste that continues to pursue in Singapore the role prescribed to them in India. You'll find them seated on the floor before decrepit desks, but don't let the simplicity of their style fool you: Some of them are very, very rich.

❹ **Burmese Buddhist Temple.** Built in 1878, this temple houses a 3.3-meter (11-foot) Buddha carved from a 10-ton block of white marble from Mandalay. The other, smaller Buddhas were placed here by Rama V, the king of Siam, and high priests from Rangoon, Burma (now called Yangon, Myanmar).

Campbell Lane. This street is full of shops selling spices, nuts, flower garlands, plastic flowers, and plastic statues.

Clive Street. On this byway off Sungei Road, you'll find shops selling sugar, prawn crackers, rice, and dried beans. The older Indian women you'll notice with red lips and stained teeth are betel-nut chewers. If you want to try the stuff, you can buy a mouthful from street vendors.

❾ **Dhobi-wallahs.** Alas, Singapore loses some of its romance every day. No. 39 Norris Road used to house Singapore's last remaining traditional Indian laundries, where clothes are boiled in a cauldron and beaten on stone slabs. Now it's an office. But Norris Road does offer many open-air cafés specializing in *chapati,* flat Indian bread.

❺ **Farrer Park.** This is the site of Singapore's original racetrack and where the first aircraft to land in Singapore came to rest en route from England to Australia in 1919.

❻ **Leong San See Temple.** Its main altar is dedicated to Kuan Yin—also known as Bodhisattva Avalokitesvara—and framed by beautiful, ornate carvings of flowers, a phoenix, and other birds.

❸ **Mahatma Gandhi Memorial Hall.** The foundation stone was laid by Prime Minister Nehru in 1950.

⑩ **P. Govindasamy Pillai.** This shop, moved to Dunlop Street, is famous for Indian textiles, especially saris.

❽ **Sri Srinivasa Perumal Temple.** Dedicated to Vishnu the Preserver, the temple is easy to recognize by the 18-meter-high (60-foot-high) monumental gopuram, with tiers of intricate sculptures depicting Vishnu in the nine forms in which he has appeared on earth. Especially vivid are the depictions of Vishnu's manifestations as Rama, on his seventh visit, and as Krishna, on his eighth. Rama is thought to be the personification of the ideal man; Krishna was brought up with peasants and, therefore, was a manifestation popular with laborers in the early days of Singapore. Sri Srinivasa Perumal is very much a people's temple. Inside you will likely find devotees making offerings of fruit to one of the manifestations of Vishnu. This is done either by handing the coconuts or bananas, along with a slip of paper with one's name on it, to a temple official, who will chant the appropriate prayers to the deity and place holy ash on your head, or by walking and praying, coconut in hand, around one of the shrines a certain number of times, then breaking the coconut (a successful break symbolizes that Vishnu has been receptive to the incantation).

❷ Sri Veeramakaliamman Temple. Built in 1881 by indentured Bengali laborers working the lime pits nearby, the temple is dedicated to Kali the Courageous, a ferocious incarnation of Shiva's wife, Parvati the Beautiful. Inside is a jet-black statue of Kali, the fiercest of the Hindu deities, who demands sacrifices and is often depicted with a garland of skulls. More cheerful is the shrine to Ganesh, the elephant-headed god of wisdom and prosperity. Perhaps the most popular Hindu deity, Ganesh is the child of Shiva and Parvati. (He was not born with an elephant head but received it in the following way: Shiva came back from a long absence to find his wife in a room with a young man. In a blind rage, he lopped off the man's head, not realizing that it was his now-grown-up son. The only way to bring Ganesh back to life was with the head of the first living thing Shiva saw; he saw an elephant.) Unlike Singapore's other temples, which are open all day, this one is open 8 AM–noon and 5:30–8:30 PM. At these times, you will see Hindus going in to receive blessings: The priest streaks devotees' foreheads with *vibhuti,* the white ash from burned cow dung.

❼ Temple of 1,000 Lights. The **Sakya Muni Buddha Gaya** is better known by its popular name because, for a small donation, you can pull a switch that lights countless bulbs around a 15-meter (50-foot) Buddha. The entire temple, as well as the Buddha statue, was built by the Thai monk Vutthisasala, who, until he died at the age of 94, was always in the temple, ready to explain Buddhist philosophy to anyone who wanted to listen. The monk also managed to procure relics for the temple: a mother-of-pearl-inlaid cast of the Buddha's footprint and a piece of bark from the bodhi tree under which the Buddha received Enlightenment. Around the pedestal supporting the great Buddha statue is a series of scenes depicting the story of his search for Enlightenment; inside a hollow chamber at the back is a re-creation of the scene of the Buddha's last sermon.

❶ Zhu Jiao Centre. One of the largest wet markets in the city, it has a staggering array of fruits, vegetables, fish, herbs, and spices. On the Sungei Road side of the ground floor are food stalls that offer Chinese, Indian, Malay, and Western foods. Upstairs are shops selling brass goods, "antiques," porcelains, and textiles.

THE ARAB DISTRICT

Long before the Europeans arrived, Arab traders plied the coastlines of the Malay Peninsula and Indonesia, bringing with them the teachings of Islam. By the time Raffles came to Singapore in 1819, to be a Malay was also to be a Muslim. Traditionally, Malays' lives have centered on their religion and their villages, known as kampongs. These consisted of a number of wood houses, with steep roofs of corrugated iron or thatch, gathered around a communal center, where chickens and children would feed and play under the watchful eye of mothers and the village elders while the younger men tended the fields or took to the sea in fishing boats. The houses were usually built on stilts above marshes and reached by narrow planks serving as bridges. If the kampong was on dry land, flowers and fruit trees would surround the houses.

Except for a Malay community on Pulau Sakeng (reachable only by private boat), all traditional kampongs have fallen to the might of the bulldozer in the name of urban renewal. Though all ethnic groups have had their social fabrics undermined by the demolition of their old communities, the Malays have suffered the most, since social life centered on the kampong.

The area known as the Arab District, or Little Araby, while not a true kampong, remains a Malay enclave, held firmly together by strict observance of the tenets of Islam. At the heart of the community is the Sultan Mosque, or Masjid Sultan, originally built with a grant from the East India Company to the Sultan of Jahore. Around it are streets whose very names—Bussorah, Baghdad, Kandahar—evoke the fragrances of the Muslim world. The pace of life is slower here: There are few cars; people gossip in doorways; and closet-size shops are crammed with such wares as Javanese batiks, leather bags from Jogjakarta (Indonesia), *songkok* hats (the white skullcaps presented to those who have made the pilgrimage to Mecca), and Indonesian herbs whose packages promise youth and beauty or lots of children.

The Arab District is a small area, bounded by Beach and North Bridge roads to the south and north and spreading a couple of blocks to either side of Arab Street. It is a place to meander, taking time to browse through shops or enjoy Muslim food at a simple café.

Numbers in the text and in the margin correspond to points of interest on the Arab District map.

A Good Walk

This walk begins at the foot of **Arab Street,** just across Beach Road from the Plaza Hotel. (From Collyer Quay, take Bus 20 or Bus 50; from Raffles Boulevard or the Stamford and Orchard roads intersection, take Bus 107.)

The first shops on Arab Street are bursting with baskets of every description, either stacked on the floor or suspended from the ceiling. Farther along, shops selling fabrics—batiks, embroidered table linens, rich silks and velvets—dominate. Turn right onto Baghdad Street and watch for the dramatic view of the **Sultan Mosque** ① where **Bussorah Street** opens to your left. Leaving the mosque, turn left on Muscat Street, right on Kandahar Street, and then left on Baghdad Street. At Sultan Gate, you will find **Istana Kampong Glam** ②, the sultan's Malay-style palace, built in the 1840s. Baghdad Street becomes Pahang Street at Sultan Gate, where traditional Chinese stonemasons create statues curbside. At the junction of Pahang Street and Jalan Sultan, turn right and, at Beach Road, left, to visit the endearing **Hajjah Fatimah Mosque** ③, built in 1845. It leans at a 6° angle. Return to Jalan Sultan and take a right. Past Minto Road is the **Sultan Plaza** ④, which houses fabric stores. Continue along Jalan Sultan, crossing **North Bridge Road,** to the junction of Victoria Street and the **Malabar Jama-Ath Mosque** ⑤.

Three blocks beyond where **Bugis Street** ⑥ becomes Albert Street—past the Fu Lu Shou shopping complex (mostly for clothes) and the food-oriented Albert Complex—is Waterloo Street. Near the corner is the **Kuan Yin Temple** ⑦, one of the most popular Chinese temples in Singapore.

TIMING

This walking tour should not take more than two hours, including some time to look around the temples and mosques, but take your time. This is one of the friendliest places in Singapore.

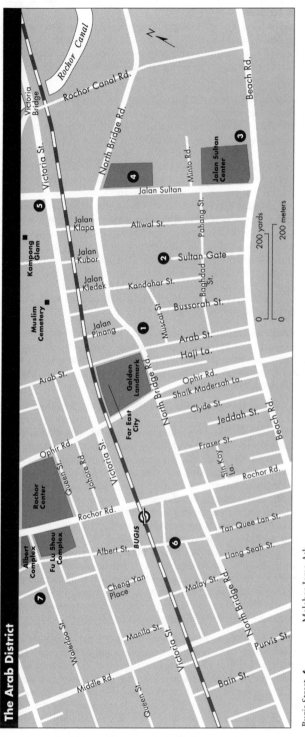

The Arab District

Bugis Street, **6**
Hajjah Fatimah
Mosque, **3**
Istana Kampong
Glam, **2**
Kuan Yin Temple, **7**

Malabar Jama-Ath
Mosque, **5**
Sultan Mosque, **1**
Sultan Plaza, **4**

Sights to See

Arab Street. This is a street of specialty shops. At the end of the street close to Beach Road you'll find baskets galore. At number 18, **Habib Handicrafts** sells leather goods, especially those made from camel hides. Farther along, shops selling fabrics—batiks, embroidered table linens, rich silks and velvets—dominate.

⑥ Bugis Street. Until recently Bugis Street was the epitome of Singapore's seedy but colorful nightlife; tourists (and Singaporeans, too, for that matter) used to delight in its red lights and bars, where transvestites would compete with the most attractive women for attention and favors. The government was not delighted, though, and the area was razed to make way for a new MRT station. So strong was the outcry that Bugis Street has been re-created, approximately 137 meters (150 yards) from its original site, between Victoria and Queen streets, Rochor Road, and Cheng Yan Place. The shophouses have been resurrected; hawker food stands compete with open-fronted restaurants (Kentucky Fried Chicken has a dominant corner). The streets in the center of the block are closed to traffic. But pedestrians look in vain for the old Bugis: Plainclothes security staff make sure that the drunken brawls and general sleaziness remain things of the past. The area has failed to attract the night revelers and performers, and trade hasn't boomed as anticipated. Still, it's convenient for lunch or an early evening meal, but not worth a detour or a special trip.

Bussorah Street. Interesting shops include a Malay bridal shop and purveyors of batiks and Arab-designed cushion covers, and an importer of leather goods from Jogjakarta. At No. 45 is the Malay-crafts store of Haija Asfiah, who will gladly explain in detail the origin and traditional uses of his goods.

③ Hajjah Fatimah Mosque. In 1845 Hajjah Fatimah, a wealthy Muslim woman married to a Bugis trader, commissioned a British architect to build this mosque. (Haj is the honorific title given a man who makes the pilgrimage to Mecca; hajjah is the title given to a woman.) The minaret is reputedly modeled on the spire of the original St. Andrew's Church in colonial Singapore, but it leans at a 6° angle. No one knows whether this was intentional or accidental, and engineers brought in to see if the minaret could be straightened walked away shaking their heads. Islam forbids carved images of Allah. The only decorative element usually employed is the beautiful flowing Arabic script in which quotations from the Qur'an are written across the walls. Because the Hajjah Fatimah Mosque is relatively small, it is very intimate and an oasis of quiet in bustling Singapore. It is extremely relaxing to enter the prayer hall (remember to take your shoes off!) and sit in the shade of its dome. French contractors and Malay artisans rebuilt the mosque in the 1930s. Hajjah Fatimah, her daughter, and her son-in-law lie buried in an enclosure behind the mosque.

② Istana Kampong Glam. The sultan's Malay-style palace, rebuilt in the 1840s on a design by George Coleman, is in a sad state of repair today. Next door, faring only slightly better, is another grand royal bungalow: the home of the sultan's first minister. Notice its gateposts surmounted by green eagles. Neither building is open to the public, but through the gates you can get a glimpse of the past. There is talk of this complex being restored, but for now there is little to see.

⑦ Kuan Yin Temple. One of the most popular Chinese temples in Singapore, the dusty, incense-filled interior, its altars heaped with hundreds of small statues of gods from the Chinese pantheon, transports the visitor into the world of Chinese mythology. Of the hundreds of Chinese deities, Kuan Yin is perhaps most dear to the hearts of Singaporeans. According to legend, she was about to enter nirvana when she heard a plaintive cry from Earth. Touched with compassion, she gave up her place in Paradise to devote herself to alleviating the pain of those on Earth; thereupon, she took the name Kuan Yin, meaning "to see and hear all." People in search of help and advice about anything from an auspicious date for a marriage to possible solutions for domestic or work crises come to her temple, shake *cham si* (bamboo fortune sticks), and wait for an answer. The gods are most receptive on days of a new or full moon.

For more immediate advice, you can speak to any of the fortune-tellers who sit under umbrellas outside the temple. They will pore over ancient scrolls of the Chinese almanac and, for a few dollars, tell you your future. If the news is not good, you may want to buy some of the flowers sold nearby and add them to your bathwater. They are said to help wash away bad luck. A small vegetarian restaurant next to the temple serves Chinese pastries, including mooncakes out of season.

❺ Malabar Jama-Ath Mosque. The land on which it is built was originally granted to the Muslim Kling community in 1848 by Sultan Ally Iskander Shah as a burial ground. The mosque they erected here was abandoned and later taken over by the Malabar Muslims, who rebuilt it in 1963.

North Bridge Road. North Bridge Road is full of fascinating stores selling costumes and headdresses for Muslim weddings, clothes for traditional Malay dances, prayer beads, scarves, perfumes, and much more. Interspersed among the shops are small, simple restaurants serving Muslim food. Toward the Sultan Mosque, the shops tend to concentrate on Muslim religious items, including *bareng haji,* the clothing and other requisites for a pilgrimage to Mecca.

❶ Sultan Mosque. The first mosque on this site was built early in the 1820s with a S$3,000 grant from the East India Company. The current structure, built in 1928 by the same architects who designed the Victoria Memorial Hall, is a dramatic building with golden domes and minarets that glisten in the sunlight. The walls of the vast prayer hall are adorned with green and gold mosaic tiles on which passages from the Qur'an are written in decorative Arab script. The main dome has an odd architectural feature: Hundreds of brown bottles, stacked five or more rows deep, are seemingly jammed in neck first between the dome and base. No one seems to understand the point. Five times a day—at dawn, 12:30 PM, 4 PM, sunset, and 8:15 PM—the sound of the muezzin, or crier, calls the faithful to prayer. At midday on Friday, the Islamic sabbath, seemingly every Malay in Singapore enters through one of the Sultan Mosque's 14 portals to recite the Qur'an. During Ramadan, the month of fasting, the nearby streets, especially Bussorah, and the square before the mosque are lined with hundreds of stalls selling curries, cakes, and candy; at dusk, Muslims break their day's fast in this square. Non-Muslims, too, come to enjoy the rich array of Muslim foods and the party atmosphere.

❹ Sultan Plaza. Inside, dozens of traders offer batiks and other fabrics in traditional Indonesian and Malay designs, and one store on the third floor (No. 26) sells handicrafts from the Philippines.

ORCHARD ROAD

If "downtown" is defined as where the action is, then Singapore's downtown is Orchard Road. Here are some of the city's most fashionable shops, hotels, restaurants, and nightclubs. The street has been dubbed the Fifth Avenue or Bond Street of Singapore, but in fact, it has little in common with either of those older, relatively understated market-places for the wealthy besides the air of luxury. A much more apt comparison would be the Ginza, for, like its Tokyo counterpart, Orchard Road is an ultra-high-rent district that is very modern and very, very flashy, especially at night, when millions of lightbulbs, flashing from seemingly every building, assault the senses.

In addition to all those glittering lights and windows, Orchard Road offers a number of sights with which to break up a shopping trip.

Numbers in the text and in the margin correspond to points of interest on the Orchard Road map.

A Good Walk

We'll start at the bottom of Orchard Road (nearest subway stop: Dhoby Ghaut) and head toward the junction with Scotts Road, the hub of downtown. (Shops and complexes mentioned in this tour are discussed in detail in Chapter 7.)

Leaving the MRT Station, you'll see the enormous **Istana** ①, once the official residence of the colonial governor and now that of the president of the republic. Senior Minister Lee Kuan Yew also keeps his office here. On the other side of Orchard Road, and a few step down Cleamenceau Avenue, is the lovely old **Tan Yeok Nee House** ②. Built in 1815 for a wealthy Chinese merchant, the house used to be a museum, but now it's being redeveloped. Turn on Tank Road and continue to the **Chettiar Temple** ③, which houses the image of Lord Subramaniam. Return to Orchard Road and turn left. On the right, you'll pass the depressing **Meridien Hotel.** A bit farther along is Cuppage Road, with a market (open every morning) known for imported and unusual fruit, a row of shops selling antiques, and the Saxophone jazz club.

Returning once more to Orchard Road, you'll pass the block-long **Centrepoint**; immediately after it is **Peranakan Place** ④, a celebration of Peranakan culture. A bit farther on, across the street, is the **Mandarin Hotel** ⑤, which has an interesting art collection. Recrossing Orchard Road, walk past the seedy Lucky Plaza shopping center, to the corner of Orchard and Scotts roads. A detour up Scotts Road past the Hyatt leads to the landmark **Goodwood Park Hotel** and the most civilized high tea in town.

Retrace your steps to the intersection of Scotts and Orchard roads. On the corner is **Shaw House** ⑥, with Isetan as its major anchor. Walk up the left side of Orchard Road, past the new Lane Crawford building. Taxi drivers call it the rocket, and you'll see why. A Planet Hollywood is due to open at the **Liat Towers** on Orchard Road in early 1997. As you continue up Orchard Road, the **Hilton** will be on your left, the **Palais Renaissance** on your right. Where Orchard turns into Tanglin, you'll find the **Tanglin Shopping Centre.** The second floor is devoted to antiques shops, some of the best in town; take a look at the maps and prints on display at Antiques of the Orient.

TIMING

Orchard Road has so many shopping diversions that you should allow three to four hours for the walk. Allow a half an hour for the Chettiar Temple, and if you are an antiques fan, at least an hour for the second floor of the Tanglin Shopping Centre.

Sights to See

Centrepoint. This spacious and impressive center (⊠ 176 Orchard Rd.) has the **Robinsons** department store as its anchor tenant. One of

Orchard Road

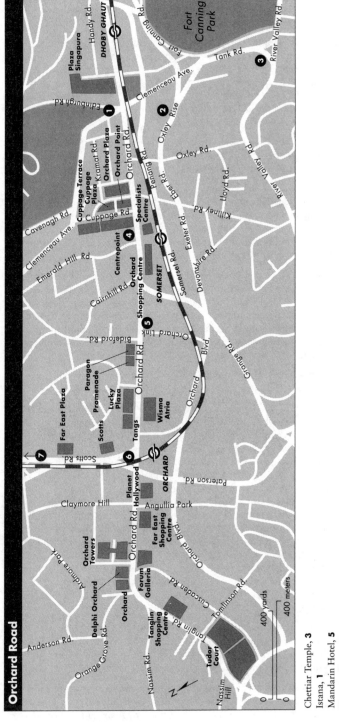

Chettiar Temple, **3**
Istana, **1**
Mandarin Hotel, **5**
Newton Circus, **7**
Peranakan Place, **4**
Shaw House, **6**
Tan Yeok Nee
House, **2**

the liveliest complexes, Centrepoint also has jewelry, silverware, and fashion shops; furniture stores selling Philippine bamboo and Korean chests; and a large basement supermarket.

❸ **Chettiar Temple.** This temple houses the image of Lord Subramaniam. The temple is a recent (1984) replacement of the original, built in the 19th century. The 21-meter-high (70-foot-high) gopuram, with its many colorful sculptures of godly manifestations, is astounding. The chandelier-lit interior is lavishly decorated; 48 painted-glass panels are inset in the ceiling and angled to reflect the sunrise and sunset. ☉ *Daily 8 AM–noon and 5:30–8:30.*

Goodwood Park Hotel. Not as well known as the Raffles and 30 years younger, this landmark hotel offers the most civilized afternoon tea in town, accompanied by a string quartet. Tea is served from 3:30 to 6 and costs about S$18.

The Hilton. This hotel's shopping gallery is home to a number of top designer names—**Giorgio Armani, Matsuda, Valentino**—and, through a boutique called **Singora,** many other Italian and French fashion houses. Among its other top-flight tenants are **Gucci, Davidoff, Louis Vuitton, L'Ultimo, Daks of London,** and **Dunhill.**

❶ **Istana.** Once the official residence of the colonial governor and now that of the president of the republic, it is open to the public only on National Day. On the first Sunday of each month, there's a changing-of-the-guard ceremony: The new guards leave Bideford Road at 5:30 PM and march along Orchard Road to the Istana, reaching the entrance gate punctually at 6. Former prime minister and senior minister Lee Kuan Yew keeps his office here.

Lucky Plaza. This shopping center is packed with camera, electronic, and watch shops.

❺ **Mandarin Hotel.** In the main lobby is an exquisite mural delineated by real gold etched into white marble. The 21-meter-long (70-foot-long) work, by Yuy Tang, is called the 87 Taoist Immortals and is based on an 8th-century Tang scroll. It depicts 87 mythical figures paying homage to Xi Wangmu, Mother of God, on her birthday. While in the Mandarin, you may want to wander around to see the other works of art displayed. In the Mezzanine Lounge is Gerard Henderson's floor-to-ceiling mural *Gift to Singapore.* Henderson, half-Chinese and half-Irish, also created a powerful series of eight canvases titled *Riders of the World.* Five of these dominate the wall adjoining the lobby. These vibrant paintings depict the untamed and unconquered, including a 13th-century Japanese samurai, a Mandarin of the Ming Dynasty, a 9th-century Moor, and a 20th-century cossack. Don't miss the huge abstract batik mural by Seah Kim Joo, one of Singapore's best-known contemporary artists, that adorns three walls of the Mandarin's upstairs gallery.

Meridien Hotel. This hotel was once home to Printemps, the French department store, and used to have some of the best art shows in town. No longer. If you want to get a feel for what overbuilding has done to business in Singapore's retail sector, come here and wander past the empty rooms that used to house shops.

❼ **Newton Circus.** This is one of the best-known hawker centers in town. (The "circus" refers to the rotary, as in Piccadilly Circus.) Some of the stalls are open all day, but the best times to go are either around 9 AM, when a few stalls serve Chinese breakfasts, or after 7 PM, when all the stores are open and the Circus is humming with the hungry.

Palais Renaissance. The Palais Renaissance is chic, opulent, and over-priced but a delight to wander through. Boutiques such as **Ralph Lauren, Dunhill, Christian Lacroix, Chanel, Gucci,** and **Karl Lagerfeld** are for the Japanese shopper seeking status labels at high prices.

❹ Peranakan Place. A celebration of Peranakan (also called Straits-born Chinese, or Baba/Nonya) culture, an innovative blending of Chinese and Malay cultures that emerged in the 19th century as Chinese born in the Straits Settlements adopted Malay fashions, cuisine, and architectural style, adapting them to their own satisfaction. At Peranakan Place, six old wooden shophouses, with fretted woodwork and painted in pastel colors, have been beautifully restored. Notice the typical Peranakan touches, like the distinctive use of decorative tiles and unusual fence doors.

Planet Hollywood. The Liat Towers, formerly home to Galleries Lafayette, the French department store, is being transformed into Planet Hollywood, to open in early 1997. (**Hermès** is here as well.)

❻ Shaw House. Isetan, a large Japanese department store, is the major anchor in this shopping complex at the corner of Scotts and Orchard roads. **Kinokuniya** bookstore, in the older Shaw Centre, is especially good for publications about Japan, but also carries English-language books.

Tanglin Shopping Centre. At the corner of Napier and Tanglin roads, this suburban shopping mall was built to cater to the surrounding wealthy neighborhood. It has an excellent food court in the basement.

❷ Tan Yeok Nee House. The house was built around 1885 for Tan Yeok Nee (1827–1902), a wealthy merchant from China who started out here as a cloth peddler and became a very wealthy man through trading in opium, gambier, and pepper. Whereas most homes built in Singapore at that time followed European styles, this town house was designed in a style popular in South China—notice the keyhole gables, terra-cotta tiles, and massive granite pillars. After the railway was laid along Tank Road in 1901, the house became the stationmaster's. In 1912, St. Mary's Home and School for Girls took it over. Since 1940 the Salvation Army has made the place its local headquarters. The house is now being redeveloped.

THE EAST COAST

Two decades ago, Singapore's eastern coastal area contained only coconut plantations, rural Malay villages, and a few undeveloped beaches. Now it has been totally transformed by the dramatic changes that have altered every aspect of Singapore. At the extreme northeastern tip of the island is Changi International Airport, one of the finest in the world. Between the airport and the city, numerous satellite residential developments have sprung up, and vast land-reclamation projects along the seashore have created a park 8 kilometers (5 miles) long, with abundant recreational facilities.

A Good Tour

An excursion along the east coast can make for a relaxing and enjoyable morning or afternoon outside the bustling metropolis. The tour is best done by taxi (S$8–S$15 each way, depending on how far out you go). Catch one near the junction of Nicoll Highway and Bras Basah Road, near the Raffles Hotel and Marina Square. Nicoll Highway leads onto East Coast Road, and heading east along it, you come to the Kallang area. Cross the Rochar and Kallang rivers by the Merdeka (Independent) Bridge and you'll see, to the left and right, an estuary that was

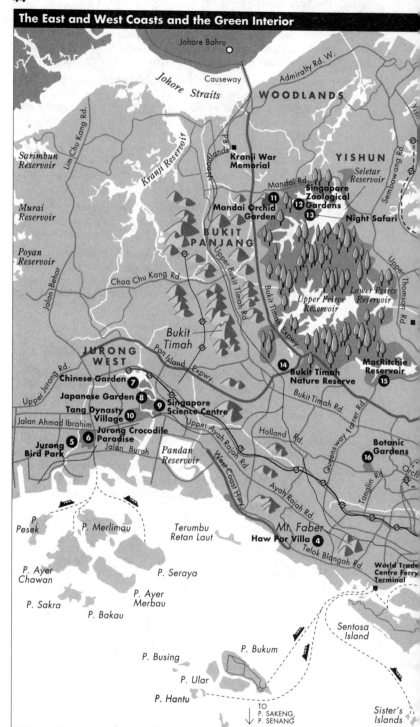

Johore Bahru

Johore Straits

Causeway

Admiralty Rd. W.

WOODLANDS

YISHUN

Sarimbun
Reservoir

Lim Chu Kang Rd.

Kranji Reservoir

Woodlands Rd.

Kranji War
Memorial

*Seletar
Reservoir*

Murai
Reservoir

Mandai Rd.

11

**Mandai Orchid
Garden**

12 **Singapore
Zoological
Gardens**

13

Night Safari

Poyan
Reservoir

**BUKIT
PANJANG**

Upper Bukit Timah Rd.

Sembawang Rd.

Yishun

Jalan Behar

Choa Chu Kang Rd.

*Bukit
Timah*

Bukit Timah Expwy.

*Upper Peirce
Reservoir*

*Lower Peirce
Reservoir*

Upper Thomson Rd.

**JURONG
WEST**

Pan Island Expwy.

Chinese Garden **7**

Upper Jurong Rd.

Japanese Garden **8**

**Tang Dynasty
Village** **10**

9 **Singapore
Science Centre**

14 **Bukit Timah
Nature Reserve**

Bukit Timah Rd.

**MacRitchie
Reservoir**

15

Jalan Ahmad Ibrahim

Upper Ayah Rajah Rd.

Holland Rd.

Queensway

Farrer Rd.

Jurong
Bird Park **5**

6 **Jurong Crocodile
Paradise**

Jalan Buroh

*Pandan
Reservoir*

**Botanic
Gardens**

16

West Coast Hwy.

Ayah Rajah Rd.

Tanglin Rd.

Orch

*P.
Pesek*

P. Merlimau

*Terumbu
Retan Laut*

Ayah Rajah Rd.

Mt. Faber

Haw Par Villa **4**

Telok Blangah Rd.

*P. Ayer
Chawan*

P. Seraya

**World Trade
Centre Ferry
Terminal**

P. Sakra

*P. Ayer
Merbau*

P. Bakau

*Sentosa
Island*

P. Busing

P. Bukum

P. Ular

P. Hantu

TO
↓ P. SAKENG,
P. SENANG

*Sister's
Islands*

0 | 4 miles
0 | 6 km

WEST MALAYSIA

P. Seletar

Johore Straits

TO DESARU, MALAYSIA

TO P. TEKONG

S. Seletar

P. Ubin

P. Serangoon

P. Ketam

Yio Chu Kang Rd.

PUNGGOL

Punggol Rd.

Serangoon Harbour

SERANGOON

CHANGI

Upper Serangoon Rd.

Tampines Rd.

S. Serangoon

Loyang Ave.

U. Changi Rd.

Changi Airport

eng

re

Central Expwy.

■ Crocodile Farm

Paya Lebar Rd.

Changi Prison
①

Airport Blvd.

■ **Siong Lim Temple**

BEDOK

Changi Rd.

New Upper Changi

Changi Coast Rd.

Pan Island Expressway

Serangoon Rd.

Sims Ave.

Geylang Rd.

East Coast Rd.

N

Kallang Rd.

KATONG

Mountbatten Rd.

East Coast Parkway

②

East Coast Park

Nicoll Hwy.

■ **National Stadium**

③

Crocodilarium

Strait   of   Singapore

ani

Buran Darat

kukor

P. Renggit

Kusu Island

Lazarus Island

St. John's Island

Subway & Rail Lines

- - - - North-South MRT line
——— East-West MRT line
——— Railroad lines
⊕ Subway stop

once the haunt of pirates and smugglers. A few shipyards are visible to the left, where the old Bugis trading schooners used to anchor. (The Bugis, a seafaring people from the Celebes [now Sulawesi], Indonesia, have a long history as great sea traders; their schooners, called prahus, still ply the Indonesian waters.) To the right is the huge National Stadium, where major international sporting events are held. Just past the stadium, Mountbatten Road crosses Old Airport Road, once the runway of Singapore's first airfield. One of the old British colonial residential districts, this area is still home to the wealthy, as attested by the splendid houses in both traditional and modern architectural styles. Ask the driver to take you up East Coast Parkway, the road that runs along East Coast Park. Here, you can ask the driver to stop at the **Crocodilarium** ③ or the **East Coast Park** ② or stop to eat at either the **East Coast Park Food Centre** or the **UDMC Seafood Centre.** Catch another taxi to take you farther east to the infamous **Changi Prison** ①. A few organized tours can take you into a part of the prison (but not on Saturday, Sunday, or public holidays)—if you're interested, check itineraries before choosing a tour.

TIMING

Allow two to three hours for this tour.

Sights to See

① **Changi Prison.** This home to Nick Leeson, the young Englishman who broke the Barings Bank, is well worth a visit. This sprawling, squat, and sinister-looking place, built in 1927 by the British, was used by the Japanese in World War II to intern some 70,000 prisoners of war, who endured terrible hardships here. Today it houses some 2,000 convicts, many of whom are here under Singapore's strict drug laws. This is where serious offenders are hanged at dawn on Friday.

On organized tours you may also pass through the old British barracks areas to the former RAF camp at Changi. Here, in **Block 151**—a prisoners' hospital during the war—you can see the simple but striking murals painted by a British POW, bombardier Stanley Warren. In going through this area, one marvels at the huge scale of military spending in the 1930s by the British, who put up these well-designed barracks to accommodate tens of thousands of men. It is hardly surprising that the British believed Singapore to be impregnable! This is still a military area; most of the barracks are used by Singapore's servicemen during their 2½-year compulsory military duty.

Most tour groups and all visitors not part of a tour are allowed to see only **Changi Prison Chapel,** whose walls hold poignant memorial plaques to the regiments and individuals interned here during the war. It is a replica of one of 14 chapels where 85,000 Allied prisoners of war and civilians gained the faith and courage to overcome the degradation and deprivation inflicted upon them by the Japanese. The **Chapel Prison Museum** contains drawings, sketches, and photographs by POWs depicting their wartime experiences.

☎ 545–1441. ✉ *Donations accepted.* ⊙ *Chapel and museum weekdays 8:30 AM–12:30 PM and 2 PM–4:45 PM, Sat. 8:30 AM–12:30 PM; visitors welcome at the Sun. service, 5:30 PM. Take Bus 13 from Orchard Rd., with a transfer to Bus 1 or 2 at Victoria St. or Bus 1 or 2 from Raffles City.*

③ **Crocodilarium.** More than 1,000 of the jaw-snapping crocodiles are bred to be skinned. Feeding time is 11 AM every Tuesday, Thursday, and Saturday. Watch crocodile wrestling Tuesday through Sunday at 1:15 and 4:15 PM. Naturally, there is a place to buy crocodile-skin bags and belts—at inflated prices. ☎ 447–3722. ✉ *S$2.* ⊙ *Daily 9–5:30.*

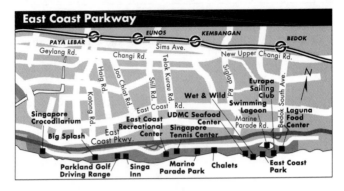

East Coast Parkway

2 **East Coast Park.** Between the highway and the sea, this park has a wide variety of recreational facilities. A cool sea breeze makes it the best place in town for running. (For more information, *see* Chapter 6.)

East Coast Park Food Centre. Next to the Europa Sailing Club, this alfresco center offers dining from many stalls and a great view of the harbor.

UDMC Seafood Centre. This gathering of eight outdoor restaurants is a popular evening destination (☞ Chapter 3).

THE WEST COAST

The satellite city of Jurong is Singapore's main industrial area. It is estimated that more than 70% of the nation's manufacturing workforce is employed here by more than 3,000 companies. One would think this an unlikely tourist area, except perhaps for visitors specializing in industrial design or city planning. However, a number of attractions have been created in or around Jurong as part of the overall planning of the island, and the concept of the garden environment has been continued here to demonstrate that an industrial area does not have to be ugly.

A Good Tour
Numbers in the text and in the margin correspond to points of interest on the East and West Coasts and the Green Interior map.

The attractions on the West Coast are far from the center of town and far from one another. The best way to visit is by either arranging a tour through your hotel or taking taxis alone or in combination with the MRT. A taxi from the center of town to Jurong will cost about S$15. **Haw Par Villa** ④, an amusement park and Chinese heritage center popular with small fry, is much closer to town than the rest of the sites and is best paired with a visit to Sentosa. The nearest MRT station is Outram Park, and from there, a taxi will cost about S$4 to the villa. After visiting the villa, Mt. Faber, one of the main entrances to Sentosa, is a short ride away.

On another day, you might want to try visiting the **Jurong Bird Park** ⑤. An MRT ride to Clementi will cost about S$1.50, depending on where you start your journey, and the taxi ride to the bird park will cost another S$5 or so, depending on traffic. If you want to take a taxi the whole way, the round trip will cost about S$30. The **Jurong Crocodile Paradise** ⑥ is directly across the parking lot from the bird park. Exploring the bird park is tiring, so plan some time-outs in the park's restaurants. A shuttle bus runs three times a day to the **Chinese Garden** ⑦ and the **Japanese Garden** ⑧, but a taxi is your best bet. This will cost about S$4.

Alternatively, you can choose to visit the **Singapore Science Center** ⑨ or the **Tang Dynasty Village** ⑩ for your afternoon. You can take the MRT to Boon Lay Station for the latter, if you don't want to spring for a taxi.

TIMING

Allow a half day for each of the sites, except the Crocodile Paradise, which deserves about one hour, at most. The Chinese and Japanese gardens can be visited in combination.

Sights to See

⑦ **Chinese Garden.** This 34.6-acre garden reconstructs an ornate Chinese imperial garden, complete with temples, courtyards, bridges, and pagodas. (One inspiration was the garden of the Beijing Summer Palace.) Within the main garden are theme areas, such as the **Ixora Garden**, with several varieties of the showy flowering ixora shrub; the **Herb Garden,** showcasing plants used in herbal medicines; and the **Garden of Fragrance**, where many newlyweds have their photographs taken against stone plaques with auspicious Chinese engravings. The Chinese Garden is beautifully landscaped, with lotus-filled lakes, placid streams overhung by groves of willows, and twin pagodas. Rental rowboats allow a swan's-eye view of the gardens, and refreshment facilities are available. The garden is especially popular during such festive occasions as Chinese New Year and the Lantern Festival. ⊠ *Off Yuan Ching Rd., Jurong,* ☎ *265–5889.* ▧ *Combined ticket with Japanese Garden, S$4.* ☉ *Mon.–Sat. 9–7, Sun. 8:30–7.*

④ **Haw Par Villa.** Also known as the Tiger Balm Gardens, the villa, near the West Coast Highway, is a modern rendition of Chinese folklore presented in theme-park fashion. The original Haw Par Villa was an estate owned by two eccentric brothers in the 1930s. After World War II, the gardens were opened to the public. The gardens fell into disarray and were sold to a soft-drink-bottling company, which spent S$85 million on their transformation. The Haw Par Villa reopened in late 1990 as a cross between an amusement park and a multimedia presentation of Chinese mythology. The most popular attractions are a boat ride ("Tales of China") through the inside of a dragon whose entrails have scenes from the 10 courts of hell; a slide presentation ("Legends and Heroes") of Chinese mythology that explains why we have only one sun; the tragedy of the Lady White Snake; a three-dimensional movie ("Creation of the World"); and a ride on the water roller coaster ("Wrath of the Water Gods Flume Ride"). These and six other attractions are excellent for keeping your child's interest, though you will be either bored or amused by the corniness of the sanitized production sets. The best time to start your visit is at 9:30 AM, before the crowds and long lines. ⊠ *262 Pasir Panjang Rd.,* ☎ *774–0300.* ▧ *S$16.50 (includes all attractions).* ☉ *Daily 9–6. A taxi from Orchard Rd. will run S$10, or take Bus 10 or 30 from the Padang to Pasir Panjang Rd. (S$1.10).*

⑧ **Japanese Garden.** Adjacent to the Chinese Garden, this delightful formal garden is one of the largest Japanese-style gardens outside Japan. Its classic simplicity, serenity, and harmonious arrangement of plants, stones, bridges, and trees induce tranquility. (Indeed, the garden's Japanese name, Seiwaen, means "Garden of Tranquility.") A miniature waterfall spills into a pond full of water lilies and lotus. ⊠ *Off Yuan Ching Rd., Jurong,* ☎ *265–5889.* ▧ *Combined ticket with Chinese Garden, S$4; camera charge, S$.50.* ☉ *Mon.–Sat. 9–7, Sun. 8:30–7; last admission at 6.*

⑤ **Jurong Bird Park.** Built on 50 landscaped acres, the park contains the world's largest walk-in aviary, complete with a 30-meter (100-foot) man-made waterfall that cascades into a meandering stream. More than 3,600 birds from 365 species are here, including the colorful, the rare, and the noisy. It is quite a shock to stand atop Jurong Hill, amid the park's twittering birds and lush green vegetation, and look down on the factories cranking out Singapore's economic success.

If you get to the bird park early, try the breakfast buffet from 9 to 11 at the **Song Bird Terrace,** where birds in bamboo cages tunefully trill as you help yourself to sausages, eggs, and toast. Breakfast with the birds is free, but you have to pay for your food. From there you can walk over to the **Free Flight Show** (held at 10:30), featuring eagles and hawks. In the afternoon, at 3:30, you might catch the **Parrot Circus,** complete with bike-riding bird-gymnasts—if you can stand the jabbering. The nocturnal-bird house allows a glimpse of owls, night herons, frogsmouth, kiwi, and other birds usually cloaked in darkness. Pelicans get fed at 10:15 AM and 2:15 PM; visitors can do so throughout the day at the **Waterfront Cafe** or the **Burger King.** ⊠ *Jurong Hill, Jalan Ahmad Ibrahim,* ☎ *265–0022.* ☜ *S$6; Panorail fare, S$2.* ⊙ *Daily 9–6.*

🖐 ❻ **Jurong Crocodile Paradise.** Singaporeans seem to be fascinated with crocs, for at this 5-acre park you'll find 2,500 of them in various environments—in landscaped streams, at a feeding platform, in a breeding lake. You can feed the crocodiles, watch muscle-bound showmen (and a showlady) wrestle crocodiles, or buy crocodile-skin products at the shop. You can also watch the beasts through glass, in an underwater viewing gallery. A seafood restaurant and fast-food outlets provide refreshments, and there is an amusement center with rides for children. ⊠ *241 Jalan Ahmad Ibrahim,* ☎ *261–8866.* ☜ *S$6.* ⊙ *Daily 9–6; crocodile-wrestling shows at 11:45, 2, and 4.*

New Ming Village. At this small complex of buildings not far from the Jurong Bird Park, demonstrations of the art of Chinese pottery making are given, and copies of Ming Dynasty blue and white porcelain are produced and sold. ⊠ *32 Pandam Rd.,* ☎ *265–7711.* ☜ *Free.* ⊙ *Daily 9–5:30.*

Singapore Mint Coin Gallery. Minting operations can be viewed here, along with coins, medals, and medallions from Singapore and around the world. ⊠ *249 Jalan Boon Lay, Jurong,* ☎ *663–4638.* ☜ *Free.* ⊙ *Weekdays 9:30–4:30.*

🖐 ❾ **Singapore Science Centre.** The center is dedicated to the space age and its technology. Subjects such as aviation, nuclear sciences, robotics, astronomy, and space technology are entertainingly explored through audiovisual aids and computers that you operate. Visitors can walk into a "human body" for a closer look at the vital organs; there is also a flight simulator of a Boeing 747, plus computer quiz games and other computer/laser displays. The Omni Theatre presents two programs: "Oasis in Space," which travels to the beginning of the universe, and "To Fly," which simulates the feel of travel in space. The center is designed as a learning experience for schoolchildren, but children of any age are sure to get a thrill from the brave new world of science presented here. ⊠ *Science Centre Rd., off Jurong Town Hall Rd.,* ☎ *560–3316.* ☜ *S$3; Omni Theatre S$9.* ⊙ *Tues.–Sun. 10–6.*

🖐 ❿ **Tang Dynasty Village.** This theme park re-creates the 7th-century Chinese village of Chang'an (present-day Xian) with pagodas, gilded imperial courts, and an underground palace of the royal dead guarded by 1,000 terra-cotta warriors. The Imperial Palace includes a cluster of six palaces built to original scale. Restaurants and entertainment facilities are modern intrusions, but artisans make and sell traditional wares, and acrobats, rickshaws, and oxcarts all add to the authenticity. A tramway takes you around. ☎ 261–1116. ✉ S$15.45, with tramway. ☉ Daily 9 AM–10 PM.

INTO THE GARDEN ISLE

Singapore is called the Garden Isle, and with good reason. Obsessed as it is with ferroconcrete, the government has also established nature reserves, gardens, and a zoo. This excursion from downtown Singapore takes you into the center of the island to enjoy some of its greenery. Should you desire a detailed understanding of Singapore's natural habitats and plant life, contact the Nature Society (☎ 253–2179). If you have only a little time to spare, do try to fit in the zoo, at least—it is exceptional.

A Good Tour

Much of Singapore's natural world is miles from the center of the city, especially the zoo, the Night Safari and the Orchid Garden. Taxis or a hotel tour are the favored ways of getting to these sites. The **Mandai Orchid Garden** ⑪ is a must for flower-lovers; a taxi from the center of town will cost about S$16. Spend about an hour there, then head off to the **Singapore Zoological Gardens** ⑫. The ride will cost about $6. If you arrive at the zoo at 2:30 PM, you'll be in time to have tea with the orangutans and get a good look at the zoo before closing time at 6:00 PM. Next door, the **Night Safari** ⑬ opens at 7:30 PM. In the meantime, you can have dinner at the restaurant at the entrance to the Safari.

Walking through nature in Singapore is tiring because it is so hot, so the **Bukit Timah Nature Reserve** ⑭, **MacRitchie Reservoir** ⑮ and **Botanic Gardens** ⑯ should be done on separate days.

To get to the Nature Reserve from the zoo or the Mandai Orchid Garden, take Bus 171. The same bus departs from the Orchard and Scotts roads intersection.

To get to MacRitchie, take a S$6.50 taxi from the Orchard MRT station or Bus 171 from the intersection of Orchard and Scotts roads. Take a taxi back from the main parking lot.

To get to the Botanic Gardens, take a taxi or the number 7 bus from the Orchard MRT station. The taxi will cost S$2.80.

TIMING

The Mandai Orchid Garden, Zoological Gardens, and Night Safari can be experienced in an afternoon and an evening. Allow at least half a day for the Botanic Gardens and another half day for the MacRitchie Reservoir.

Sights to See

⑯ **Botanic Gardens.** This is an ideal place to escape the bustle of downtown Singapore. The gardens were begun in Victorian times as a collection of tropical trees and plants. (Today a 19th-century bandstand perpetuates the image of carefully conceived British gardens.) Later, botanist Henry Ridley came here to experiment with rubber-tree seeds from South America; his experiments led to the development of the region's huge rubber industry and the decline of the Amazon basin's importance as a source of the commodity.

The beautifully maintained gardens are spread over some 74 acres, with a large lake, masses of shrubs and flowers, and magnificent examples of many tree species, including 30-meter-high (98-foot-high) fan palms. Locals come here to stroll along nature walks, jog, practice *tai chi* (the Chinese shadow-boxing exercise), feed the geese that inhabit the small pond, or just enjoy the serenity. An extensive orchid bed contains specimens representing 250 varieties, some of them very rare. The combined fragrances of frangipani, hibiscus, and aromatic herbs that pervade the gardens are a delight. ⊠ *Corner of Napier and Cluny Rds.,* ☎ *1800/479–7100.* ☒ *Free.* ☉ *Weekdays 5 AM–11 PM, weekends 5 AM–midnight.*

Inside the Botanic Gardens, the 7.4-acre **Singapore Orchid Garden** was opened by Senior Minister Lee Kuan Yew, the former prime minister, in 1995. Its splendid display of more than 3,000 orchids makes it well worth the visit. ⊠ *Botanic Gardens.* ☒ *S$2.* ☉ *Daily 8:30–6; last ticket sold at 6, last person out at 7.*

⑭ Bukit Timah Nature Reserve. This is the place for those who prefer their nature a little wilder than what the carefully manicured parks around the city can offer. In these 148 acres around Singapore's highest hill (175 meters, or 574 feet), the tropical forest runs riot, giving a feel for how things were before anyone besides tigers roamed the island. Wandering along structured, well-marked paths, you may be startled by flying lemurs, civet cats, or—if you're really lucky—a troupe of long-tailed macaques. The view from the hilltop is superb. Wear good walking shoes—the trails are not smooth gravel but rocky, sometimes muddy, paths. ⊠ *Km 12, Upper Bukit Timah Rd., no phone.* ☒ *Free.* ☉ *Daily dawn–dusk.*

Kong Meng San Phor Kark See Temple. This relatively modern complex of Buddhist temples is typical of the ornate Chinese style, with much gilded carving. ⊠ *Bright Hill Drive, about 1½ km (about 1 mi) west of the Bishan MRT station.*

Kranji War Memorial. This cemetery, a tribute to the forces who fought to defend Singapore in World War II, is in the north of the island, near the causeway off Woodlands Road. Rows of Allied dead are grouped with their countrymen in plots on a peaceful, well-manicured hill. This is a touching experience, a reminder of the greatness of the loss in this and all wars.

☙ ⑮ MacRitchie Reservoir. This 30-acre park has a jogging track with exercise areas, a playground, and a tea kiosk. The path around the reservoir is peaceful, with only the warbling of birds and chatter of monkeys to break your reverie. Crocodile spotting became a favorite pastime after baby crocs were found in the reservoir in early 1996. Don't go in the water. ⊠ *Lornie Rd., near Thomson Rd., no phone.* ☒ *Free.* ☉ *Daily dawn–dusk.*

⑪ Mandai Orchid Garden. Less than a kilometer down the road from the zoo (Bus 171 links the two) is a commercial orchid farm. The hillside is covered with the exotic blooms, cultivated for domestic sale and export. There are many varieties to admire, some quite spectacular. However, unless you are an orchid enthusiast, and since it is a good 30-minute taxi ride from downtown, a visit here is worth it only when combined with a visit to the zoo. The Botanic Gardens (☞ *above*) are closer to downtown and also have orchids. ⊠ *Mandai Lake Rd.,* ☎ *269–1036.* ☒ *S$2 (refunded if you make a purchase).* ☉ *Weekdays 9–5:30.*

OFF THE
BEATEN PATH

Near the Mandai Orchid Garden is the **Artists Village** (⊠ 61-B Lorong Gambas, ☎ 257–2503), where Singaporean and expatriate artists work together in a cluster of huts on a working farm. Shows and workshops are held from time to time, but because of the artists' desire to involve the viewer in the process of creating art, they welcome visitors anytime. The nearest MRT stop is Yi Shun; from there, take a taxi.

☙ ⑬ Night Safari. Right next to the zoo, the safari claims to be the world's first nighttime wildlife park. Here 80 acres of secondary jungle provide a home to 100 species of wildlife that are more active at night than during the day. Some 90% of tropical animals are, in fact, nocturnal, and to see them active—instead of snoozing, which is what you are likely to catch them doing if you visit during the day—gives their behavior a new dimension. Night Safari uses the same moat concept as the zoo to create an open natural habitat; the area is floodlit with enough light to see the animals' colors, but not enough to limit their nocturnal activity. Visitors are transported on a 45-minute tram ride along 3 kilometers (2 miles) of loop roads, stopping frequently to admire the beasts and their antics. On another 1.3 kilometers (⅞ mile) of walking trails you can observe some of the small cat families, primates (like the slow loris and tarsier), and the pangolin, or scaly anteater. Larger animals include the Nepalese rhino (the largest of rhinos, with a single, mammoth horn) and the beautifully marked royal Bengal tigers—which are somewhat intimidating to the nearby shy mousedeer, babirusa (pig deer with curled tusks protruding through the upper lip), gray gorals (wild mountain goats), and bharals (mountain sheep). ⊠ *80 Mandai Lake Rd.,* ☎ *269–3411.* ☜ *S$15.* ☽ *Daily 7:30 PM–midnight.*

Seletar Reservoir. Larger and wilder than the MacRitchie Reservoir, the Seletar is the largest and least developed natural area on the island. ⊠ *Mandai Rd., near the zoo, no phone.* ☜ *Free.* ☽ *Daily dawn–dusk.*

☺ **Singapore Crocodile Farm.** Yet more of these popular creatures—plus alligators, snakes, and lizards—are on view at this 1-acre breeding farm. Feeding time is 11 AM Tuesday through Sunday. At the factory, observe the process of turning hides into accessories that are sold at the farm shop, along with imported eel-skin products. ⊠ *790 Upper Serangoon Rd.,* ☎ *288–9385.* ☜ *Free.* ☽ *Daily 8:30–5:30.*

☺ ⑫ **Singapore Zoological Gardens.** Cliché though it may be, here the humans visit animals as guests in their habitat. One gets the impression that animals come here for a vacation and not, as is often the case elsewhere, to serve a prison sentence. What makes the Singapore zoo different is that it is designed according to the open-moat concept, wherein a wet or dry moat separates the animals from the people. (Interestingly, a mere 1-meter-deep [3-foot-deep] moat will keep humans and giraffes apart, for a giraffe's gait makes even a shallow trench impossible to negotiate. A narrow water-filled moat prevents spider monkeys from leaving their home turf for a closer inspection of visitors.)

Few zoos have found it possible to afford the huge cost of employing this system, developed by Carl Hagenbeck, who created the Hamburg (Germany) zoo at the turn of the century: Moated exhibits take up much more space per animal than cages do. The Singapore zoo has managed by starting small and expanding as more funds became available. It now sprawls over 69 acres of a 220-acre forested area, and the visitor has the pleasurable feeling that the animals are in their natural environments and having a good life.

Try to arrive at the zoo in time for the buffet breakfast. The food itself is not special, but the company is. At 9:30 AM, Ah Meng, a 24-year-old orangutan, comes by for her repast. She weighs about 250 pounds, so she starts by taking a table by herself, but you are welcome to join her for a snack. Afterward, from glass windows beneath their watery grotto, you can watch the polar bears dive for their own fishy breakfast. At the reptile house, be sure to see the Komodo dragon lizards, which can grow to 3 meters (10 feet) in length. Then it will be time for the primate-and-reptile show, in which monkeys, gibbons, and chimpanzees have humans perform tricks, and snakes embrace volunteers from the audience.

There are performances by fur seals, elephants, free-flying storks, and other zoo inhabitants at various times throughout the day. In numerous miniparks reproducing different environments, giraffes, Celebese apes, bearded pigs, tigers, lions, and other of the zoo's 1,700 animals from among 160 species take life easily. Elephant rides are available for S$2 adults, S$1 children. For S$1.50, visitors can travel from one section of the zoo to another by tram. ⊠ *80 Mandai Lake Rd.,* ☎ *269–3411.* ▣ *S$9; breakfast or tea S$15 before 9 AM or after 4 PM.* ☯ *Daily 8:30–6; breakfast with an orangutan Tues.–Sat. 9–10 AM; high tea at 3.*

Siong Lim Temple and Gardens. This is the largest Buddhist temple complex in Singapore, built by two wealthy Hokkien merchants between 1868 and 1908. Set among groves of bamboo, the temple is guarded by the giant Four Kings of Heaven, in full armor. There are a number of shrines and halls, with many ornate features and statues of the Lord Buddha. The goddess of mercy, Kuan Yin, has her shrine behind the main hall; another hall houses a number of fine Thai Buddha images. The oldest building in the complex is a small wood shrine containing antique murals of the favorite Chinese legend "Pilgrimage to the West." ⊠ *184 E. Jalan Toa Payoh, about 1 km (½ mi) east of the Toa Payoh MRT station.*

SENTOSA

Connected to Singapore by bridge, this highly developed island is Singapore's best-known amusement park.

In 1968 the government decided that Sentosa, the Isle of Tranquillity, would be transformed from the military area it was into the Disney-type resort playground it has become, with museums, parks, golf courses, restaurants, and hotels. A tremendous amount of money has been poured into the island's development, and some Singaporeans find Sentosa an enjoyable place to spend some of their free time. However, this "pleasure park" is likely to hold little interest for travelers who have come 10,000 miles to visit Asia, a fact lost on the Singapore government. Though Sentosa is certainly not a must-see in Singapore, there are two good reasons to go: the visual drama of getting there and the fascinating wax museum.

In addition to historical and scientific exhibitions, Sentosa offers a nature walk through secondary jungle; a *pasar malam* (night market) with 40 stalls (☯ Fri.–Sun. 6–10 PM); campsites by the lagoon and tent rentals; and a wide range of recreational activities. Canoes, paddleboats, and bicycles are available for hire. There is swimming in the lagoon and at a small ocean beach, though the waters leave a lot to be desired, considering the hundreds of cargo ships at anchor off the coast. Golf is available at the Tanjong Course, and for anyone with balance, there is a roller-skating rink, said to be the largest in Southeast Asia. (For detailed information on Sentosa's recreational offerings, *see* Chapter 6.)

Admission

There are two main types of all-day (8:30 AM–10 PM) admission passes to the island, plus cheaper evening-only (5–10 PM) versions of the same. The Day Charges Ticket (S$6) covers round-trip shuttle bus, unlimited monorail and beach train rides, swimming in the lagoon, and admission to the fountain shows and the Maritime Museum. The Sentosa Saver (a day package; S$9.50) includes the above, plus admission to the Pioneers of Singapore/Surrender Chambers, the Coralarium, and Fort Siloso. You may also choose the Sentosa Discovery Package (S$21.50), which includes transfer to and from the city's major hotels and admission to major attractions. Reservations may be made through your hotel desk or by telephoning 235–3111. For further information about Sentosa and its facilities, call 270–7888.

Arriving and Departing

To bridge the 1.8 kilometers (about 1 mile) to Sentosa from Singapore, you can take the cable car (with small gondolas holding four passengers each), the ferry, or a shuttle bus. Traveling out by cable car, the more dramatic method, heightens the anticipation; for convenience, return via the causeway, or for variety, via the ferry.

BY CABLE CAR

The cable car picks up passengers from two terminals on the Singapore side: the Cable Car Towers, next to the World Trade Centre, and the Mt. Faber Cable Car Station. As the trip from Cable Car Towers starts at the edge of the sea and is a bit shorter, it does not afford the spectacular, panoramic views you get swinging down from Mt. Faber. At 113 meters (377 feet), Mt. Faber is not particularly high, but it offers splendid views of Singapore city to the east and of industrial Jurong to the west. At sunset it is a very romantic spot. A small café offers simple fare. There is no bus to the Mt. Faber Cable Car Station, and it's a long walk up the hill, so a taxi is the best way to get there. The Cable Car Towers station is accessible by bus: From Orchard Road, take Bus 10 or 143; from Collyer Quay, Bus 10, 20, 30, 97, 125, or 146. ⊠ *Cable Car Towers: Off Kampong Bahru Rd.,* ☎ *270–8855.* ☞ *S$6.50 round-trip, S$5 one-way.* ☉ *Mon.–Sat. 10–7, Sun. and public holidays 9–9.*

BY FERRY

Ferries ply between Jardine Steps at the World Trade Centre and Sentosa every 15 minutes from 7:30 AM, seven days a week; the crossing takes four minutes. The last ferry back from Sentosa departs at 11 PM Monday through Thursday. From Friday through Sunday and on public holidays, there are two extra return ferries, one at 11:15 PM, the other at midnight. Cost: S$2 one-way.

BY SHUTTLE BUS

To reach Sentosa by land, take a bus to the World Trade Centre—number 10, 97, 100, or 125 from Shenton Way, or number 65 or 143 from Orchard Road—and transfer from there onto a shuttle bus across the causeway. The S$5 round-trip fare includes admission to the island. The shuttle operates 7 AM–11 PM (midnight on weekends). You can also get to Sentosa by taxi (there's a $S6 toll in addition to the fare), but only between 7 PM and 10 AM, and cabs may drop or collect passengers only at the two island hotels, the Beaufort and the Rasa Sentosa. (An unofficial method of reaching Sentosa is to take the shuttle bus from the Shangri-La Hotel off Orchard Road to its sister hotel, the Rasa Sentosa.)

Getting Around

Sentosa has Southeast Asia's first monorail. Its six stations cover most of the major attractions (operates daily 9 AM–10 PM). Unlimited rides are included in the price of the admission ticket—you may get on and off at any of the stations at will. A free bus (daily 9–7) also provides transportation to most of the attractions. A small train runs along the island's south coast for about 3 kilometers (2 miles). Bicycles are available for rent at kiosks throughout the island. And, of course, you can walk.

A Good Tour

Start at the World Trade Centre, where you'll take a ferry or cable car (from the nearby station) to Sentosa. Between the ferry terminal and the cable car station on the Sentosa side is the **Asian Village** ①, a mini-theme park. Follow the signs up the hill until you get to the **Rare Stone Museum** ②. It is exactly what it says, and not something to write home about, but if you have a yearning to see rare stones, this is the place for you. Follow the signs again, until you arrive at the **Pioneers of Singapore/Surrender Chambers** ③, a wax museum that gives you an idea of what Singapore was like 100 years ago. Close by, you will find the **Butterfly Park and World Insectarium** ④ with both live and dead butterflies. After this, board the monorail for the trip to **Underwater World** ⑤, a popular aquarium. Next to that, you will find **Fort Siloso** ⑥, an old British fort that amuses the French to no end. Much as at the famous Maginot Line, the cannons on this fort were pointing the wrong way during World War II. From there, take the monorail again, to stop 5 and the swimming lagoon.

After a drink at the **Sunset Bar**, where you can sit on the wooden deck, gaze out at the view, and watch the nonstop volleyball game, head up the hill behind the bar to the **Merlion** ⑦, Singapore's 10-story mascot. The view is from the top is good—the city and the container port on one side, the harbor, the refineries, and the Indonesian islands of Bintan and Bataam on the other.

A three-hour guided tour of Sentosa covers the other major attractions, including the **Maritime Museum** ⑧ and the **Coralarium** ⑨. These tours depart daily at 10:30 AM. Tickets (S$15) may be purchased at the Sentosa Cable Car Station ticket booth. You can certainly do as well on your own, however: A recording on the monorail points out sights as you pass, and audiovisual displays accompany many exhibits in the museums.

TIMING
Depending on your schedule and your tolerance for kitsch, you can spend a half an hour or all day on Sentosa. This tour will take three to four hours, or longer if you linger at the beach.

Sights to See
Numbers in the margin correspond to points of interest on the Sentosa Island map.

❶ Asian Village. Adjacent to the ferry terminal, this village contains three independent "communes" representing East Asia, South Asia, and Southeast Asia. In each village, street performances, demonstrations, merchandise, and food stalls do what they can to add life to an eclectic mix that, for example, combines Thai and north Sumatran architecture in one village and a Japanese torii gate and a Chinese teahouse in another. 🎟 S$4. ☉ Daily 10–9.

❹ Butterfly Park and World Insectarium. This park has a collection of 2,500 live butterflies from 50 species, 4,000 mounted butterflies and insects, plus lots of other insects—like tree-horn rhino beetles, scorpions, and tarantulas—that still creep, crawl, or fly. The park is landscaped on an Oriental theme, with moon gate, streams, and bridges. 🎟 S$4. ☉ Weekdays 9:30–5:30, weekends and holidays 9:30–7.

❾ Coralarium. The Coralarium has more than 2,500 specimens of seashells and corals on display. Exhibits demonstrate how coral grows, how shells have evolved, and how typical coral reefs are structured. 🎟 S$1.50. ☉ Daily 9–7.

Fantasy Island. This is one of the truly fun places on Sentosa and a great place to escape Singapore's heat. Among other attractions, there's a water slide and an action river with white-water rapids. 🎟 S$16. ☉ Fri.–Tues. 10–7.

Sentosa Island

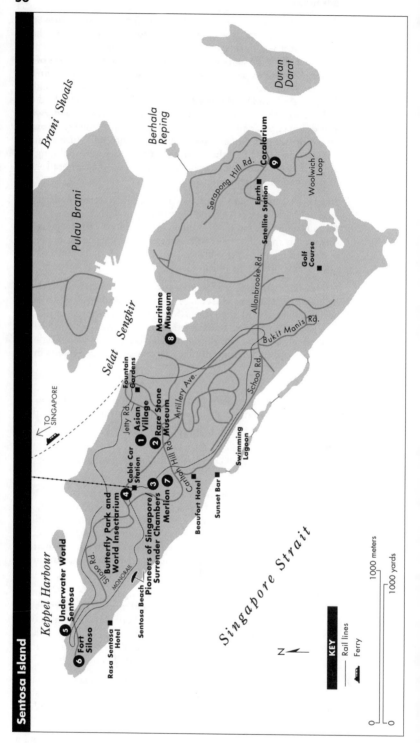

Brani Shoals

Pulau Brani

Duran Darat

Berhala Reping

Selat Sengkir

Keppel Harbour

TO SINGAPORE

Serapong Hill Rd.

Coralarium ❾

Earth Satellite Station ■

Woolwich Loop

Golf Course ■

Allanbrooke Rd.

Bukit Manis Rd.

School Rd.

Maritime Museum ❽

Fountain Gardens ■

Jetty Rd.

Asian Village ❶

Rare Stone Museum ❷

Artillery Ave.

Cable Car Station ■

❹

❸ ❼ Merlion

Pioneers of Singapore/
Surrender Chambers

Carlton Hill Rd.

Beaufort Hotel ■

Sunset Bar ■

Swimming Lagoon

Butterfly Park and
World Insectarium

Underwater World Sentosa ❺

Fort Siloso ❻

Siloso Rd.

MONORAIL

Sentosa Beach

Rasa Sentosa Hotel ■

Singapore Strait

KEY

—— Rail lines

⚓ Ferry

N

0   1000 meters

0   1000 yards

NEED A
BREAK? You may want to enjoy high tea or an early dinner at the **Rasa Sentosa Food Centre** (☉ Daily 10 AM–10:30 PM), next to the ferry terminal. More than 40 stalls offer a variety of foods for alfresco dining amid groomed tropical surroundings. Two stalls worth noting are Fatty's from Albert Street, for Cantonese, and Charlie's Peranakan, for authentic Nonya food.

⑥ Fort Siloso. The fort covers 10 acres of gun emplacements and tunnels created by the British as a fortress against invasion by the Japanese. Unfortunately, the Japanese arrived by land (through Malaysia) instead of by sea, so the huge guns were pointed in the wrong direction. (In fact, the guns could have been redirected, but they were designed to fire shells that pierced ships' armor, not to deal with land forces.) Gun buffs will enjoy the range of artillery pieces in the fort. Photographs document the history of the war in the Pacific, and dioramas depict the life of POWs during the harsh Japanese occupation. 🖾 S$1. ☉ Daily 9–7.

Fountain Gardens. Several times each evening, visitors to the gardens, conveniently close to the ferry terminal, are invited to dance along with the illuminated sprays from the fountains to classical or pop music. This activity is not for introverts. Performances by traditional-dance groups are sometimes held during the evening.

⑧ Maritime Museum. A small but interesting collection of ship models, pictures, and other items document Singapore's involvement with the sea in business and in war. A fishing gallery displays nets, traps, and spears used in the area throughout the centuries; a collection of full-size native watercraft traces the development of local boatbuilding from dugout canoes to Indonesian *prahus* (schooners). 🖾 S$1. ☉ Daily 10–7.

⑦ Merlion. This monument to bad taste is Singapore's tourism mascot—a 10-story, 37-meter off-white sea lion that emits laser beams from its eyes and smoke from its nostrils. It even glows in the dark. To get to the observation tower, you'll have to walk through a pirate cave exhibition. The walls are covered with television screens, some showing "the Legend of the Merlion," others showing advertisements for the rest of Sentosa. The ride up to the 10th story is by elevator, then you climb up two stories to the top of the Merlion and a view of Singapore and the Indonesian islands of Bataam and Bintan. 🖾 S$3. ☉ Daily 9–10.

③ Pioneers of Singapore/Surrender Chambers. This wax museum stands out from all the rest of Sentosa's attractions. A series of galleries traces the development of Singapore and portrays the characters whose actions profoundly influenced the island's history. Though the wax figures are not the most lifelike you'll ever see, the scenes and audio narrative offer a vivid picture of life in Singapore in the 19th century and a rare opportunity, in the modernized Singapore of today, to ponder the diversity of cultures that were thrust together in the pursuit of trade and fortune. The second part of the museum is the Surrender Chambers, with wax tableaux depicting the surrender of the Allies to the Japanese in 1942 and the surrender of the Japanese in 1945. Photographs, documents, and audiovisuals highlight significant events in the Japanese occupation of Singapore and the various battles that led to the eventual defeat. Originally, there was only the scene representing the Japanese surrender; as Japan became the number-one source of foreign visitors to Singapore, it was wisely decided to show both surrenders. 🖾 S$3. ☉ Daily 9–9.

② Rare Stone Museum. Here you'll find some 4,000 rare and unique stones and other rocks that have been given interesting designs and shapes by nature. Among these shapes, the imaginative have recognized deities, animals, and historical figures, including Confucius and Winston Churchill. The collection is the work of five generations and includes a display of large rocks, such as 600,000-year-old stalactites and stalagmites, and of fossils and dinosaur bones. ☒ S$3. ☉ Daily 9–7.

Rasa Sentosa. This 450-room hotel, popular with families, has one of the better island beaches and a big pool.

☯ **Sentosa Orchid Garden.** This exotic garden is filled with orchids from around the world, a flower clock, a carp pond, and a Japanese teahouse. ⊠ Monorail Station 1. Bus 2 or C. ☒ S$2. ☉ Daily 9:30–6:30.

☯ **Singapore Maritime Showcase.** At the World Trade Centre on the Singapore side, the showcase consists of high-tech interactive exhibits and displays designed to enlighten visitors about the past, present, and future of Singapore's shipping industry. The **Shipbridge Simulator** lets visitors operate sophisticated navigational controls to guide megaton ships through computerized versions of famous waterways. Another exhibit shows how Singapore could become a space port. At the **TechnoPort,** visitors play simulated games working dockside equipment in a detailed model of Singapore's Tanjong Pagar and Brani terminals. ☒ Free. ☉ Daily 9–5.

Sunset Bar. Expatriates hang out here to play volleyball and other beach games, to the background drone of rap music.

☯ ➎ **Underwater World Sentosa.** Completed in 1991, Underwater World reverses the traditional aquarium experience by placing the visitor right in the water. Two gigantic tanks house thousands of Asian Pacific fish and other marine life; visitors walk through a 91-meter (100-yard) acrylic tunnel that curves along the bottom. ☒ S$10. ☉ Daily 9–9.

THE OUTER ISLANDS

Singapore consists of one large island and some 60 smaller ones. Though the STPB, ever striving to make Singapore more attractive to tourists, has begun targeting the islands for development as beach destinations, most of them are still off the beaten track, with few facilities for visitors. Exceptions are Kusu and St. John's, which can be reached by a ferry departing from the Cruise Centre at the World Trade Centre (☞ below).

Kusu, also known as Turtle Island, is an ideal retreat (except on weekends) from the traffic and concrete of Singapore. There is a small coffee shop on the island, but you may want to bring a picnic lunch to enjoy in peace on the beach. A number of different stories explain the association with turtles, all in some way relating to a turtle that saved two shipwrecked sailors, one Chinese and one Malay, who had washed up on the island. Turtles now are given sanctuary here, and an artificial pond honors them with stone sculptures. There are two ferries, at 10 AM and 1:30 PM, Monday through Saturday. On Sunday and public holidays there are nine, the first departing at 6 AM and the last at 8 PM. The trip takes about 30 minutes each way (☒ S$6, ☎ 270–7888).

On top of the hill on Kusu Island, a **shrine** (called a *keramat*) is dedicated to a Malay saint, a pious man by the name of Haji Syed Abdul Rahman, who, with his mother and sister, is said to have disappeared supernaturally from the island in the 19th century. To reach the shrine, you must climb the 122 steps that snake their way up the hill through a forest of trees. Plastic bags containing stones have been hung on the trees by devotees who have come to the keramat to pray for forgiveness of sins and the correction of wayward children. If their wishes are granted, believers must return the following year to remove their bags and give thanks.

Tua Pek Kong, a small, open-fronted Chinese temple on Kusu Island, was built by Hoe Beng Watt in gratitude for the birth of his child. The temple is dedicated to Da Bo Gong, the god of prosperity, and the ever-popular Kuan Yin, goddess of mercy. Here she is also known by her Chinese surname, Sung Tzu Niang ("giver of sons"), and is associated with longevity, love of virtue, and fulfillment of destiny. Sung Tzu had a difficult childhood. She was determined to become a nun, but her father forbade it. When she ran away to join an order, he tried to have her killed. In the nick of time she was saved by a tiger and was able to fulfill her destiny. In gratitude, she cut off her arm as a sacrifice. This so impressed the gods that she was then blessed with many arms. Hence, when you see her statue in many of the Chinese temples in Singapore, she is depicted with six or eight arms. This temple has become the site of an annual pilgrimage. From late October to early November, some 100,000 Taoists bring exotic foods, flowers, joss sticks, and candles, and pray for prosperity and healthy children.

Lazarus Island is being redeveloped as a resort area. Since there is no regular ferry service, you'll have to hire a bumboat (☞ Bumboats *in* Smart Travel Tips A to Z). If you plan to stay awhile, make sure to arrange to have the boat come back for you!

St. John's is the most easily reached island for beach activities, and the one to which Singaporeans go for weekend picnics. The same ferries that go to Kusu go to St. John's. The trip takes an hour and a bit from the Singapore Cruise Centre at the World Trade Centre.

St. John's was first a leper colony, then a prison camp for convicts. Later it became a place to intern political enemies of the republic, and now it has become an island for picnicking and overnight camping. Without any temples or particular sights, it is quieter than Kusu. There are plans to develop camping facilities, which will surely take away some of the peaceful solitude one can experience here now.

Sisters' Island, one of the most beautiful of the southern islands, is also one of the best for snorkeling and diving. To get there, you'll have to hire a bumboat or take an organized day cruise (check with your hotel). Some of the boatmen know where to find the best coral beds, but the quality of these is not outstanding compared with that of those in nearby Malaysia. If you dive off the islands to the south, be careful of the currents—they can be very strong.

3 Dining

In Singapore, eating is a national pastime, and you'll soon discover why. From breakfast in Chinatown to high tea in your hotel to a late-night snack in a hawker center, you can sample the international array of cuisines virtually around the clock.

SINGAPORE OFFERS THE GREATEST FEAST in the East, if not in the world. Here you'll find excellent restaurants specializing in home-grown fare (known as *Nonya,* or *Peranakan,* cuisine) and foods from Malaysia, Indonesia, Thailand, Vietnam, Korea, Japan, all parts of China, and North and South India, as well as from France, Germany, Italy, Britain, and the United States. At the hawker centers—indoor/outdoor markets with as many as 200 vendors selling wonderfully cooked, authentic foods—you can sample almost all the local and regional cuisines in the same meal.

Updated by
Wendy Hutton

The Cuisines of Singapore

Singapore's dining scene reflects the three main cultures that have settled here—Chinese, Indian, and Malay—as well as the many other influences that contribute to the island's diverse cultural mix.

Chinese

Chinese make up about 76% of Singapore's population, and this predominance is reflected in the wide assortment of restaurants representing their ethnic groups. The following is a sampling of the many Chinese cuisines represented in Singapore.

The best-known regional Chinese cuisine is **Cantonese,** with its fresh, delicate flavors. Vegetable oil, instead of lard, is used in the cooking, and crisp vegetables are preferred. Characteristic dishes are stir-fried beef in oyster sauce; steamed fish with slivers of ginger; and deep-fried duckling with mashed taro.

If you walk around Ellenborough Market, you'll notice the importance of dried ingredients in Chinese cooking. The people here are **Teochew** (or Chao Zhou), mainly fisherfolk from Swatow in the eastern part of Guangdong Province. Though their cooking has been greatly influenced by the Cantonese, it is quite distinctive. Teochew chefs cook with clarity and freshness, often steaming or braising, with an emphasis on fish and vegetables. Oyster sauce and sesame oil—staples of Cantonese cooking—do not play a large role in Teochew cooking; Teochew chefs pride themselves on enhancing the natural flavors of the foods.

Characteristic Teochew dishes are *lo arp* and *lo goh* (braised duck and goose), served with a vinegary chili-and-garlic sauce; crispy liver or prawn rolls; stewed, preserved vegetables; black mushrooms with fish roe; and a unique porridge called *congee,* which is eaten with small dishes of salted vegetables, fried whitebait, black olives, and preserved-carrot omelets.

Szechuan food is very popular in Singapore, as the spicy-hot taste suits the local palate. This style of cooking is distinguished by the use of bean paste, chilies, and garlic, as well as nuts and poultry. The result is dishes with pungent flavors of all sorts, harmoniously blended. Simmering and smoking are common forms of preparation, and noodles and steamed bread are preferred accompaniments. Characteristic dishes to order are hot-and-sour soup, sautéed chicken or prawns with dried chilies, camphor- and tea-smoked duck, and spicy fried string beans.

Pekingese cooking originated in the imperial courts. It makes liberal use of strong-flavored roots and vegetables, such as peppers, garlic, ginger, leeks, and coriander. Dishes are usually served with noodles or dumplings and baked, steamed, or fried bread. The most famous dish is Peking duck: The skin is lacquered with aromatic honey and baked until it looks like dark mahogany and is crackly crisp. Other choices are clear winter-melon soup, emperor's purses (stir-fried shredded beef with shredded red chili, served with crispy sesame bread), deep-fried minced shrimp on toast, and baked fish on a hot plate.

The greatest contribution to Singaporean cuisine made by the many arrivals from China's **Hainan** island, off the north coast of Vietnam, is "chicken rice": Whole chickens are lightly poached in a broth flavored with ginger and spring onions; then rice is boiled in the liquid to fluffy perfection and eaten with chopped-up pieces of chicken, which are dipped into a sour and hot chili sauce and dark soy sauce.

Also popular here are Fukienese and Hunanese restaurants. **Fukien** (also known as Hokkien) cuisine emphasizes soups and stews with rich, meaty stocks. Garlic and dark soy sauce are often used, and seafood is prominent. Dishes to order are braised pork belly served with buns, fried oyster, and turtle soup. **Hunanese** cooking is dominated by sugar and spices and tends to be more rustic. One of the most famous dishes is beggar's chicken: A whole bird is wrapped in lotus leaves and baked in a sealed covering of clay; when it's done, a mallet is used to break away the hardened clay, revealing a chicken so tender and aromatic that it is more than worthy of an emperor. Other favorites are pigeon soup in bamboo cups, fried layers of bean-curd skin, and honey ham served with bread.

Hakka food is very provincial in character and uses ingredients not normally found in other Chinese cuisines. Red-wine lees are used to great effect in dishes of fried prawns or steamed chicken, producing gravies that are delicious when eaten with rice. Stuffed bean curds and beef balls are other Hakka delicacies.

Indian

Most Indian immigrants to Singapore came from the south, from Madras (now known as Tamil Nadu) and Kerala, so **South Indian** cultural traditions tend to predominate here. In Little India, many small and humble restaurants can be found. Race Course Road is a street of curries: At least 10 Indian restaurants, most representing this fiery-hot cooking tradition, offer snacks or meals served on banana leaves. The really adventurous should sample the Singapore Indian specialty fish-head curry. Like all the food served here, this dish, with its hot, rich, sour gravy, is best appreciated when eaten without utensils—somehow, eating with the fingers enhances the flavor!

South Indian cuisine, generally more chili-hot than northern food, relies on strong spices like mustard seed and uses coconut milk liberally. Meals are very cheap, and eating is informal: Just survey the cooked food displayed, point to whatever you fancy, then take a seat at a table. A piece of banana leaf will be placed before you, plain rice will be spooned out, and the rest of your food will be arranged around the rice and covered with curry sauce.

Vegetarian cuisine is raised to a high art by South Indian cooks. Other tempting South Indian dishes include fish *pudichi* (fish in coconut, spices, and yogurt), fried prawns and crabs, mutton or chicken *biryani* (a meat-and-rice dish), *brinjal curry* (spiced eggplant), *keema* (spicy minced meat), *vindaloo* (hot spiced meat), *dosai* (savory pancakes), *appam* (rice-flour pancakes), sour lime pickle, and *papadam* (deep-fried lentil wafers). Try a glass of *rasam* (pepper water) to aid digestion and a glass of *lassi* (yogurt drink) or beer to cool things down.

Since the 1960s, **North Indian** food has made a mark in Singapore. Generally found in the more posh restaurants, this cuisine blends aromatic spices with a subtle Persian influence. The main differences between northern and southern Indian cuisine are that northern food is less hot and more subtly spiced than southern and that cow's milk is used as a base instead of coconut milk. North Indian cuisine also uses yogurt extensively to tame the pungency of the spices and depends more on puréed tomatoes and nuts to thicken gravies.

The signature North Indian dish is Tandoori chicken (marinated in yogurt and spices and cooked in a clay urn, or *tandoor*) and fresh mint chutney, eaten with *naan, chapati,* and *paratha* (Indian breads). Another typical dish is *rogan josh,* lamb braised gently with yogurt until the spices blend into a delicate mix of aromas and flavors. *Ghee,* a nutty clarified butter, is used—often in lavish quantities—to cook and season rice or rice-and-meat dishes (*pulaos* and *biryanis*).

In general, North Indian food is served more elegantly than is South Indian food. The prices are also considerably higher. (Beware of ordering prawns in South Indian restaurants, though—they often cost as much as S$8 apiece.)

The **Indian Muslim** tradition is represented in the Arab Street area. Opposite the Sultan Mosque, on North Bridge Road, are small, open-fronted restaurants serving *roti prata* (a sort of crispy, many-layered pancake eaten with curries), *murtabak* (prata filled with spiced, minced mutton and diced onions), *nasi biryani* (saffron-flavored rice with chicken or mutton), and various curries. These places are for the stouthearted only; they are cramped and not really spic-and-span.

Japanese

Over the past few years in Singapore, there has been a sudden interest in all things Japanese, no doubt partly because of the influx of Japanese tourists, but also because of the very large Japanese community here. Japanese restaurants (and supermarkets stocking imported Japanese produce) are all over the island, and Singapore can now offer Japanese cuisine equal to the best served in Japan.

The Japanese eat with studied grace. Dishes look like still-life paintings; flavors and textures both stimulate and soothe. Waitresses quietly appear and then vanish; the cooks welcome you and chat with you.

In Singapore you can savor a modified form of the high art of *kaiseki* (the formal Japanese banquet) in popular family restaurants. It was developed by the *samurai* class for tea ceremonies and is influenced by Zen philosophy. The food is served on a multitude of tiny dishes and offered to guests as light refreshments. Regulations govern the types of foods that can be served: The seasoning is light, the color schemes must be harmonious, and the foods, whenever possible, must be in their natural shapes. Everything presented is intended for conscious admiration. This stylistic approach is the perfect way to mark a special occasion.

More fun for some are the forms of Japanese dining in which guests can watch the chef exercise his skills right at the table. At a *sushi* bar, for example, the setting and the performance of the chef as he skillfully wields the knife to create the elegant, colorful pieces of *sushi* (vinegared rice tinged with *wasabi,* or green horseradish, and topped with a slice of raw fish) make the meal special. Savor the incredibly fresh flavor and you will be hooked forever. Also watch the chef perform stylistic movements, including knife twirling, at places serving *teppan-yaki:* On a large griddle around which diners are seated, fish, meat, vegetables, and rice are lightly seared, flavored with butter and *sake. Sukiyaki,* too, is grilled at the table, but the meat is strictly beef and the soup is sweeter; noodles and bean curd are served at the end of the meal as fillers.

Yakitori, a Japanese satay, is meat and vegetables grilled to perfection and glazed with a sweet sauce. *Yakiniku* is a grill-it-yourself meal of thin slices of beef, chicken, or Japanese fish. *Shabu-shabu* is a kind of fondue: Seafoods and meats are lightly swished in boiling stock, then dipped in a variety of sauces. *Tempura* is a sort of fritter of remarkable lightness and delicacy; the most popular kinds are made of prawns and vegetables. The dipping sauce is a mix of soy sauce and *mirin* (sweet rice wine), flavored with grated giant white radish and ginger.

Malay and Indonesian

Malay cuisine is often hot and rich. Turmeric root, lemongrass, coriander, *blacan* (prawn paste), chilies, and shallots are combined with coconut milk to create fragrant, spicy gravies. A basic method of cooking is to gently fry the *rempah* (spices, herbs, roots, chilies, and shallots ground to a paste) in oil and when the mixture is fragrant, add meat and either a tamarind liquid, to make a tart spicy-hot sauce, or coconut milk, to make a rich spicy-hot curry sauce. Dishes to look for are *gulai ikan* (a smooth, sweetish fish curry), *sambal telor* (eggs in hot sauce), *empalan* (beef boiled in coconut milk, then deep-fried), *tauhu goreng* (fried bean curd in peanut sauce), and *ikan bilis* (crispy fried anchovies).

Perhaps the best-known Malay dish is *satay*—slivers of marinated beef, chicken, or mutton threaded onto thin coconut sticks, barbecued, and served with a spicy peanut sauce. At most hawker centers, you will find at least one satay seller sitting over his charcoal fire and fanning the embers to grill sticks of satay. Tell the waiter how many of each type of meat you want, and he'll bring the still-smoking satay to your table.

Unlike the Chinese, who have a great tradition of eating out and a few classical schools of restaurant cooking, most Malay families continue to entertain at home, even when celebrating special events, such as marriages. As a consequence, there are very few stylish Malay restaurants.

Indonesian food is very close to Malay; both are based on rice and cooked with a wide variety of spices, and both are Muslim and thus do not use pork. A meal called *nasi padang*—consisting of a number of mostly hot dishes, such as curried meat and vegetables with rice, that offer a range of tastes from sweet to salty to sour to spicy—originally comes from Padang in the Indonesian province of West Sumatra. Ready-cooked dishes are usually displayed in glass cases from which customers make their selections.

Nonya

The first Chinese immigrants to this part of the world were the Hokkien. When they settled on the Malay Peninsula, they acquired the taste for Malay spices and soon adapted Malay foods to their cuisine. Nonya food is one manifestation of the marriage of the two cultures, which is also seen in language, music, literature, and clothing. This blended Peranakan culture was called *baba,* as were the men; the women were called *nonya,* and so was the cuisine, because cooking was considered a feminine art.

Nonya cooking combines the finesse and subtlety of Chinese cuisine with the spiciness of Malay cooking. Many Chinese ingredients are used—especially dried foods like Chinese mushrooms, fungus, anchovies, lily flowers, soybean sticks, and salted fish—along with the spices and aromatics used in Malay cooking. A favorite Chinese ingredient is pork, and pork satay is made for the Peranakan home (you won't come across Malay pork satay, since Muslims do not eat pork).

The ingenious Nonya cook uses *taucheo* (preserved soybeans), garlic, and shallots to form the rempah needed to make *chap chye* (a mixed-vegetable stew with soy sauce). Other typical dishes are *husit goreng* (an omelet fried with shark's fin and crabmeat) and *otak otak* (a sort of fish quenelle with fried spices and coconut milk). Nonya cooking also features sourish-hot dishes like *garam assam,* which is a fish or prawn broth made with pounded turmeric, shallots, *galangal* (a type of ginger), lemongrass, and shrimp paste. The water for the broth is mixed with preserved tamarind, a sour fruit that adds a delicious tartness.

A few years ago, Nonya cuisine appeared to be dying, like Peranakan culture itself, but since the publication of many Nonya cookbooks, there has been a resurgence of interest.

Thai

Thai cuisine, while linked with Chinese and Malay, is distinctly different in taste. Most Thai dishes are hot and filled with exciting spices and fish aromatics. On first tasting a dish, you may find it stingingly hot (tiny chilies make the cuisine so fiery), but the taste of the fresh herbs will soon surface. Thai food's characteristic flavor comes from fresh mint, basil, coriander, and citrus leaves; extensive use of lemongrass, lime, vinegar, and tamarind keeps the sour-hot taste prevalent.

Thai curries—such as chicken curry with cashews, salted egg, and mango—use coconut milk and are often served with dozens of garnishes and side dishes. Various sauces are used for dipping; *nam pla,* one favorite, is a salty, fragrant amber liquid made from salted and fermented shrimp.

A popular Thai dish is *mee krob,* crispy fried noodles with shrimp. Other outstanding Thai dishes: *tom yam kung,* hot and spicy shrimp soup (few meals start without it); *gai hor bai toey,* fried chicken wrapped in pandanus leaves; *pu cha,* steamed crab with fresh coriander root and a little coconut milk; and *khao suey,* steamed white rice, which you'll need to soothe any fires that may develop in your mouth.

The larger Thai restaurants are actually seafood markets where you can pick your own swimming creature and tell the waitress how you want it cooked. For drinks, try Singha beer, brewed in Thailand, or *o-liang,* the national drink—very strong black iced coffee sweetened with palm-sugar syrup.

European

Singaporeans recognize that through the stomach lies the path to all other satisfactions. Culinary skills have been developed to superlative levels—not only for Chinese or Indian or other Asian cooking styles but also for European cuisine. If you long for steak or fish-and-chips or fondue, you'll find it here.

The many Continental restaurants have impeccable service and high-quality food. In the 1980s, French cuisine made the greatest impact in Singapore. But the European food of the '90s is Italian, and many new restaurants have opened. Except for **Fosters Restaurant** in the Specialists Shopping Centre, Singapore does not really have a full-fledged English restaurant, but the Goodwood Park Hotel's **Gordon Grill** serves a fantastic sherry trifle, and their English roast beef is famous. **The Baron's Table** at the Royal Holiday Inn Crowne Plaza offers traditional German and Austrian dishes.

Seafood

Seafood is among Singapore's greatest contributions to the gourmet world, and generally very inexpensive (though elegant and expensive seafood meals featuring delicacies like shark's fin, dried abalone, and lobster are served in some Chinese restaurants). Most accessible to the visitor is the **UDMC Seafood Centre** on the East Coast Parkway, with no less than eight restaurants in terracelike pavilions looking out toward the sea. Dishes marked "market price" on the menu are the premium items. Before ordering, be sure to find out exactly how much each dish will cost.

Other Choices

In Singapore, you'll find that you can get pretty much whatever kind of cuisine you're in the mood for, including fast food from America's best-known outlets. Other Asian options include Korean and Vietnamese. For Mexican food, try **Cha Cha Cha** in Holland Village.

Dining Out

While some cultures consider atmosphere, decor, and service more important than food, in Singapore, the food's the thing. To us, a good meal means good food cooked with fresh ingredients. Gourmet cooking can be found as easily in small, unpretentious, open-front coffee shops as in the most elegant restaurants in the world, with service that's second to none. Many of the poshest restaurants are in hotels—Singaporeans love to make a grand entrance through a sparkling, deluxe hotel lobby. The Westin's **Compass Rose** and the Marina Mandarin's **Bologna Restaurant** are excellent examples of fine European-style dining, complete with displays of roses and orchids, polished silver and gleaming crystal, waiters dressed in tuxedos, and impeccable service in the best European tradition. The food itself is of the highest standard, with ingredients flown in fresh from France, Scotland, Australia, and elsewhere.

Recent widespread restoration of the older buildings of Singapore has given rise to chic dining-out addresses in areas like Boat Quay, Clarke Quay, and Tanjong Pagar. Boat Quay, a riverside strip of cafés, restaurants, and bars, is perhaps the busiest place in town at night; names to look out for here are the **Opera Cafe, Our Village** (for North Indian food), and **Warung Wayan** (for Indonesian food). Clarke Quay is another massive restoration project. Three restaurants of note are **Key Largo,** for seafood; **Thanying Restaurant,** for exquisite Thai cuisine; and **Bastiani's,** for Mediterranean food. You can even dine on a moored *tongkang,* one of the old boats that used to ply the river, or sample the controversial durian fruit at Clarke Quay's **Durian House.** Two trendy restaurants in the Tanjong Pagar area are **Fratini La Trattoria** (Italian) and **L'Aigle d'Or** (French).

Food Centers and Wok-and-Roll

At the bargain end of the scale are the **hawker centers,** agglomerations of individual vendor-chefs selling cooked foods in the open air. These vendors originally traveled from door to door selling their wares from portable stalls. Each hawker would serve only one dish, sometimes made from a secret recipe handed down through generations. The hawker would advertise his or her wares by sounding a horn, knocking two bamboo sticks together, or simply shouting. Hearing the sound, people would dash out of the house to place an order. After everyone had eaten, the hawker would collect and wash the crockery and utensils, then continue up the road. As many as 10 different hawkers might pass one's house in a day.

Some years ago, Singapore decided to gather the hawkers in food centers for reasons of hygiene. (And these new centers *are* all perfectly clean—the health authorities are very strict.) Visitors and locals alike find the food centers a culinary adventure. You can check out each stall— see the raw materials and watch the cooking methods—then choose whatever strikes your fancy from as many different stalls as you like. Find a seat at any of the tables (the government owns the centers and the seats; the hawkers rent only their stalls). Note the number of your table so you can tell the hawkers where to deliver your orders, then sit down and wait for food to arrive. Someone will come to your table to take your drink order. You pay at the end of the meal. Most dishes cost S$4 or slightly more; for S$12, you can get a meal that includes a drink and a slice of fresh fruit for dessert.

An excellent hawker center is at **Marina South,** where hundreds of stalls in a covered area offer a vast selection of Chinese and Malay foods. The area is not easy to reach by public transport, but if you'd rather not take an S$8 (from Orchard Road) taxi ride, you could take the evening shuttle bus to Marina Village that collects passengers from most major hotels, and then walk 10 minutes along the waterfront to the hawker center.

The most touristy open-air center is **Newton Circus.** Many people find Newton *the* place to see life at night—it's raucous and noisy and festive. Go to Newton if you must for the experience, but avoid the seafood stalls: They are known to fleece tourists. Feast instead at stalls offering the traditional one-dish meals, such as fried Hokkien noodles, roast-duck rice, *rojak,* or Malay *satay* (☞ Glossary of Food Terms, *below*). These stalls have prices displayed prominently. When you place your order, specify whether you want a S$2, S$3, or S$4 portion.

Other open-air centers include the historic **Lau Pa Sat Festival Market** in the downtown financial district, **Telok Ayer Transit Food Centre,** on Shenton Way, and **Bugis Square,** at Eminent Plaza (this one's open 7 AM–3 AM).

Offering the same sort of food as the open-air centers for only fractionally higher prices, air-conditioned food centers (generally in shopping malls) have become very popular in the past decade. They're particularly busy at lunchtime, when the midday heat makes the older-style fan-cooled food centers less appealing. Those in the Orchard Road area include **Picnic,** in the basement of Scotts Centre, and the **Food Chain** in the basement of Orchard Emerald, opposite and just down from the Mandarin Hotel.

Another experience in Singaporean dining is a visit to the **stir-fry stalls,** fondly called "wok-and-roll" by Americans. These stalls, most half-restaurant and half–parking lot, can be found in abundance on East Coast Road. The most popular dish at the stir-fry stalls is chili crab, with crusty bread to dip into a hot, rich, tasty sauce. Who can resist it? Other favorites are deep-fried baby squid and steamed prawns or fish, accompanied by fried noodles. There is certainly no elegance here—just good, fresh food cooked according to tried-and-true recipes. Prices are very reasonable. Stalls open for business at 5 PM.

Dim Sum

Called *dian xin* ("small eats") in Singapore, dim sum is a particularly Cantonese style of eating, featuring a selection of bite-size steamed, baked, or deep-fried dumplings, buns, pastries, and pancakes, with a variety of savory or sweet flavorings. Popular items are the *cha shao bao* (a steamed bread bun filled with diced, sweetened barbecued pork) and *shao mai* (a steamed mixture of minced prawns, pork, and sometimes water chestnuts). The selection, which might comprise as many as 50 separate offerings, may also include such dishes as soups, steamed pork ribs, and stuffed green peppers.

Traditionally, dim sum are served three on a plate in bamboo steamer baskets on trolleys that are pushed around the restaurant. You simply wait for the trolleys to come around, then point to whichever item you would like. The more elegant style now is to order dim sum à la carte so that they will be prepared freshly for you. Dim sum is usually served for lunch from noon to 2:30 PM, though in some teahouses in Chinatown, it is served for breakfast from 5 to 9. Dim sum is usually priced between S\$2 and S\$6 per dish of three pieces, though the fancier restaurants will have a higher range. An excellent place for dim sum in the financial district is the **Noble House** (⊠ #04–02 DBS Bldg., 6 Shenton Way, ☎ 227–0933), a huge room heavy with Chinese decor. Also see the recommendations below.

High Tea

High tea has become very popular in Singapore, especially among women of leisure, who find it a pleasant way to pass the time with friends. In many hotels, such as the **Goodwood Park Hotel** and the **Holiday Inn Park View,** high tea is accompanied by light Viennese-style music. Though British-inspired, the Singapore high tea is usually served buffet style and includes dim sum, fried noodles, and other local favorites in addition to the regulation finger sandwiches, scones, and cakes. For delicious pastries and tea or coffee, try the **Canopy Bar** at the Hyatt Regency on Scotts Road or the **Tiffin Room** at the Raffles. Teas are usually served between 3 and 6 PM and cost about S\$20 per person, including tax. The **Oriental** at Marina Square has its own version of high tea, and, with an array of Chinese, Nonya, Malay, Indian, and Western delicacies, it ranks as one of the best around.

The Flavors of Asia

It will not take you long to discover that Singaporeans love spices. This is not surprising in light of Singapore's history as a port through which the products of the famed Spice Islands were traded. But spicy doesn't necessarily mean hot. The dozens of spices used in the various cuisines can yield tastes mellow, as in thick, rich coconut gravies; pungent, as in Indian curries; tart, as in the sour and hot tamarind-, vinegar-, and lime-based gravies of Thailand, Malaysia, Indonesia, and Singapore; or sweet and fragrant, as in Indian desserts and beverages.

Basically, there are two main schools of spicy cooking, both well represented in Singaporean cuisine. The first is the **Indian tradition,** emphasizing dried-seed spices: cardamom, cloves, cumin, fennel, fenugreek, white and black pepper, chili peppers, powdered turmeric root, and mustard and poppy seeds. These spices are sometimes used whole but are more often ground into a powder (broadly referred to as curry powder) or made into a paste used as a base for gravies.

The second tradition is **Southeast Asian** and depends mainly on fresh roots and aromatic leaves. Typically, lemongrass, turmeric root, galangal, ginger, garlic, onions, shallots, and other roots are pounded into smooth pastes with candlenuts and shrimp paste to form a base for gravies and soups. (In Asia, gravies are thickened not with flour or cream but usually with these pastes.) The leaves—turmeric, lime, coriander, several varieties of basil—add a distinctive bouquet. How exciting this juxtaposition of flavors and aromas is!

Glossary of Food Terms

The following are dishes and food names you will come across often at the hawker centers. *Also see* The Cuisines of Singapore, *above,* for descriptions of other dishes.

char kway teow—fried flat rice noodles mixed with soy sauce, chili paste, fish cakes, and bean sprouts and fried in lard.
Hokkien prawn mee—fresh wheat noodles in a prawn-and-pork broth served with freshly boiled prawns.

laksa—a one-dish meal of round rice noodles in coconut gravy spiced with lemongrass, chilies, turmeric, galangal, shrimp paste, and shallots. It is served with a garnish of steamed prawns, rice cakes, and bean sprouts.

mee rebus—a Malay version of Chinese wheat noodles with a spicy gravy. The dish is garnished with sliced eggs, pieces of fried bean curd, and bean sprouts.

rojak—a Malay word for "salad." The Chinese interpretation of rojak consists of cucumber, lettuce, pineapple, *bangkwang* (jicama), and deep-fried bean curd, tossed with a dressing made from salty shrimp paste, ground toasted peanuts, sugar, and rice vinegar. Indian rojak consists of deep-fried lentil and prawn patties, boiled potatoes, and deep-fried bean curd, all served with a spicy dip thickened with mashed sweet potatoes.

roti prata—an Indian pancake made by tossing a piece of wheat-flour dough into the air until it is paper-thin and then folding it to form many layers. The dough is fried until crisp on a cast-iron griddle, then served with curry gravy or sugar. An ideal breakfast dish.

satay—small strips of meat marinated in fresh spices and threaded onto short skewers. A Malay dish, satay is barbecued over charcoal and eaten with a spiced peanut sauce, sliced cucumbers, raw onions, and compressed rice cakes.

thosai—an Indian rice-flour pancake that is a popular breakfast dish, eaten with either curry gravy or brown sugar.

Dining Essentials

Alcohol

Liquor is very expensive in Singapore. In a restaurant, a glass of wine costs from S$8–S$12, a bottle of wine costs a minimum of S$50, a cocktail, S$8–S$12. It generally costs more to drink than to eat.

Dress

Except at the fancier hotel dining rooms, Singaporeans do not dress up to eat out. The weather calls for lighter wear than a jacket and tie. (Some restaurants tried to enforce a dress code for men but found that their customers went elsewhere to eat. Now an open-neck shirt and a jacket represent the upper limit of formality.) Generally, though, shorts, thongs, singlets (sleeveless cotton T-shirts), and tracksuits are not appropriate. Those sensitive to cold might bring a sweater, since many restaurants are air-conditioned to subarctic temperatures.

Hours

Most restaurants are open from noon to 2:30 or 3 for lunch and from 7 to 10:30 PM (last order) for dinner. Seafood restaurants are usually open only for dinner and supper, until around midnight or 1 AM. Some hotel coffee shops (and the Indian coffee shops along Changi Road) are open 24 hours a day; others close between 2 and 6 AM. At hawker centers, some stalls are open for breakfast and lunch while others are open for lunch and dinner. Late-night food centers like Eminent Plaza in Jalan Besar are in full swing until 3 AM. Unless otherwise stated, restaurants listed below are open daily for lunch and dinner.

Ordering

Asians, particularly Chinese and not including Japanese, order food to be shared. Generally plan on small servings of four to five dishes for four people or three dishes for two people. Food is either served family-style—placed all at once at the center of the table so everyone can dip in—or, for more formal meals, served a course at a time, again with diners sharing from a single dish at the center of the table. Each diner is given a plate or bowl of rice.

Price Categories

CATEGORY	COST*
$$$$	over S$60
$$$	S$35–S$60
$$	S$15–S$35
$	under S$15

All prices are per person, including first course, main course, and dessert, excluding tax, service charge, and drinks.

Reservations

Reservations are always a good idea; we note only when they're essential or when they are not accepted.

Smoking

Smoking is banned in air-conditioned restaurants and banquet/meeting rooms.

Taxes and Charges

Hawker stalls and small restaurants do not impose a service charge. Most medium-size and larger restaurants, however, add 10% service charge as well as a 4% government tax to the bill. Most Chinese restaurants also automatically add a charge of about S$2 per person for tea, peanuts, pickles, and rice.

Tipping

Tipping is actively discouraged in Singapore. Do not tip in restaurants and hawker centers unless you really feel the service deserves an extra bit of recognition. (The 10% service charge is shared by a restaurant's staff.)

RESTAURANTS

Chinese: Cantonese

$$$$ ✕ **Hai Tien Lo.** Sit in the right place at this 37th-floor restaurant in the round and you'll get a view of the sea, the Padang, and City Hall. The cuisine, decor, and service are all superelegant: Plates are changed with every course; waitresses wear *cheongsams* (traditional Chinese sheath dresses with high collars and side slits) of celadon green to match the decor; and the delicate white china is hand-painted with cherry blossoms. For lunch, opt for the dim sum, priced at a premium because top-quality ingredients are used. The specialties are Cantonese roast chicken with crispy golden-brown skin and tender, juicy flesh; cubes of beef fillet fried with black pepper and oyster sauce; and deep-fried fresh scallops stuffed with minced prawns and tossed in a salty black-bean sauce. The pièce de résistance is Monk Jumps over the Wall—dried abalone, whole chicken, Chinese ham, fish stomach lining, dried scallops, and shark's fin steamed together for hours until tender. At S$100 per serving (or S$1,000 for 10 people), it is one of the most expensive dishes in town, but the broth is the best in the world—the really rich simply drink it and leave the rest. ✉ #01–300 Pan Pacific Singapore, Marina Square, 6 Raffles Blvd., ☎ 336–8111. AE, DC, MC, V.

$$$–$$$$ ✕ **Li Bai.** Its dining room evokes richness without overindulgence:
★   deep maroon wall panels edged with black and backlighted; elaborate floral displays that change with the seasons; jade table settings; ivory chopsticks. The service is very fine, as is the cooking, which is modern and innovative, yet deeply rooted in the Cantonese tradition. The chef's unusual creations include deep-fried diamonds of egg noodles in a rich stock with crabmeat and mustard greens; fried lobster in black-bean paste; and double-boiled shark's fin with Chinese wine and *jin-*

hua ham. The extensive menu also features barbecued sliced duckling with fresh mango; suckling pig on prawn toast; and Monk Jumps over the Wall with abalone, mushrooms, fish maw, sea cucumber, Chinese herbs, and shark's fin. The restaurant is small, seating fewer than 100 people. ⊠ *Sheraton Towers Hotel, 39 Scotts Rd.,* ☎ *737–6888. AE, DC, MC, V.*

$$–$$$ ✕ **Lei Garden.** This aesthetically pleasing restaurant has built up a devoted following. The food represents the nouvelle Cantonese style with its pristine tastes and delicate textures. One old-fashioned item is the soup of the day, cooked just the way mother did—assuming that mother had the time to stew a soup lovingly for many hours over low heat. The menu also offers a long list of double-boiled tonic soups (highly prized by the Chinese), barbecued meats, seafoods, and a variety of shark's fin dishes. Dim sum is available; recommendations include Peking duck, grilled rib-eye beef, and fresh scallops with bean curd in black-bean sauce. ⊠ *Boulevard Hotel, 200 Orchard Blvd., Basement 2,* ☎ *235–8122. AE, DC, MC, V.*

$$–$$$ ✕ **Tsui Hang Village.** This well-regarded restaurant in Marina Square has a decor of green tiles, brick walls, and rooflike overhangs that give it a courtyard ambience. The braised superior shark's fin is among the best in town. Roast suckling pig and braised abalone are served here as well but are usually reserved for banquet dining. The fresh seafood is flown in from Hong Kong. At lunch, try the inexpensive dim sum or one of the set menus. The deep-fried roast chicken pleases most palates. ⊠ *#02–142 Marina Square, 6 Raffles Blvd.,* ☎ *338–6668. AE, DC, MC, V.*

$$–$$$ ✕ **Xin Cuisine.** The most innovative Chinese food in Singapore is served here. The cooking is excellent, the service expert, the setting cloistered and restful with elegant overtones; and you can be sure of getting a good meal. Dishes change regularly; watch for the monthly specials. We recommend the wok-fried salmon with shiitake and pickled ginger. The steamed fish is a good bet, and the desserts are all good for you—they either improve your complexion or cool you down. Double-boiled bird's nest, Chinese herbal pudding, and double-boiled *hasma* (snow frog jelly) with ginkgo nuts are just some of the endings to sample. ⊠ *Concorde Hotel, 317 Outram Rd.,* ☎ *733–0188. AE, DC, MC, V.*

$ ✕ **Loy Sum Juan Restaurant.** This is not the place to go for glamour (it's tucked away on the second floor of a low-rent block of apartments on the fringe of Chinatown), but the food is both cheap and totally delicious. This is a good bet for traditional Cantonese cooking: Song Yu fish head steamed Hong-Kong style, abalone salad, and deep-fried chicken with prawn paste are among the specialties. The restaurant, which is just a stone's throw away from the Outram Park MRT station, is open for lunch and dinner. ⊠ *#02–88 Block 31, Outram Park,* ☎ *273–7231. Reservations not accepted. No credit cards.*

$ ✕ **New Nam Thong Tea House.** This Chinatown teahouse is absolutely inelegant and totally authentic. Breakfast here between 5 and 9:30 AM for a view of real Singapore life. Older folk, mainly men, congregate daily to gossip with friends and read the Chinese papers. Situated above an open-front shophouse, the teahouse is not air-conditioned and can be muggy, but it serves hearty, giant-size dim sum—*char siew pow* (steamed barbecued pork buns), *siew mai* (prawn-and-minced-pork dumplings), and other assorted dishes. Wash it all down with piping-hot Chinese tea. They don't understand English here, so just point. ⊠ *8–10A Smith St.,* ☎ *223–4229. Reservations not accepted. No credit cards.*

Chinese: Hakka

$$ ✕ **Moi Kong.** At this unpretentious and honest family eatery, try the prawns fried with red-wine lees, the steamed chicken with wine, or the

Singapore Dining

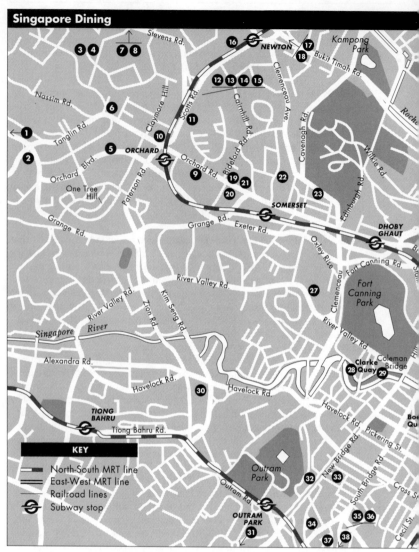

Al Forno Trattoria, **17**
Alkaff Mansion, **31**
Annalakshmi, **39**
Aziza's, **22**
Banana Leaf
Apollo, **25**
Bastiani's, **28**
Beng Hiang, **36**
Chang Jiang, **12**
Cherry Garden, **46**

Compass Rose
Restaurant, **40**
Dragon City, **7**
Fratini
La Trattoria, **34**
Golden Phoenix
Sichuan
Restaurant, **8**
Gordon Grill, **14**
Guan Hoe Soon, **54**
Hai Tien Lo, **50**

Imperial Herbal, **43**
Ivin's Restaurant, **18**
Keyaki, **51**
La Brasserie, **2**
L'Aigle d'Or, **37**
Latour, **3**
Lei Garden, **5**
Li Bai, **16**
Long Jiang, **21**

Loy Sum Juan
Restaurant, **32**
Madras New
Woodlands
Restaurant, **26**
Min Jiang, **13**
Moi Kong, **35**

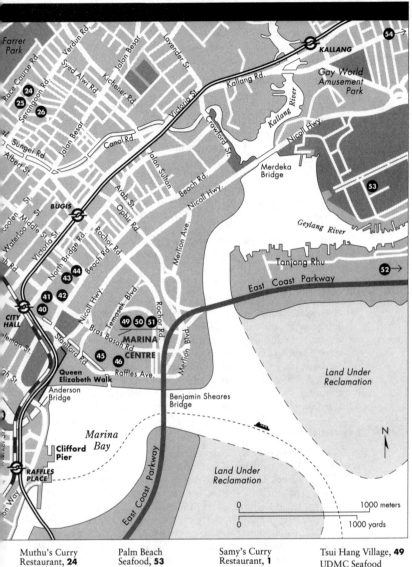

Muthu's Curry
Restaurant, **24**
Nadaman, **4**
New Nam Thong Tea
House, **33**
Nonya and Baba, **27**
Our Village, **48**

Palm Beach
Seafood, **53**
Pete's Place, **11**
Pine Court, **20**
Prego Restaurant, **41**
Raffles Tiffin
Room, **42**
Ristorante
Bologna, **45**

Samy's Curry
Restaurant, **1**
Shima, **15**
Sukmaindra, **10**
Suntory, **6**
Sushi Nogawa, **9, 19**
Tandoor, **23**
Thanying, **29, 38**

Tsui Hang Village, **49**
UDMC Seafood
Centre, **52**
Warung Wayan, **47**
Xin Cuisine, **30**
Yhingthai Palace, **44**

khong bak mui choy (braised pork in dark soy sauce with a preserved salted green vegetable), delicious with rice. ⊠ *22 Murray St.,* ☎ *221–7758. Reservations not accepted. AE, DC, V.*

Chinese: Herbal

$$–$$$ ✕ **Imperial Herbal Restaurant.** The Chinese traditionally believe that "you are what you eat" and that food can be used to maintain or restore one's health. In this unique restaurant, the kitchen is presided over by an herbalist rather than a chef, and there is a traditional pharmacy near the entrance where the herbs are stored (they can also be purchased for home cooking). The menu includes a wide range of dishes, some decidedly exotic, others deceptively simple. A must is the delicate quick-fried egg white with scallops and herbs, served in a crunchy nest of potato threads. Eel fried with garlic and fresh coriander and eggplants with pine nuts are equally delicious, while the crispy fried ants on prawn toast are not only a conversation piece but totally inoffensive. There's nothing bland or bitter about the food, and it's nice to know that it's not only satisfying your taste buds but doing you good. Beer and wine are available as well as restorative tonics and teas. ⊠ *Metropole Hotel, 41 Seah St., 3rd floor,* ☎ *337–0491. AE, MC, V.*

Chinese: Hokkien

$$ ✕ **Beng Hiang.** Like Hakka food, Hokkien cooking is peasant-style: hearty, rough, and delicious. *Kwa huay* (liver rolls) and *ngo hiang* (pork-and-prawn rolls) are very popular and are eaten dipped in sweet plum sauce. *Hay cho* (deep-fried prawn dumplings) are another Hokkien staple. Beng Hiang also serves *khong bak* (braised pig's feet) and what is reputedly the best roast suckling pig in Singapore. The restaurant is in a restored shophouse just outside the main financial district. ⊠ *112–116 Amoy St.,* ☎ *221–6695. Reservations not accepted. No credit cards.*

Chinese: Hunanese

$$$ ✕ **Cherry Garden.** The Cherry Garden restaurant is a beautiful setting
★ for a meal: A wood-roofed pavilion with walls of antique Chinese brick encloses a landscaped courtyard. Artwork is tastefully chosen and displayed. The service is impeccable, and the food is a welcome change from the usual Cantonese fare. An unusual dish is the steamed rice in woven bamboo baskets. Also try the minced-pigeon broth with dry scallops steamed in a bamboo tube or, in season, served in a fragrant baby melon; the superior Yunnan honey-glazed ham served between thin slices of steamed bread; or the camphor-smoked duck in a savory bean curd crust. ⊠ *The Oriental, 6 Raffles Blvd., Marina Square,* ☎ *338–0066. AE, DC, MC, V.*

Chinese: Pekingese

$$$ ✕ **Pine Court.** Baked tench, marinated lamb, and fried dry scallops are just a few of the dishes that distinguish the cooking of the Pine Court. The restaurant's Peking duck is famed for its crisp, melt-in-your-mouth skin and delicate pancake wrapping. Dinner is the Pine Court's best meal; the more economical lunch (frequently a buffet) is less inspired. The carved-wood wall panels will make you feel as if you're in a Chinese mansion; the award-winning service is fine and caring. ⊠ *Mandarin Hotel, 333 Orchard Rd.,* ☎ *737–4411. AE, DC, MC, V.*

Chinese: Shanghainese

$$$$ ✕ **Chang Jiang.** Meals in this stylish restaurant are served Western-
★ style—portions are presented on dinner plates, and patrons do not serve
themselves from a central platter. The kitchen staff was trained by the
chef of Shanghai's leading restaurant, Yang Zhou. Recommended
dishes are the chicken and goose surprise, fresh crabmeat in a yam basket, baby kale with scallops, lion's head (beef balls) in consommé, and
sliced beef fillet stir-fried and served with leeks. Presentation is an art
here. Even the chopsticks are gold-plated. Children are not welcome—
the management wants to preserve the valuable furnishings and the serene
atmosphere. If you must bring your child, a cover of S$25 will be added
to the bill. ⊠ *Goodwood Park Hotel, 22 Scotts Rd.,* ☎ *737–7188.*
AE, DC, MC, V.

Chinese: Szechuan

$$–$$$ ✕ **Dragon City.** Many Singaporeans consider Dragon City the best place
★ for Szechuan food. Set in a courtyard and entered through a flamboyant
red moongate door, the restaurant is a large room that looks Chinese
but is not particularly appealing. The food is where all the artistry is.
Choose from such Szechuan staples as *kung po* chicken and prawns,
in which the meat is deep-fried with whole dried chili peppers and coated
with a sweet-and-sour sauce, or try the delicious minced-pork soup in
a whole melon, steamed red fish with soybean crumbs, or smoked
Szechuan duck. The service is fast. If you don't quite know how to order
your meal, ask for Wang Ban Say, the restaurant's manager and one
of the owners. ⊠ *Novotel Orchid Inn, Plymouth Wing, 214 Dunearn*
Rd., ☎ *250–3322. AE, DC, MC, V.*

$$–$$$ ✕ **Golden Phoenix Sichuan Restaurant.** The first Szechuan restaurant
to open in Singapore, the Golden Phoenix has a reputation for large
portions. It is known for its braised pork, fresh abalone with vegetables, and Szechuan desserts. ⊠ *Hotel Equatorial, 429 Bukit Timah Rd.,*
☎ *732–0431. AE, DC, MC, V.*

$$–$$$ ✕ **Long Jiang.** Perhaps the greatest draw of this restaurant in the heart
of the Orchard Road shopping area is the "all you can eat" offer. For
a set price (around S$20), you can sample nearly 40 items on the
menu, including hot-and-sour soup, shark's fin soup, smoked duck,
and kung po chicken. It's not unlike most other Chinese restaurants
in appearance, but the service is above average. ⊠ *Crown Prince*
Hotel, 270 Orchard Rd., ☎ *732–1111. AE, DC, MC, V.*

$$ ✕ **Min Jiang.** Housed in a Chinese pavilion on the grounds of the Good-
wood Park, Min Jiang is always packed, thanks to its delicious food, fast
service, and reasonable prices. The decor is attractive, a restrained and
elegant interpretation of Chinese style. The camphor-smoked duck, kung
po chicken, and long beans fried with minced pork are favorites. ⊠ *Good-*
wood Park Hotel, 22 Scotts Rd., ☎ *737–7411. AE, DC, MC, V.*

Continental

$$$$ ✕ **Latour.** Floor-to-ceiling windows provide a spectacular view of the
★ palm-fringed swimming pool and the garden of the Shangri-La Hotel.
Inside, an eclectic luxury reigns: salmon-pink walls, comfortable rat-
tan chairs, batik paintings, and Austrian chandeliers, plus elegant crys-
tal, china, and silver table settings. The food is French-based nouvelle
cuisine. Thinly sliced beef marinated in lemon pepper à la Cipriani, cream
of smoked salmon soup, fresh warm goose-liver salad enhanced with
truffles, and deboned rack of lamb with herbed morello sauce are
some of the star dishes. At lunch, appetizers and desserts are offered
buffet style while the main course is ordered à la carte from a small

but well-chosen menu. The wine list is one of the best in town and includes a fine selection from France's Château Latour. ⊠ *Shangri-La Hotel, 22 Orange Grove Rd.,* ☏ *737–3644. Reservations essential. AE, DC, MC, V.*

$$$ ✕ **Bastiani's.** Mediterranean food with a New World accent stars in
★ this gorgeous restaurant in a restored riverside warehouse on Clarke Quay. A comfortable downstairs bar and outdoor patio are adjacent to Bastiani's cellars, while upstairs, the spacious dining room has a delightful terrace (where renegade smokers can indulge while eating). With its Oriental rugs on polished wooden floors, eclectic blend of furniture, and open kitchen hung with garlic, salamis, and the like, Bastiani's has a casual elegance hard to find in Singapore. The menu changes every two months, but always emphasizes fresh vegetables, herbs, grains such as couscous and polenta, and plenty of grilled or baked poultry, meat, and fish. Pizza is cooked in a wood-fired oven. The more than 4,000 bottles of wine in the cellar should satisfy the most fastidious wine buff. ⊠ *Bastiani's, Clarke Quay,* ☏ *433–0156. AE, DC, MC, V.*

$$$ ✕ **Compass Rose Restaurant.** This elegant restaurant, spread out over three floors of the Westin Stamford, is decorated in subtle sunset shades of peach and purple to complement the 70th-floor view it offers—on a clear day, you can see Malaysia and some of the Indonesian islands. Indulge in the luxurious lounge (where high tea and drinks are served) or in the more formal dining room, where the artistically presented meals preside. "East meets West" is the dominant theme in such dishes as sautéed filet mignon wrapped in lotus leaf, lobster ravioli soup, and grilled king prawns. The presentation is painterly. There's always a line at night for seats in the lounge. ⊠ *Westin Stamford Hotel, 2 Stamford Rd.,* ☏ *338–8585. AE, DC, MC, V.*

$$$ ✕ **Gordon Grill.** The Scottish country/hunting lodge look, with heavy draped curtains, is lightened with celadon and soft apple greens, lightwood chairs, and glass panels etched with delicate drawings of Scottish lairds. The Goodwood Park's restaurant has changed decor and location within the hotel many times, but tradition is served up here very much as it always has been, including excellent roast beef, perfect steaks, and the best sherry trifle in town. The service is also very good. ⊠ *Goodwood Park Hotel, 22 Scotts Rd.,* ☏ *737–7411. AE, DC, MC, V.*

French

$$$ ✕ **L'Aigle d'Or.** Glittering crystal contrasts with gaily decorated floral plates at this small, cheerful restaurant in the Duxton Hotel (in the Tanjong Pagar area of Chinatown). A five-course *menu dégustation* for about S$100 may include chestnut soup, sautéed fresh foie gras, a delicate fillet of sea bass in a basil sauce, and a panfried medallion of veal. Desserts come in pairs; you'll rave about the chocolate cake in licorice sauce. ⊠ *Duxton Hotel, 83 Duxton Rd.,* ☏ *227–7678. AE, DC, MC, V.*

$$–$$$ ✕ **La Brasserie.** Often named as the favorite French restaurant in Sin-
★ gapore, this is an informal place, with garçons clad in ankle-length aprons serving hearty traditional fare like French onion soup, *émincé de veau à la crème* (sliced veal with mushrooms in cream sauce), and *crème brûlée.* Here you'll dine on the spirit of Paris as well as the food: Red-checked tablecloths, wrought-iron lamps, exuberant French art, lace curtains, gleaming copper pans, and two attractive bar counters bring this brasserie to life. ⊠ *Omni Marco Polo, Tanglin Rd.,* ☏ *474–7141. AE, DC, MC, V.*

Indian

$$$ ✕ **Tandoor.** The food has a distinctly Kashmiri flavor at this luxuri-
★ ous restaurant, where Indian paintings, rust and terra-cotta colors, and
Indian musicians at night create the ambience of the Moghul court.
The tandoor oven, seen through glass panels across a lotus pond, dom-
inates the room. After you place your order for tandoori chicken, lob-
ster, fish, or shrimp—marinated in yogurt and spices, then roasted in
the oven—sit back and watch the chef at work. Also cooked in the oven
is the northern Indian leavened bread called *naan*; the garlic naan is
justifiably famous. The tender spice-marinated roast leg of lamb is a
favorite of the regulars. Spiced masala tea is a perfect ending to the
meal. Service is exceptionally attentive. ✉ *Holiday Inn Park View, 11
Cavenagh Rd.,* ☎ *733–8333. AE, DC, MC, V.*

$$–$$$ ✕ **Annalakshmi.** This Indian vegetarian restaurant, run by a Hindu re-
ligious and cultural organization, is considerably more elegant and
consequently somewhat more expensive than most serving vegetarian
cuisine. The lunch buffet, which costs around S$20, is very popular with
Indian businessmen working in the vicinity. At night, the paper-thin *dosai*
pancakes are delicious in the special Sampoorna dinner (S$35), limited
to 30 servings and presented on silver. The selection often includes cab-
bage curry, potato roast, *channa dhal* (chickpea stew), *kurma* (a mild
vegetable curry spiced with cumin, coriander, cinnamon, and cardamom
and cooked with yogurt or cream), *poori* (puffy, deep fried bread), *samosa*
(deep-fried, vegetable-stuffed patties), and *jangri* (a cold dessert). The
flavors are delicate, and spices are judiciously employed to enhance rather
than mask the taste. ✉ *#02–10 Excelsior Hotel & Shopping Centre,
5 Coleman St.,* ☎ *339–9993. AE, DC, MC, V. Closed Thurs.*

$$ ✕ **Our Village.** There are considerably more attractive—and expensive—
★ Indian restaurants along Boat Quay, but aficionados declare that the
food here is definitely superior. Look for the narrow corridor leading
to the restaurant's elevator, which will take you to the fifth floor, where
the rooftop terrace is delightfully cool and gives an excellent view at
night. The menu contains all the usual North Indian favorites, yet the
food, cooked home-style rather than prepared hours in advance, has a
particular freshness and intensity of flavor. The *sag paneer* (spinach with
homemade cheese) and *bhindi bhartha* (okra) are very good; so are the
naan breads and any of the dishes cooked in the tandoor. ✉ *46 Boat
Quay, 4th and 5th floors,* ☎ *538–3058. AE, MC, V.*

$ ✕ **Banana Leaf Apollo.** Along Race Course Road are a host of South
★ Indian restaurants that serve meals on fresh rectangles of banana leaf.
The specialty here is fish-head curry (S$18–S$25, depending on size),
and the taste is gutsy and chili-hot. Recently this down-home cafete-
ria-style restaurant has undergone a transformation, and it's now posh
and stylish. The food itself is fabulous, though be warned that you may
wind up with tears streaming! Each person is given a large piece of banana leaf; steaming-hot rice is spooned into the center; then two *papadam* (deep-fried lentil crackers) and two vegetables, with delicious
spiced sauces, are arranged neatly around the rice. Optional extras such
as the fish-head curry or spicy mutton may be added. ✉ *56/58 Race
Course Rd.,* ☎ *293–8682. Reservations not accepted. No credit cards.*

$ ✕ **Madras New Woodlands Restaurant.** Locals have formed an alle-
★ giance to this simple restaurant in the heart of Little India. The zesty
food is vegetarian, combining northern (Punjabi) and southern styles.
For a full meal, order a *thali:* a large platter of dosai pancakes served
with three spiced vegetables, curd, dhal, *rasam* (hot and sour soup),
sambar (spicy sauce), sweet *raita* (chopped vegetables with yogurt), and
papadam. The dosai are superb. Ask for the paper dosai, which is particularly crisp and comes in an enormous roll; it is served with two spiced

coconut sauces and a rasam. Or ask for the potato-stuffed or masala dosai. They're all wonderful enough to make a meal on their own. The milk-based sweetmeats are irresistible. ⊠ *14 Upper Dickson Rd.,* ☎ *297–1594. Reservations not accepted. No credit cards.*

$ ✕ **Muthu's Curry Restaurant.** Curry aficionados argue endlessly over which sibling serves the better food, Muthu or his brother, who owns the Banana Leaf Apollo (☞ *above*) down the street. The decor is similar, and Muthu's also has air-conditioning. ⊠ *78 Race Course Rd.,* ☎ *293–7029. Reservations not accepted. AE, MC, V.*

$ ✕ **Samy's Curry Restaurant.** It's *très* chic to lunch at this restaurant on the grounds that used to be home to the Ministry of Defence, not least because there's no way you can stumble upon it by chance—you have to be in the know. The old, no-fuss Civil Service clubhouse is a legacy of the British rule. The decor and service are equally no-fuss. The food—South Indian curries that are chili-hot and spicy and served on banana leaves—is excellent. There's no air-conditioning, which means that you sweat it out in true colonial fashion. It's cooler in the evening, but you have to arrive no later than 7 PM for the best dishes. ⊠ *Singapore Civil Service Club House, Block 25, Dempsey Rd.,* ☎ *472–2080 or 296–9391. Reservations not accepted. AE, DC, V. No dinner Thurs.*

Italian

$$$ ✕ **Ristorante Bologna.** The Bologna insists on making pastas fresh and on using fresh herbs in dishes like *spezzatino di sogliola ai peperoni e zucchini* (panfried strips of sole fillet with sweet bell pepper and zucchini) and *agnello al dragoncello* (roasted rack of lamb stuffed with snow peas and tarragon). Ingredients are flown in from Italy to ensure authenticity. Waiters in waistcoats provide impeccable service. The decor is light, airy, and luxurious; Renaissance-inspired murals adorn the walls, Carrera marble tiles the floor, and a cascading waterfall tops off the view. ⊠ *Marina Mandarin Hotel, 6 Raffles Blvd., Marina Square,* ☎ *338–3388. Reservations not accepted. AE, DC, MC, V.*

$$–$$$ ✕ **Al Forno Trattoria.** A favorite with Singapore's Italian community, and anyone else who likes unpretentious yet delicious food in relaxed surroundings, Al Forno recently moved from its original location to larger premises nearby. It's only two stops by MRT from Orchard Station to Novena Station, or less than five minutes by taxi from Orchard Road. Handmade tiles set into the floor of the entrance are the restaurant's most striking feature, unless one considers the wood-fired oven for baking superb pizzas (17 to choose from) and crusty country bread. Don't miss the mixed *antipasti* to start with, and if you love desserts, you'll go wild over the Coppa Amaretto. ⊠ *1 Goldhill Plaza, corner of Thomson and Newton Rds., ground floor,* ☎ *256–2838. Reservations not accepted. AE, V.*

$$ ✕ **Fratini La Trattoria.** These days the trend is moving away from splendid hotel dining rooms and toward intimate establishments, like this exciting restaurant in Tanjong Pagar. The chef is Gabriel Fratini himself, and his traditional cuisine has established a strong following. The antipasto selection is always splendid, especially the thinly sliced veal in a tuna sauce. Make sure you order one of the fabulous pastas or pizzas. For dessert, there's a splendid *tiramisù.* ⊠ *51 Neil Rd.,* ☎ *323–2088. AE, DC, MC, V.*

$$ ✕ **Pete's Place.** This is one of the city's most popular restaurants. The look is cozy Italian-country, with rustic brick walls and checkered tablecloths. The food is Italian-American, with staples like pizza and pastas. A salad bar with crisp, fresh vegetables, a wide array of dressings, and a large selection of breads is particularly popular, especially at lunchtime, when you can opt for a light luncheon of soup and salad.

The service is friendly, yet full of finesse, making this restaurant a fun, relaxed place. A plus is Pete's proximity to two of the best shopping centers—Scotts and Far East. ⊠ *Hyatt Regency Singapore, 10–12 Scotts Rd.,* ☎ *738–1234. AE, DC, MC, V.*

$$ ✕ **Prego Restaurant.** On the ground floor of the Westin Plaza hotel, Prego is very popular for its reasonable prices and informality. The S$2 million transformation of the site of the former Palm Grill is a gamble that's paid off for the Westin. Italian staples include *focaccia all origano* (flat oregano bread with whole roasted garlic), ravioli, *pollo al rosmarino* (roast chicken with rosemary), and skewered prawns. ⊠ *Westin Plaza, 2 Stamford Rd.,* ☎ *338–8585. AE, DC, MC, V.*

Japanese

$$$–$$$$ ✕ **Suntory.** Owned by the famous Japanese beer company, this is reputedly the most expensive Japanese restaurant in town. Choose from among several different Japanese dining styles: There's a teppanyaki room, a sushi counter, shabu-shabu tables, tatami rooms, and a very attractive lounge. The decor is exquisite, the staff well trained, and the food excellent. ⊠ *#06–01/02 Delfi Orchard, 402 Orchard Rd.,* ☎ *732–5111. AE, DC, MC, V.*

$$$ ✕ **Keyaki.** A Japanese farmhouse has been re-created in a formal Japanese garden with a golden-carp pond on the rooftop of the Pan Pacific Hotel. The waitresses dressed in kimonos, waiters in *happi* coats, and Japanese lacquerware and porcelain make you feel as though you're in Japan (despite the European-looking wood chairs). The teppanyaki may be the best in Singapore, with excellent beef, scallops, salmon, large shrimps, and a distinctive Japanese fried garlic rice. ⊠ *Pan Pacific Hotel, 7 Raffles Blvd., Marina Square,* ☎ *336–8111. AE, DC, V.*

$$$ ✕ **Nadaman.** There's nothing quite so exciting as watching a teppanyaki
★ chef perform his culinary calisthenics at this 24th-floor restaurant, with the Singapore skyline as a backdrop. The Nadaman offers sushi, sashimi (the fresh lobster sashimi is excellent), teppanyaki, tempura, and kaiseki. Those on a budget should try one of the *bento* lunches—fixed-price meals (around S$30) beautifully decorated in the Japanese manner and served in lacquer trays and boxes. The decor is distinctly Japanese, and the service is discreetly attentive. ⊠ *Shangri-La Singapore, 22 Orange Grove Rd., 24th floor,* ☎ *737–3644. AE, DC, MC, V.*

$$$ ✕ **Sushi Nogawa.** Chef Nogawa himself presides, and his clientele is
★ so discerning that he is able to fly in tons of fresh Japanese produce throughout the year. The best dishes are seasonal (hence it's difficult to say what to expect). The small original restaurant, where aficionados sit cheek by jowl, is in the Crown Prince Hotel; the new, larger branch, at Takashimaya Shopping Centre on the opposite side of Orchard Road, offers less expensive food. If you're nervous, you can order the superb sushi or sashimi. The adventurous can leave it all to the restaurant manager and hope to be surprised. Prices are steep, but you can expect the best. There's *dobinmushi* (teapot soup) as well as tempura, more unusual stews, and even a fish-head dish. Over at Takashimaya, in addition to the incomparable sushi and sashimi selections, you can choose from a number of set menus, including the most elegant of Japanese meals, the kaiseki banquet. ⊠ *Crown Prince Hotel, 270 Orchard Rd.,* ☎ *732–1111;* ⊠ *Takashimaya Shopping Centre, 391 Orchard Rd., Level 4,* ☎ *735–5575. AE, DC, MC, V.*

$$–$$$ ✕ **Shima.** "German baronial" is perhaps the best way to describe the look of this Japanese restaurant. Teppanyaki, shabu-shabu, and yakiniku are the only items on the menu. You sit around a teppanyaki grill, watching the chef at work, or at the shabu-shabu and yakiniku tables, doing the cooking yourself. Copper chimneys remove the smoke and smell.

The all-you-can-eat yakiniku lunch is one of the best buys in town. ☒ *Goodwood Park Hotel, 22 Scotts Rd.,* ☎ *734–6281/2. Reservations essential for buffet lunch. AE, DC, MC, V.*

Malay and Indonesian

$$$ ✕ **Alkaff Mansion.** Once the estate of wealthy merchants, this 19th-century house on Mt. Faber Ridge opened as a restaurant in 1991. You can sit inside under twirling fans or out on a veranda decorated to reflect the diverse tastes of the old Arab traders. Downstairs there's a huge Malay-Indonesian dinner buffet; on the balconies upstairs, 10 sarong-clad waitresses serve a multicourse *rijstaffel*. Western food is also offered, from the three-course luncheon to a more elaborate à la carte menu (from steaks to seafood bordelaise) at dinner. Overall, the delightful turn-of-the-century ambience and the presentation are more rewarding than the food. ☒ *10 Telok Blangah Green,* ☎ *278–6979. AE, DC, MC, V.*

$$$ ✕ **Raffles Tiffin Room.** For a taste of nostalgia and of a typical British "curry tiffin," part of the Malay colonial tradition, a visit to the Tiffin Room at the exquisitely restored landmark hotel, the Raffles, is a must. Despite its popularity with tour groups, the light, airy restaurant with its marble floors is still gracious, the service courteous if a fraction slow during busy luncheons. A self-service buffet available for both lunch and dinner, the tiffin is a tempting spread of largely Indian dishes. Forget that concession to modern tastes, the salad bar, and head straight for the mulligatawny, a spicy curry soup. There's a large array of spicy (but not necessarily chili-hot) vegetable, meat, poultry, and seafood dishes, and far more pickles, chutneys, and other condiments than a genuine Indian meal would provide. If you've still got room, the dessert table offers one or two local desserts as well as Indian and international favorites. ☒ *Raffles Hotel, 1 Beach Rd.,* ☎ *337–1886. AE, DC, MC, V.*

$$ ✕ **Aziza's.** Hazizah Ali has brought elegant Malay cooking out of the home and into her intimate street-front restaurant on the charming Emerald Hill Road, just up from Peranakan Place. It's the spicy cooking of the Malay Peninsula you get here—lots of lemongrass, galangal, shallots, pepper, coriander, cloves, and cinnamon. Try the *rendang* (beef simmered for hours in a mixture of spices and coconut milk), *gado gado* (a light salad with a spiced peanut sauce), or *bergedel* (Dutch-influenced potato cutlets). The oxtail soup is especially delicious. Ask for *nasi ambang* and you'll get festive rice with a sampling of dishes from the menu. The Orchard Road location and the friendly setting make this an easy place to experiment with Malay food. ☒ *36 Emerald Hill Rd.,* ☎ *235–1130. AE, DC, MC, V.*

$$ ✕ **Sukmaindra.** You'd expect this restaurant, in one of the many hotels owned by the Sultan of Brunei, reputedly the world's richest man, to be opulent. And you won't be disappointed; there are acres of marble with Moorish arches and marble columns supporting a sculptured geometric ceiling. The atmosphere is a trifle cold, but this is the swankiest Muslim restaurant in town. Dishes to sample include oxtail soup stewed in a light blend of spices, satays, and *kepala ikan* (fish-head curry). For dessert, *chendol* (a noodle-like jelly) served with palm sugar and coconut milk is a delight. No alcoholic beverages are served. ☒ *Royal Holiday Inn Crowne Plaza, Level 3, 25 Scotts Rd.,* ☎ *737–7966. AE, DC, MC, V.*

$$ ✕ **Warung Wayan.** Indonesian cuisine and Balinese specialties reign in this riverside restaurant along popular Boat Quay. The charcoal-grilled items are particularly good. If you want to sample Balinese as opposed to Javanese or Indonesian Chinese food, order the Balinese satay (but don't eat it with peanut sauce; they don't go together in Balinese cooking) and barbecued chicken (*ayam panggang Wayan*) with its wonderful tangy sambal sauce. A Javanese speciality, *tahu telor,* is a must: meltingly soft bean curd deep-fried with a crunchy egg coating. Prices for wine and beer are very reasonable by Singapore standards. ⊠ *Warung Wayan, 50A Boat Quay,* ☎ *538–3889. AE, DC, MC, V.*

Nonya

$$ ✕ **Ivin's Restaurant.** Housed in the remote, upmarket suburb of Bukit Timah, beyond the Turf Club (you'll need a cab to get there), this casual restaurant serves traditional Nonya food à la carte. Specialties include *ayam buah keluak,* chicken in a spicy, sour gravy with a black Indonesian nut that has a creamy texture and the smokiness of French truffles; *babi pongteh,* pork stewed in soy sauce and onions; *udang masak nanas,* prawns cooked with pineapple; and *pong tauhu* soup, a prawn soup with julienned bamboo shoots and minced chicken, prawn, and bean-curd dumplings. Prices are reasonable. ⊠ *19/21 Binjai Park,* ☎ *468–3060. AE, DC, MC, V.*

$$ ✕ **Nonya and Baba.** This restaurant serving the authentic food of the Babas is situated near the Tank Road Hindu Temple. It's intimate but not particularly well decorated. Habitués like it for the food and the basic comforts it provides. Try the ayam buah keluak, *bakwan kepiting* (soup of crabmeat and pork dumplings), *babi pongtay, satay ayam* (fried chicken satay), or sambal "lady's fingers" (okra with a spicy sauce). ⊠ *262 River Valley Rd.,* ☎ *734–1382/6. Reservations not accepted. V.*

$–$$ ✕ **Guan Hoe Soon.** The heartland of the Baba culture is Katong, a suburb about 20 minutes by cab from the city center. This long-established restaurant is air-conditioned, simple, and comfortable, with authentic Nonya food at a reasonable price. The specialty is the *otak otak* (charcoal-grilled fish quenelle mixed with spices and wrapped in banana leaves). Also taste the ayam buah keluak and the fried noodles. Next door is Peter Wee's absolutely must-visit **Katong Antique House.** Inside this house, in the terrace style of the Babas, Peter Wee has lovingly displayed his collection of antique Baba beaded slippers, embroidered blouses (called *kebayas*), Chinese export porcelain, carved-wood furniture inlaid with mother-of-pearl, embroidered wedding-bed hangings, and much more. ⊠ *214 Joo Chiat Rd.,* ☎ *344–2761. Reservations not accepted. No credit cards. Closed Tues.*

Seafood

$$–$$$ ✕ **Palm Beach Seafood.** Forty years ago, this restaurant was on a beach, with tables set under coconut trees—hence the name. It is now in a shopping and leisure complex next to the National Stadium and covers three floors, the downstairs restaurant seating around 550. What the place lacks in ambience, it more than makes up for in food, and the prices must be the best in town for seafood. The most popular dishes include chili crabs served with French bread to mop up the sauce (although you may prefer the black pepper crab); prawns fried in black soy sauce or in butter and milk with curry leaves; and deep-fried crisp squid. Don't miss the *yu char kway,* deep-fried crullers stuffed with a mousse of squid and served with a tangy black sauce. ⊠ *Leisure Park, 5 Stadium Walk, Kallang Park,* ☎ *344–3088. Reservations not accepted. AE, MC, V.*

$$–$$$ ✕ **UDMC Seafood Centre.** You *must* visit this place at the East Coast Parkway, near the entrance to the lagoon, to get a true picture of the way Singaporeans eat out, as well as real value (prices here are cheaper than in most other seafood restaurants). Walk around the eight open-fronted restaurants before you decide where to eat. Chili crabs, steamed prawns, steamed fish, pepper crabs, fried noodles, and deep-fried squid are the specialties. ⊠ *East Coast Pkwy. Restaurants include Chin Wah Heng,* ☎ *444–7967;* ⊠ *Gold Coast Seafood,* ☎ *242–7720;* ⊠ *Golden La-*

goon Seafood, ☎ 448–1894; ✉ Jumbo Seafood, ☎ 442–3435; ✉ Kheng Luck Seafood, ☎ 444–5911; ✉ Lucky View Seafood Restaurant, ☎ 241–1022; ✉ Ocean Park Seafood Restaurant, ☎ 242–7720; and ✉ Red House Seafood Restaurant, ☎ 442–3112. Reservations not accepted. AE, DC, MC, V. No lunch.

Thai

$$–$$$ ✗ **Thanying.** Possibly the best Thai restaurant in Singapore (the own-
★   ers and chefs are Thai), the Thanying is decorated in exquisite aristo-
cratic Thai taste, and the food—redolent of kaffir lime leaves, basil, mint
leaves, ginger, and coriander leaves—is cooked in the best palace tradition. The restaurant has been such a success that there is now a second Thanying along the attractive Clarke Quay. As with Chinese food,
you normally order one dish per person plus one extra and share the
entire meal. Try the *gai kor bai toey* (marinated chicken wrapped in pandanus leaves and char-grilled to perfection), an exquisite Thai salad like
yam sam oh (shredded pomelo tossed with chicken and prawns in a spicy
lime sauce), *pla khao sam rod* (garoupa, or grouper, deep-fried until it's
so crispy you can practically eat the bones), and one of the Thai curries. And of course, don't miss out on the sour and hot *tom yam* soup.
✉ Amara Hotel, Level 2, 165 Tanjong Pagar Rd., ☎ 222–4688; ✉
Clarke Quay, Block D, ☎ 336–1821. AE, DC, MC, V.

$$ ✗ **Yhingthai Palace.** The no-nonsense decor of this small, simple
restaurant—just around the corner from the famous Raffles Hotel—
makes it clear that food is the prime concern. Although the service can
be a little slow, the well-prepared and moderately priced Thai food is
worth waiting for. The *yam ma muang* (sour mango salad) is an ex-
cellent and refreshing dish, while *hor mok talay*, seafood mousse served
in charming terra-cotta molds, is light and full of flavor. If you enjoy
spicy dishes with plenty of herbs, try the *phad kra kai* (stir-fried minced
chicken). The *kuay teow phad Thai* (fresh rice noodles fried with
seafood) are delicious, and one of the lemony tom yam soups is almost
obligatory. ✉ 13 Purvis St., ☎ 337–1161. AE, MC, V.

4 Lodging

Singapore's hotels are a true delight, offering charm, efficiency, and every modern creature comfort—all at prices to suit a wide range of budgets.

Updated by
Nigel Fisher

OVER THE YEARS Singapore has been transformed from a popular destination for individual tourists to a conventioneers' mecca teeming with tour groups and delegates. Singapore's lodging has visibly changed to accommodate this profitable market: Extensive refurbishment and growth with less personal, more automated service has been the trend. Although at times hotel rooms can be scarce, with the overall decline in the number of tourists visiting Singapore, attractive discounts are usually available—and no thrifty visitor ever pays the published price.

So unless you visit during a large convention—and the island republic invests heavily in wooing them—or in August or December, the most popular tourist months, you should be able to obtain a reservation at the hotel of your choice. If you use a travel agent, make sure that he or she asks for a discount. If you gamble and arrive without reservations, the Singapore Hotel Association maintains two reservations counters at Changi Airport that can set you up with a room—and often a discount—with no booking fee.

Even with the discounts, Singapore's hotels are no longer inexpensive compared to New York's. The average price ranks just under Hong Kong's and considerably above those of Jakarta, Bangkok, Manila, and Kuala Lumpur. At deluxe hotels, a superior double room runs more than S$400 a night. A room with a private bath in a modest hotel should cost no more than S$200. At budget hotels with shared bathroom facilities, the rates are under S$85. And if all you're looking for is a bunk, walk along Bencoolen Street, where there are dormitory-style guest houses that charge no more than S$25 a night.

Colonial-Style Hotels

Most of the better hotels are new, but two notable exceptions have been witness to—and sometimes the scene of—a good chunk of Singapore's history: the 97-year-old Goodwood Park, and the Raffles Hotel, which has been around for 110 years. The Goodwood Park has been renovated to bring its facilities up to world-class standing; the Raffles has been completely gutted and resurrected as a theme-park version of its former self, charging the highest rates in Singapore.

Modern Hotels

Among the newer hotels, five are on Marina Square, a minicity created by a vast reclamation project that pushed back the seafront. More than 200 shops and a multitude of restaurants surround these towering atrium hotels, of which the newest is the Ritz-Carlton. The Inter-Continental has attempted to blend its new high-rise building unobtrusively with the surrounding shophouses of the Bugis Street neighborhood. Rivaling the luxury found at the Ritz-Carlton and other top hotels is the new Four Seasons, tucked behind the Hilton off Orchard Road. Close by is the new Traders Hotel, offering a new concept—it cuts out the frills and frippery found at luxury hotels but gives all the basic comforts at affordable rates.

Other modern hotels, some a decade or two old by now, have undergone additions and renovations to keep up with the newcomers. The Shangri-La, for example, was built in 1971, but its new Valley Wing has some of the most luxurious accommodations that Singapore—and perhaps the world—has to offer. The Hyatt Regency on Scotts Road has reconfigured half of its rooms into suites for business travelers, a big part of the city's hotel trade, especially as corporations move their offices from Hong Kong to Singapore.

Conventions are big business in Singapore, and there are megahotels geared specifically to handling hundreds of delegates. The Westin Plaza and Westin Stamford in Raffles City together offer more than 2,000 guest rooms and a ballroom that can accommodate 3,000 people. Marina Square, now home to the Suntec City convention complex, was opened with conventions in mind: its Pan Pacific has 800 rooms and a meeting hall for 1,000 delegates. Also here are the more upscale Marina Mandarin, with 640 rooms to satisfy higher-level delegates, and the Oriental, with 640 rooms suitable for the most persnickety CEOs, though some may now prefer the new Ritz-Carlton.

Restaurants

All of the major hotels have several restaurants, each specializing in a different cuisine (☞ Chapter 3). Although relatively expensive, they serve some of Singapore's best food in opulent surroundings. Hotel coffee shops generally offer a mix of Western and local foods, and many are open 24 hours a day.

Service

Service in the deluxe properties is excellent; it used to be exemplary, but as the number of luxury hotels has grown, dedicated employees have become few and far between. However, deluxe hotels are still a pleasure: The staff at the better hotels go to great lengths to meet guests' needs. A 10% charge is added to your bill to cover service. Tipping is frowned upon, except for bellmen who bring luggage to the rooms. Guest rooms are spacious, with the latest amenities, from bedside remote-control panels for lights and television to marble-tiled bathrooms with telephone extensions and TV speakers. Many hotels have business and fitness centers loaded with the latest technology and equipment. The most recent addition is modem outlets in the guest rooms.

Where to Stay

Singapore's hotels have developed in clusters throughout the city. The best-known grouping is around the popular tourist belt at the intersection of Orchard and Scotts roads. Another cluster is at Raffles City, where the megalithic Westins stare down at Raffles, the grande dame of Singapore's hotels, and the Inter-Continental's black-and-white marble gleams alongside turn-of-the-century shophouses. At the south end of the Shenton Way commercial district are a number of business-oriented hotels; to the west of Chinatown and the south of the Singapore River, another cluster has sprung up. The newest hotel area is Marina Square, where a half dozen hotels and a vast shopping-mall complex have established an independent hub within the city.

Your choice of hotel location may be influenced by your reason for visiting Singapore. Certainly the Orchard and Scotts roads area favors the shopper and night reveler. Marina Square would be the logical choice for those attending conventions in the complex or who simply prefer the area's open space and harbor views. For those doing business in the financial district, a hotel close to Shenton Way is ideal; likewise, hotels along the Singapore River are convenient for anyone making trips to the industrial city of Jurong.

But location should not be overemphasized. Singapore is a relatively compact city, and taxis and public transportation, especially the new subway, make travel between areas a matter of minutes. Furthermore, no hotel is more than a 30-minute cab ride from Changi Airport. If you are between planes and this is too far, the new Transit Hotel within the airport departure area charges on the basis of six-hour periods.

Amenities

All hotels listed, unless otherwise noted, have rooms with private baths. All deluxe hotels have International Direct Dial (IDD) telephones with bathroom extensions, color televisions with Teletext for world news and information, room service, and minibars. The top luxury hotels have recently added database ports for modems and are currently connecting their business centers to the Internet. Most hotels have a travel desk.

Price Categories

CATEGORY	COST*
$$$$	over S$375
$$$	S$275–S$375
$$	S$175–S$275
$	S$100–S$175
¢	under S$100

*All prices are for a standard double room, excluding 4% tax and 10% service charge.

HOTELS

$$$$ 🏨 **Four Seasons.** Opened in 1995 by the owner of the adjacent Hilton,
★ the Four Seasons is quieter and—dare we say it?—more refined, with luxuries intended to outshine the city's older hotels. Guest rooms are as gracious as home: spacious, with soft fabrics and peaceful Asian art, large bathrooms, two-line speakerphones with modem hookups, laser video, and CD players. Of the three restaurants, the Cantonese **Jiang-Nam Chun** is the most memorable for its stunning art deco and art nouveau decor and its exotic fare—bird's nest soup, shark's fin, and abalone—and don't miss the popular dim sum lunch. Some of the tennis courts are air-conditioned, and there is even a golf simulator. The hotel is linked to Orchard Road via an elevated passageway to the Hilton. ⊠ 190 Orchard Blvd., 2486, ☎ 734–1110, ℻ 733–0682. 257 rooms. 3 restaurants, pool, 4 tennis courts, health club, meeting room. AE, DC, MC, V.

$$$$ 🏨 **Goodwood Park.** This venerable Singapore institution began in
★ 1900 as a club for German expatriates and has since hosted the likes of the Duke of Windsor, Edward Heath, Noël Coward, and the great Anna Pavlova, who performed here. Today the hotel may be overshadowed by the glitz of the high-rises, but for personal service and refinement, it stands alone. Guests are greeted by name, high tea is accompanied by a string quartet, and guest rooms are as comfortable as those in a country house, with all amenities. One caveat: the staff can be condescending to those who don't appreciate tradition. Parklane suites, each with a separate bedroom and living-dining room, can be rented for long-term or shorter stays, for less than a double room in the main hotel; the drawback is the five-minute walk to the hotel's facilities. Restaurants include the **Gordon Grill,** the **Min Jiang,** and the **Chang Jiang** (☞ Chapter 3). It is just off Scotts Road and within minutes of Orchard Road. ⊠ 22 Scotts Rd., 0922, ☎ 737–7411, ℻ 732–8558; U.S. reservations 800/323–7500. 171 rooms, 64 suites. 3 restaurants, coffee shop, tea shop, 3 pools, beauty salon, baby-sitting, business services, meeting rooms. AE, DC, MC, V.

$$$$ 🏨 **Hotel Inter-Continental Singapore.** Most of Singapore's luxury hotels cluster around Orchard Road or Marina Square. Not so for this Bugis Junction hotel, built in 1995. Part of the government's re-creation of Bugis Street, it is on Asia's first air-conditioned walkway, topped with a glass dome and lined with shops and cafés. It appears to be just another modern marbleized, albeit posh, hotel with all the latest comforts and technology, but the concept is to incorporate Singapore's multicultural heritage: Each of the 83 "shophouse" rooms is different, but the Peranakan style prevails, along with polished wood floors, throw rugs, louvered windows, reproduced turn-of-the-century furnishings, and balconies. There is a S$45 surcharge for these rooms, which includes a complimentary American breakfast. The remaining guest rooms on the club floors are classical European, with clean, simple lines; there is a surcharge of S$65 for more attentive service, continental breakfast, evening cocktails, and use of the exercise room. Among three hotel restaurants, of special note is **Pimai Thai,** which interprets Royal Thai dishes such as deep-fried crab legs with sweet-and-sour sauce and roasted duck with red curry. ⊠ *80 Middle Rd., Bugis Junction, 1889,* ☎ *338–7600,* ℻ *338–7366. 406 rooms. 3 restaurants, pool, exercise room, business services, meeting rooms. AE, DC, MC, V.*

$$$$ 🏨 **Hyatt Regency.** The rates here are among the most expensive in town, but promotional packages are frequently offered. Regency Suites consist of 421 one-, two-, and three-room apartments with telecommunications equipment, two-line telephones, Reuters services, separate guest bathrooms, work areas, and private mailboxes. The remaining standard rooms are adequate but small. Other highlights are the tropical garden with 16 miniwaterfalls and the **Canopy Bar,** which overlooks Scotts Road and serves afternoon tea and evening cocktails. Dine at **Pete's Place,** for the best pasta in town (☞ Italian *in* Chapter 3); the elegant **Ruyi; Nutmegs,** for steaks and seafood; **Plums,** a 24-hour café-restaurant-lounge; and **Brannigan's,** a lively watering hole. ⊠ *10–12 Scotts Rd., 0922,* ☎ *738–1234,* ℻ *732–1696. 738 rooms. 3 restaurants, coffee shop, pool, beauty salon, massage, sauna, 2 tennis courts, badminton, exercise room, squash, business services. AE, DC, MC, V.*

$$$$ 🏨 **The Oriental.** Inside this pyramid-shaped Marina Square hotel, ar-
★ chitect John Portman has created a 21-story atrium with interior balconies that are stepped inward as they ascend; glass elevators glide from floor to floor. The reception area and lobby are on the fourth floor, free from the bustle of transients. Subdued, modern elegance and personalized attention are the keynotes of this smaller deluxe hotel. Rooms are understated, with soft hues of peach and green, hand-woven carpets, and paintings of old Singapore. Of special note are the Italian-marble-tiled bathrooms, with telephones, radio and television speakers, and an array of toiletries, plus terry-cloth bathrobes. One-bedroom suites have lovely sitting rooms and a separate guest washroom. The **Cherry Garden** (☞ Chinese: Hunanese *in* Chapter 3) prepares some of the best Hunanese food in Singapore. **Fourchettes** is fancy, with haute Continental cuisine. More casual dining is available at **Café Palm,** which serves Chinese, Nonya, Malay, and Western delicacies, a variety of teas, and a high tea, and **Pronto,** a rustic Italian restaurant on the terrace near the pool. The **Captain's Bar,** decorated with portraits of famous Singaporean sea traders, serves a roast beef luncheon, and international entertainers perform in the evening. ⊠ *#01–200, 6 Raffles Blvd., 0103,* ☎ *338–0066,* ℻ *339–9537. 640 rooms. 5 restaurants, pool, massage, sauna, golf privileges, 2 tennis courts, exercise room, jogging, squash, business services, meeting rooms, travel services. AE, DC, MC, V.*

$$$$ 🏨 **Raffles Hotel.** Opened by the Sarkies brothers in 1887 and visited by Conrad, Kipling, and Maugham, Raffles was the belle of the East during its heyday in the '20s and '30s but fell on hard times after World War II. True to form in this planned republic, millions of dollars have been spent to replace Singapore's noble old charm with a sanitized version of colonial ambience. The new Raffles is a glistening showpiece, especially from the outside; inside, it's sterile (☞ Exploring Colonial Singapore *in* Chapter 2). The polished-marble lobby seems cold; guest

88

Singapore Lodging

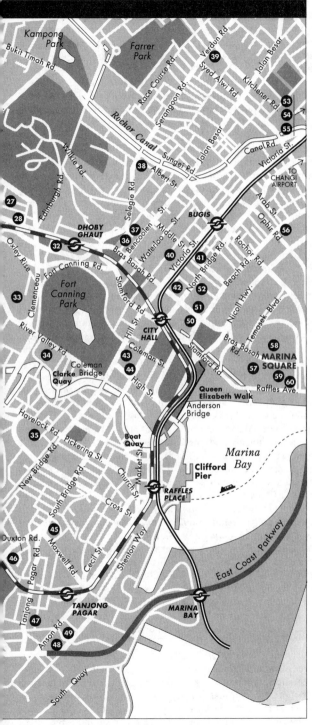

suites have teak floors, 14-foot ceilings, overhead fans, and '20s-style furnishings that tend to be stiff. The rectangular layout, with a small living room facing directly into the bedroom and the bathroom beyond, is awkward. For this you pay S$750—if you'll accept a suite facing the busy street. S$100 less will get you a suite in one of Singapore's truly superb deluxe hotels. The hotel's **Elizabethan Grill** is very posh indeed. ⊠ *1 Beach Rd., 0718,* ☎ *337–1886,* 𝔽𝔸𝕏 *339–7650. 104 suites. 2 restaurants, pool, exercise room, business services. AE, DC, MC, V.*

$$$$ 🏨 **Ritz-Carlton.** The most dramatic of the new spate of luxury hotels ★ is the Marina Square Ritz-Carlton. It opened in 1996 to a fanfare so impressive that taxi drivers dubbed it the "wanna-be six-star hotel." All rooms are unusually large, with unobstructed views—from the tall beds and even the tubs—of the skyline or Marina Bay. Modern, minimal appointments are softened by Tibetan-style woven rugs and wooden floors. Floors 30 to 32 are Club Floors where, for a S$50 premium, guests enjoy complimentary breakfast, evening cocktails, and personalized concierge services. For dining, there is **Snappers** for seafood, the **Summer Pavilion** for Cantonese cuisine, and the Asian- and European-accented **Greenhouse.** ⊠ *7 Raffles Ave., 0397,* ☎ *337– 8888,* 𝔽𝔸𝕏 *338–0001. 610 rooms. 3 restaurants, pool, tennis court, health club, business services, meeting rooms. AE, DC, MC, V.*

$$$$ 🏨 **Shangri-La.** Exceptionally attentive service characterizes this hotel, ★ consistently ranked among the top three in Singapore since its opening in 1971. The main lobby is handsome and pleasant, with easy chairs and tables for morning coffee and afternoon tea. The most attractive rooms are in the newer Valley Wing, which has its own entrance, check-in counter, concierge, boardrooms, and spacious guest rooms. Rooms in the Garden Wing are replete with warm fabrics and maple, cherry wood, and rattan furniture. The Tower Wing is the oldest, with the smallest rooms, but it was refurbished in 1994. The **Coffee Garden,** designed after an English conservatory, has light meals and a lunch buffet; the **Waterfall Café** serves breakfast and snacks all day in a delightful outdoor setting. Formal haute cuisine is served at the **Shang Palace,** noted for its dim sum lunches and fine Cantonese cuisine, and the Japanese **Nadaman** (☞ Japanese *in* Chapter 3). Amid 15 acres of gardens in a residential area at the top of Orchard Road, the Shangri-La is a pleasant 10-minute walk from the shopping areas; taxis are always on call. ⊠ *22 Orange Grove Rd., 1025,* ☎ *737–3644,* 𝔽𝔸𝕏 *733–7220. 821 rooms (136 in the Valley Wing). 4 restaurants, poolside bar and café, 4 tennis courts, putting green, exercise room, squash, dance club, nightclub, business services, meeting rooms. AE, DC, MC, V.*

$$$ 🏨 **ANA Singapore.** Don't be disconcerted by the antique tapestries and wood-paneled walls in the lobby of this ostentatiously glistening 14-story hotel—it, too, offers a full range of modern facilities. The guest rooms are furnished in light colors with separate writing desks, bedside remote controls, and coffee and tea makers. The **Hubertus Grill** serves seafood, prime rib, and Continental cuisine. The **Unkai** specializes in Japanese food. The hotel is near the Botanic Gardens and the embassies. ⊠ *16 Nassim Hill, 1025,* ☎ *732–1222,* 𝔽𝔸𝕏 *732–2222. 445 rooms, 17 suites. 2 restaurants, coffee shop, outdoor café, pool, exercise room, dance club, business services. AE, DC, MC, V.*

$$$ 🏨 **The Beaufort.** This resort hotel on Sentosa Island is aimed at tourists, but its remote location makes it seem more suited to business seminars. The best feature is the swimming pool overlooking the Malacca Straits, flanked by a romantic open-air seafood restaurant that serves Asian and Western fare. The rooms—down concrete corridors, past pond-filled courtyards, and in two symmetrical low-rise wings—don't share these fine views; instead they look onto tropical parkland. Standard rooms (called deluxe) aren't very large, except for the bathrooms,

In case you want to be welcomed there.

We're here to see that you're always welcomed at establishments everywhere. That's why millions of people carry the American Express® Card – for peace of mind, confidence, and security, around the world or just around the corner.

do more

Cards

In case you're running low.

We're here to help with more than 118,000 Express Cash locations around the world. In order to enroll, just call American Express before you start your vacation.

do more

Express Cash

and have undistinctive pastel furniture. The Garden Rooms have larger bedrooms and work areas with better-quality furniture like handmade tortoiseshell desks, mosaic tables, and French banquette sofas. There are also four luxurious two-bedroom villas, each with its own pool. ✉ *Sentosa Island, 0409,* ☎ *275–0331,* 🖷 *275–0228; U.S. reservations 800/637–7200, U.K. reservations 0800/220–761. 175 rooms, 34 suites, 4 villas. 3 restaurants, pool, 2 tennis courts, exercise room, squash. AE, DC, MC, V.*

$$$ 🏨 **Carlton Hotel.** This stark, pristine hotel near Raffles City has achieved a more relaxed ambience than when it first opened in 1989. The lobby is still an echo chamber for footsteps, but the lounges to the side are quiet enclaves for sipping afternoon tea. All the amenities of this hotel are up-to-date and modern. The upper five stories are concierge floors, with express check-in, complimentary breakfast, and evening cocktails. Published prices have climbed recently and, unless you can obtain a decent discount, they are rather steep for what the hotel offers. ✉ *76 Bras Basah Rd., 0718,* ☎ *338–8333,* 🖷 *339–6866; U.S. reservations 800/637–7200. 467 rooms, 53 suites. 2 restaurants, bar, coffee shop, lobby lounge, outdoor café, wine shop, pool, exercise room, business services, meeting rooms. AE, DC, MC, V.*

$$$ 🏨 **The Duxton.** This was Singapore's first boutique hotel—eight smartly
★ converted shophouses in the Tanjong Pagar district of Chinatown. It remains a breath of fresh air: intimate and tasteful with a whiff of old Singapore's character before it sold out to steel girders and glass. The standard rooms, at the back of the building, are small, with colonial reproduction furniture. You may want to spend the extra S$50 for one of the small duplex suites. Since windows aren't double glazed, you can hear some street noise and a few vocal alley cats. Breakfast is included, and afternoon tea is served in the lounge. The excellent French restaurant, L'Aigle d'Or (☞ French *in* Chapter 3), is off the lobby. ✉ *83 Duxton Rd., 0208,* ☎ *227–7678,* 🖷 *227–1232; U.S. reservations 800/272–8188, U.K. reservations 0181/876–3419. 48 rooms. Restaurant, business services. AE, DC, MC, V.*

$$$ 🏨 **Hilton International.** It may be short on glitter and dazzle, but the rooms have all the standard amenities of a modern deluxe property— and highly competitive rates. It's near Orchard and Scotts roads and shopping arcades with some of Singapore's most exclusive boutiques. The rooms on the street side still have views, but those on the back have been blocked by the adjacent Four Seasons; however, in back you can sleep with the sliding windows open, unlike in most Singapore hotels, which rely solely upon air-conditioning for ventilation. The former Givenchy suites are now executive club floors with 72 rooms and suites and a clubroom all decked out in contemporary furniture with black steel trim. Executive rooms are equipped with two telephone lines and a modem connection. Within the hotel is a Chinese restaurant, a spot for rooftop and poolside dining, and the **Harbour Grill** for seafood and French cuisine. Vodka aficionados can choose from 50 varieties at the **Kaspia** bar; locals come here for afternoon tea and the best cheesecake in Singapore. ✉ *581 Orchard Rd., 0923,* ☎ *737–2233,* 🖷 *732–2917. 435 rooms. 4 restaurants, 2 bars, pool, health club, business services, meeting rooms. AE, DC, MC, V.*

$$$ 🏨 **Hotel New Otani.** Off by itself on the north bank of the Singapore River, this orange-brick-fronted hotel is striking against the greenery of Fort Canning Park. It attracts many Japanese travelers as part of the Liang Court complex, which houses more than 40 specialty shops and the large Japanese department store Daimaru. Rooms come with coffee, tea, and soup makers. The hotel's location is best suited to business travelers wishing to be close to Shenton Way. ✉ *177A River Valley Rd., 0617,* ☎ *338–3333,* 🖷 *339–2854. 408 rooms.*

2 restaurants, bar, pool, exercise room, business services, meeting rooms. AE, DC, MC, V.

$$$ 🏨 **Mandarin Singapore.** Centrally located on Orchard Road, the Mandarin has a grand main lobby with translucent white-and-black Italian marble and a huge mural, *87 Taoist Immortals*, based on an 8th-century Chinese scroll. Otherwise, the Mandarin is a little disappointing, even though the guest rooms on the upper floors command fabulous views of the harbor, the city, and Malaysia beyond. The best rooms have safes, VCRs, and bedside remote controls. The South Wing's Renaissance rooms are furnished with colorful silk cushions and black lacquer furniture. But all show the wear and tear of the thousands of tour groups that are the hotel's mainstay. There are many restaurants: the **Pine Court** (☞ Chinese: Pekingese *in* Chapter 3); the **Top of the M**, Southeast Asia's only revolving restaurant, for Continental fare; **Stables Grill** for steaks and prime rib; the **New Tsurunoya** for Japanese specialties; the 24-hour **Chatterbox** coffeehouse for Western food; and hawker-stand Chinese food. ⊠ *333 Orchard Rd., 0923,* ☏ *737–4411,* 🖷 *732–2361. 1,208 rooms. 4 restaurants, coffee shop, pool, beauty salon, massage, sauna, miniature golf, 3 tennis courts, exercise room, squash, dance club, nightclub, business services, meeting rooms. AE, DC, MC, V.*

$$$ 🏨 **Marina Mandarin.** The John Portman–designed atrium is the Marina Mandarin's focal point: It narrows as it ascends 21 floors to a tinted skylight. The lobby area is relatively peaceful. Pastel guest rooms are modern and smart, with tea and coffee makers. For the best views get a room overlooking the harbor. Rooms on the concierge floor—the Marina Club—cost about 25% more and have additional amenities, such as terry-cloth bathrobes, butler service, and complimentary breakfasts and cocktails. Also available are accommodations for the businessperson who does not need the extras of the concierge floor but wants hotel services streamlined for efficiency. The **House of Blossoms** has an excellent Cantonese lunch and dinner. The **Ristorante Bologna** (☞ Italian *in* Chapter 3) serves northern Italian cuisine and fresh seafood. The **Cricketeer** pub is pleasant for evening drinks or an English buffet lunch. For homesick American travelers: **Champions** bar serves drinks and snacks to a backdrop of TV sports. ⊠ *#01-100, 6 Raffles Blvd., 0103,* ☏ *338–3388,* 🖷 *339–4977. 640 rooms. 3 restaurants, coffee shop, no-smoking floor, pool, massage, sauna, 2 tennis courts, exercise room, squash, dance club, business services. AE, DC, MC, V.*

$$$ 🏨 **Meridien Singapore Orchard.** On Orchard Road, slightly away from the center of activity, this French hotel is part of a shopping complex that includes the department store Printemps. The large atrium lobby is reminiscent of a train station. Guest rooms are decorated in salmon, pink, and blue, with silk-screened murals. Rooms on the Le Club Président concierge level have extra amenities. On the other floors, some rooms have private balconies loaded with potted plants. Aside from French haute cuisine served in the formal dining room, there is the relaxed **Brasserie Georges,** for local and French fare, and the **Spice Garden** for Cantonese cuisine. ⊠ *100 Orchard Rd., 0923,* ☏ *733–8855,* 🖷 *732–7886. 419 rooms. 3 restaurants, coffee shop, outdoor café, pool, exercise room, business services. AE, DC, MC, V.*

$$$ 🏨 **Omni Marco Polo.** The word on the street is that this hotel may be transformed into separate apartments for long-term stays. In the meantime, the rooms in the Continental Wing have Chippendale reproductions, marble-tiled bathrooms, writing desks, and remote controls for television and lights. The Omni Continental Club concierge floor has a handsome split-level lounge for complimentary breakfast and cocktails, and a separate business center. There are three restaurants: the smart, formal **Le Duc,** with haute Continental cuisine; the cheerful **La**

Brasserie, with bistro-style cooking (☞ French *in* Chapter 3); and the coffee shop, serving local cuisine. At night, a basement bar turns into a private disco for hotel guests. Perhaps because the British and Australian High Commissions are right across the road, guests are frequently from the Commonwealth. This hotel is set apart from the center of action, about a 15-minute walk from the Scotts and Orchard roads intersection. ⊠ *Tanglin Rd., 1024,* ☎ *474–7141; in U.S., 800/843–6664;* ℻ *471–0521. 573 rooms, 30 suites. 2 restaurants, bar, coffee shop, lobby lounge, in-room safes, pool, exercise room, dance club, business services, meeting rooms. AE, DC, MC, V.*

$$$ 🏨 **Orchard Hotel.** Close to the bustle of Orchard Road, several embassies, and the Botanic Gardens, this hotel, one of the largest in Singapore, is a popular spot. A recent renovation has inflated the prices but quelled the frequent mob scenes in the otherwise nondescript lobby. The light pastel rooms here are comfortable and functional. The Claymore Wing, a 300-room 17-story tower extension, is more expensive, with slightly larger rooms with built-in safes. The top four Claymore floors form the Premier Club, which has separate check-in, complimentary breakfast, and evening cocktails. The formal **Hua Ting** serves Cantonese and Shanghainese cuisine. **Ficus Cafe** is open until 1 AM for light meals, and the **Sidewalk Café** goes all night. The outdoor **Orchard Terrace** has casual dining, and a downstairs pub plays music nightly. ⊠ *442 Orchard Rd., 0923,* ☎ *734–7766,* ℻ *733–5482. 679 rooms. 3 restaurants, outdoor café, pool, dance club, business services, travel services. AE, DC, MC, V.*

$$$ 🏨 **Pan Pacific.** Of the three Marina Square hotels, this one is the least expensive and the largest, its size giving it an impersonal feeling. It caters to group tours and large conventions, with accommodations to please the budgets and needs of business travelers, from junior executives to senior management. It has a rooftop Chinese restaurant, Japanese and Polynesian restaurants, a grill room, and six other food and beverage spots. Upper-floor guest rooms have better views and more amenities, such as minibars and bathrobes. The Pacific Floor has butler service and complimentary breakfast and cocktails. ⊠ *7 Raffles Blvd., 0103,* ☎ *336–8111,* ℻ *339–1861. 800 suites and rooms. 4 restaurants, coffee shop, outdoor café, pool, 4 tennis courts, exercise room, business services, meeting rooms. AE, DC, MC, V.*

$$$ 🏨 **The Regent.** This hotel is relaxed and comfortable, with soft tones, Oriental carpets, wood paneling, and flower beds. Obtrusive glass elevators bob up and down the spacious atrium lobby, but guests can relax in the quiet tea and lobby lounges. The clubby second-floor cocktail lounge, **The Bar,** is another refuge. Rooms are done in Singapore's ever-pervasive pastel, with big beds, writing desks, and marble bathrooms; some have balconies. Try the **Tea Garden** for informal Continental and Asian food and buffet breakfasts; the **Steak Corner** for U.S. prime beef; the **Summer Palace** for Cantonese cuisine prepared by Hong Kong chefs; and **Maxim's de Paris** for French cuisine in an opulent Belle Epoque setting. A good 10-minute walk from the Scotts and Orchard roads intersection, the hotel appeals to those who want a quiet haven. ⊠ *1 Cuscaden Rd., Singapore 1024,* ☎ *733–8888 or 800/545–4000,* ℻ *732–8838. 397 rooms, 44 suites. 4 restaurants, lobby lounge, pool, spa, business services. AE, DC, MC, V.*

$$$ 🏨 **Royal Holiday Inn Crowne Plaza.** This popular hotel has an expansive lobby with Italian marble floors, Burmese teak wall paneling, stained-glass skylights, and hand-woven tapestries. The coffee shop lounge is bustling until 1 AM, and tour groups seem a permanent fixture at the reception counters. An "executive club" floor has a private lounge for complimentary breakfast and evening cocktails. All rooms are light-colored and compact, with high-tech remote controls. The **Baron's Table**

serves a mix of German and French cuisines. **The Bar** offers noisy live entertainment, including karaoke on weekends. The hotel's prime asset remains its location at the junction of Scotts and Orchard roads. ✉ *25 Scotts Rd., 0922,* ☎ *737–7966; in the U.S., 800/465–4329; in the U.K., 0171/722–7755;* FAX *737–6646. 493 rooms. 3 restaurants, bar, in-room safes, pool, miniature golf, exercise room, business services, travel services. AE, DC, MC, V.*

$$$ 🏨 **Sheraton Towers.** Formerly one of our favorites thanks to the superior service, the hotel has changed: those little touches—like early morning coffee brought to your room—are gone. The pastel-decorated guest rooms have all the deluxe amenities, including a small sitting area with sofa and easy chairs. (Room 1816 is particularly pleasant.) The best vantage point for the dramatic cascading waterfall—the rocks are fiberglass—is from the **Terrazza** restaurant, which is especially welcoming for a superb high tea. Other restaurants are **Domus** for Italian food and **Li Bai** (☞ Chinese: Cantonese *in* Chapter 3) for refined Cantonese. The hawker stalls at Newton Circus are close by. A large, comfortable lounge has live music in the evening. ✉ *39 Scotts Rd., Singapore 0922,* ☎ *737–6888,* FAX *737–1072. 406 rooms. 2 restaurants, coffee shop, outdoor café, pool, massage, sauna, dance club, business services, meeting rooms. AE, DC, MC, V.*

$$$ 🏨 **Singapore Marriott.** Formerly The Dynasty, this striking 33-story, pagoda-inspired property dominates Singapore's "million-dollar corner"—the Orchard and Scotts roads intersection. Before Marriott took over, the hotel's three-story lobby was decked out in rich, deep red— the Chinese color for good fortune—with 24 remarkable carved-teak wall panels. This detail is gone, and what is left are light-colored walls and a typical marble floor. The rooms are Western in style, with light gray carpets, pink vinyl wallpaper, pink-gray upholstery, and ample wood. The hotel's central location—rather than its character—is now its selling point. ✉ *320 Orchard Rd., 0923,* ☎ *735–5800,* FAX *735– 9800. 359 rooms, 15 suites. 2 restaurants, coffee shop, outdoor café, in-room safes, pool, exercise room, dance club, business services, meeting rooms. AE, DC, MC, V.*

$$$ 🏨 **Westin Plaza** and **Westin Stamford.** Catering to business executives, the Plaza is the smaller and higher-priced of these Raffles City twins; the 70-story Stamford, one of the tallest hotels in the world, attracts tours and conventions. These hotels are a hub of their own, with more than 100 shops, convention facilities, and 16 restaurants, the highlight being the **Compass Rose** (☞ Continental *in* Chapter 3). The complex also has one of the largest column-free meeting rooms in the world. The hotels are about 10 minutes by taxi or five by subway from the Orchard and Scotts roads intersection. ✉ *2 Stamford Rd., 0617,* ☎ *338–8585,* FAX *338–2862. Stamford, 1,257 rooms; Plaza, 796 rooms. 16 restaurants and lounges, 2 pools, 6 tennis courts, exercise room, squash, dance club, convention center, meeting rooms. AE, DC, MC, V.*

$$ 🏨 **Allson.** This hotel's published room rates are lower than at similar hotels, such as the nearby Carlton. All rooms have rosewood furniture and little extras such as coffee and tea makers and IDD phones. Rooms on the Excellence Floor are more expensive, but more spacious. This hotel is near Raffles City Tower, Marina Square, the colonial historic district, Little India, Bugis Street, and the Arab District, and it's only a 10-minute subway or bus ride to Orchard Road. ✉ *101 Victoria St., 0718,* ☎ *336–0811,* FAX *339–7019. 500 rooms. 3 restaurants, coffee shop, outdoor café, pool, exercise room, dance club, business services. AE, DC, MC, V.*

$$ 🏨 **Amara Hotel.** At the south end of the business district, this 18-story hotel, ideal for business travelers, is convenient to the train station and the commercial and port facilities. This is one of Singapore's better deals if you get the discount that's usually available. The hotel is characterless, but it is part of a vibrant shopping and entertainment complex and close to Chinatown's Tanjong Pagar. Rooms are warm, with pastel colors, wide sofas, two queen-size beds or a single king-size one, and bedside remote-control panels. The concierge floor, the Royal Club, has butler service. Don't miss the bargain S$22 poolside steamboat and barbecue buffet with more than 40 items nightly. ⊠ *Tanjong Pagar Rd., 0208,* ☎ *224–4488,* FAX *224–3910. 337 rooms. 2 restaurants, coffee shop, pool, 2 tennis courts, exercise room, jogging, squash, nightclub, playground, business services. AE, DC, MC, V.*

$$ 🏨 **Apollo Singapore.** As the Tanjong Pagar section of Chinatown develops, so does the appeal of the Apollo. Another business traveler haven, this semicircular 19-story hotel has relatively inexpensive, clean, and bright rooms. There are Chinese, Indonesian, and Japanese restaurants, a coffee shop serving Nonya food and the local Tamalak cuisine, and evening entertainment. The hotel is south of the Singapore River and west of Chinatown and the business district. A day shuttle bus runs hourly to Orchard Road. ⊠ *405 Havelock Rd., 0316,* ☎ *733–2081,* FAX *733–1588. 317 rooms. 3 restaurants, coffee shop, exercise room, dance club. AE, DC, MC, V.*

$$ 🏨 **Boulevard Hotel.** A floor-to-ceiling sculpture dominates the airy atrium lobby of this hotel, which caters to the traveling executive. Guest rooms have large work desks, IDD telephones, and pantries with coffee and tea makers. Rooms come in three sizes: standard; deluxe, with a corner pantry; and executive, with a work desk area. This hotel has not pushed up its rates like some of its competitors. It's at the top end of Orchard Road, away from the main thoroughfare. ⊠ *200 Orchard Blvd., 1024,* ☎ *737–2911,* FAX *737–8449. 528 rooms. 3 restaurants, coffee shop, 2 pools, beauty salon, exercise room, dance club, business services, travel services. AE, DC, MC, V.*

$$ 🏨 **Crown Prince Hotel.** The large, sparse lobby greets you with Italian marble and glass chandeliers. For drama, glass elevators run along the outside of the building, enabling you to check out the traffic congestion on Orchard Road. The pastel rooms are neat and trim, with amenities like Teletext television subtitles. Efficiency outweighs warmth here. The **Cafe de Prince** serves local and Western food, the **Long Jiang** (☞ Chinese: Szechuan *in* Chapter 3) offers Szechuan food from a set menu, and the **Sushi Nogawa** (☞ Japanese *in* Chapter 3) is Japanese-owned. ⊠ *270 Orchard Rd., 0923,* ☎ *732–1111,* FAX *732–7018. 297 rooms, 6 executive suites. 3 restaurants, pool, business services, meeting rooms. AE, DC, MC, V.*

$$ 🏨 **Furama Hotel.** This modern curvilinear building, on the doorstep of Chinatown and a 10-minute walk from the commercial district, stands out amid the surrounding shophouses. Unfortunately, the ubiquitous tour groups have left smudges on the walls of the otherwise attractive rooms. The helpful staff will direct you to the interesting sites, and there are daily guided walking tours through Chinatown. The popular poolside café provides a good rest stop after hoofing it around Chinatown. ⊠ *10 Eu Tong Sen St., 0105,* ☎ *533–3888,* FAX *534–1489. 354 rooms. 2 restaurants, bar, outdoor café, pool, beauty salon, sauna, steam room, business services, meeting rooms. AE, DC, MC, V.*

$$ 🏨 **Harbour View Dai Ichi.** This 29-story hotel is ideal for business travelers who want to be away from the hoi polloi but near the business district. Rooms are small, neat, and functional; two are in Japanese tatami style. Most of the clientele is from Japan, and the hotel's main restaurant is the **Kuramaya,** with kaiseki (formal Japanese banquet cuisine). There is also a Continental restaurant. ⊠ *81 Anson Rd., 0207,* ☎ *224–1133,* FAX *222–0749. 420 rooms. 2 restaurants, coffee shop, pool, massage, sauna, exercise room, business services. AE, MC, V.*

$$ 🏨 **Le Meridien Changi.** Aside from its location 10 minutes from the airport, this hotel has no particular merits, except for golfers. It is in need of a general sprucing up. ✉ *1 Netheravon Rd., 1750,* ☎ *542–7700,* ⓕ *542–5295. 280 rooms. Restaurant, coffee shop, pool, golf privileges, exercise room, bicycles, baby-sitting, business services. AE, DC, MC, V.*

$$ 🏨 **Melia Scotts.** Not far from Newton Circus, this modern, oblong hotel is rather cold and sterile. The guest rooms have IDD telephones, and the MRT station next door provides quick access to the whole island. ✉ *45 Scotts Rd., 0922,* ☎ *732–5885,* ⓕ *732–1332. 245 rooms. Restaurant, bar, coffee shop, pool, business services, meeting rooms. AE, V.*

$$ 🏨 **Plaza Hotel.** The rooms in this Little Araby hotel include IDD telephones, coffee and tea makers, and sensor-touch bedside control panels. Service is friendly, though a bit laid-back. Its three restaurants offer Cantonese and Thai cuisine, Western and regional fare, and spicy Oriental-style steaks. With a full house, the hotel can be quite lively. There is live entertainment in the evenings and a jumping disco. ✉ *7500A Beach Rd., 0719,* ☎ *298–0011,* ⓕ *296–0208. 350 rooms. 3 restaurants, 2 bars, refrigerators, pool, steam room, badminton, exercise room, squash, dance club, business services. AE, MC, V.*

$$ 🏨 **Rasa Sentosa.** A vast, arc-shaped building facing the sea and ships, this Sentosa Island hotel is a resort getaway: "When in Singapore, Stay Overseas" is the promotional slogan. It is ideal for Singaporean families escaping to the beach—although most stick to the pool—or for conventions whose delegates are not encouraged to make forays downtown. The motel-like rooms are quite small, with balconies facing either the water or a grassy knoll. The main restaurant serves Cantonese fare, and the café prepares Western and Asian dishes. It's dreamy for children, to whom the resort caters: there's a pool with water slides, playground, nursery, and video games room. For parents, a new hydrotherapy spa offers a range of body tonics, from seaweed facials and body wraps to rejuvenating mineral programs. Get to Sentosa either by the free shuttle-bus to the Shangri-La or by taxi (you'll have to pay the S$6 toll in addition to cab fare); there is also a S$5 charge to get onto the island. Room rates are lower during the week. ✉ *101 Siloso Rd., Sentosa 0409,* ☎ *275–0100; in the U.S., 800/942–5050;* ⓕ *275–0355. 459 rooms. 2 restaurants, pool, health club, recreation room, playground. AE, DC, MC, V.*

$$ 🏨 **Traders Hotel.** For value and service, this hotel is hard to beat. It
★　has all the necessary comforts but no frills. For example, there's no turn-down service; laundry is self-service; and toiletries are limited to the essentials. There's only one coffee shop for dining and no fancy room service, but scores of restaurants, a deli, and a supermarket are just steps away. Rooms are comfortable, with writing desks and plenty of light from the bay windows. There are spacious gardens and a pool—and proximity to the Orchard Road hub. Try to take advantage of frequent promotional rates. ✉ *1A Cuscaden Rd., 1024,* ☎ *738–2222; U.K. reservations, 181/747–8485; U.S. reservations, 800/492–5050;* ⓕ *831–4314. 543 rooms. Coffee shop, pool, exercise room, business services, meeting rooms. AE, DC, MC, V.*

$$ 🏨 **York Hotel.** Near bustling Orchard Road, the York is a quiet oasis. This classic European hotel is divided into two parts: The tower has only suites, and the poolside wing has split-level cabanas and "superior" rooms surrounding a garden. The **White Rose Cafe** serves Asian and Western fare, and the Balalaika Room offers Russian specialties. All rooms have two queen-size beds. ✉ *21 Mt. Elizabeth, 0923,* ☎ *737–0511,* ⓕ *732–1217. 400 rooms. 2 restaurants, bar, pool, beauty salon, sauna, exercise room. AE, DC, MC, V.*

$ ★ **Albert Court Hotel.** Rare in Singapore are small hotels that have gone to the expense and effort to restore existing structures. The Albert Court is one. Furnishings are simple, but wood panels create a warm, comfortable atmosphere. The staff is enthusiastic, and this attitude infects the guests. You can relax and grab a bite at the small coffee shop, open all day. ⊠ *180 Albert St., 0718,* ☎ *339–3939,* ℻ *339–3253. Coffee shop, bar. AE, MC, V.*

$ ★ **Cairnhill Hotel.** Not a particularly attractive building in itself, this hotel on a hill commands good views of downtown Singapore. Its restaurant serves Pekingese and Szechuan food, as well as regional fare. It's a 10-minute walk from Orchard Road. ⊠ *19 Cairnhill Circle, 0922,* ☎ *734–6622,* ℻ *235–5598. 220 rooms. Restaurant, coffee shop, pool, exercise room, business services, meeting room. AE, V.*

$ **The Concorde.** Once appropriately called the Glass Hotel, the Concorde has a glass canopy curving down from the ninth story over the entrance, which faces southeast for good fortune. Guest rooms in autumn hues are modern, with standard amenities. On the three executive floors, complimentary breakfast and cocktails are available. For dining and entertainment, head for the fourth floor, where there are French, Japanese, and Chinese restaurants; the last offers frequent floor shows. The hotel lies just south of the Singapore River and west of the business district. ⊠ *317 Outram Rd., 0316,* ☎ *733–0188,* ℻ *733–0989. 509 rooms (4 Japanese style). 3 restaurants, pool, massage, sauna, steam room, exercise room, tennis court, business services, meeting rooms. AE, MC, V.*

$ **Excelsior Hotel.** This economical central-city hotel is across the street from nearly 1,000 shops, close to its older sister hotel, the Peninsula, and a few blocks from Raffles City. The rooms are reasonably large and well maintained, with IDD telephones. Its popular **Annalakshmi** serves vegetarian Indian fare (☞ Indian *in* Chapter 3). ⊠ *5 Coleman St., 0617,* ☎ *338–7733,* ℻ *339–3847. 300 rooms. 3 restaurants, piano bar, in-room safes, pool, dance club, travel services. AE, MC, V.*

$ **Hotel Equatorial.** In a residential area a good 10-minute drive from Orchard Road, the Equatorial offers reasonably priced rooms equipped with IDD telephones and televisions with Teletext. ⊠ *429 Bukit Timah Rd., 1025,* ☎ *732–0431,* ℻ *737–9426. 224 rooms. 3 restaurants, coffee shop, outdoor café, minibars, pool. V.*

$ **Hotel Grand Central.** This hotel offers clean rooms with IDD telephones and extensive convention facilities. The lobby is populated with name-tagged delegates and unattached women. In addition to the **Omei Sichuan,** there are Italian and Mongolian restaurants. It's within easy strolling distance of Orchard Road's shopping centers. ⊠ *22 Cavenagh Rd., 0922,* ☎ *737–9944,* ℻ *733–3175. 365 rooms. 3 restaurants, coffee shop, outdoor café, room service, mini-refrigerators, pool, massage, sauna, exercise room, convention center. MC, V.*

$ **Hotel Royal.** This modest hotel has the standard amenities and in-room IDD telephones. On the premises is an International Forwarding Service, which can be useful for anyone—especially shoppers—wishing to send excess baggage back home. It's near Newton Circus and a 20-minute walk from Orchard Road. ⊠ *36 Newton Rd., 1130,* ☎ *253–4411,* ℻ *253–8668. 331 rooms. 3 restaurants, coffee shop, minibars, mini-refrigerators, pool, massage, sauna. AE, MC, V.*

$ **Imperial Hotel.** Set on a small hill between Orchard Road and Shenton Way, the Imperial has pastel-colored rooms with mirrored walls. Air-conditioning is individually controlled, and the rooms have free videos and large windows with expansive views of Singapore. The **Hill-Top Lounge** has a bar with live entertainment in the evenings, backgammon and chess during the day. ⊠ *1 Jalam Rumbia, 0923,* ☎ *737–1666,*

FAX 757–4761. *558 rooms, 42 suites. 3 restaurants, coffee shop, mini-bars, pool, dance club, business services. AC, DC, MC, V.*

$ 🏨 **The Inn of the Sixth Happiness.** Original Chinese paintings, rosewood furniture, and antiques from the mainland adorn this hotel, which pays tribute to Singapore's Chinese heritage. Standard rooms are spacious; they aren't overdecorated and tend to be a little dark. The staff is laid-back, as though the initial enthusiasm has waned. Prices are quite reasonable if you negotiate a discount. The inn is in Chinatown at the top end of Tanjong Pagar, in a converted stretch of former shophouses. ⊠ *33–35 Erskine Rd., 0106,* ☎ *223–3266,* FAX *223–7951. 44 rooms, 9 suites. Restaurant, coffee shop, pub, nightclub. AE, DC, MC, V.*

$ 🏨 **Ladyhill Hotel.** Unlike most other Singapore hotels, Ladyhill em-
★   phasizes home comforts and relaxation. In the main building are the intimate Swiss-style restaurant **Le Chalet**, a cozy split-level bar with a Filipino band in the evening, and guest rooms. "Superior" rooms in the surrounding cottages are spacious enough for an extra bed, perfect for families. There is usually a poolside barbecue at night. The Ladyhill is in a residential area a good 10-minute walk uphill from Orchard Road (a hotel bus shuttles the weary back and forth). ⊠ *1 Ladyhill Rd., 1025,* ☎ *737–2111,* FAX *737–4606. 171 rooms. Restaurant, bar, coffee shop, pool, nightclub, meeting rooms. AE, V.*

$ 🏨 **New Park Hotel.** Formerly the President Merlin Hotel, this 19-story hotel has clean and fairly spacious rooms. The **Huang Palace** serves Chinese fare, and the **Terrace Garden Coffee House** has regional and Continental food. There is live entertainment every night in the lounge. The hotel is on the northern edge of Little India and a good 10-minute taxi ride to Orchard Road (a free shuttle bus is provided) and another 10 minutes to the city's commercial center and Chinatown. ⊠ *181 Kitchener Rd., 0820,* ☎ *291–5533,* FAX *297–2827. 525 rooms. 2 restaurants, lobby lounge, room service. AE, V.*

$ 🏨 **RELC International House.** This is less a hotel than an international
★   conference center often used by Singapore's university for seminars. However, the upper floors of the building are bargain guest rooms: large and basically comfortable, with plenty of welcomed light, but be prepared for slapdash plaster repair work in the otherwise clean and functional bathrooms. The building is in a residential neighborhood, up a hill beyond the Shangri-La Hotel, a 10-minute walk to the Orchard and Scotts roads intersection. Because of its good value, it is often booked, so reservations are strongly advised. ⊠ *30 Orange Grove Rd., 1025,* ☎ *737–9044,* FAX *733–9976. 128 rooms. Coffee shop, coin laundry. No credit cards.*

$ 🏨 **River View Hotel.** Rooms are equipped with modern amenities, including convenient telephone extensions in the bathrooms. This high-rise hotel is on the south bank of the Singapore River and is about 10 minutes by taxi from both the commercial center and Orchard Road. ⊠ *382 Havelock Rd., 0316,* ☎ *732–9922,* FAX *732–1034. 476 rooms. 2 restaurants, coffee shop, outdoor café, room service, minibars, pool, exercise room, dance club, business services, meeting rooms. AE, DC, MC, V.*

$ 🏨 **Seaview Hotel.** Off the East Coast Parkway, midway between Changi Airport and Singapore city, this high-rise hotel is more convenient for travelers in transit than for visitors. Guest rooms offer the basic amenities. There are restaurants, nightclubs, and shops on the premises and in the area. The nearby East Coast Park has golf, tennis, cycling, and water-sports facilities. ⊠ *Amber Close, 1543,* ☎ *345–2222,* FAX *345–1741. 435 rooms. 2 restaurants, bar, coffee shop, room service, pool, nightclub. MC, V.*

$ 🏨 **Singapore Peninsula Hotel.** Near the Padang and between the fashionable Orchard Road and commercial district areas, this hotel offers the basic creature comforts. The lobby area is small and nondescript. The fairly spacious guest rooms are clean—the best are on the 17th floor—though you may have to tolerate water stains in the bathtub. All rooms have televisions with Teletext. There is no restaurant, but a coffee shop serves the basics. ⊠ *3 Coleman St., Singapore 0617,* ☎ *337–2200,* ℻ *339–3580. 311 rooms, 4 suites. Bar, coffee shop, room service, minibars, in-room safes, pool, massage, sauna, exercise room, nightclub. AE, MC, V.*

$ 🏨 **Transit Hotel.** This is the answer for bleary-eyed long-distance travelers who arrive at Changi Airport in the middle of the night, only to be taking off again within the next few hours. This new hotel is inside the airport on Level 3 of the Departure Lounge in Terminal 1. Note: passengers staying at this hotel do not go through immigration control. Rooms are clean, fresh, and basic but do have private bathrooms and television. Rates are for six-hour periods—a double is S$56—and include use of the swimming pool, sauna, and fitness center. Nonguests may also use the pool (S$10), sauna and showers (S$10), or just the shower (S$5). ⊠ *Terminal 1, Changi Airport,* ☎ *543–0911, U.K. reservations, 0800/96–3562; U.S. reservations, 800/690–6785;* ℻ *545–8365. Pool, sauna, health club, nursery. AE, DC, MC, V.*

¢ 🏨 **Hotel Asia.** Next to the Sheraton Towers, between Orchard Road and Newton Circus, the Hotel Asia is a modest economy hotel. Guest rooms have few luxuries, and unless you can negotiate a discount, it's a little overpriced for the scant offerings. The **Tsui Hang Village** serves Cantonese cuisine. ⊠ *37 Scotts Rd., 0922,* ☎ *737–8388,* ℻ *733–3563. 146 rooms. Bar, coffee shop. MC, V.*

¢ 🏨 **Hotel Bencoolen.** On the commercial street that leads from Orchard Road to Little India, this hotel's highlights are in-room IDD phones, its central location, and helpful staff. Usually one can negotiate a discount on the room rate, making the Bencoolen a fine value. A rooftop restaurant serves Chinese and Continental fare. ⊠ *47 Bencoolen St., 0718,* ☎ *336–0822,* ℻ *336–4384. 86 rooms. Restaurant. MC, V.*

¢ 🏨 **Metropole Hotel.** This is a very modest and basic hotel near Raffles City. The rooms are simply furnished and have televisions. The staff is quite helpful, which isn't always the case in budget hotels. ⊠ *41 Seah St., 0718,* ☎ *336–3611,* ℻ *339–3610. 54 rooms. Restaurant, coffee shop, room service. AE, DC, MC, V.*

¢ 🏨 **Metropolitan YMCA, International Centre.** This is the oldest of the three Singapore YMCAs. Most rooms are singles and for men only; single females get a double room at a single rate. Bathrooms are shared, except for the double rooms (a bargain at S$70). Most of the rooms have air-conditioning but no telephones. This Y is at the end of Shenton Way in the central business district. ⊠ *70 Palmer Rd., 0207,* ☎ *224–4666. 52 rooms, including 16 doubles. Restaurant. No credit cards.*

¢ 🏨 **Metropolitan YMCA, Tanglin Centre.** A 10-minute walk to Orchard Road, this YMCA (which admits women) has rooms with air-conditioning and private baths. There are even a few suites. The budget restaurant offers wholesome English breakfasts for only a few Singapore dollars, as well as Chinese, Malay, Nonya, and Western meals. ⊠ *Tanglin Centre, 60 Stevens Rd., 1025,* ☎ *737–7755,* ℻ *235–5528. 88 rooms. Coffee shop, pool, exercise room, squash, meeting rooms. No credit cards.*

¢ 🏨 **Queen's Hotel.** In a quiet area off Orchard Road, this hotel is a friendly, homey place. The rooms are quite modest but do have air-conditioning and television. In the "deluxe" four-story wing, the rooms even have refrigerators; since these rooms are newer, they're worth the extra S\$10. ⊠ *24 Mt. Elizabeth, 0922,* ☎ *737–6088. 61 rooms. Coffee shop, pool, massage, sauna. MC, V.*

¢   🏨 **Strand Hotel.** This hotel's simple, clean rooms have IDD telephones and color televisions with in-house videos. The location, between Raffles City and Orchard Road, is central, though a 10-minute walk is required to reach either. The service tends to be rather curt. ⊠ *25 Bencoolen St., 0718,* ☎ *338–1866,* FAX *336–3149. 130 rooms. Bar, coffee shop. No credit cards.*

¢   🏨 **YMCA International House.** This well-run YMCA at the bottom end of Orchard Road offers hotel-like accommodations for men and women, with double (S\$70) and single (S\$45) rooms, plus dormitories for budget travelers (S\$20). S\$5 will buy you temporary YMCA membership. All rooms have private baths, color TVs, and IDD phones. In addition to an impressive gym, there are a rooftop pool and squash and badminton courts. And there's a McDonald's at the entrance. ⊠ *1 Orchard Rd., 0923,* ☎ *336–6000,* FAX *337–3140. 60 rooms. Pool, exercise room, squash. AE, DC, MC, V.*

5 Nightlife and the Arts

Risqué nightlife is a thing of the past in Singapore. Now it's good, clean fun in new areas for managed frivolity. Jazz bars, discos, and nightclubs abound, along with a symphony orchestra and dance and theater troupes. Whatever your tastes, you'll find plenty of choices.

Updated by
Christine Hill

PERHAPS BECAUSE EATING OUT consumes so much of Singaporeans' time and money, there is less variety in other forms of entertainment. Still, there's enough to keep visitors busy. The Singapore Tourist Promotion Board (STPB; ☎ 736–6622) has listings of events scheduled for the current month. You can also find the schedules of major performances in the local English-language newspaper, the *Straits Times,* or in the free monthly *Arts Diary* brochure available at most hotel reception desks.

Every year there seem to be more cultural events, especially orchestral and dramatic performances—perhaps as a result of the government's decree that Singaporeans become more genteel. And it's a lot easier now to obtain tickets to performances, thanks to SISTIC, a ticketing service that operates Monday–Friday 10–5 and Saturday 10–1. You can book over the hot line (☎ 348–5555) for a S$2 handling fee, or go to one of the convenient ticket offices at designated shopping centers (☞ Concerts *in* The Arts, *below*).

In an attempt to counteract the perception that Singapore is strictly regimented, the government has created new areas for managed frivolity. **Bugis Street,** once a center of risqué nightlife, was closed and partly torn down, and now has been resurrected—some say sanitized beyond repair—with boutique shopping, cafés, bars, and the only air-conditioned outdoor mall in Asia. More authentic is Chinatown's **Tanjong Pagar;** here shophouses have been turned into hotels, shops, restaurants, teahouses, and bars. Though not very lively in the evenings, Chinatown's Duxton Hill is home to two or three bars with good jazz. The third area planned under the auspices of the government's STPB is **Clarke Quay** on the Singapore River. Former godowns and shophouses have been transformed into upscale shops, restaurants, and bars, there's an open-air hawker food court, and the streets are lined with stalls selling trinkets.

Whet your whistle with a beer or a glass of wine on one of the four *tongkangs* (old Chinese cargo vessels) before an early-evening walk along **Boat Quay,** which was developed with less stringent government supervision; the result is a more interesting—and more reasonably priced—mix of restaurants and bars, some with live music. If you want to enjoy the natural flavor of Singapore, Boat Quay is your best bet.

NIGHTLIFE

Music clubs, offering everything from serious listening to jazz to the thumping and flashing of discos, are becoming more popular as Singaporeans take up the Western custom of dating. The increasingly popular *karaoke* (empty orchestra) bars, where guests grip real microphones and sing along to the music track of a video, offer chronic shower singers the chance to go public.

Nightclubs with floor shows are also popular, and the bigger the place is, the better—some accommodate as many as 500 revelers. Often these clubs have hostesses, affectionately called public relations officers, or PROs, available for company. Depending on the establishment, "booking the hostess" requires either a flat hourly fee or a gratuity at the end of the evening.

At nightclubs or music bar/lounges, there is usually a cover charge or a first-drink charge (cover plus one free drink) of about S$15 weeknights and S$25 weekends. At the nightclubs where there are floor shows and hostesses, the common practice is to buy a bottle of brandy—Chinese consider brandy a high-status drink, whereas whiskey is "bad smelling and shows poor taste." A bottle of brandy may cost as much as S$300. You are advised to let your hostess drink from your bottle, rather than order her own.

Risqué nightlife disappeared long ago from Singapore. Prostitution is not exactly legal, but certain areas, such as Geylang, do have red-light districts. However, the fear of AIDS has made Westerners suspect, and when they're not downright unwelcome, they must pay a higher price. The bars along Keppel Road are not recommended.

Comedy

Boom Boom. Don't expect the delightful unsavoriness of the old Bugis Street, but this comedy house usually offers a few belly laughs with its twice-nightly schedule. A DJ spins disks between shows. ⊠ *Bugis Village,* ☎ *339–8187.* ⊞ *Varies, starting about S$15.* ☉ *Tues.–Sun. 8 PM–2 AM.*

Country-and-Western

Golden Peacock Lounge. This has long been a favorite of those who enjoy country music. The star attraction is Matthew Tan, Singapore's own singing cowboy, who has a vintage country twang. ⊠ *Shangri-La Hotel, 22 Orange Grove Rd.,* ☎ *737–3644.* ⊞ *Drinks from S$15.* ☉ *Nightly 8–2.*

Dance and Theater Nightclubs

The most popular nightclubs among Singaporeans are those with floor shows and hostesses. You are under no obligation to select a hostess, however. The cost of going to these clubs is in the bottle of brandy you are expected to buy; if you don't mind losing face, you can forgo the brandy and order whatever you want from the bar. There are also "dinner theater" evenings held periodically at the Hilton, Hyatt, and Shangri-La hotels; dinner and a show at the **Shangri-La,** which often has some good comics, runs about S$85.

Apollo Theatre Restaurant and Nightclub. This club is very popular with Chinese businessmen, who come here to be entertained by a steady stream of Chinese singers and hostesses and to enjoy the Hunanese cuisine. ⊠ *Apollo Singapore Hotel, 405 Havelock Rd., 17th floor,* ☎ *235–7977.* ⊞ *Brandy S$270; hourly hostess fee S$25.* ☉ *Nightly 8–2.*

Golden Million. Here you can either dine or just listen to Hong Kong bands play a mixture of Mandarin, Cantonese, and Western music. The decor is expansive and rich, with lots of gold and red, oozing extravagance. This was one of the clubs that started the hostess concept; it has become well established among Chinese and Singaporean businessmen. ⊠ *Peninsula Hotel, 3 Coleman St., 5th floor,* ☎ *336–6993.* ⊞ *Brandy S$250; hourly hostess fee S$25.* ☉ *Nightly 8–2.*

Kasbah. The decor is Moroccan in this long-established, tiered nightclub where, on occasion, good artists from abroad entertain. Dancing is both fast and slow, and the music allows for conversation. The crowd, too, is more subdued and "properly" dressed. ⊠ *Mandarin Hotel, Orchard Rd.,* ☎ *737–4411.* ⊞ *1st drink: Sun.–Thurs. S$16, Fri.–Sat. S$22.* ☉ *Nightly 9–2.*

Lido Palace Niteclub. Promoting itself as the "palace of many pleasures," this lavish establishment offers Chinese cabaret, a band, DJ-spun disco, hostesses, karaoke, and, for those who wish to dine, Cantonese cuisine. ⊠ *Concorde Hotel, 317 Outram Rd., 5th floor,* ☎ *732–8855.* 🍸 *1st drink S$30.* 🕐 *Nightly 9–3, shows at 9:30 and 12:30.*

Marco Polo. A four-piece band plays popular dance music to which diners can take a turn on the floor between courses in the formal and elegant split-level Le Duc Continental restaurant in the Omni Marco Polo Hotel. Tables are at either side of center stage, some discreetly positioned in alcoves, others overlooking the dance floor. ⊠ *Tanglin Rd.,* ☎ *464–7141.* 🍸 *Dinner for 2 approximately S$70.* 🕐 *Nightly 8–11.*

Neptune. This sumptuous two-story establishment, designed as an Oriental pavilion, is reputed to be the largest nightclub in Southeast Asia. Cantonese food is served, and there is a gallery for nondiners. Local, Taiwanese, and Filipino singers entertain in English and Chinese; occasionally a European dance troupe is added to the lineup. For the most fun, go with a group. It's operated by the Mandarin Hotel, so call ahead to be sure it's not already booked for private functions. ⊠ *Overseas Union House, Collyer Quay,* ☎ *224–3922 or 737–4411 (information and reservations).* 🍸 *S$8, dinner S$15.* 🕐 *Nightly 8–2.*

Discos and Dance Clubs

The distinction between a disco and a place with live music and a dance floor has become blurred. At all the following establishments, the decibel levels allow for only snatches of conversation.

Caesars. The decor and the waitresses clad in lissome togas give this disco an air of decadent splendor. DJ-spun music plus imported live bands make it a hot venue for entertainment. ⊠ *#02–36 Orchard Towers, front block, 400 Orchard Rd.,* ☎ *235–2840.* 🍸 *1st drink: Sun.–Thurs. S$15, Fri.–Sat. S$24.* 🕐 *Sun.–Thurs. 8 PM–2 AM, Fri.–Sat. 8 PM–3 AM.*

Celebrities. This establishment, in the swank Orchard Towers, is considered a sophisticated nightspot. Dance music spun by a DJ is interspersed with live pop music; one of the key attractions is the all-girl band Heaven Knows. There is ample room to drink at the 150-foot-long bar. ⊠ *#B1–41 Orchard Towers, rear block, 400 Orchard Rd.,* ☎ *734–5221.* 🍸 *1st drink: Sun.–Thurs. S$15, Fri.–Sat. S$24.* 🕐 *Sun.–Thurs. 8 PM–2 AM, Fri.–Sat. 8 PM–3 AM.*

Chinoiserie. This is currently the in place for yuppies. Outside, lines of people wait to enter and be entertained by a variety of musical groups. ⊠ *Hyatt Hotel, 10–12 Scotts Rd.,* ☎ *733–1188.* 🍸 *1st drink: Sun.–Thurs. S$20, Fri.–Sat. S$30.* 🕐 *Nightly 8–3.*

East-West Express. This is both a restaurant and a disco. A changing menu each month reflects the cuisines of various countries, and the decor adapts to suit the cuisine. After about 10:15 PM, disco dancing becomes the focus of attention. ⊠ *#03–119, 121 Marina Square,* ☎ *339–1618.* 🍸 *Mon.–Thurs. S$11, Fri. S$16, Sat. S$20.* 🕐 *Mon.–Sat. 6 PM–2 AM.*

Fire. One of Singapore's steady favorites, Fire has live music danced to by a lively crowd. Drinks are paid for by coupons, so work out the cost before making the purchase. Upstairs, would-be artists sing their lungs out in 12 computerized karaoke rooms. ⊠ *Orchard Plaza #04-19, 150 Orchard Rd.,* ☎ *235–0155.* 🍸 *Drink prices higher weekends.* 🕐 *Nightly 9–2.*

Rumours. One of the largest discos in Singapore, this is a favorite among the younger set. The two-level glass dance floor is designed to make you feel as though you are dancing in space; the play of mirrors adds to the distortion. ⊠ *#03–08 Forum Galleria, 483 Orchard Rd.,*

☎ 732–8181. ☒ *1st drink: Sun.–Thurs. S$15, Fri.–Sat. S$20.* ☺
Sun.–Thurs. 8–2, Fri.–Sat. 8–3.

Shock! Odyssey. This ultramodern disco with live entertainment uses
high-tech effects and robots to startle the senses. ☒ *Orchard Hotel,*
442 Orchard Rd., ☎ *739–7766.* ☒ *Price of 1st drink varies, but high-*
est on weekends. ☺ *Nightly 8–2.*

Sparks. An offshoot of the popular Fire disco, this club has karaoke
rooms, live music, and laser shows. It's on the 7th floor of the upmarket Takashimaya Shopping Centre where, so it would seem, the revelers have just made purchases. ☒ *Ngee Ann City, Tower B,* ☎ *735–6133.*
☒ *Depending on band S$12, weekends S$20.* ☺ *Mon.–Sat. 8 PM–2 AM.*

Studebakers. This lavish penthouse disco is quite the yuppie playground.
Disco music booms throughout the week; live shows heighten the ex-
citement on the weekends. ☒ *Pacific Plaza, Scotts Rd.,* ☎ *736–0300.*
☒ *S$15, weekends S$25.* ☺ *Mon.–Sat.*

TGIF. This establishment is strictly for drinking from lunchtime to 7:30,
whereupon it turns into a disco. However, the action rarely begins before 10. Dinner is also available, if you like to eat amid flashing lights.
☒ *Far East Plaza, 14 Scotts Rd.,* ☎ *235–6181.* ☒ *1st drink S$7.* ☺
Daily noon–2 AM.

Top Ten. This old, converted cinema is decorated with cityscapes, including the Manhattan skyline, and now contains a four-tier bar, a dance
floor, and a stage. Imported bands alternate with disco music. The happy
hour in the lobby bar between 5 and 9 is popular. ☒ *#04–35/36 Or-*
chard Towers, 400 Orchard Rd., ☎ *732–3077.* ☒ *1st drink:*
Sun.–Thurs. S$15, Fri.–Sat. S$25. ☺ *Nightly 9–3.*

The Warehouse. Two former riverside warehouses now store up to 500
disco fanatics and the largest video screen in Singapore. This is a popular nightspot, especially for the younger crowd. ☒ *332 Havelock Rd.,*
next to the River View Hotel, ☎ *732–9922.* ☒ *Sun.–Thurs. S$12 with*
1 drink, Fri.–Sat. S$24 with 2 drinks. ☺ *Sun.–Thurs. 8 PM–2 AM,*
Fri.–Sat. 8 PM–3 AM.

Xanadu. The reputation of the Shangri-La Hotel and the intricate,
high-tech lighting system of this popular disco bring in a steady, sophisticated crowd. They come partly for the "changing environment":
With the flip of a switch, the American Western scene—complete with
square dancing—is transformed into a tropical island night suitable for
smooching. Gimmicky perhaps, but it works—each time the switch is
pulled (twice nightly), the ambience changes and the clientele reacts with
amused delight. ☒ *Shangri-La Hotel, 22 Orange Grove Rd.,* ☎ *737–*
3644. ☒ *1st drink: Sun.–Thurs. S$18, Fri.–Sat. S$24.* ☺ *Nightly 9–3.*

Jazz

Captain's Bar. For a sophisticated evening of jazz and rhythm and blues,
this elegant but comfortable bar and lounge is just the place. ☒ *Ori-*
ental Hotel, Marina Square, ☎ *338–0066.* ☒ *Drinks from S$12.* ☺
Nightly 9–1.

Club 3992. Owned by the same people as Caesars, this club maintains
a high jazz profile with international artists. ☒ *Orchard Towers, 400*
Orchard Rd., ☎ *235–2840.* ☒ *Drinks from S$10.* ☺ *Nightly 9–2.*

Duxton's Chicago Bar & Grill. In the renovated Tanjong Pagar district,
this bar serves up barbecued spare ribs to the tune of jazz and blues
American style. ☒ *6 Duxton Hill,* ☎ *222–4096.* ☒ *No cover.* ☺
Nightly 5–1.

Harry's Quayside. This is a comfortable place to hang out to a mix of jazz, blues, and old-time rock and roll. Occasionally the live band gets carried away and produces a good old-fashioned jam session. Upstairs, food is served with fine waterfront views. ⊠ *28 Boat Quay,* ☎ *538–3029.* ⊘ *Daily 11 AM–midnight.*

Saxophone. At this club, which offers both jazz and popular rock, the volume is loud and the space is compact, with standing room only. However, there is a terrace outside where you can sit and still hear the music. Saxophone was a pioneer of the Singapore jazz scene, and the customers keep coming, so the sound must be right. ⊠ *23 Cuppage Terr.,* ☎ *235– 8385.* ▣ *Drinks about S$10.* ⊘ *Nightly 6–1.*

Somerset Bar. The New Orleans–style jazz played here has attracted a loyal following. With a larger space than the Saxophone, it offers room to sit and relax, making it popular with the older crowd. ⊠ *Westin Plaza, 4 Stamford Rd., 3rd floor,* ☎ *338–8585.* ▣ *Drinks from S$10.* ⊘ *Nightly 5–2.*

Karaoke Bars

Dai-Ichi Karaoke. Patrons climb onto a revolving platform to sing along with videos and lyrics flashed on a screen. Understanding Mandarin helps one appreciate the vocalists. ⊠ *Dai-Ichi Hotel, 81 Anson Rd.,* ☎ *222–8931.* ▣ *Drinks from S$9.* ⊘ *Nightly 8–2.*

Park Avenue. Formerly the Peppermint Park, this is a large, cavernous karaoke lounge, with imitation facades of old houses setting the mood. Different sections permit different kinds of crooning, from French love songs in a library setting to John Denver in a Western landscape. ⊠ *#04–08, 80 Marina Parade,* ☎ *440–9998.* ▣ *Drinks from S$15.* ⊘ *Nightly 8–2.*

Pubs and Beer Gardens

Brannigans. Decorated with knickknacks from around the world to celebrate the adventures of Captain David Brannigan, British wanderer, this popular watering hole is a convenient meeting spot before a night of revelry or a friendly place for a nightcap. ⊠ *Hyatt Regency, 10–12 Scotts Rd.,* ☎ *733–1188.* ⊘ *Daily 11 AM–1 AM.*

Champions. There are 20 Champions in the United States, but only one existed elsewhere (in Dubai) until Singapore's became the second. Fans enjoy video sports, drinks, and snacks surrounded by sports paraphernalia. ⊠ *Marina Mandarin Hotel, Marina Square, 6 Raffles Blvd.,* ☎ *331–8567.* ⊘ *Mon.–Sat. 5 PM–2 AM.*

The Coolies' Pub. The Inn of the Sixth Happiness in Tanjong Pagar has devoted the top floors of four shophouses to this friendly, casual café, where light music is offered most evenings. ⊠ *Eskine Rd.,* ☎ *223– 3266.* ▣ *Drinks from S$8.* ⊘ *Nightly 7–midnight.*

Dickens Tavern. At this pub and lounge, regulars listen to bands while being served by friendly waitresses (not hostesses). It's a good place to visit if you do not want to have a raucous and expensive evening. ⊠ *#04–01 Parkway Parade, 80 Marina Parade Rd.,* ☎ *440–0215.* ▣ *No cover, drinks from S$7.* ⊘ *Nightly 8–2.*

Flag & Whistle. Down in the renovated part of Chinatown, this English-style pub chatters with expat conversations punctuated with pints and fortified with British snacks. ⊠ *10 Duxton Hill,* ☎ *223– 1126.* ▣ *Drinks from S$5.* ⊘ *Daily 11 AM–midnight.*

Hard Rock Cafe. Hamburgers and light fare are served at this pub/café, and a live band plays in the evenings. The atmosphere here doesn't deviate from the chain—casual, young, and festive—with a bar, booth tables, and souvenir shops. ⊠ *#02–01, 50 Cuscaden Rd.,* ☎ *235–5232.* 🖾 *S$12 with 1 drink, drinks from S$8.* ☾ *Nightly 6–1.*

Jim's Pub. Try this cozy bar, owned and managed by pianist Jimmy Chan, for an evening of light music from a vocalist or instrumentalist. ⊠ *Hotel Negara, 15 Claymore Dr.,* ☎ *737–0811.* 🖾 *Beer S$3 a glass.* ☾ *Nightly 7–1.*

Riverbank Restaurant & Pub. Boat Quay is the city's best place to wander around aimlessly, people-watch, and do some casual barhopping. The riverside terrace here is an especially good place to meet up with others and start your evening. ⊠ *Boat Quay,* ☎ *538–1135.* ☾ *Nightly 6–2.*

Wild West Tavern. One of Clarke Quay's plethora of restaurants and bars, this is less pricey than most and quite appealing for a beer and a chat. As the name may imply, expect an authentic Hollywood-style saloon—but without the cowboys. ⊠ *12 Clarke Quay,* ☎ *334–4180.* ☾ *Nightly 4–midnight.*

Rock

Anywhere. Crowds gather, especially on weekends, in this smoke-filled room to hear the music of the local rock band Tania. ⊠ *#04–08 Tanglin Shopping Centre, 19 Tanglin Rd.,* ☎ *734–8233.* 🖾 *1st drink: Sun.–Thurs. S$12, Fri.–Sat. S$18.* ☾ *Sun.–Thurs. 8 PM–2 AM, Fri.–Sat. 8 PM–3 AM.*

THE ARTS

Chinese, Indian, and Malay cultural events are limited to sporadic performances and festivals; the STPB can provide you with schedules of current and upcoming shows. Some commercial shows focusing on Asian culture are given nightly for tourists (☞ Cultural Shows, *below*). Indian music, drama, and dance performances are staged during some of the major festivals at the more important temples, including the Sri Mariamman Temple (⊠ South Bridge Road) and the Chettiar Temple (⊠ Tank Road). Themes are from the ancient epics—tales of gods, demons, and heroes.

Singapore is weakest in the area of serious international theater and classical concerts, though this is changing. The best of what there is may be found at the **Victoria Theatre and Memorial Hall** (⊠ Empress Pl., ☎ 339–6120 information, 338–8283 bookings), in two adjoining Victorian buildings at the Padang. This is home to the 85-member **Singapore Symphony Orchestra,** which since 1979 has built an excellent reputation for its large repertoire of well-known classics and works by local and Asian composers. Several times a year, festivals featuring music and dance groups from all over Southeast Asia are held in these auditoriums. Also presented here from time to time are performances by Singapore's various theatrical and operatic societies, Chinese opera, and Indian classical dance.

Chinese Opera

The dramatic *wayangs* (Chinese operas) reenact Chinese legend through powerful movement, lavish costumes, outrageous masks, and heavy makeup. Performances are held on temporary stages set up near temples, in market areas, or outside apartment complexes. They are staged all year, but most frequently in August and September, during the Festival of the Hungry Ghosts. Contact the STPB for dates and performance. Street performances are free. Performances by registered theatrical groups, such as the Chinese Theatrical Circle (☎ 235-2911), which performs at different venues, including the Victoria Theatre and Memorial Hall, are not.

The wayangs, based on legend, are full of action. Gongs and drums beat, devils leap, maidens weep, and heroes reap the praise of an enraptured audience. The characters are fancifully weird—take a look behind the stage and watch the actors apply their makeup—and gorgeously costumed. With Chinese television programming mostly in Mandarin, street wayangs—spoken in dialect, though totally different from the conversational dialect—have become popular with the older generation, who rarely have a chance to be entertained in their own language.

Do try to seek out a wayang. It is an experience you will not quickly forget. And don't be bashful about asking a fellow spectator who the characters portrayed are.

Concerts

The **Singapore Symphony Orchestra** gives concerts on Friday and Saturday evenings twice a month at the Victoria Theatre and Memorial Hall. Tickets cost S$6–S$30 and are available at SISTIC (☎ 348–5555) outlets at Scotts Shopping Centre, Forum Galleria, Raffles City, Specialists Centre, Liang Court Complex, and Takashimaya Shopping Centre (☞ Shopping Centers *in* Chapter 7) or at the box office, Monday through Saturday 10 to 6 and up to 8:30 on the night of the concert. Tickets may be reserved by telephone (☎ 338–8283); American Express and Visa are accepted.

Nanyang Academy of Fine Arts Chinese Orchestra (☎ 338–9176) gives regular concerts featuring traditional Chinese instruments producing classics and folk tunes. Performances are given at the Victoria Theatre and Memorial Hall four times a year. Tickets run from S$5 to S$15. Three times a year, the 70-member **Chinese Orchestra of the Singapore Broadcasting Corporation** (☎ 338–1230 or 256–0401, ext. 2732) performs Chinese classical music at the Victoria. Tickets are S$5–S$10.

Infrequently, the **People's Association Indian Orchestra** (☎ 440–9353) and the **Indian Fine Arts Society Orchestra** (☎ 270–0722) perform at the Victoria Theatre and Memorial Hall.

Cultural Shows

"ASEAN Night" at the Mandarin Hotel offers traditional songs and dances from the various countries of ASEAN (the Association of South East Asian Nations): Singapore, Indonesia, Malaysia, Thailand, Brunei, and the Philippines. The shows are held poolside, and dinner is available during performances ⊠ *333 Orchard Rd.,* ☎ *737–4411.* 🍴 *Dinner and show S$46.50, show S$26.25.* ☉ *Tues.–Sun., dinner at 7, show at 7:45.*

The **"Cultural Wedding Show"** is a 45-minute re-creation of a Peranakan wedding ceremony. The presentation is part of a three-hour immersion in the culture of Straits-born Chinese that includes a tour of Peranakan Place's Show House Museum and dinner at Bibi's restaurant, serving Nonya food. ⊠ *Peranakan Pl., 180 Orchard Rd.,* ☎ *732–6966.* 🍴 *S$36.* ☉ *Weeknights at 6:30.*

"Instant Asia" is a 45-minute revue of Chinese, Indian, and Malay dance at Singa Inn Seafood Restaurant. The show begins with the clash of cymbals and gongs and the beat of drums that accompany a traditional Chinese lion dance. The subsequent "Harvest Dance" sets quite a different mood as a graceful Malay troupe performs, lighted candles in each hand. Indian dancers then take the stage, telling stories in mime while snake charmers play their flutes. At the end, members of the audience are invited to participate—perhaps to dangle a python around their necks or join the dancers in mime. Although clichéd and commercial, it's fun if you've never seen this kind of thing before. ⊠ *920 East Coast Pkwy.,* ☎ *345–1111.* ▣ *S$5, free to diners.* ⊘ *Weeknights at 7:30.*

"Malam Singapura" is the Hyatt Regency's colorful 45-minute show of song and dance (mostly Malay) performed poolside with or without dinner. ⊠ *10–12 Scotts Rd.,* ☎ *733–1188.* ▣ *Dinner and show S$38, show S$18.* ⊘ *Nightly, dinner at 7, show at 8.*

Raffles Jubilee Hall, a 392-seat Victorian theater, presents an hourly audiovisual history of Raffles against the backdrop of Singapore. At noon only, 20 local artists put on the 25-minute, multiethnic "Life and Times of Singapore." ⊠ *328 North Bridge Rd.,* ☎ *331–1732.* ▣ *S$5, noon show S$10.* ⊘ *Daily (hourly) 10–3.*

Dance

Performances are given throughout the year by the **Singapore Ballet Academy** (☎ 737–5772) and the **Sylvia McCully** dance group (☎ 457–6995), which perform a combination of ballet and jazz. Periodic performances by various companies, such as the **Singapore Dance Theatre,** are given at The Green, Fort Canning Park. Notices for these are printed in the local papers. Take along a picnic before the show; they usually start at about 7 PM.

Theater

Theatreworks (☎ 280–0188) is a professional drama company focusing on contemporary works. **Act 3** (☎ 734–9090) concentrates on children's plays. **Stars** (☎ 468–9145) is a community theater that performs family shows, such as American musicals and Christmas specials, as well as classic and modern dramas. **Hi! Theatre** (☎ 468–1945) is Singapore's theater for those who are deaf; its mask, mime, black-light, and sign-language performances appeal to everybody.

Occasionally the **Kallang Theatre** (⊠ Stadium Walk, ☎ 345–8488) imports some London plays and Broadway hits, though they usually serve up local companies in a large-capacity facility. **Harbour Pavilion** (⊠ 1 Maritime Square, World Trade Centre, ☎ 321–1972) also stages local shows and sometimes brings in a foreign touring company to perform a Broadway production. To experience the work of local playwrights and actors, find out what's happening at the **Drama Centre** (⊠ Fort Canning Rise, ☎ 336–0005); tickets cost S$12–S$25. For foreign musicals, comedies, and films, check out the program at the **Raffles Jubilee Hall** (☞ Cultural Shows, *above*); tickets run S$12–S$25.

6 Outdoor Activities and Sports

From biking and hiking to golf and tennis to waterskiing and windsurfing, the Garden Isle offers land and water sports in scenic settings.

Updated by
Christine Hill

SINGAPORE IS ONE OF THE BEST CITIES IN ASIA for outdoor activities, despite the heat, for it's one of few that are not polluted. The government has taken care to set aside a significant portion of the island for recreation, so you can choose anything from waterskiing to a jungle hike to beach volleyball. Be sure to drink lots of water, and try to schedule the most strenuous activities in early morning or late afternoon.

BEACHES AND WATER PARKS

East Coast Park. This park stretches for 8 kilometers (5 miles) on recently reclaimed land between the new airport road and the seashore. Here you'll find well-planned recreational facilities, including an excellent beach and a water-sports lagoon where you can rent sailboards, canoes, and sailboats. If you prefer swimming in a pool, the **Aquatic Centre** has four—including a wave pool—as well as a giant water slide called the Big Splash. "Holiday chalets" set among the palm trees beside the beach can be rented by the day. Restaurants and changing facilities are available.

Sentosa Island. Billed as Singapore's leisure resort, Sentosa offers a range of recreational facilities in addition to its museums, waxworks, musical fountains, and other attractions (☞ Chapter 2). There is a reasonable beach and a swimming lagoon, with changing and refreshment facilities, as well as rowboats, sailboards, and canoes for rent. You can camp here, play golf or tennis, roller-skate, or join the weekend-long beach volleyball tournaments and games. Do not expect seclusion on the weekend—the island gets very crowded. Midweek is much better.

Nearby Islands. The islands of **Kusu** and **St. John's** have reasonable small beaches and swimming facilities. On weekends, they are crowded with locals. For information on transportation to the islands, *see* Chapter 2.

Desaru, Malaysia. The best beach area near Singapore is on peninsular Malaysia, 100 kilometers (60 miles) east of Johore Bahru. It takes a little over two hours to drive there (slightly longer by bus) but makes a great retreat, especially if you've got a weekend to spare. There are excellent beaches and lots of resort-type activities on the water, as well as an 18-hole golf course (rental equipment is available). You can charter a taxi from Johore Bahru for about M$60 (US$23), but it's easier to take the 450-passenger, 80-vehicle catamaran **Tropic Chief,** which makes a 45-minute run between the Marine Terminal at Changi and Tanjung Belungkar; from there a coach makes the 32-kilometer (20-mile) run to Desaru. Contact **Ferrylink** (✉ Changi Ferry Rd., ☎ 733–6744; S$18 one-way; reservations essential). For overnight accommodations, Desaru has two hotels and several chalets (the Desaru View Hotel will collect you from Singapore). For more information, *see* Chapter 8.

PARTICIPANT SPORTS

Archery
The **Archery Club of Singapore** (✉ 5 Binchang Walk, ☎ 258–1140) welcomes enthusiasts.

Bicycling
You can rent a bike from one of the many **bicycle kiosks** that dot designated bike paths. Rates are about S$3–S$8 an hour, with a deposit of S$20–S$50. The best places to look for signs pointing to the kiosks

are in the East Coast Park and around Sentosa Island. Other places to try are Pasir Ris, Bishan, and Pulau Ubin, an island on Singapore's northeast coast. Cycling through the beaches and parks along the highway to the airport is a very pleasant way to see this part of the island.

Bowling

There are a number of bowling centers in Singapore. **Kallang Bowl** (⌧ Leisure-Dome, 5 Stadium Walk, Kallang Park, ☎ 345–0545), with 62 lanes, claims to be the largest in Southeast Asia. Under the same ownership and in the same building is the **Kallang Bowlers Dome,** with 30 computerized lanes. Other alleys include **Jackie's Bowl** (⌧ 452B East Coast Rd., ☎ 241–6519; ⌧ 8 Grange Rd., ☎ 737–4744), **Pasir Panjang Bowl** (⌧ 269 Pasir Panjang Rd., ☎ 775–5555), and **Plaza Bowl** (⌧ Textile Centre, 8th floor, Jalan Sultan, ☎ 292–4821). The cost per string is about S$2.80 on weekdays before 6 PM, S$3.90 on weekends and after 7 PM weekdays.

Flying

The **Republic of Singapore Flying Club** (⌧ East Camp Bldg., 140B Seletar Airbase, ☎ 481–0502 or 481–0200) offers visiting membership to qualified pilots and has aircraft available for hire (approximately S$270 per hour plus S$65 per hour for a temporary one-month membership). You cannot fly solo unless you have a Singapore license. A piloted ride for up to three people can be arranged for about S$270 an hour and is a superb way to see the island.

Golf

Some of the top Singapore hotels, including the Oriental, have special arrangements for guests at local golf clubs. For example, they may make all the necessary bookings, including equipment reservations, at the club of your choice and arrange for a limousine to take you there (about S$225 for a round). You might check before leaving home to see whether your club has any reciprocal arrangements with a Singapore club. Several excellent Singapore golf clubs accept nonmembers, though some limit this practice to weekdays.

Changi Golf Club is a hilly nine-hole course on 50 acres that's open to nonmembers on weekdays. ⌧ *345 Netheravon Rd.,* ☎ *545–5133. Greens fee: S$41.20. Caddy fee: S$25.*

Jurong Country Club has an 18-hole, par 71 course on 120 acres. Half the holes are on flat terrain and the other nine on small hills. ⌧ *9 Science Centre Rd.,* ☎ *560–5655. Greens fee: S$123.60 weekdays, S$185.40 weekends and public holidays. Caddy fee: S$25.75.*

Keppel Club is the nearest 18-hole course to the city. ⌧ *Bukit Chermin,* ☎ *273–5522. Greens fee: S$123.60 Tues.–Fri., S$185.40 weekends and public holidays. Caddy fee: S$40. Closed Mon.*

Seletar Country Club is considered the best nine-hole course on the island. The course was laid out in 1932 by the Royal Air Force. ⌧ *Seletar Airbase,* ☎ *481–4746. Greens fee: S$45 for non-Singaporeans (for 9 holes) Tues.–Fri., S$60 on weekends and public holidays. No caddies. Trolley fee: S$4.*

Sembawang Country Club is an 18-hole, par 70 course. It is known as the commando course for its hilly terrain. There are also squash courts available. ⌧ *17 Km Sembawang Rd.,* ☎ *257–0642. Greens fee: S$113.30 weekdays, S$139.05 weekends and public holidays. Includes golf cart. No caddies.*

Sentosa Golf Club permits visitors to play on the 18-hole, par 71 **Tanjong course** on the southeastern tip of the island. The 18-hole **Serapong**

course is also open to nonmembers on weekdays; but both courses are restricted to members on weekends and public holidays. ⊠ *Sentosa Island,* ☎ *275–0022. Greens fee: Tanjong, S$164.80 mornings, S$185.50 afternoons; Serapong, S$123.60 mornings, S$144.20 afternoons. Includes golf cart. No caddies. Golf clubs: S$15 steel, S$20 graphite.*

Singapore Island Country Club has four 18-hole, par 71 courses: two at Upper Thomson Road and two (including the world-class Bukit course) on Sime Road. There are clubhouse facilities at both locations. Nonmembers can play Monday, Wednesday, and Friday before 10 AM, and must pay in cash. ⊠ *180 Island Rd.,* ☎ *459–2222; the Bukit clubhouse is at 240 Sime Rd.,* ☎ *466–2244. Greens fee: S$206. Caddy fee: S$28.*

Horseback Riding

There is no organized riding stable for visitors. However, arrangements may be made through the **Singapore Polo Club** (⊠ Thomson Rd., ☎ 256–4530).

Hotel Fitness Facilities

For all addresses and telephones, *see* Chapter 4.

The **Shangri-La** has a good-size outdoor pool and a smaller one indoors; a modern health club with a Universal gym, stationary bikes, running treadmills, and other equipment; tennis and squash courts; and a three-hole golf course, where you can jog in the early morning.

The **Oriental** has a jogging track, tennis and squash courts, and a splendid outdoor pool with an underwater sound system and a view of the harbor. The fifth-floor health club includes a hot tub, massage, steam and sauna rooms for men and for women, free weights, a Universal gym, stationary bikes, running treadmills, and individual trainers.

The **Mandarin** has squash and tennis courts, an outdoor pool, a gym with Nautilus-type equipment, a Universal gym, a running treadmill, free weights, individual trainers, steam room, sauna, massage, and a mini–golf course suitable for a quick jog.

The **Pan Pacific** has a modern fitness center with computer-monitored equipment, free weights, Nautilus, and trainers on duty, plus an outdoor pool and tennis courts; it is on the bay, a good place for an invigorating jog.

The **Hyatt Regency** has a kidney-shaped pool, tennis courts, and an ultramodern fitness center with Nautilus equipment, free weights, Universal gym, sauna, massage, and trainers on duty.

Jogging

Singapore is a great place for joggers. There are numerous parks, and a number of leading hotels offer jogging maps. Serious joggers can tackle the 10-kilometer (6.2-mile) **East Coast Parkway track,** then cool off with a swim at the park's sandy beach. One of the most delightful places to run is the **Botanic Gardens** (off Holland Road and not far from Orchard Road), where you can jog on the paths or on the grass until 11 at night. The best time to run in Singapore is in the morning or evening; avoid the midday sun. It is safe for a woman to run alone. Remember to look right when crossing the road—in the British manner, driving is on the left. Several full or half marathons are organized in Singapore during the year.

Roller-Skating

Sentosa Island has a rink that is said to be the largest in Southeast Asia. 🎫 *Free; skate rentals: S$2 per hr.* ☉ *Weekdays 9–6, weekends 9–8.*

Sailing

If you introduce yourself at the **Changi Sailing Club** (⊠ Netheravon Rd., ☎ 545–2876), you should be able to find a berth crewing on one of the weekend races. Sunfish and sailboards may be rented at the **Europa Sailing Club** (⊠ 1210 East Coast Pkwy., ☎ 449–5118). Sailboat rentals are also available on **Sentosa Island** (☞ Beaches and Water Parks, *above*).

Scuba Diving

The waters around Singapore are polluted, thanks to the thousands of ships that anchor offshore and to the oil refineries. Better diving is found off the nearby islands, though the currents are treacherous. Contact the **Singapore Club Aquanaut** (⊠ 1 Tanglin Rd., Orchard Parade Hotel Podium Block #03–253A, ☎ 733–5976) for information on local opportunities. For a dive shop that runs trips to the outer islands, try the **Great Blue Dive Shop** (⊠ 03–05 Holland Village Shopping Centre, 211 Holland Ave., ☎ 467–0767) or **Asia Aquatic** (7–37 Cuppage Centre, ☎ 536–8116).

Squash and Racquetball

Several hotels have their own squash courts (☞ Hotel Fitness Facilities, *above*), and there are numerous public squash and racquetball courts available. Among them are **Alexandra Park** (⊠ Royal Rd. off York Rd., ☎ 473–7236), **Kallang Squash and Tennis Centre** (⊠ National Stadium, Kallang, ☎ 440–6839), and **Singapore Squash Centre** (⊠ Fort Canning Rise, ☎ 336–0155). Courts cost around S$10 an hour, depending on the time of day.

Swimming

Virtually all Singapore hotels have swimming pools. There are also 19 public swimming complexes, the best of which are superb (☞ Beaches and Water Parks, *above*). The **Singapore Swimming Club** is at Tanjong Rhu Road (☎ 345–2122).

Tennis

The top hotels have their own tennis courts, and several public clubs welcome visitors: **Alexandra Park, Farrer Park,** and **Kallang Squash and Tennis Centre** (☞ Squash and Racquetball, *above*) all have courts. Also try the **Singapore Tennis Centre** (⊠ 1020 East Coast Pkwy., ☎ 442–5966) and **Tanglin Tennis Courts** (⊠ Minden Rd., ☎ 473–7236). Court costs range from S$7 to S$12 an hour, depending on the time of day.

Waterskiing

The center of activity is Ponggol, a village in northeastern Singapore. **Ponggol Water Ski Centre** (⊠ 17th Ave., Ponggol, ☎ 386–3891) charges S$60 an hour weekdays, S$70 an hour on weekends for a boat with ski equipment. Some of the local boats are for hire at considerably lower rates—about S$40 an hour. Negotiate directly, and make sure the proper safety equipment is available. Another popular venue for waterskiing is along the Kallang River, where the recent world championships were held. For rentals, try **Bernatt Boating and Skiing** (⊠ 62C Kg Wak Hassan, ☎ 257–5859); S$25 buys you six runs along a slalom course.

Windsurfing

At the **Europa Sailing Centre** (⊠ 1210 East Coast Pkwy., ☎ 449–5118), sailboards rent for S$20 for two hours, S$10 per hour thereafter. Half-day lessons are available weekdays 2–6 PM for S$90, minimum three people per class and subject to the availability of instructors. Windsurfing is available on **Sentosa Island** (☞ Beaches and Water Parks, *above*) from 9:30 to 6:30.

SPECTATOR SPORTS

In addition to the sports listed below, international matches of golf, tennis, cycling, formula motor racing, swimming, badminton, and squash are held on and off. Some of these attract top professionals from abroad, and it may be easier to see them here than in countries where competitions are more heavily attended. Most events are detailed in the newspapers; information is also available from the **National Sports Council** (☏ 345–7111). A number of tourist-oriented events—such as the International Dragon Boat Races, an international kite-flying festival, and powerboat races—are organized annually.

Cricket

From March through September, games take place on the Padang grounds in front of the old **Cricket Club** (☏ 338–9271) every Saturday at 1:30 PM and every Sunday at 11 AM. Entrance to the club during matches is restricted to members, but you can watch from the sides of the playing field. Refreshments are available in the park on the seaward side of the main road.

Polo

The **Singapore Polo Club** (✉ Thomson Rd., ☏ 256–4530) is quite active, with both local and international matches. Spectators are welcome to watch Tuesday, Thursday, Saturday, and Sunday matches, played in the late afternoon.

Rugby

Rugby is played on the **Padang** grounds in front of the Singapore Cricket Club. Kickoff is usually at 5:30 PM on Saturdays from September through March.

Soccer

Soccer is the major sport of Singapore; important matches take place in the **National Stadium** at Kallang. Details are published in the daily papers, and ticket reservations can be made through the **National Sports Council**. The main season is September through March.

Track and Field

In recent years, most Asian countries have become keen on track-and-field events. Singapore has the **National Stadium** at Kallang for major events, plus nine athletic centers with tracks. International meets are usually detailed in the daily press and arouse considerable nationalistic feeling. For information and details on how to book seats for major meets, call the **National Sports Council**.

7 Shopping

You can get just about anything you want in Singapore—for a price. Sleek shopping malls exist cheek by jowl with two-story shophouses and indoor/outdoor markets. Shopping here is a sport to be savored. With persistence and luck, you may find one of Singapore's few remaining bargains.

SINGAPORE IS TRULY A SHOPPING FANTASYLAND. What makes it so is the incredible range of goods brought in from all over the world to be sold in an equally incredible number of shops. Unfortunately, though, the bargain prices for which Singapore was once famous no longer exist. The intense competition among shops prevents them from buying and selling in volume. Also, with a growing economy and a standard of living second in Asia only to Japan's, Singapore has a strong dollar and high overheads for importing agents and retail outlets. Concerned that travelers are finally getting the message that Singapore's shopping has become expensive, the Singapore Tourist Promotion Board has initiated an annual shopping promotion in July, the "Great Singapore Sale." Bargains can be found, but it's mostly a gimmick, with banners and flags and a competition for the best dressed shop window.

Updated by Christine Hill

More often than not, prices on fashion and on most manufactured items are higher than in the United States. You should know the prices of goods you intend to buy before you leave home. This is especially true of photographic and electronic equipment. Prices do not vary a great deal from shop to shop. Compare a few shops to feel secure about your price. There are still some good buys on handcrafted rosewood furniture, Chinese objets d'art, and carpets. In general, though, if you are heading farther into Southeast Asia, you may want to delay your shopping until Kuala Lumpur or Bangkok for clothing and crafts and Indonesia for crafts and batiks.

When shopping, look for the Singapore Tourist Promotion Board logo—a gold Merlion (a lion's head with a fish tail) on a red background. This signifies that the retailer is a member of the Good Retailers Scheme. Members need to be approved by the Consumers' Association of Singapore and the STPB. Shops that have fixed prices often have a FIXED PRICE STORE sign on the entrance and on their price tags, while the price tags in stores that allow bargaining often say "recommended price."

Shopping Essentials

Bargaining

Bargaining is widely practiced in Singapore. In determining whether or not a shop discounts, the first thing to look at is the type of store. Department stores and chain stores do not offer discounts—their items are tagged with fixed prices. Other stores have the sign FIXED PRICE STORE hanging on the window and may be reluctant to discount. It's a good idea to visit a department store first to get an idea of established prices, then shop around. If you do not like to bargain, stick to the department stores, which usually have the lowest initial ("first") price.

Local shops in upscale shopping complexes or malls tend to give a 10% discount, sometimes 15%, on clothes. However, at a jewelry store, the discount can be as high as 50%, and carpet dealers also give hefty reductions. At less-upscale complexes, the discounts tend to be greater, especially if the vendors view you as a tourist—that will boost their initial asking price. Stalls and shops around tourist attractions have the highest initial prices, so bargaining here yields deep discounts.

Everyone has his or her own method of bargaining, but in general, when a vendor tells you a price, ask for the discounted price, then offer even less. The person will probably reject your offer but come down a few dollars. With patience, this can continue and earn you a few more dollars off the price. If you don't like haggling, walk away after hearing the discounted price. If the vendor hasn't hit bottom price, you'll be called back.

Complaints

Complaints about either a serious disagreement with a shopkeeper or the purchase of a defective product should be lodged with the STPB (✉ Tourism Court, 1 Orchard Spring Lane, Singapore 247729, ☎ 736–6622). Give full details of the complaint, and the STPB's Tourism Services Division will pursue it. The Consumers Association of Singapore (✉ 164 Bukit Merah Central, #04–3625, Singapore 150164, ☎ 270–4611) can also advise you regarding a vendor-related complaint. If you do encounter retailer malpractice, you can get full redress through the Small Claims Tribunals—something retailers dread, because the STPB publishes the names and addresses of miscreants ordered by the tribunals to make redress to tourists.

Electrical Goods

Singapore's current is 220–240 volts at 50 cycles, similar to Australia's, Great Britain's, and Hong Kong's. Canada, Japan, and the United States use 110–120 volts at 60 cycles. When buying electrical equipment, verify that you can acquire special adapters, if required, and that these will not affect the equipment's performance.

Guarantees

Make sure you get international guarantees and warranty cards with your purchases. Check the serial number of each item against its card, and don't forget to mail the card in. Sometimes guarantees are limited to the country of purchase. If the dealer cannot give you a guarantee, he is probably selling an item intended for the domestic market in its country of manufacture; if so, he has bypassed the authorized agent and should be able to give you a lower price, but that is not always the case. Though your purchase of the item is not illegal, you have no guarantee. If you decide to buy it anyway, be sure to check that the item is in working order before you leave the shop.

How to Pay

All department stores and most shops accept credit cards—American Express, Diners Club, MasterCard, and Visa—and many tourist shops also accept Carte Blanche. Traveler's checks are readily accepted, and many tourist shops will also accept foreign currency, but it is better to change traveler's checks and foreign currency at a bank before shopping. Check the exchange rates before agreeing to any price—some store owners try to skim extra profit by giving an unfair rate of exchange. Retailers work at a low profit margin and depend on high turnover; they assume you will pay in cash. Except at the department stores, paying with a credit card will mean that your "discounted price" will reflect the commission the retailer will have to pay the credit card company.

Imitations

Copyright laws passed in early 1987 impose stern penalties on the selling of pirated music tapes and computer software. However, Singapore still has a reputation for pirated goods. If you are buying a computer, for example, stores are quite amenable to loading it with all the software you want.

Street stalls or bargain shops have designer-label merchandise for ridiculously low prices; they are all fakes. Sport shirts with famous-name labels and logos—Lacoste, Pierre Cardin, Giordano—filter in from Thailand and Hong Kong. Deeply discounted leather goods with such labels as Cartier, Etienne Aigner, and Gucci at these shops are most certainly frauds.

Street peddlers sell quartz watches, mainly from Taiwan, bearing the names of great Swiss or French watchmakers or European design houses for about S$30; they are fakes. The greatest of the fakes is the "solid gold Rolex," which comes complete with serial number for S$100. It looks so good you could have a problem at Customs—though you're more likely to have a Customs problem (either in Singapore or at home) if you're discovered to have purchased a counterfeit item.

Receipts

Be sure to ask for receipts, both for your own protection and for Customs. Though shopkeepers are often amenable to stating false values on receipts, Customs officials are wary and knowledgeable.

Shipping

All stores that deal with valuable, fragile, or bulky merchandise know how to pack well. Ask for a quote on shipping charges, which you can then double-check with a local forwarder. Check whether the shop has insurance covering both loss and damage in transit. You might find you need additional coverage.

Touts

Touting—soliciting business by approaching people on the street with offers of free shopping tours and special discounts—is illegal (maximum fines were raised from S$200 to S$5,000 in 1989, and prison sentences of up to six months are possible). Nevertheless, it continues inside one or two shopping centers, especially Lucky Plaza. Each shopping center has its band of men looking for people to interest in their special stash of fake designer watches. The touts in front of the Tudor Court Shopping Centre at the top of Tanglin Road can be particularly bothersome. Some taxi drivers tout as well. Avoid all touts and the shops they recommend. The prices will end up being higher—reflecting the tout's commission—and the quality of the goods possibly inferior. A reputable shop does not need touts.

Shopping Districts

Throughout the city are complexes full of shopping areas and centers. Many stores will have branches carrying much the same merchandise in several of these areas.

Orchard Road

The heart of Singapore's preeminent shopping district, Orchard Road is bordered on both sides with tree-shaded tiled sidewalks lined with modern shopping complexes and deluxe hotels that house exclusive boutiques. Also considered part of this area are the shops on Scotts Road, which crosses Orchard, and two shopping centers—**Supreme House** on Penang Road and **Singapore Shopping Centre** on Clemenceau Avenue—at the end of Orchard Road, where it detours at Plaza Singapura, next to the Istana.

Orchard Road is known for fashion and interior design shops, but you can find anything from Mickey Mouse watches to Chinese paper kites and antique Korean chests. The interior design shops have unusual Asian bric-a-brac and such original items as a lamp stand made from an old Chinese tea canister or a pair of bookends in the shape of Balinese frogs. Virtually every Orchard Road complex, with the exception of the Promenade, has a clutch of department stores selling electronic goods, cigarette lighters, pens, jewelry, cameras, and so on. Most also have money changers, a few inexpensive cafés, and snack bars.

Though there is reference to an "Orchard Road price," which takes into account the astronomical rents some shop tenants have to pay, the department stores have the same fixed prices here as at all their branches. Small shops away from the center may have slightly cheaper prices.

Chinatown

Once Singapore's liveliest and most colorful shopping area, Chinatown lost a great deal of its vitality when the street stalls were moved indoors, but it is still fun to explore. The focus is on the Smith, Temple, and Pagoda street blocks, but nearby streets—Eu Tong Sen Street, Wayang Street, and Merchant Road on one side, and Ann Siang Hill and Club Street on another—can yield some interesting finds.

The old street vendors have moved into the **Kreta Ayer Complex,** off Neil Road; the **Chinatown Complex,** off Trengganu Street; and the **People's Park Centre,** on Eu Tong Sen Street. Most sell market goods, but here and there you'll find a booth with odds and ends of jade or porcelain.

Chinese kitchenware can be fascinating. On Temple Street in particular you can find a wealth of unusual plates, plant pots, teapots, lacquered chopsticks, and so on.

All the paraphernalia for Chinese funerals is sold in a number of shops in Chinatown, especially around Sago Street. Nearby Sago Lane was lined, not so long ago, with "death houses," where elderly people went to await death. This may sound gruesome, but these funerary items are among the most creative examples of folk art in the world. They include paper replicas of life's necessities, to serve the dead in their afterlife. You can even buy paper servants, a paper Mercedes, or—the height of this artwork—a paper Boeing 747. There are some famous funeral-paper craftsmen on Ann Siang Hill, where there is also a shop that can sell you a lion's head (made of fabric over a wire frame) like those used in the Chinese lion dance.

Just around the corner, on Club Street, are several wood-carvers who specialize in creating idols of Chinese gods. On Merchant Road, a vendor of costumes for Chinese operas welcomes customers. And on Chin Hin Street, you can buy a package of fragrant Chinese tea direct from the merchant.

South Bridge Road in Chinatown is the street of goldsmiths. There are dozens of jewelers here, specializing in 22K and even 24K gold ornaments in the characteristic orange color of Chinese gold. Each assistant, often shielded by a metal grill, uses an abacus and a balance to calculate the value of the piece you wish to buy. You must bargain here. South Bridge Road is also home to many art galleries.

At **Fook On** (✉ 83–85 South Bridge Rd., ☎ 532–3239) you can buy all your winter clothes, whether you prefer Chinese or Western styles. Seal carvers in the **Hong Lim Shopping Centre** will carve your name into your own personal "chop."

Of the shopping areas along Eu Tong Sen Street, the most famous is the **People's Park Complex,** where every shop promises a bargain. There are lots of watch and camera shops here, and the **Overseas Emporium** (☎ 535–0555) is a wonderful place to explore. In the next block is **People's Park Centre,** which is not as lively but has an emporium, too, as well as shopkeepers who are easier to deal with. Neither complex opens before noon.

Little India

Serangoon Road is affectionately known as Little India. For shopping purposes, it begins at the **Zhu Jiao Centre,** on the corner of Serangoon and Buffalo roads. Some of the junk dealers and inexpensive-clothing stalls from a bazaar known as Thieves Market were relocated here when the market was cleared out. This is a fun place to poke about.

All the handicrafts of India can be found on Serangoon Road: intricately carved wood tables, shining brass trays and water ewers, hand-loomed table linens, fabric inlaid with tiny mirrors, brightly colored pictures of Hindu deities, and even garlands of jasmine for the gods.

And the sari shops! At dozens of shops here you can get the 6 meters (6.5 yards) of voile, cotton, Kashmiri silk, or richly embroidered Benares silk required to make a sari. For the variety, quality, and beauty of the silk, the prices are very low. Other Indian costumes, such as long or short kurtas (men's collarless shirts) and Punjabi trouser sets, are unusual and attractive buys.

Should you overspend and find yourself with excess baggage, there are several luggage shops on Serangoon Road where you can buy an old-fashioned tin trunk big enough to hide a body in.

Arab Street
The Arab Street shopping area really begins at Beach Road, opposite the Plaza Hotel. This old-fashioned street is full of noteworthy buys. A group of basket and rattan shops first catches your eye. There are quite a few jewelers here, and even more shops selling loose gems and necklaces of garnet and amethyst beads. The main business is batiks (textiles bearing hand-printed designs) and lace.

Brassware, prayer rugs, carpets, and leather slippers are sold in abundance on Arab Street and its side streets, which have appealing names like Muscat Street and Baghdad Street. Two noteworthy complexes in the vicinity are the **Golden Mile Food Centre,** on Beach Road, devoted to good food on the lower floors and junk and antiques on the top floors, and the **Textile Centre,** on Jalan Sultan, offering a wide variety of batiks.

Katong
The quiet east-coast suburb of Katong, just 15 minutes from town via the expressway, has old-fashioned shophouses along its main street, some selling inexpensive children's clothes and one dealing in antiques. Off the main road is an even more old-fashioned street called Joo Chiat Road, which gets more and more interesting as it approaches Gelang Road. Its shops sell Chinese kitchenware, antiques, baby clothes, and lots of offbeat items.

Holland Village
Holland Village, 10 minutes from town by taxi, is a bit of a Yuppie haunt, but it is the most rewarding place to browse for unusual and inexpensive Asian items, large and small. Many shops here specialize in Korean chests. Behind the main street is Lorong Mambong, a street of shophouses jammed with baskets, earthenware, porcelain, and all sorts of things from China and Thailand. The **Holland Village Shopping Centre** on Holland Avenue has quite a few shops, including **Lim's Arts and Crafts** (☎ 467–1300), selling inexpensive gifts and souvenirs; there always seems to be something out of the ordinary to pick up here. A 10-minute walk from Holland Village is **Cold Storage Jelita** (⊠ 293 Holland Rd.), with several stores, including **Jessica Art 'N Craft** (☎ 469–0689).

Shopping Centers

Note: Shops in multilevel buildings and shopping complexes are often listed with a numerical designation such as #00-00. The first part of this number indicates what floor the shop is on. The second part indicates its location on the floor. When the phone number of an individual shop is not given in this section, you'll find it listed with the shop under a specific merchandise category, below.

Centrepoint
This spacious and impressive center (⊠ 176 Orchard Rd.) has the **Robinsons** department store as its anchor tenant. One of the liveliest complexes, Centrepoint also has jewelry, silverware, and fashion shops; furniture stores selling Philippine bamboo and Korean chests; and a large basement supermarket.

Delfi Orchard
Also on Orchard Road (⊠ #402), Delfi is full of wedding boutiques and jewelry shops, but **Waterford Wedgwood** and **Selangor Pewter** are also here, along with a well-stocked golf shop.

Far East Plaza
This center (⊠ 14 Scotts Rd.) is where the young and trendy gather to see and be seen. The shops are geared to them, and there's a bargain-basement atmosphere about the place. A forecourt offers fast-food restaurants (including a McDonald's), outdoor tables, and entertaining people-watching.

Forum Galleria
This center (⊠ 583 Orchard Rd.) has a huge **Toys 'R' Us** (☎ 235–4322), as well as an assortment of boutiques.

Liang Court Complex
Liang Court (⊠ 177 River Valley Rd.) is off the beaten track but only five minutes by cab from Orchard Road and worth the drive. The department store **Daimaru** is here, with half of its floor transformed into selected designer boutiques, a pearl specialist, a bookstore, and a silk store.

Lucky Plaza
At this center (⊠ 304 Orchard Rd.), the tenant mix is aimed specifically at the tourist market but has been moving progressively downmarket as shops move to trendier, newer buildings. This is a place to bargain furiously. The many jewelers here are involved in a perpetual price-cutting war, to the delight of shoppers. The American store Kmart is moving out, another victim of Singapore's shopping slump.

Marina Square
Part of an elegant complex, this shopping center includes **Metro** (⊠ ☎ 337–2868) and 200 smaller shops, including the English store **Mothercare** (☎ 337–0388).

Ngen An City
New in 1994, this complex at 391 Orchard Road is taken up mostly by the Japanese store **Takashimaya** (☎ 738–1111), but there are a number of small boutiques as well.

Orchard Point and Orchard Plaza
Side by side on Orchard Road (⊠ #220 and #150), these centers don't have the popular appeal of some other complexes but will reward dedicated shoppers with good finds. Reptile bags can be found in the basement shops of Orchard Point. Orchard Plaza houses a number of brothels. At night, you might want to avoid it.

Palais Renaissance
Across the road from the Hilton Hotel (⊠ 390 Orchard Rd.) is Singapore's newest haute-fashion center. Targeted at the Japanese shopper seeking status labels at high prices, the Palais Renaissance is chic, opulent, and overpriced but a delight to wander through. Boutiques for **Prada, DKNY, Gianni Versace,** and **Krizia** compete as much in the

It helps to be pushy in airports.

Introducing the revolutionary new TransPorter™ from American Tourister.® It's the first suitcase you can push around without a fight. TransPorter's™ exclusive four-wheel design lets you push it in front of you with almost no effort – the wheels take the weight. Or pull it on two wheels if you choose. You can even stack on other bags and use it like a luggage cart.

Stable 4-wheel design.

TransPorter™ is designed like a dresser, with built-in shelves to organize your belongings. Or collapse the shelves and pack it like a traditional suitcase. Inside, there's a suiter feature to help keep suits and dresses from wrinkling. When push comes to shove, you can't beat a TransPorter.™ For more information on how you can be this pushy, call 1-800-542-1300.

Shelves collapse on command.

American Tourister®

Making travel less primitive.®

Your passport around the world.

- Worldwide access
- Operators who speak your language
- Monthly itemized billing

MCI Calling Card

415 555 1234 2244
J.D. SMITH

Use your MCI Card® and these access numbers for an easy way to call when traveling worldwide.

Bahrain†	800-002
Brunei	800-011
China (CC)†	108-12
(Available from most major cities)	
For a Mandarin-speaking operator	108-17
Cyprus ♦†	080-90000
Egypt (CC) ♦†	355-5770
Federated States of Micronesia	624
Fiji	004-890-1002
Guam (CC)†	950-1022
Hong Kong (CC)†	800-1121
India (CC)†	000-127
(Available from most major cities)	
Indonesia (CC) ♦†	001-801-11
Iran ✣	(Special Phones Only)
Israel (CC)†	177-150-2727
Japan (CC) ♦†	
To call U.S. using KDD ■	0039-121
To call U.S. using IDC ■	0066-55-121
Jordan	18-800-001
Korea (CC)†	
To call using KT ■	009-14
To call using DACOM ■	0039-12

Phone Booths ✣	Press Red Button 03, then ✳
Military Bases	550-2255
Kuwait†	800-MCI (800-624)
Lebanon (CC) ✣	600-624
Macao†	0800-131
Malaysia (CC) ♦†	800-0012
Philippines (CC) ♦†	
To call using PLDT ■	105-14
To call using PHILCOM ■	1026-12
For a Tagalog-speaking operator	105-15
Qatar ★	0800-012-77
Saipan (CC) ✣†	950-1022
Saudi Arabia (CC)†	1-800-11
Singapore†	8000-112-112
Sri Lanka	(within Colombo) 440100
	(outside of Colombo) 01-440100
Syria	0800
Taiwan (CC) ♦†	0080-13-4567
Thailand ★†	001-999-1-2001
United Arab Emirates ♦	800-111
Vietnam ●	1201-1022

To sign up for the MCI Card, dial the access number of the country you are in and ask to speak with a customer service representative.

http://www.mci.com

†Automation available from most locations. (CC) Country-to-country calling available. May not be available to/from all international locations. (Canada, Puerto Rico, and U.S. Virgin Islands are considered Domestic Access locations.)
♦ Public phones may require deposit of coin or phone card for dial tone. ✣ Limited availability. ■ International communications carrier.
★ Not available from public pay phones. ● Local service fee in U.S. currency required to complete call.

design of their store as in the design of their merchandise. Perfumes, jewelry, and travel accessories are also expensively represented in this extravagant marbled emporium to make it a one-stop shopping spree for the well-heeled.

The Paragon

One of the glossiest of the shopping centers, the Paragon (⊠ 290 Orchard Rd.) has more than 15 men's fashion boutiques and numbers among its more popular tenants **Gucci** (☎ 734–2528) and the **Metro** department store (☎ 235–2811).

Parkway Parade

This excellent and very attractive center is on Marine Parade Road, 15 to 20 minutes east of town by expressway. On weekdays you can shop here in peace and quiet; on weekends, it is uncomfortably crowded. The focus is on up-to-date and affordable fashions. Things get started around noon.

People's Park Complex

This Chinatown center (⊠ Eu Tong Sen St.) has an international reputation. It's not new and glossy like most of the other complexes, but it's always entertaining. Everything is sold here: herbs, Chinese medicines, cameras, stereo equipment, clothes, luggage. Shopkeepers are much more aggressive here than in town, and if you haven't done your homework, you can get taken.

The Promenade

The Promenade (⊠ 300 Orchard Rd.) is Singapore's most elegant shopping center, in both design (a spiral walkway with a gentle slope instead of escalators) and tenants. Its fashion stores carry some of the hottest names. Home-decor shops sell a superb collection of Asian odds and ends.

Raffles City

Bordered by Stamford, North Bridge, and Bras Basah roads, this complex has a confusing interior. If you get lost, you're sure to come across many shopping finds, some of them in the Japanese department store **Sogo.** Also here are a **Times** bookshop, fashion boutiques, a post office, and the STPB on the ground floor next to Singapore Airlines. Across the road is the **Raffles Hotel Shopping Complex,** with 60 boutiques selling high fashion and art.

Raffles Place

Overlying the Raffles Place MRT stop, this complex caters mainly to the daily business crowd. One interesting find is **Ming Blue** (⊠ P1-22 Raffles Place, MRT station, ☎ 533–7153), a super place for knick-knacks from all over the Orient.

Scotts Shopping Centre

One of the best places in Singapore for affordable fashion that stops just short of haute couture, Scotts (⊠ 6–8 Scotts Rd.) also has a basement food court with local and delicatessen food, plus activities and demonstrations to keep shoppers entertained.

Shaw Centre

This center (⊠ 1 Scotts Rd.) has been around since the tourist boom of the early 1970s. Among its offerings are a rosewood showroom and a quaint antiques shop.

Shaw House

Isetan (⊠ 350 Orchard Rd., ☎ 733–1111), a large Japanese department store, is the major anchor in this new shopping complex at 350 Orchard Road. You will also find a **Kinokuniya** bookstore (☎ 735–0426) here, excellent for volumes on Japan.

Specialists Centre
This center (⌧ 277 Orchard Rd.) is the home of the **John Little** department store (☏ 737–2222), better known as JL, and assorted boutiques. There is also a **Times** bookshop, where you can pick up something to read over tea and scones at nearby **Fosters** (☏ 737–8939).

Tanglin Shopping Centre
This center, where Orchard Road meets Tanglin Road, has a good selection of antiques shops, especially in a small, self-contained section at ground level. **Moongate**, one of the oldest dealers in fine antique porcelain in Singapore, is here, as is **Antiques of the Orient**, the city's only shop specializing in antique maps. The contemporary interior-design shops are excellent, too.

Wisma Atria
Also on Orchard Road (⌧ #435), this center has several fashion names, such as **Dior** (☏ 734–0374), and the **Isetan** department store. An added attraction of the complex is an aquarium that wraps around the elevator.

Department Stores

Singapore has one homegrown chain. **Metro** offers a wide range of affordable fashions and household products. When shopping for locally designed and manufactured fashion as well as brands such as Esprit, Metro is the best bet. The designs are up-to-the-minute, and the prices are good by local standards and unbelievably good by international standards. Look for Metros in Far East Plaza, Marina Square, and the Paragon.

Tang's (☏ 737–5500), also known as Tang's Superstore or C. K. Tang's, is locally owned, with just one store, next to the Dynasty hotel on Orchard Road (⌧ #320). It looks upmarket, but some of the best buys in town are found here. Its fashions are, at best, improving, but its accessories are excellent—especially the costume jewelry—and its household products are unsurpassed.

Two Chinese department stores under different ownership, but with the same name, **Overseas Emporium,** are in the People's Park Complex (☏ 535–0555) and the People's Park Centre (☏ 535–0967). Both offer basically the same goods: Chinese silk fabric, silk blouses, brocade jackets, crafts, children's clothes, and china.

Singaporeans enjoy Japanese department stores. **Isetan**—in Wisma Atria (⌧ 435 Orchard Rd., ☏ 733–7777), Shaw House (⌧ 350 Orchard Rd., ☏ 733–1111), and Parkway Parade (⌧ Marine Parade Rd., ☏ 345–5555)—always has good specials, and the fashion departments for men and women are well stocked. **Daimaru** (☏ 339–1111), in Liang Court, has some very unusual goods. **Yaohan,** whose biggest store is in Plaza Singapura (☏ 337–4061; others are at Parkway Parade and at Thomson Plaza on Thomson Rd.), is by far the most popular chain; its appliances and audio equipment are very competitive in price. **Sogo** (☏ 339–1100) has opened in Raffles City. The giant **Tokyu** (☏ 337–0077) is in Funan Center.

Both **Printemps,** formerly in the Hotel Meridien on Orchard Road, and **Galeries Lafayette,** formerly in Liat Towers, have fled Singapore's high costs.

The English **Robinsons** (☏ 733–0888), in Centrepoint, is Singapore's oldest department store. It recently shed its fuddy-duddy image and rethought its pricing and is once again one of the best. **John Little** (☏ 737–2222), at the Specialists Centre, has a full range of offerings but is now targeting the young and trendy. The **Marks & Spencers** in the basement of Lane Crawford at the corner of Scotts and Orchard is the biggest of several outlets in town.

Hotel Shopping Arcades

Most of Singapore's hotels have one or two boutiques in their lobbies, but the Hilton has an extensive shopping arcade with designer boutiques.

The **Hilton Shopping Gallery** (⊠ 581 Orchard Rd., ☎ 737–2233) is home to a number of top designer names—**Giorgio Armani, Matsuda, Valentino**—and, through a boutique called **Singora,** many other Italian and French fashion houses. Among its other top-flight tenants are **Gucci, Davidoff, Louis Vuitton, L'Ultimo, Daks of London,** and **Dunhill.**

Other hotels with shopping arcades include the **Hyatt Regency** (⊠ 10–12 Scotts Rd.), with a large shop for **Lanvin** and **Cartier.**

Markets

Food Markets

Stalls crowd upon stalls in a covered, open space to make a hectic, colorful scene where everything edible is sold. The range of foodstuffs is staggering, and some of the items may turn your stomach. The live animals eyed by shoppers will tug at your heartstrings. Usually a food market is divided into two sections: the dry market and the wet market. It is in the latter that squirming fish, crawling turtles, strutting chickens, and cute rabbits are sold for the pot and the floors are continually being sluiced to maintain hygiene. The wet market at the **Chinatown Centre** is the most fascinating; the dry market at **Cuppage Centre** (⊠ on Cuppage Rd., off Orchard Rd.), where the flower stalls are particularly appealing, is a better choice for the squeamish.

Street Markets

Old-style street bazaars have gone now, but in the **Sungei Road** area, site of the once-notorious Thieves Market, a few street vendors creep back each weekend. The stalls sell mainly inexpensive shirts, T-shirts, children's clothes, and underwear, as well as odds and ends such as inexpensive watches, costume jewelry, and sunglasses. A few sell plastic household items.

The **Kreta Ayer** complex in Chinatown may be modern, but it has all the atmosphere of a bazaar. All the street vendors from Chinatown were relocated here. The shops sell cassette tapes, clothing from China, toys, and a lot of gaudy merchandise.

Some of Chinatown's elderly junk peddlers refuse to leave the streets. In the afternoon, they line up along **Temple Street** and lay out a strange variety of goods—old bottles, stamps, bits of porcelain or brass, old postcards, and the like—on cloths.

Shops and stalls also cluster at the new **Bugis Street** mall and at **Telok Ayer,** but the merchandise tends to be overpriced.

There is a small market of souvenir stalls near the food center on **Sentosa Island** on Friday and Saturday nights.

Specialty Shops

Antiques

Some curio dealers style themselves as antiques shops, as do some vendors selling rosewood items or reproduction furniture. Good places to see the genuine articles, if you have no time to explore outside Orchard Road, are the Tanglin Shopping Centre's **Antiques of the Orient** (☎ 734–9351), specializing in maps, ceramics, and furniture, and **Moon-**

gate (☎ 737–6771), for porcelain. Off Orchard Road on Cuppage Road is a row of restored shophouses. Here, **Babazar** (✉ 31A–35A Cuppage Terr., ☎ 235–7866) is full of wonderful finds in jewelry, furniture, clothes, art, knickknacks, and antiques, and **Aizia Discoveries** (✉ 29B Cuppage Rd., ☎ 734–8665) has yet more antiques. **Keng of Tong Mern Sern** (✉ 226 River Valley Rd., ☎ 734–0761), near the Chettiar Temple, has a rabbit warren full of antiques. The store's sign says, "We buy junk, we sell antiques." Strictly speaking, antiques in Singapore are defined as being more than 80 years old. For museum-quality Asian antiques, visit the **Paul Art Gallery** in Holland Park (✉ 62–72 Greenleaf Rd., ☎ 468–4697).

Most antiques stores have a variety of small items—porcelain, brassware, idols, and so on—as well as Chinese furniture, which may be of blackwood inlaid with mother of pearl, or namwood stained red with elaborate carvings picked out in gold. There is a fashion now for Chinese "country furniture," which is carried by **Aizia Discoveries** (☞ *above*). For primitive art and antique Indonesian batik and ikat (a woven fabric of tie-dyed yarns), there is **Tatiana** (☎ 235–3560) in the Tanglin Shopping Centre.

Art

Singapore has more than its share of fine artists. Established names, such as **Chen Wen Hsi** for Chinese brush painting, **Thomas Yeo** for abstract landscapes, and **Anthony Poon** for contemporary graphics, fetch high prices. Among the artists who are gaining recognition are **Wan Soon Kam, Ng Eng Teng** (a sculptor who re-creates the human figure in cement, stoneware, and bronze), **James Tan** (known for his traditional and abstract Chinese brush paintings), and **Teng Juay Lee** (who specializes in orchids). Nostalgic scenes of the Singapore of yesteryear are captured in watercolors and oils by artists such as **Gog Sing Hoi, Ang Ah Tee,** and **Ong Kim Seng,** known for his scenes of the Singapore River and Chinatown. Some delightful paintings can be had for as little as S$300.

For a range of art, try **Art Forum** (☎ 737–3448) and **Raya Gallery** (☎ 732–0298), both in the Promenade. There are also many galleries on South Bridge Road in Chinatown. If you wish to see Chinese calligraphy in action, Yong Cheong Thye works his art at the **Yong Gallery** (✉ 17 Erskin Rd., ☎ 226–1718) in Chinatown.

Batik

A traditional craft item of Singapore, Malaysia, and Indonesia, batik is now also important in contemporary fashion and interior design. **Blue Ginger Design Centre** (☎ 334–1171) and **Design Batik** (☎ 776–4337), both at the Raffles Hotel, sell clothes and fabrics in modern designs. Blue Ginger is especially innovative. Traditional batik sarong lengths can be bought in the shops on Arab Street and in the **Textile Centre** on Jalan Sultan. **Tang's** stores sell inexpensive batik products, including a good range of men's shirts.

Cameras

Photographic equipment may not be the bargain it once was, but the range of cameras and accessories available can be matched only in Hong Kong. It is especially important that you establish the price at home before buying here. Film and film processing remain excellent buys. All department stores carry cameras, and there are so many in Lucky Plaza that you can do all your comparison-shopping in one spot.

If you do not care for negotiating prices, **Cost Plus Electronics** (✉ #B1–21 Scotts Shopping Centre, ☎ 235–1557), something of a supermarket of cameras and electronics, is a good place to shop. The prices are just about as low as you'll find listed in Singapore; no further discounts are given. For more-personalized service try Cathay Photo (☎ 339–6188) in Marina Square. For camera repairs, Goh Gin Camera Service Center (✉ 160 Orchard Rd., ☎ 732–6155) may be able to help you.

Carpets
Carpets are very attractively priced in Singapore. Afghan, Pakistani, Persian, Turkish, and Chinese carpets—both antique and new—are carried by reputable dealers. Carpet auctions, announced in the newspapers, are good places to buy if you know your stuff.

Other good shops include **Qureshi's** (✉ #05–12, ☎ 235–1523) in Centrepoint, **Hassan's** (✉ #01–15, ☎ 737–5626) in the Tanglin Shopping Centre, and **Amir & Sons** (✉ #03–01, ☎ 734–9112) in Lucky Plaza. It is quite acceptable to bargain in these shops—in fact, it's integral to the rather lengthy proceedings.

Curios
Falling halfway between souvenir shops and antiques stores, curio shops sell a fascinating variety of goods, mainly from China. Reverse-glass paintings, porcelain vases, cloisonné, wood carvings, jewelry (agate, jade, lapis lazuli, malachite), ivory carvings, embroidery, and idols represent just a fraction of the treasure trove. These shops, such as the Orchard Towers' **Chen Yee Shen** (✉ #01–12, ☎ 737–1174) and **Ivory Palace** (✉ ☎ 737–1169), are great places for those who seek the unusual.

Fun Fashion
In department stores and small boutiques all over the island—but especially on Orchard Road—locally made women's fashions and Japanese imports sell for a song. Brands like Chocolate and Ananas offer colorful, reasonably made, very fashionable garments. Two of the better-known boutiques are **Mondi** (✉ 300 The Promenade, ☎ 738–1318; #03–36 Centrepoint, ☎ 734–9672) and **Trend,** with two locations (✉ Centrepoint, ☎ 235–9446; ✉ Plaza Singapura, ☎ 337–1038).

Shoes are good buys, too, especially in the **Metro** and **Tang's** department stores, but sizes here are smaller than in the West, and some women have a problem getting the right fit.

High Fashion
Singapore has its own designers: **Tan Yoong** has his shop in Lucky Plaza (☎ 734–3783), and **Benny Ong** (who is based in London) sells through Tang's and China Silk House (☞ Silk, *below*).

For European couture, check the arcades of the Hilton International and the Mandarin, as well as the more fashionable shopping centers, especially the Palais Renaissance. **Lanvin** (☎ 235–4039) is at the Hyatt Regency; **Gucci** is in the Hilton (☎ 732–3298) and the Paragon (☎ 734–2528); **L'Ultimo** (☎ 734–0456) is in the Hilton; **Sonia Rykiel** (☎ 235–9300) is in the Paragon; **Dior** (☎ 734–0374) is in Wisma Atria; **Nina Ricci** (☎ 732–9555) is in Isetan Scotts and Takashimaya. Boutiques carrying a number of designers include **Singora** (☎ 737–0768) in the Hilton, **Link** (☎ 235–4648) in Palais Renaissance, **Club 21** (☎ 235–0753) in the Four Seasons Hotel, and **Glamourette** (☎ 734–3137) in the Promenade. For resort clothing and swimwear, stop in at any major department store. Lane Crawford (☎ 735–8735) has a nice collection of bathing suits on the second floor.

Men's fashions are represented by **Dunhill** (☎ 459–2038) in the Hilton; **Mario Valentino** (☎ 338–4457) in Marina Square; **Hermès** (☎ 734–1353) in Liat Towers; and **Ralph Lauren** (☎ 738–0298) in

128

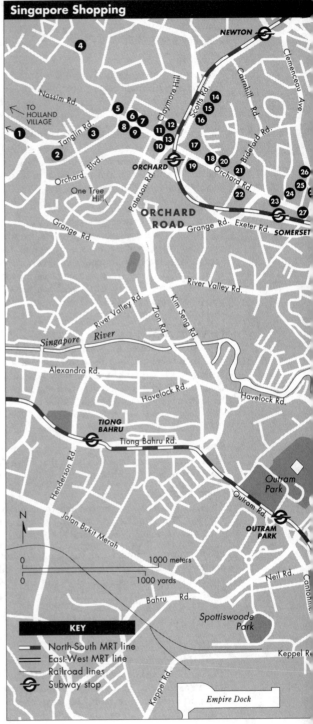

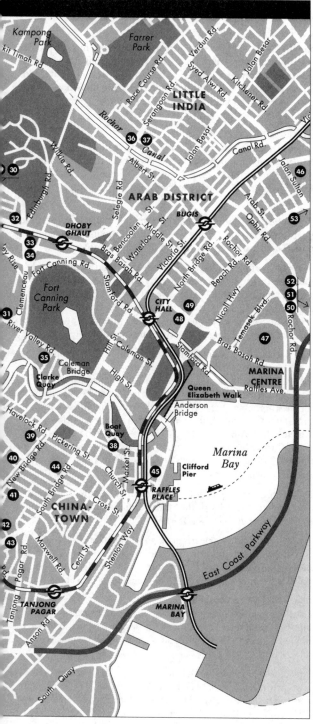

Takashimaya. The Wisma Atria department store also carries Ralph Lauren, Givenchy, and Valentino.

Ivory

Singapore has accepted the international ban on ivory imports, so demand for antique ivory may increase. Be aware that ivory can be smoked to make it appear old. A lot of curio shops carry ivory, too: Souvenir shops have ivory jewelry, and high-class curio shops have carved tusks and figurines. Japanese netsuke (small carved figures) in ivory are found in the better curio shops.

Jewelry

Singapore is a reliable place to buy jewelry, and there are so many jewelers that prices are competitive. Never accept the first price offered, no matter how posh the store. All jewelers give enormous discounts, usually 40% or more, but some, especially in hotels, don't mention this until pressed.

The Singapore Assay Office hallmarks jewelry, though the procedure is time-consuming and not many jewelers submit to it unless required for export. There are a number of gem-testing laboratories as well.

In Chinatown, particularly along South Bridge Road and in People's Park, there are dozens of Chinese jewelers selling 22K gold. Many of these are old family firms. Chinese jewelers of this kind can be found in all the suburbs and are patronized by all ethnic groups. Prices are calculated by abacus based on the weight of the ornament and the prevailing price of gold. The bargaining procedure can take quite some time.

On Orchard Road, the jewelry shops are often branches of Hong Kong firms or are local firms modeled along the same lines. They sell 18K set jewelry, often in Italian designs, as well as loose investment stones. **Larry's** (☎ 734–8763), with branches in Orchard Towers and other malls, is one popular store. One of the many small jewelers in Takashimaya is the **Hour Glass** (☎ 734–2420), which carries a large selection of designer watches. **Je T'Aime** (☎ 734–2275) in Wisma Atria is also a reputable firm. **Cartier** has shops in Takashimaya (☎ 734–2427) and in the Hilton (☎ 235–0295). **Tiffany's**, which is also in Takashimaya, recently opened a two-story store at Ngen An City (☎ 735–8823).

Antique European jewelry is not often seen in Singapore, but the antique silver and gold jewelry of the Straits Chinese can be seen in **Petnic's** (⊠ 41A Cuppage Rd., ☎ 235–6564).

Like other forms of jewelry, pearls are a good buy in Singapore. Small jewelers in Lucky Plaza and other complexes use freshwater pearls as "loss leaders," selling a strand for just a few dollars. Mikimoto pearls are available at **Kampooli Jewelers** (☎ 336–1381) in the Singapura Plaza.

Luggage and Accessories

It is not well known that luggage is a bargain in Singapore. Every complex contains several stores carrying all the designer names in luggage and leather accessories. Department stores carry such brands as Samsonite and Delsey.

Dunhill (☎ 339–1111) is in the Daimaru in Liang Court; **Etienne Aigner** is in Shaw Centre (☎ 737–6141); **Louis Vuitton** (☎ 737–5820) is in the Hilton and in Takashimaya; **Hermès** is at Liat Towers (⊠ 541 Orchard Rd., ☎ 734–1353) and at Daimaru in Liang Court (☎ 339–1111); and **Charles Jourdan** (☎ 737–4988) is in the Promenade. The **Escada** boutique (☎ 336–8283) at the Promenade and the Millennia Walk has a range of accessories and custom-made luggage.

Pewter and Dinnerware

Malaysia is the world's largest tin producer, and pewter is an important craft item in the region. **Selangor Pewter,** the largest pewter concern in Singapore, has a great product range displayed at the main showrooms in the Paragon, Delphi, Clarke Quay, Raffles Hotel, Marina Square, and Raffles City (☎ 339–3958). The main office is at 7500A Beach Road (☎ 334–1183).

Modern pewter items are heavily influenced by Scandinavian design. Items range from jewelry and tiny figurines to coffee and tea sets. Sake sets, bowls, vases, ornamental plates, clocks, and traditional beer tankards are also available. Some items are specifically aimed at the tourist trade, such as Raffles plates and Chinese zodiac plaques.

For dinnerware, **Christofle** (☎ 733–7257) has a boutique in the Hilton. Also try the **Waterford Wedgwood Shop** (⊠ #01–01 Delfi Orchard, ☎ 734–8375).

Reptile-Skin Products

Check the import restrictions on these goods. Singapore issues no export certificate for these or for ivory. The price of alligator, crocodile, and snake skins is lower here than anywhere else except Hong Kong.

In the old shops around the Stamford Road–Armenian Street area, hard bargaining will yield dividends. The range is widest at big stores such as the showroom at the **Crocodilarium** (⊠ 730 East Coast Pkwy., ☎ 447–3722). You can have bags and belts made to your specifications. The existing designs, especially for shoes, are often old-fashioned.

Silk

Chinese silk is easy to find in Singapore. All the emporiums have special departments for fabrics and tailored clothes. **China Silk House** (⊠ Tanglin Shopping Centre, ☎ 235–5020, and Centrepoint, ☎ 733–0555) has a wide range of fabrics in different weights and types, plus silk clothing, including a line designed for the shop by Benny Ong.

Indian silk, in sari lengths, is found in the dozens of sari shops in the Serangoon Road area. For 6 meters (6.5 yards) of silk, which could be the thin Kashmiri silk or the heavier, embroidered Benares silk, you pay only a fraction of what you would elsewhere. The major store for Indian textiles is **P. Govindasamy Pillai** (⊠ 153 Dunlop St., ☎ 297–5311).

Thai silk, in different weights for different purposes, comes in stunning colors. Specialty shops sell it by the meter or made up into gowns, blouses, and dresses. **Jim Thompson** (☎ 737–1133), in the Orchard Parade Hotel, has these well-known, branded Thai silks. A much more extensive collection can be found at the **Miss Ming** shops in the Orchard Towers (☎ 235–2865).

Tailoring

There are tailors and tailors—what you end up with depends on how well you choose. Tailors who offer 24-hour service rarely deliver, and their quality is pretty suspect. Another indication of danger is not seeing a tailor on the premises. Anyone can set up shop as a tailor by filling a store with fabrics and then subcontracting the work; the results from such places are seldom felicitous. Allow four to five days for a good job. **Justmen** (☎ 737–4800) in the Tanglin Shopping Centre is one of a number of excellent men's tailors. For women, shops such as the Tanglin branch of **China Silk House** (☎ 235–5020) offer good tailoring.

8 Side Trips to Indonesia and Malaysia

Singapore offers possibilities for excursions to neighboring countries. To the southeast, in Indonesian waters, is Bintan Island, with pristine shores, mangrove swamps, and hideaway resorts. A short drive north of Singapore, across the Johore Straits, is peninsular Malaysia, with its white-sand beaches, hill towns, and rich cultural heritage. Sprawling, clamorous Kuala Lumpur is strongly Islamic, while strategically located Malacca retains deep traces of its colonial and precolonial past.

BINTAN ISLAND

Updated by
Christine Hill

FROM THE TALLEST BUILDING IN SINGAPORE, you can see the nearby islands of Indonesia. In 30 minutes, you can cross the straits on a hydrofoil ferry south to the Bataam Islands. Bataam is undergoing a vast development project that includes a duty-free industrial zone and a tourist complex. However, Bataam and its resorts have been overshadowed by the more interesting island of Bintan, which is farther east, 45–90 minutes by hydrofoil.

Both Bintan and Bataam are part of Indonesia's Riau archipelago, islands south of Singapore with a colorful history. Overnight trips to Bintan, more than twice the size of Singapore, can include a stay at a five-star hotel with your own private pool or a more adventurous jaunt in a sampan to the 16th-century palace of a Malaysian sultan. The islands are home to the *orang laut,* or sea people, the descendants of pirates and traders who now live in houses on stilts over the sea.

Bintan Resorts Management (✉ 1 Temasek Ave., #03-01 Millenia Tower, Singapore 039192, ☎ 339–1368, ℻ 339–1551), a Singapore-Indonesia joint venture, has been given rights to develop the northern third of the islands. BRM provides the basic infrastructure and sells development rights. The resort is being developed with typical Singaporean efficiency and attention to details such as how to keep the environment clean. For example, unlike most Southeast Asia developments, the area's sewers do not empty straight into the sea. Instead, the system is centralized and treated, and the waters off the island are clear and free from garbage.

Bintan's main town is **Tanjung Pinang,** where the primary activity is shopping at **Pasar Pelantar Dua.** Tanjung Pinang is a jumping-off point for some interesting nearby sites. You can rent a motorboat at the pier to take you up the **Snake River** through the mangrove swamps to the oldest Chinese temple in Riau; as the boatman poles his way up the small tributary choked with mangroves, the sudden view of the isolated 300-year-old temple with its murals of hell will send chills down your spine. Have the boatman take you back down the river to **Tanjung Berakit,** where tiny huts perch on stilts. Friendly villagers live in spartan homes without electricity or water—this only an hour and a half from Singapore.

Another good stop by motorboat is **Pulau Penyengat** (Wasp Island), once the heart of the Riau sultanate and the cultural hub of the Malay empire. In the 16th century, the Malay sultanate fled here after being defeated by the Portuguese in Malacca. The island is just 15 minutes by motorboat from Tanjung Pinang's Pelentar pier. Sites include royal graves, banyan-shrouded ruins of the istana (palace), and the Sultan's Mosque, or **Mesjid Raya.** This bright yellow building was plastered together with egg yolks.

Lodging

If you are going to stay overnight, it is best to take a taxi (about S$50) from Tanjung Pinang to the resorts on the northern part of the island, as the hotels in Tanjung Pinang are unclean and known for their nefarious nightly activities. So far, four resorts have been completed, and several more are in the pipeline. All dot Bintan's wide sandy beaches and clear ocean waters. Most resorts are full on weekends with Singaporeans and expatriates, all amazed to find such beautiful resorts and clean water just 45 minutes from the world's busiest port.

Where you stay depends on what sort of holiday you want. All the resorts have their marketing offices in Singapore. Since opening in 1996, most of these resorts have been fully booked on weekends, and prices may go up.

CATEGORY	COST*
$$$$	over S$375
$$$	S$275–S$375
$$	S$175–S$275
$	under S$175

*All prices are for a standard double room, excluding 10% tax and 10% service charge.

$$$–$$$$ ⊞ **Banyan Tree.** This is the place to stay if you are looking for a ro-
★ mantic weekend. Individual cottages stand on stilts overlooking a horseshoe-shape bay. Each villa is designed in Balinese style and comes with its own whirlpool tub or pool. This resort caters to expatriates and Singaporeans. The 27 villas with whirlpools go for S$300 on weekdays, S$410 on weekends. The three pool villas, which include two bedrooms and a kitchen, go for about S$700 a night. Some visitors have complained that other guests can see into their private Jacuzzis. The pool villas are safe. ☎ 226–6123, FAX 226–6128. 32 rooms. Restaurant, pool, 18-hole golf course (under construction at press time), beach, dive shop.

$$ ⊞ **Sedona.** This enormous hotel caters mainly to Japanese and the local Singaporean crowds. In addition to a giant pool, attractions include water sports, a mah-jongg hall, tennis, golf, and karaoke. Although right next to the beach, this hotel lacks the aesthetic appeal of the Banyan Tree and the relaxed atmosphere of Mayang Sari and Mana Mana. Rooms go for S$182–S$232. ☎ 337–3577. 416 rooms. 10 restaurants (not all opened yet), 2 pools, 4 tennis courts, 9 holes of golf (56 planned), beach.

$–$$ ⊞ **Mayang Sari.** This accommodation is on a bay, right next to the ocean. The atmosphere is relaxed and friendly. The chalet-style rooms go for S$150–S$180 on weekdays and S$170–S$200 on weekends. ☎ 732–8515. 50 rooms. Restaurant.

$ ⊞ **Mana Mana.** This is a good destination for those looking to do water sports at the **Mana Mana Beach Club,** which has scuba diving and sailing. Air-conditioned huts with televisions and showers go for S$130–S$150 per night. ☎ 346–1984. 50 rooms. Restaurant, beach, snorkeling.

Bintan Island A to Z

Arriving and Departing

How you get to Bintan depends on whether you want to visit the new resort developments or the older historical sites. To go directly to any of the resorts listed above from Singapore, take a taxi (S$15 or so) to the **Tanah Merah Ferry Terminal** (☎ 542–4369) on Changi Road on the East Coast. The round-trip fare for the 45-minute ferry trip to the island is S$54. Call ahead and have your hotel arrange for land transfer, which will cost you about S$10. Do not go without a reservation and arrangements for land transfer.

Ferries to Tanjung Pinang leave from Singapore's World Trade Centre. On **Dino Ferries** (☎ 270–2228) the trip will cost you S$63 round trip, and the ferries leave at 8:50, 2:40, and 2:55. **Auto Bataam** (☎ 271–4866) costs S$68 round trip, leaving Singapore each day at 8:40,

10:10, and 2:50. Both ferries take 90 minutes to get to the islands. Reservations are a good idea on weekends.

Currency

Lodgings accept Singapore dollars, and most of the prices on menus are listed in Singapore dollars. However, you will need Indonesian rupiahs to make purchases in shops outside the resorts. At press time, there were 2,000 rupiahs (Rps) to the US$1.

Passports and Visas

Passports but no visas are required for citizens of Great Britain, Canada, or the United States wishing to enter Indonesia for less than one month.

Visitor Information

For tourist, passport and visa, health, and currency information, go to Singapore's **Indonesian Tourist Promotion Office** (⊠ #15–07 Ocean Bldg., 10 Collyer Quay, Singapore 0104, ☎ 534–2837). Visitors, be wary about malaria. If you are coming to Bintan, either take pills or bring some bug spray with you.

When to Go

The climate is pleasant year-round, with periods of intense sunshine alternating with cooling rain.

PENINSULAR MALAYSIA

Updated by
Nigel Fisher

In culturally diverse Malaysia, Malay, Chinese, Indian, and British influences confront you at every turn. Contrasts are endless: businessmen in Western garb and teenagers in T-shirts and jeans; Malay women in floral-print sarongs and Muslim women with traditional head coverings; Chinese men in the pajama-type outfits called *samfoo* and Indian men in dhotis. This vibrant cultural mix is readily apparent in the varied street-food scene, with its proliferation of vendors selling everything from exotic fruits and juices to Hokkien noodles to Malay satay to fish grilled with pungent Asian spices. And diversity proclaims itself joyously in the street festivals and religious ceremonies celebrated throughout the year.

Malaysia's racial and political power balance is delicate, but the government has promoted ethnic Malay interests and has based much of its state law on Islam. Further strengthening of Muslim law (for example, by arresting Muslims who break the Ramadan fast) is occurring, and greater emphasis is being placed on the Malay language at the expense of Mandarin and English. Over the last few years, the press has been increasingly muzzled and criticism of politicians suppressed; citizens are becoming more careful about what they say, and to whom. Nonetheless, the Chinese have been able to push Malaysia's economy forward, making the nation's economic growth a success story of the 1990s.

Malaysia has traditionally welcomed visitors, and since the country started to solicit tourists in earnest a decade ago, more and more facilities have become available for the traveler. Since many people speak some English, it is easy to get around by public transportation.

This side trip into southern peninsular Malaysia (as West Malaysia, the 11 Malaysian states that, with southern Thailand, make up the Malay Peninsula, is called) takes you to some of the beautiful beaches of the east coast and to the beach resort island of Tioman in the South China Sea. Crossing the peninsula from east to west, we pass the hill-town resort of Genting Highlands, then continue on to Malaysia's capital, Kuala Lumpur (called KL), and the west coast. North of Kuala Lumpur are several resort islands, of which the best known is Penang, but this excursion instead heads south, toward the historic city of Malacca, where the Portuguese established the first European settlement. From there we return to Singapore.

However, you may wish to choose just a part of this excursion. Those seeking sun, surf, and sand should head for the east and stay at Tioman or Kuantan. If you're looking for history, make for Malacca, and if you want a busy metropolis, visit Kuala Lumpur.

Pleasures and Pastimes

Dining

The center for dining in Malaysia is its capital city. Though it isn't by the sea, centrally located Kuala Lumpur still reaps its benefits, and seafood washed down with ice-cold beer is the rage with city folk. Thai as well as Japanese food has made its mark. Nonya food (the cuisine of the Straits-born Chinese), which is a combination of Malay, Chinese, and Thai, is gaining in popularity; the cooking methods are traditional and laborious, but fine cuisine is the reward.

Three styles of Indian cooking can be found in KL—South Indian, Mughal, and Indian Muslim, the last a blend of South Indian and Malay.

Eating Indian rice and curry with your hands on a banana leaf is an experience to be savored.

European, primarily Italian and French, dining has found favor with an increasingly affluent city population. Outside KL, four-star hotels usually have one restaurant serving Continental-style cooking with some Malay dishes included and another restaurant serving Chinese (Cantonese) fare. Breakfasts are usually buffet-style.

Eating out, even in Kuala Lumpur, is an informal affair. Jackets and ties are hardly ever worn, except perhaps in a formal restaurant at a five-star hotel.

Credit cards are accepted in most but not all restaurants, which are usually open for lunch from 11:30 AM to 2:30 PM and for dinner from 6:30 to 11, depending on business. Seafood restaurants are usually open from 5 PM to 3 AM.

In the more expensive restaurants, a service charge of 10% and a sales tax of 5% are added to the bill. Tipping is not necessary and is entirely up to you.

CATEGORY	COST*
$$$$	over M$100
$$$	M$60–M$100
$$	M$30–M$60
$	under M$30

per person, not including tax, service, or drinks

Lodging

Malaysia's slow start in attracting tourists probably accounts for the paucity of charming, architecturally attractive hotels. International hotels for the business traveler, though, are springing up in Kuala Lumpur. A Hyatt, a Ritz-Carlton, and a Ramada Renaissance are scheduled to open their doors by 1997, adding themselves to the existing Shangri-La, Hilton, Istana, and Kuala Lumpur's top hotel, the Regent. Outside Kuala Lumpur—with a few exceptions—the best hotels reach only a four-star level, but in all major cities or resort areas, you'll always be able to find modern, clean hotels of an international standard. Often, too, you will find them less than half full, enabling you to negotiate a discount. For anyone traveling on a budget, there is an ample supply of inexpensive Chinese hotels that offer an iron bedstead, a couple of chairs, and a washbasin, perhaps even a bathroom with an Asian toilet en suite. (Note: "Asian toilet" refers to the type with no seat.)

On the plus side, hotels across the board are considerably less expensive than those in Singapore; for example, in Kuala Lumpur a room at the Regent runs US$170, whereas the Regent in Singapore charges US$340. Please be aware that while we list the facilities that are available, we don't specify whether they cost extra: When pricing accommodations, always ask what's included.

CATEGORY	COST*
$$$$	over M$300
$$$	M$220–M$300
$$	M$150–M$220
$	M$75–M$150
¢	under M$75

All prices are for a standard double room with bath, excluding 10% service charge and 5% government tax.

The East Coast and Highlands

Numbers in the margin correspond to points of interest on the Peninsular Malaysia map.

Johore Bahru

❶ *368 km (221 mi) southeast of Kuala Lumpur, 30 km (18 mi) north of central Singapore.*

At the end of the causeway from Singapore, the town of Johore Bahru, an old royal and administrative capital, begins. The apparent lack of town planning stands in sharp contrast to the orderliness of Singapore. There are no right angles; streets follow no grid or other logical plan but run into one another higgledy-piggledy. The pace, too, is noticeably different: Here, watches seem to have no minute hands. However, because labor costs are lower than in Singapore, the last four years have seen rapid commercial and industrial development. The pace is picking up, taxis are smarter, and first-rate hotels are springing up.

The town's major sight is the **Istana Besar** (✉ Jalan Tun Dato Ismail), the old palace of the sultans of Johore. This neoclassical, rather institutional-looking building, erected in 1866, has been converted into a museum; it holds the hunting trophies of the late sultan as well as ceremonial regalia and ancient weapons. The new sultan's palace, the **Istana Bukit Serene** (✉ Jalan Straits View), was built in 1933 and is noted for its gardens, which are popular with joggers.

The **Sultan Abu Bakar Mosque** (✉ Jalan Gerstak Merah, off Jalan Tun Dato Ismail), built in 1900 in European Victorian style, is one of Malaysia's most beautiful, with sparkling white towers and domes surrounding the main prayer hall. It can accommodate more than 2,000 worshipers. At the cemetery on Jalan Muhamadiah, the **Royal Mausoleum** (Sultan Abu Bakar Mausoleum) has been the final resting place of the Johore royal family since they left Singapore. Visitors may not enter the mausoleum, but a number of impressive Muslim tombs surround it.

Dining and Lodging

$$ ✕ **Stulang Seafood.** While smart dining may be found at Johore's best hotels, the top local choice is outdoor dining at one of the restaurants clustered together along Jalan Stulang Laut. Two of the popular restaurants are **Makunan Laut Ocean Garden** (☏ 07/222–7482) and **Khye Cheang** (☏ 07/222–4732). Seafood is the specialty—be sure to ask the prices before committing yourself—but Malay curries and Chinese pork and chicken dishes are also offered. ✉ *Jalan Stulang Laut. No credit cards.*

$$$$ ▦ **Hyatt Regency Johore Bahru.** Opened in mid-1994, this is the grandest of Johore Bahru's modern hotels. Built on a slight rise facing the Straits of Johore, the mammoth building forms an arc around landscaped gardens through which a two-tier pool meanders. The guest rooms are large (34 meters square), with all the latest technological gadgetry in bedside controls. The bathrooms are a pleasure—plenty of room and with a separate shower stall. It is also worthwhile to pay a little more for a room facing the pool, the gardens, and, beyond, the Straits separating the Malay Peninsula from Singapore. The Regency Rooms on the top floors have access to the **Club Lounge,** with an outside terrace. The hotel is designed for the business traveler, with four restaurants (Western, Japanese, Szechuan, and Italian) for entertaining and meeting rooms for business. ✉ *Jalan Sungai Chat, Box 222, 80720 Johore*

Peninsular Malaysia

0 — 100 miles
0 — 150 km

N

THAILAND

Langkawi Island

Kangar

George Town
Penang Island

Butterworth

Kota Bharu

MALAYSIA

Kuala Terengganú

South China Sea

Taiping

Ipoh

Cameron Highlands

Kuala Lipis

Telok Anson

Fraser's Hill

Pancing Caves

9 **Chendor Beach**
8 **Cherating**
7
6 **Kuantan**

Kuala Lumpur
11 — 38

10
Genting Highlands

5 **Pekan**

S. Pahang

Tioman Island
4

Klang

NEGRI SEMBILAN

Seremban 39
41
Port Dickson

40
Sri Menanti

Gemas

Segamat

3 **Mersing**

42
Pengkalan Kempas
43
Malacca

Keluang

Strait of Malacca

Dumai

Johore Bahru 1 **Desaru**
2
SINGAPORE ☆ Strait
Singapore Batam

SUMATRA

Bintan

Pakanbaru

INDONESIA

KEY
— Rail Lines

Bahru, ☎ *07/223–1234,* FAX *07/223–2718. 406 rooms. 4 restaurants, bar, pool, 2 tennis courts, health club, business services, meeting rooms. AE, DC, MC, V.*

$$$ 🏨 **Puteri Pan Pacific.** This 500-room hotel opened in 1991 adjacent to the Kotaraya Complex—the city's newest and most prestigious office and shopping mall. The design makes use of round, timber-clad columns and colorful batiks in an open court lobby. Guest rooms, decorated in popular pastel colors, are fully equipped with modern amenities. The **Newsroom Café** features local and international foods; the **Selasih** offers traditional Malay cuisine; the **Hai Tien Lo** presents Cantonese food in elegant surroundings; and the **Poolside Terrace** has evening barbecues. ✉ *Jalan Salim, Box 293, 80000 Johore Bahru,* ☎ *07/223–3333,* FAX *07/233–6622. 500 rooms. 4 restaurants, in-room safes, room service, pool, business services. AE, DC, MC, V.*

Shopping
There are several handicraft centers where demonstrations of batik making and *songket* weaving (in which gold and silver threads are twined through the pattern) are given. A good one to visit is Sri Ayu Batik Industries (✉ 136 Jalan Perwira Satu); who knows, you may buy something.

Desaru

❷ *94 km (58 mi) east of Johore Bahru, 436 km (282 mi) southeast of Kuala Lumpur.*

An hour out of Johore on the road to Kota Tinggi (45 km or 30 mi) there is a junction. The right fork goes to Desaru. Since Singapore has no decent beaches, the hope of developers has been that Desaru would fill the bill. For a time, it seemed that their wish might come true, and fast ferries brought Singaporeans over in droves on weekends. Plans were made to add a Disney-style playground, complete with artificial snow, two additional golf courses, and more water-sports facilities; an additional 4,000 holiday homes; and more hotels along its 17-kilometer (10½-mile) stretch of jungle-fringed beach. So far, that has not materialized.

Lodging
$$$–$$$$ 🏨 **Desaru View Hotel.** At this full-service luxury resort hotel set in seaside gardens, all rooms have balconies and views of the South China Sea, plus air-conditioning, color TV and video, and minibar. A wide variety of facilities—including the longest swimming pool in Malaysia—is available, and pickup in Singapore can be arranged. ✉ *Tanjong Penawar, 81900 Kota Tinggi,* ☎ *07/822–1221,* FAX *07/822–1237. 134 rooms. 4 restaurants, bar, pool, 18-hole golf course, miniature golf, 4 tennis courts, horseback riding, bicycles, dance club, recreation room, meeting rooms. AE, MC, V.*

$$–$$$ 🏨 **Desaru Golf Hotel.** This medium-class, family-oriented hotel is in a two-story building with double-peaked roof. Not all guest rooms have sea views. ✉ *Tanjong Penawar, 81900 Kota Tinggi,* ☎ *07/822–1101,* FAX *07/822–1480. 100 rooms. Restaurant, coffee shop, 18-hole golf course, 2 tennis courts, dive shop, playground, convention center. AE, MC, V.*

Golf
The **Desaru Resort Golf Club** (✉ Box 57, 81907 Kota Tinggi, ☎ 07/821–187, FAX 07/821–855) has an undulating 18-hole course designed by Robert Trent Jones Jr., made more difficult by strong sea breezes.

Mersing

3 *353 km (212 mi) southeast of Kuala Lumpur, 161 km (100 mi) north of Johore Bahru.*

The low-key market town of Mersing is a good three-hour drive from Johore Bahru on a road that cuts through rubber and palm plantations. An occasional monkey scampering across the road keeps you alert. Mersing still has its roots as a fishing village, but it has also become the gateway to Tioman Island and the other smaller islands lying offshore. The local tourist office, **Mersing Tourist Information Center** (✉ 01 Jalan Abu Bakar, ☎ 07/799–5212, FAX 07/799–3975), is especially helpful. It's a good idea to drop in here to get maps, your bearings, and reliable information on hotels; it's about 400 yards before you reach the ferry wharf.

Lodging

$ 🏨 **Timotel.** The only reason to stay overnight in Mersing is if you have missed the ferry to the offshore islands. While there are several inexpensive Chinese hotels on Mersing's main street, Timotel, on the edge of town in a small shopping center and on the road to Kuantan, is the newest (1995) and cleanest hotel in the area. All rooms have air-conditioning and either a king-size or twin beds. Furnishings are basic—carpet on the floor, TV on a side cabinet, coffee table, and chairs. Bathrooms have a tub and hand-held shower. A small dining area serves meals all day long. ✉ *839 Jalan Endau, 86800 Mersing,* ☎ *07/799–5888,* FAX *07/799–5333. 44 rooms. Coffee shop. AE, MC, V.*

Tioman Island

4 *Two hours by ferry from Mersing.*

Boats are scheduled to leave Mersing harbor for the two-hour trip to Tioman and the other islands every day around noon, though because they are dependent on the tides, the actual departure time varies. The cost to any of the islands is M$25. Because the boats must wait for the morning tides to make the return from Tioman, a day excursion is not possible; you must stay overnight.

Tioman Island was Bali Hai in the movie *South Pacific*. This lush tropical island hasn't changed much since then, except for the tourists, and it is large enough to absorb them. Sunbathe on the sandy coves, swim in the clear waters, try the 9-hole golf course (☎ 09/445–445, FAX 09/445–718), or hike through the jungle-clad hills (the highest is Gunjung Kajang at 1,037 meters, or 3,400 feet). Plenty of water sports are available; brightly colored fish and coral make for enjoyable snorkeling. Boats and bicycles—your transportation around the island—are available for rent.

Tioman is the farthest and largest of the offshore islands. The ferry boat makes five stops up the island's west coast at the various resorts. The island has only one major resort, known as the Tioman Island Resort, but more accurately by its new name, the **Berjaya Imperial Beach Resort.** It's in the center of the island. Guesthouses—clusters of small chalets—are to the north and south.

Tioman, while peaceful and quiet by most standards, does get a little busy with tourists. Those seeking quieter havens head for the other islands. Three of them, which have one resort offering simple bungalow accommodation, are **Pulau Cibu** (☎ 07/799–3167), **Pulau Rawa** (☎ 07/799–1204), and **Pulau Besar** (☎ 07/799–4995). The last has slightly more spacious bungalows than the others.

Lodging

You can book the ferry ride and the lodging of your choice at one of the many tourist offices around Mersing's harbor and in the adjacent Plaza R&R. You may want to try **Zaid Mohammed Lazim** (⊠17 Jalan Abu Bakar, Plaza R&R, 86800, ☎ 07/799–4280, ℻ 07/799–4434).

$$$$ 🏨 **Berjaya Imperial Beach Resort.** The Tioman Island Resort used to be a casual, family place with accommodations of varying sizes to meet all budgets. Then, in 1993, it changed its name and was completely redone to become a full-service hotel and resort complex at prices to match. With rooms decorated in soft colors and equipped with telephones, televisions, and minibars, two restaurants (Asian and Western), a coffee lounge, and a conference center, the resort is designed for individuals, business seminars, and conferences. An attractive nine-hole golf course and a large swimming pool keep most guests occupied, but the activities desk can arrange pony rides, diving and snorkeling, and boat trips around the island. If the room prices here are too high for you, come for the facilities and stay at one of the inexpensive chalets around Kampung Telek and Kampung Air Batang. ⊠ *Pulau Tioman, 86807 Mersing, Johor,* ☎ *09/414–5445,* ℻ *09/414–5718. 375 rooms. 2 restaurants, bar, coffee shop, pool, 9-hole golf course, 2 tennis courts, dive shop, jet skiing. AE, MC, V.*

Pekan

❺ *107 km (63 mi) north of Mersing.*

Though there are numerous traditional kampongs and colorful fishing villages along the east coast between Mersing and Kuantan, the only main town is Pekan, the home of the sultan. You can see his modern palace, with its manicured lawns and, of course, its polo field, but only from outside the gates. Don't bypass this town, as the signposts invite; drive through the center instead. Built on the western shore of a river, it is delightfully old-fashioned, with two-story shophouses lining the main street. At the **Silk Weaving Centre** at Pulau Keladi, traditional Pahang silk is woven into intricate designs.

Kuantan

❻ *259 km (156 mi) east of Kuala Lumpur, 70 km (42 mi) north of Pekan, 325 km (155 mi) north of Johore Bahru.*

The major beach and holiday resort on Malaysia's east coast is Kuantan. The first hotel area begins just north of the city at the crescent-shaped sandy bay of **Telok Chempedak.** To get there, take Jalan Telok Sisek, just past the Hotel Suraya. This small community consists of several hotels (including the Hyatt Kuantan), four or five restaurants and bars, discos, and a small but attractive curving beach. Sunbathers come for the company of other vacationers rather than solitude. If you prefer privacy, continue a few miles north. Here, smaller hotels dot a long stretch of virtually untrodden sands.

Dining and Lodging

$$$ ✕ **The Kampong Café.** A soft candlelit setting, with rattan chairs, taupe linens, and sparkling crystal and silver, creates a romantic ambience. The restaurant is built on stilts; the view is of the South China Sea. The food is a mix of Malay and European, and the seafood dishes are the best. ⊠ *Hyatt Kuantan, Telok Chempedak,* ☎ *09/525–211. Reservations essential. AE, DC, MC, V.*

$$$ ⊞ **Hyatt Regency Kuantan.** The low-rise hotel opened in 1980, and
★ though the architects were Malaysian and the lobby uses Malaysian
redwood, the design gives you a feeling of Hawaii. Full advantage of
the sea breezes is taken with an open side facing the South China Sea.
Lush, cultivated gardens surround the hotel, and two swimming pools
are steps back from the golden sandy beach. Rooms line three court-
yards running parallel to the beach and away from the lobby and
restaurant area. Two pools separate the courtyards from the beach it-
self. The rooms farthest from the lobby are in the Regency Court ex-
tension. The distinct advantage in staying here is the lounge, which serves
an ample continental breakfast and an array of evening cocktails with
hors d'oeuvres. The carpeted guest rooms have either king-size or twin
beds and bathrooms with a separate shower stall. Since you have come
here for the sea, it's worth the premium to reserve a room facing it—
sleep with the balcony doors open to the sounds of the surf—rather
than one overlooking the vegetation and hills at the back of the court-
yards. A six-story business wing to the rear of the main hotel has con-
ference rooms and 52 business suites. The Chinese restaurant, **Yue Yuen,**
offers Cantonese food; the **Kampong Café,** built on stilts on the beach,
is a romantic spot for local and European fare; and the **Coco Loco Bistro**
offers pizza. A Filipino band plays for the late night crowd. ⊠ *Telok
Chempedak, 25730 Kuantan, Pahang Darul Makmur,* ☎ *09/513–1234,*
℻ *09/567–7577. 327 rooms. 2 restaurants, outdoor café, room ser-
vice, 2 pools, water sports, sauna, golf privileges, 3 tennis courts, ex-
ercise room, squash, dance club. AE, MC, V.*

$–$$ ⊞ **Coral Beach Resort.** Formerly a Ramada-managed property, this modern resort hotel has a wide-open lobby area and a light-filled coffee
lounge serving Malay and European fare. A Japanese and a Chinese
restaurant are the venues for more elaborate dining. The resort's chief
pleasure is fronting the endless sands on the shores of the South China
Sea. Rooms are similar to what you may expect of a former Ramada.
Beds are either king-size or twins, furniture is utilitarian, and the bathrooms are adequate. The hotel promotes itself to tourists as well as for
business seminars, and the mix of earnest, shirted delegates and fun-
loving sunbathers seems a bit strained during the day, but by night—
with bars scattered around the property—the tension is relieved. The
Coral Beach is 12 kilometers (7½ miles) north of Kuantan. ⊠ *152 Sungai Karang, 26100 Beserah, Kuantan,* ☎ *09/544–7544,* ℻ *09/544–
7543. 162 rooms. 2 restaurants, pool, 2 tennis courts, water sports,
health club, squash, meeting rooms. AE, DC, MC, V.*

¢ ⊞ **Tanjong Gelang Motel.** This small, Chinese-owned motel has simple chalets packed rather tightly together, facing the beach. There are
no frills, just the basics and a small restaurant that serves mostly Chinese and European food, but the Coral Bay Resort and all its facilities
are right next door. To reach this motel from Kuantan, you do need a
car. ⊠ *15 Km Jalan Kemaman, 26100 Kuantan, Pahang Darul Mak-
mur,* ☎ *09/544–7254,* ℻ *09/544–7388. 40 rooms. Restaurant. AE,
MC, V.*

Pancing Caves

❼ *25 km (15 mi) west of Kuantan.*

Several excursions inland to the jungled hills and small Malay kampongs can be arranged out of Kuantan. One is to the Pancing Caves
(or, more correctly, **Gua Charah**). Traveling from Kuantan, first you
pass rubber and oil-palm plantations before arriving at the bottom of
a small hill. Now comes the hard part. To reach the caves you must
climb 220 steps. Buddhists still live here, and there are many altars.

Don't miss the cave with the reclining Buddha some 9 meters (30 feet) long, carved by a Thai Buddhist monk who devoted his life to the task.

Cherating

8 *30 km (19 mi) north of Kuantan.*

Half an hour's drive north of Kuantan is the peaceful village of Cherating, which used to be a rustic haven for beachcombing along miles of white, clean beaches, fanned by gentle breezes through the coconut trees. But inevitably, hotels sprang up, and Club Med was one of the first to stake its claim on a fine stretch of beach here, responding to the spirit of the place with its Malay-style bungalows built on stilts. Now, off the main highway, there are numerous three- and four-star hotels that get a mix of British and German tour groups, but always seem to have more than enough empty rooms to offer good discounts.

Turtle-watching—one of the east coast's most popular attractions— begins at Cherating and continues north. The best viewing place is said
9 to be **Chendor Beach,** an hour north of Kuantan or 20 minutes up from Cherating. Most nights between May and September (peak month is August), enormous leatherback turtles slowly make their way ashore to lay as many as 200 eggs each. Signs at the hotels will tell when and where to go, and the crowds do gather to watch as the 1,000-pound turtles laboriously dig their "nests" before settling down to their real work.

Lodging

$$$$ 🏨 **Club Med Cherating.** This traditional Malaysian-style Club Med village is set on its own bay, surrounded by 200 acres of parkland. Accommodations are in twin-bedded bungalows with air-conditioning and showers. As with all Club Meds, the package is inclusive, with full sporting facilities, arts-and-crafts workshops, and buffet-style dining. The year-round resort was refurbished in 1994 and is quieter and more low-key than the Club Meds found in the Caribbean. ⊠ *29th Mile, Jalan Kuantan-Kemaman, Cherating, 26080 Kuantan,* ☎ *09/439–133 or 800/258–2633,* 𝔽𝔸𝕏 *09/439–524. 300 rooms. 2 restaurants, pool, 6 tennis courts, aerobics, archery, exercise room, squash, windsurfing, children's program (ages 4–9 and 10–11). AE, MC, V.*

$$$$ 🏨 **Impiana Resort.** Offering more independence than Club Med is this low-rise sprawl of modern luxury on 32 acres at the edge of Cherating's beach. The vast lobby, flooded by natural light and cooled by sea breezes, is the focal point. Beyond is the two-tier swimming pool, and beyond that the sea. Guests have the choice of Malay, Chinese, or Western food from the three restaurants, or a selection of everything from the evening buffet. Standard rooms are in the main building; there are also two- and three-bedroom chalets. Most rooms and chalets face the sea, and all have four-poster wooden beds, a ceiling fan, and air-conditioning. For recreation, there is a fully equipped water sports center, which sadly includes jet-skiing. ⊠ *Km 32, Jalan Kuantan-Kemaman, Cherating, 26080 Pahang,* ☎ *09/439–000,* 𝔽𝔸𝕏 *09/439–090. 250 rooms, including chalets. 3 restaurants, bar, meeting rooms. AE, DC, MC, V.*

$$ 🏨 **Cherating Holiday Villa Beach Resort.** Formerly affiliated with the Holiday Inn in Kuala Lumpur, this hotel has undergone a metamorphosis. A central building houses the reception/dining area; guest rooms are in smaller buildings built around a swimming pool and gardens. Each building takes some architectural aspect, mostly in the roof styles, from the different regions of Malaysia. Most of the rooms are wood paneled with sliding glass doors facing the pool—more privacy, therefore, is found in the rooms on the second floor. Your choice of rooms varies from modern hotel-style rooms to chalets designed in the Malay style with bare wood floors and minimum furniture. At night the restaurant offers a mix of Italian-inspired fare and Malay cooking. Twice a week there is a beach barbecue. As at the other hotels on the east coast of Malaysia, you'll need a car to get off the property. ⊠ *Lot 1303, Mukim Sungei Karang, Cherating, 26080 Kuantan,* ☎ *09/581–9500,* FAX *09/581–9178; in KL,* ☎ *03/262–2922,* FAX *03/262–2937. 94 rooms. 2 restaurants, coffee shop, 2 pools, 3 tennis courts, badminton, exercise room, squash. AE, MC, V.*

¢ ⊡ **Cherating Beach Mini-Hotel.** If the reason for staying in Cherating is to be a beachcomber, then this small hotel is the place for you. The rooms are tiny and sparsely furnished, but the beach is at the front door. The staff are wonderfully low-key and friendly, and the restaurant does its best to cook up European food (though it's better at Malay food). ⊠ *Batu 28 Kampung, Jalan Kemaman, Cherating, 26080 Kuantan, Pahang Darul Makmur,* ☎ *09/592–527. 35 rooms, most with shower and toilet. Restaurant. No credit cards.*

Genting Highlands

➓ *50 km (30 mi) east of Kuala Lumpur, 209 km (125 mi) west of Kuantan.*

In the thickly forested hills a little more than an hour's drive out of Kuala Lumpur and some three hours from Kuantan is Genting Highlands. Twenty minutes off the main highway and up a winding paved road, with the heat and humidity dropping as you rise, you'll reach this hill resort at 1,711 meters (5,614 feet). It's popular mostly with Southeast Asians. It is very much a family resort, with an artificial lake full of paddleboats, an amusement park for the young, and a gambling casino—the only one in Malaysia—for adults. Given that gambling is against the laws of Islam, Genting Highlands is an anomaly, but an influential and wealthy Chinese owns the property. While the views from Genting Highlands are dramatic and the air is a cool contrast to the humidity and heat of the lowlands, the resort is modern and probably not what the overseas visitor has come to Asia to see. If you do come, you'll find the 700-room **Genting Highlands Resort,** a hive of activity on weekends, but quiet, even deserted, during the week. Discounts and packages are always available and considerably less than the published room rates, which begin at M$250 and climb up to M$1,650 for a suite. ⊠ *69000 Genting Highlands,* ☎ *03/211–1118,* FAX *03/211–1888.*

Kuala Lumpur

The capital of Malaysia, Kuala Lumpur is a repository for much of the country's artifacts, colonial architecture, Chinese shophouses, impressive mosques, criminal elements, and newfound wealth—as attested to by soaring skyscrapers and traffic jams. The city's rapid growth seemingly has no logical plan—multitower complexes rise high next to single-story houses.

Because of the sprawl that is Kuala Lumpur, it is a tough city to explore. It's not made for walking—sidewalks have potholes, crossing streets is hazardous, distances between sights seem long in the heat and humidity. On the other hand, you don't want to sit in a taxi, stalled in traffic, even though the meter fare is low—M$1.30 for the first 1.6 kilometers (1 mile) or M$12 an hour. However, taxi drivers are notorious for not using their meters and charging tourists more than twice the correct fare. The best plan is to arm yourself with a map, choose the sights that you wish to see, wear comfortable walking shoes and loose, light clothing (cotton breathes and keeps you cooler than synthetics), and when the distances are great, hop on a "bas mini" (minibus) and alight from it when it deviates from the direction in which you want to go.

A Good Walk

Numbers in the text and in the margin correspond to points of interest on the Kuala Lumpur map.

The ideal place to begin exploring the city is the national museum, **Muzim Negara** ⑪, a short walk from the Kuala Lumpur Visitors Center. The museum provides an opportunity to place the nation in historical perspective and gives an introduction to the country's culture. Relax afterward in the Lake Gardens behind the museum before visiting the **National Art Gallery** ⑫ next door to the visitors center. The imposing Moorish structures across the street contain the **main railway station** ⑬ and the administrative offices of KTM, the national rail system. Walk up Jalan Sultan Hishamuddin, a pleasant street lined with hibiscus bushes, to the **National Mosque** ⑭, with its distinctive star-shaped dome. At Jalan Cenderasari, go under the road via the pedestrian walkway to the **Kompleks Dayabumi** ⑮, which contains the city's main post office and a stamp museum. Stroll through the glistening red-marble lobby of the Dayabumi tower to the shopping-arcade level. On the town side of the plaza that connects the post office and the office tower, cross the pedestrian bridge to the **Central Market** ⑯, a renovated Art Deco building that holds a lively bazaar with tempting food stalls. After browsing here, exit through the far door onto a street called Leboh Pasar Besar ("big market"), cross the river, and walk up a block to the high-tech twin-story Petronas Twin Towers complex, from where you'll see the *padang* (playing field) of the **Selangor Club** ⑰.

Pass by **Masjid Jamek Bandaraya** ⑱, the city's oldest mosque, **St. Mary's Anglican Church** ⑲, **Masjid India** ⑳ (another mosque), and the vendors selling herbal medicine and cosmetics then head north up Jalan Tuanku Abdul Rahman, past a few remaining turn-of-the-century, two-story shophouses with decorative flourishes along the roofline. You'll be in the center of the city when you reach the massive **Sultan Abdul Samad Building** ㉑, where you may want to stop in at Infokraf Malaysia, a branch of the national handicrafts center.

Continuing north on Jalan Tuanku Abdul Rahman, also called **Batu Road** ㉒, you'll come to the **Coliseum Theatre** ㉓, a city landmark. Around the theater's parking lot, near the traffic signal, are *tandas* (public toilets). Across the road, on Jalan Bunus, little shops and vendors compete with the modern and bustling **Mun Loong department store** ㉔.

Farther along Batu Road, look in at the Peiping Lace Shop (No. 217) and the **Selangor Pewter showroom** ㉕ (No. 231), where you can watch pewter objects being made. At the intersection of Batu Road and Jalan Dang Wangi, where the Odeon Theatre occupies one corner and the giant **Pertama Komplex** ㉖ the other, turn right onto Jalan Dang Wangi then left onto Jalan Ampang. The next corner is the beginning of Jalan Sultan Ismail, Kuala Lumpur's "gold coast."

Caution: Travelers should watch their handbags and shoulder bags in this district. Thieves on motorcycles are known to ride up alongside strollers, snatch their goods, and buzz off. Police advise walkers to carry bags under the arm, on the side away from the street, to forestall such incidents.

Walk down Jalan Sultan Ismail past the **Concorde Hotel** ㉗ to Jalan Raja Chulan, where you'll see **Anak Ku** ㉘, a row of outdoor food stalls in

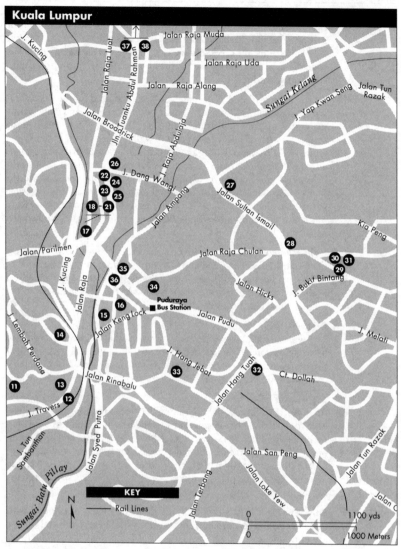

Kuala Lumpur

Jalan Raja Muda

Jalan Raja Uda

Jalan Raja Alang

Jalan Broadrick

J. Dang Wangi

Jalan Sultan Ismail

Jalan Ampang

Jalan Parilmen

Jalan Raja Chulan

Jalan Hicks

J. Bukit Bintang

Jalan Keng Lock

Puduraya Bus Station

Jalan Pudu

J. Hang Jebat

Jalan Rinabalu

Ct. Dollah

Jalan San Peng

Jalan Loke Yew

KEY

Rail Lines

0   1100 yds

0   1000 Meters

Anak Ku, **28**
Bank Bumiputra, **35**
Batik Malaysia Berhad, **36**
Batu Caves, **37**
Batu Road, **22**
Central Market, **16**
Coliseum Theatre, **23**
Concorde Hotel, **27**
Crafts Museum, **30**
International Crafts Museum, **31**

Karyaneka Handicraft Centre, **29**
Kompleks Dayabumi, **15**
Main railway station, **13**
Masjid India, **20**
Masjid Jamek Bandaraya, **18**
Maybank Building, **34**

Mun Loong department store, **24**
Muzim Negara, **11**
National Art Gallery, **12**
National Mosque, **14**
Pertama Komplex, **26**
Pudu Prison, **32**
St. Mary's Anglican Church, **19**
Selangor Club, **17**

Selangor Pewter Factory, **38**
Selangor Pewter showroom, **25**
Stadium Negara, **33**
Sultan Abdul Samad Building, **21**

the parking lot behind the Hilton Hotel. Continue on to the **Karyaneka Handicraft Centre** ㉙, which has displays and demonstrations by local artisans. Behind the handicraft center, across a little stream, are two small museums, the **Crafts Museum** ㉚ and the **International Crafts Museum** ㉛. The botanical gardens that border the stream offer a quiet spot to rest and reflect.

As you leave the handicraft center, turn left and head for the next block, which is Jalan Bukit Bintang, a jumble of shops, offices, and malls. Heading east up Jalan Pudu from Jalan Bukit Bintang, you'll see the **Pudu Prison** ㉜, with its beautifully painted wall—topped with barbed wire. Going west on Jalan Pudu takes you past a series of private hospitals and the Selangor Chinese Recreation Club, with its modest Tudor-style clubhouse and playing field. At Jalan Pudu Lama you can see the dome of **Stadium Negara** ㉝, an indoor arena said to be the largest such structure in Southeast Asia. On the imposing hill beyond the Pudu Raya bus station is the new **Maybank Building** ㉞, housing the Numismatic Museum.

Continue along Jalan Pudu toward the Kelang River. To your right is the **Bank Bumiputra** ㉟ and across from the bank, on the other side of Jalan Tun Perak, you'll see Wisma Batik, with the **Batik Malaysia Berhad** ㊱ on the first and second floors. At the next intersection the loop of the walk is completed.

TIMING

The walk, which covers the area known as the Golden Triangle, can be completed in two hours, but it will take several hours longer to visit the museums and experience the activities of the city. Note: The Friday afternoon prayer break usually lasts from 12:15 to 2:45.

Sights to See

㉘ **Anak Ku.** This hawker area is among the best in the city. First-time visitors to Asia might be alarmed at the standards of cleanliness. As a general rule, food handlers are inspected by health enforcement officers, but it's best to patronize popular places: Consumers everywhere tend to boycott stalls that have a reputation for poor hygiene. Because Muslims do not eat pork, the word "ham" is offensive, so Malaysians call hamburgers simply "burgers" or sometimes "beef burgers."

㉟ **Bank Bumiputra.** This is built in the shape of a kampong house, with its tower next door. Trading corporations that deal in natural rubber are in this area.

㊱ **Batik Malaysia Berhad (BMB).** This shop has a wide selection of batik fabrics, shirts, dresses, and handicrafts upstairs.

㉒ **Batu Road** (Jalan Tuanku Abdul Rahman). This is a pleasant street by day, filled with shopping families. In front of the **Globe Silk Store,** a troupe of blind musicians with bongo drums and electric piano entertains passersby. The **Peiping Lace Shop** (⊠ No. 217) stocks Chinese linens, lace, jewelry, and ceramics. **China Arts** next door is a branch of Peiping Lace that sells furniture; the rambling shop is filled with decorative coromandel screens, carved writing desks, teak and camphor chests, and antique vases. At midnight the street life changes dramatically, as *pondans* (transvestites) chat up men who cruise by in cars.

NEED A BREAK?

Off Batu Road on Jalan Bunus Enam is the open-air **Restoran Lebat,** where folks on their way to work pause for a breakfast of *roti canai,* a fried bread dipped in curry sauce. Across the street is the **Restoran Al-isan,** which is ringed by hawkers' stalls. Street food is a main event in Malaysia, and locals share tables when it's crowded. You don't need to know what the dishes are; look at what others are eating, and if it looks good, point and order. One favorite is the *popiah*, a soft spring roll filled with vegetables. The *meehom* or *kweh teow* (grilled fish and fried noodles) are especially tasty and cheap. The shop owner sells only drinks and dessert, so when you order two or three different dishes, you have to pay each provider. Be cautious with the *nasi kandar*, a local favorite, for the chilies rule the spicy prawns and fish-head curry.

16 **Central Market.** This renovated Art Deco building served as the city's produce market until it was converted into a series of stalls and shops in 1986, and today the 50-year-old market, painted apricot and baby blue, serves as the commercial, cultural, and recreational hub of downtown. Some 250 tenants, mostly retail shops and stalls, do business within the two-story, block-long market. This is a great place to sample dishes you have never tried before, whether Chinese dim sum or *laksa,* a noodle dish with fish paste. At night, there are cultural performances given outside on the riverside, and the Central Market becomes a popular gathering spot for inexpensive dining. (The small **Riverbank Restaurant** offers light Continental fare and live jazz.)

23 **Coliseum Theatre.** The Coliseum showcases the Malaysian and Indonesian film industries.

27 **Concorde Hotel** (formerly the Merlin). The Concorde's coffee shop and lobby lounge are popular meeting spots, and in front of the hotel, in the early morning hours, a makeshift stand hawks Malaysia's favorite breakfast dish, *nasi lemak*—a bundle of rice with salt fish, curry chicken, peanuts, slices of cucumber, and boiled egg—for one ringgit. Diagonally across the road is the **Shangri-La** hotel, marking the beginning of Kuala Lumpur's "gold coast," with its ritzy high-rise luxury hotels and modern skyscraper offices. If you are not already convinced by Malaysia's new wealth, you will be now.

30 **Crafts Museum.** The museum shows changing exhibits of the work of Malaysian artisans.

31 **International Crafts Museum.** This museum has a modest collection of work from other parts of the world, especially Asia, Africa, and Europe.

Jalan Bukit Bintang. This street is a jumble of modest hotels, goldsmiths and other shops, and finance companies. In addition, it contains several jumbo shopping complexes. The **Bukit Bintang Plaza** and the **Sungai Wang Centre** behind it form one of the largest shopping areas in the city. Among the tenants are fast-food restaurants, boutiques, bookstores, and the **Metrojaya** and **Parkson** department stores, possibly the city's finest. Outside, just across from the taxi stand, are racks of a strange green produce that more resembles a porcupine than a fruit. The Malaysian durian, the "king of fruits," grows in the jungle and is prized highly by city dwellers. But be prepared: The smell of a durian is not sweet, even though its taste is.

Jalan Bunus. Saturday nights this street is closed off for a *pasar malam*, a night market that begins at about 6 and ends at about 11. Here you'll find many goods, from bootleg tapes of the latest music to homemade sweets.

29 **Karyaneka Handicraft Centre.** On entering, you'll notice that each of the 13 little houses is labeled with the name of a Malaysian state. Inside, as might be expected, goods from that area are on display and demonstrations are regularly conducted by local artisans. The main building of the center, shaped like a traditional Malay house, stocks goods from the entire country.

NEED A
BREAK?

Fu Kwee Siang, two blocks east of the Karyaneka Handicraft Centre on Jalan Bukit Bintang, specializes in dried and minced pork and stocks Asian dried fruits, cookies, and candies, all displayed decoratively in huge glass jars with red plastic tops. Salesgirls will sell you small amounts so that you can sample the dried nutmeg, the mango, or—for the more adventurous—the roast cuttlefish and the dried pork floss. This taste experience should not be missed.

🕕 **Kompleks Dayabumi.** Constructed in 1984, the complex has three parts: the main post office building, the gleaming white office tower with its Islamic motif, and the plaza that connects the two. In the post office, just around the corner from the main lobby, the tiny stamp museum, **Galeri Setem,** will be opened for viewing on request. A huge fountain stands at the center of the two-level plaza area. From the upper level, you can get a close-up view of the commercial district dominated by banks, with the Bangkok Bank building at the center.

🕙 **Main railway station.** The station complex includes the administrative offices of **KTM (Kereta-api Tanah Melayu),** the national rail system. Built early in this century, the Islamic-influenced buildings were designed by a British architect to reflect the Ottoman and Mogul glory of the 13th and 14th centuries. The KTM building blends Gothic and Greek designs and features the wide verandas common in tropical climates. ☎ *03/274–7435.*

🕑 **Masjid India.** A modern structure, this mosque is the linchpin of the Little India district, where the attractions include street vendors who sell the local concoctions *ubat* (medicine) and *jamu* (cosmetics).

🕘 **Masjid Jamek Bandaraya.** The two minarets of this traditional-style mosque are only slightly taller than the coconut palm trees on the grounds.

🕓 **Maybank Building.** This office building was designed to resemble the handle of a *kris* (a Malay knife). Up the escalators, you can enter and walk around the soaring five-story bank lobby during banking hours. Of special interest is the **Numismatic Museum** in 1 South East, which exhibits Malaysian bills and coins from the past, offers information on the nation's major commodities, and adjoins a gallery that shows contemporary art. ☎ *03/280–8833, ext. 2023.* 🎫 *Museum free.* 🕙 *Daily 10–6.*

🕤 **Mun Loong department store.** This emporium carries such international goods as polyester dress shirts and French perfumes. A convenient bank of telephones is just outside the Mun Loong entrance.

🕚 **Muzim Negara.** The national museum building is modeled on an old-style Malay village house, enlarged to institutional size; the two mosaic murals on its facade depict significant elements in the country's history and culture. The cultural gallery, to the left as you enter, emphasizes traditional Malay folk culture. At the far end of the gallery, a model Nonya home shows classical Chinese furniture, exquisite antique carved canopy beds, and a table and chair set with inlaid pearl.

Across the lobby, the historical gallery has more models of regional-style homes; a collection of ceramic pottery, gold and silver items, and other artifacts; and traditional costumes (now seen only at festivals or on hotel doormen). Exhibits trace the stages of British colonization from the old East India Company in the late 18th century to its withdrawal in the mid-20th century. Photos and text outline the Japanese occupation during World War II and Malaysia's move toward federation status in 1948 and independence in 1957.

The natural history exhibit upstairs shows the country's indigenous animals. The other upstairs gallery, more like a trade show, deals with the national obsession with sports and recreation. A number of exhibits are behind Muzim Negara. The transportation shed houses an example of every form of transport in the country. You'll also see a model tin dredge, which represents one of Malaysia's main industries. Don't miss the Malay-style house, **Istana Satu** ("first palace"). ⊠ *Jalan Damansara,* ☎ *03/238–1067.* ☎ *Free.* ☉ *Daily 9–6 (except during Fri. prayers, 12:15–2:45).*

Behind the national museum, in the scenic **Lake Gardens** park (Tasek Perdana), you can find city dwellers relaxing and picnicking. Boating on the lake is popular (M$7 for an hour's boat rental), and at night Lake Gardens becomes a lover's lane. In the northern portion of the area stands the **National Monument,** a bronze sculpture dedicated to the nation's war dead. Nearby is the modern **Parliament** complex, with its 18-story office tower. When Parliament is in session, visitors can go into the gallery, provided they make arrangements in advance (inquire at the visitor center) and are properly attired.

⑫ **National Art Gallery.** The large permanent collection suggests the country's pluralistic style and its palette, its vistas, and its issues of concern. One recognizes quickly that the local artists reflect a refined sensibility while working in contemporary modes: conceptual pieces, pop images, bold sculptures, humorous graphics, landscapes, and realism. ⊠ *Jalan Hishamuddin,* ☎ *03/230–0157.* ☎ *Free.* ☉ *Daily 10–6 (except during Fri. prayers).*

⑭ **National Mosque** (Masjid Negara). The mosque's contemporary architecture features a 73-meter (240-foot) minaret spire, convoluted purple roof, and geometric grillwork. The main dome is designed as an 18-pointed star, representing the 13 states in Malaysia and the Five Pillars of Islam. The entrance is on the left, up Jalan Lembah Perdana. The mosque complex houses a meeting hall, ceremonial rooms, offices, a library, and a mausoleum and can accommodate 10,000 worshipers. ☉ *Sat.–Thurs. 9–6, Fri. 2:45–6.*

㉖ **Pertama Komplex.** Pertama ("first") is typical of most town shopping centers: clothing, shoe, appliance and record shops, plus several recreational spots, including a video-games room, a pool hall, and a nightclub.

㉜ **Pudu Prison.** A tropical landscape graces the wall of this otherwise forbidding place. The mural, painted by inmates, is the longest in the world, according to the *Guinness Book of World Records.* You'll also note a warning that death is the mandatory sentence for drug trafficking in Malaysia, and the news reports will confirm that the law is enforced.

⑲ **St. Mary's Anglican Church.** This gem-like church has a red-tile roof and manicured grounds. Services are now held in Tamil as well as in English.

⑰ **Selangor Club.** This private club housed in a rambling, Tudor-style building is a vestige of colonial days. The padang now covers an underground parking lot for the central business district. A new garden proclaims the area as Merdeka Square, commemorating national independence.

㉕ **Selangor Pewter showroom.** The showroom has a full range of pewter products, which have been made in Malaysia for more than 100 years. Most designs are simple and of world-class quality; a few items are pure kitsch. In the back of the shop you can watch a demonstration of the process of pewter making: the casting, soldering, and polishing. ⊠ *231 Batu Rd.*

㉝ Stadium Negara. This indoor arena, said to be the largest such structure in Southeast Asia, is used for concerts, conventions, and trade fairs as well as sports events. On the sidewalk near the Voon Radio shop a Chinese fortune-teller works from a little table.

㉑ Sultan Abdul Samad Building. This massive 1897 structure, with its Moorish arches, copper domes, and clock tower, is considered the center of the old city. Within it, the **Dewan Bandaraya,** or state secretariat, houses the judicial department and high courts. Preservationists fought to have the stylish brick building restored in the early 1980s, and it now also accommodates a small crafts museum, a branch of the national handicrafts center, on the corner of Jalan Tun Perak.

Excursions from Kuala Lumpur

㊲ Batu Caves. These vast caverns in a limestone outcrop are approached by a flight of 272 steps, but the steep climb is worth it. A wide path with an iron railing leads through the recesses of the cavern. Stalagmites, such as the fancifully named Onyx Rock, have been tinted over the years by internal chemical processes and now can be viewed in all their glory. It is here, during January or February, that the spectacular but gory Thaipusam festival (☞ Festivals and Seasonal Events *in* Chapter 1) takes place in its most elaborate form. In the main cave is a **Hindu temple** dedicated to Lord Subramaniam. Behind the **Dark Cave** lies a third cave called the **Art Gallery,** displaying colorful and elaborate sculptures of figures from Hindu mythology. The caves are staggering in their beauty and immensity: The Dark Cave is 366 meters (1,200 feet) long and reaches a height of 122 meters (400 feet). To reach them, take a taxi (about M$35) or a local bus from Pudu Raya Bus Terminal. ⊠ *About 11 km (7 mi) due north of the city.*

㊳ Selangor Pewter Factory. Here, in the world's largest such factory, visitors can see artisans designing the pewter as well as demonstrations of the manufacturing process. At the end of the tour comes the duty-free shop. ⊠ *8 km (5 mi) northeast of Kuala Lumpur.*

Dining and Lodging

$$$ ✕ **Lai Ching Yuen.** Master chef Choi Wai Ki came from Hong Kong to
★ establish Kuala Lumpur's foremost Cantonese restaurant. The extensive menu draws on shark's fin, bird's nest, abalone, pigeon, chicken, and duck, as well as barbecue specialties; the drunken prawns are superb. The elegant dining room is designed as two Chinese pavilions, with illuminated glass etchings, modern Chinese art, silver panels, a Burmese teak ceiling, and silver-and-jade table settings. Traditional music on Malay instruments accompanies dinner. ⊠ *The Regent, 126 Jalan Bukit Bintang,* ☏ *03/241–8000. Reservations essential. Jacket and tie. AE, DC, MC, V.*

$$ ✕ **Coliseum Cafe.** The aroma of countless sizzling steaks—the house
★ specialty—clings to the walls of this old café, established before World War II. Enter through the swing door and hang your jacket and hat on the antique coat hanger. A nostalgic British colonial ambience prevails. The waiters still dress in starched white jackets, though the latter are a bit frayed at the seams. Steaks are served with brussels sprouts, chips, and salad. Crab baked with cheese is another favorite. On Sunday the curry tiffin lunch is not to be missed. ⊠ *98–100 Jalan Tuanku Abdul Rahman,* ☏ *03/292–6270. No credit cards.*

$$ ✕ **Restoran Makanan Laut Selayang.** Dine under the stars on a clear night or inside the zinc-roofed building in an air-conditioned room that seats 30 at three tables. The black chicken soup steamed in a coconut is wonderful. Also good are the deep-fried soft-shell crabs or the prawns fried with butter, milk, and chili. For those into exotica, there are steamed river frogs and soups of squirrel, pigeon, or turtle. For a taste of luxury, try the *fatt thieu cheong* ("monk jumps over the wall"), a soup of shark's fin, sea cucumber, dried scallops, mushrooms, and herbs; this must be ordered in advance. ⊠ *Lot 11, 7½-mi Selayang,* ☎ *03/627–7015. AE, V.*

$$ ✕ **Yazmin.** It's housed in a sparkling white colonial bungalow on shady, sprawling grounds. A cozy kampong-style terrace extension of dark timber with a dried-palm roof offers a buffet lunch and dinner to guests who can also watch traditional Malay dances at night. Within the house, guests dine in a large, airy hall upstairs, whose windows overlook a wonderful bamboo grove at the front. Evocative black-and-white pictures taken by a sultan grace the walls. Unfortunately, Yazmin has gotten on the tour circuit, and some evenings crowds swamp the buffet tables. The best dishes are the *rendang tok* (tender beef chunks simmered in spices and coconut), *roti canai* (unleavened bread), and *rendang pedas udang* (prawns cooked in coconut cream, chili, lemongrass, and turmeric leaves). There is high tea daily and Sunday brunch. ⊠ *6 Jalan Kia Peng,* ☎ *03/241–5655. Reservations essential. AE, DC, MC, V. Closed 4 days at the end of Ramadan.*

$ ✕ **Kedai Makanan Yut Kee.** This 60-year-old family-run coffee shop–restaurant is one of the few that have not been pulled down in the name of progress. Large and airy but rather noisy from the city traffic, the place has marble-top tables and old customers who insist on their favorite seats. Recommended are *roti babi* (a sandwich with pork filling dipped in egg and deep-fried) and *asam* prawns, hot, sour, and fragrant with spices. The local black coffee is the best around, and the kaya Swiss roll makes a fine dessert. Open 7 AM–6 PM. ⊠ *35 Jalan Dang Wangi,* ☎ *03/298–8108. Reservations not accepted. No credit cards. Closed Mon.*

$$$$ 🏨 **Carcosa Seri Negara.** This member of the Amanresorts group is KL's most prestigious address and the priciest—the least expensive room is US$380. On 40 acres of landscaped gardens, the hotel has been converted from the former British Governor's House, with only 13 suites split between the two handsome late-19th-century mansions. The ambience is elegant colonial, with furnishings in Regency style. Every guest gets a personal butler. The sports center, with a small pool, sauna, and gym, is genteel, and dining is a jeweled occasion. ⊠ *Taman Tasik Perdana, 50480 Kuala Lumpur,* ☎ *03/282–1888,* FAX *03/282–7888. 13 suites. Restaurant, tea shop, pool, 2 tennis courts, exercise room, business services. AE, DC, MC, V.*

$$$$ 🏨 **Kuala Lumpur Hilton.** KL's first high-rise luxury hotel still maintains its world-class standards for service and quality. Conveniently located in the Golden Triangle, the hotel offers bird's-eye vistas of the city from its 36th-floor **Paddock Room.** The pastel-decorated rooms have a bay window and sitting area, plus a desk. The **Aviary Bar,** just off the lobby, is a popular meeting lounge, and the **Melaka Grill** offers gourmet dining. The hotel's cosmopolitan reputation is enhanced by an English pub and Chinese, Japanese, and Korean restaurants. ⊠ *Jalan Sultan Ismail, 50250 Kuala Lumpur,* ☎ *03/248–2322,* FAX *03/244–2157. 581 rooms, including executive suites. Restaurants, bar, coffee shop, pool, 2 tennis courts, exercise room, squash, business services, meeting rooms. AE, DC, MC, V.*

$$$$ 🏨 **The Regent.** At KL's leading hotel, a quiet grace permeates the public areas: The marble floors and pillars glisten, and light floods in through the high glass front. Color is everywhere, with flower-filled terraces staggered up from the main lobby. Guest rooms are furnished in soft, elegant hues; the king-size beds come with six fluffy pillows.

There is a desk with a two-line telephone in the triangular bay formed by two windows at right angles; the unusual design fills the rooms with light and provides wide-angled views. Bathrooms have huge tubs and separate showers, terry-cloth robes, and an extravagant array of toiletries. The staff is wonderfully attentive. There are three formal restaurants—Chinese, Japanese, and Continental—and a brasserie. ✉ *126 Jalan Bukit Bintang,* ☎ *03/241–8000 or 800/545–4000,* 🏧 *03/242–1441. 454 rooms. 4 restaurants, coffee shop, tea shop, pool, business services, meeting rooms. AE, DC, MC, V.*

$$$$ 🏨 **Shangri-La.** The smartest and plushest hotel in Kuala Lumpur back in the 1980s, the Shangri-La still has its loyal following and attracts local high society. Its location is prime, right in the heart of the business and shopping district. The spacious and glittering lobby sparkles with jeweled guests. Guest rooms are spacious, some decorated in warm pastels, others with splashes of color and floral designs. All are equipped with every convenience. Ask for a room on the upper floors, since the lower ones can be noisy from street traffic. Though the size of the hotel causes a certain impersonality, service is attentive and efficient. The Chinese restaurant is excellent for a dim sum lunch, and for evening dining on French fare, the **Lafite Restaurant** is hard to beat. For light snacks and a chat, visit the **English Pub.** ✉ *11 Jalan Sultan Ismail, 50250 Kuala Lumpur,* ☎ *03/232–2388,* 🏧 *03/230–1514. 722 rooms. 3 restaurants, outdoor café, coffee shop, pub, room service, pool, 2 tennis courts, exercise room, squash, dance club, laundry service, business services, meeting rooms, travel services. AE, DC, MC, V.*

$$ 🏨 **Concorde Hotel.** Once the government-owned Merlin Hotel, this large, centrally located building has been completely—and impersonally—refurbished. But the rooms are bright and fresh, and the price is right. The large coffee shop has floor-to-ceiling windows, making you feel good at breakfast time while watching the stalled traffic! Next door is the **Hard Rock Café,** offering cheer and conviviality. Pay more for the concierge floor and you'll enjoy more personalized service, including complimentary breakfasts. The large lobby is often filled with tour groups. ✉ *2 Jalan Sultan Ismail, 50250 Kuala Lumpur,* ☎ *03/244–2200,* 🏧 *03/244–1628. 600 rooms, including suites. 3 restaurants, coffee shop, pool, exercise room, 3 concierge floors, parking (fee). AE, DC, MC, V.*

$$ 🏨 **Holiday Inn City Centre.** On the banks of the Gombak River, a good 10-minute walk from the city's main shopping and entertainment area, this inn has suffered from the passage of many tour groups, and, despite refurbishing in 1995, still looks downtrodden. However, for basic Holiday Inn–style amenities at a reasonable price, the hotel delivers. ✉ *12 Jalan Raja Laut, Box 11586, 50750 Kuala Lumpur,* ☎ *03/293–9233 or 800/465–4329,* 🏧 *03/293–9634. 250 rooms. Restaurant, outdoor café, Western coffee shop, pool, exercise room, squash, business services. AE, DC, MC, V.*

$ 🏨 **Lodge Hotel.** Across from the Hilton in the Golden Triangle, this hotel offers basic air-conditioned accommodations. Everything is a little shabby—carpets have stains and bathrooms need some plaster repair—but the rooms are clean and service is friendly. Its coffee shop has been smartened up and stays open 24 hours for nightclub revelers to drop in. ✉ *Jalan Sultan Ismail, 50250 Kuala Lumpur,* ☎ *03/242–0122,* 🏧 *03/241–6819. 50 rooms. Bar, coffee shop, pool. DC, V.*

The West Coast

Numbers in the margin correspond to points of interest on the Peninsular Malaysia map.

Negri Sembilan

64 km (37 mi) south of Kuala Lumpur.

Between Kuala Lumpur and Malacca is an area called Negri Sembilan ("Nine States"). Negri Sembilan is unique in Malaysia, for it's an internal union of ancient states, and it is a matriarchy—tribal lines descend from women rather than from men. **Seremban,** its capital, is a pleasant city with attractive botanical gardens. An old Malay palace has been moved to the gardens and serves as a museum; there also is a reconstructed Malay house, an example of early Minangkabau (or Sumatran) architecture. The people of this area are related to the inhabitants of west Sumatra; homes in both places have the same buffalo-horn-shape peaked roofs.

At **Sri Menanti,** a few miles west of Seremban, is the sultan's headquarters, where both a new and an old *istana* (palace), the latter in Sumatran style, as well as an ancient royal burial ground may be visited. The drive to Sri Menanti takes you through hilly country, where bougainvillea and hibiscus abound. **Port Dickson,** on the coast, is a seaside resort area where casuarina trees line the shore. Near the Malacca border, south of Port Dickson, is **Pengkalan Kempas.** Here are three famous stones, inscribed in cuneiform, that remain an archaeological mystery, and the **tomb of Sheik Ahmad,** dated 1467.

Malacca

155 km (97 mi) south of Kuala Lumpur, 245 km (153 mi) northwest of Singapore.

Malacca (Melaka) was once the most important trading port in Southeast Asia, but it lost out to Raffles's Singapore. After a long period of languishing in the doldrums, Malacca is having a rebirth. Construction has sprawled out along the coast, and a vast land reclamation project is taking place at the mouth of the Melaka River estuary.

Created as the capital of a Malay sultanate, it was captured in 1511 by the Portuguese, who built fortifications and held it until 1641, when the Dutch invaded and took possession. The British took over in Victorian times and remained in control until Malay independence was declared in 1957. It was here, in fact, that the Sultan of Johore, the man who signed over the rights of the island of Singapura (Singapore) in 1819 to Raffles, has his tomb in the **Tranquerah Mosque,** a 150-year-old building of Sumatran design. In this, Malaysia's most historic town, you'll find impressive buildings and ruins dating from all these periods of colonial rule.

One of the oldest of Malacca's Portuguese ruins, dating from 1521, is **St. Paul's Church,** atop Residency Hill. The statue at the summit commemorates St. Francis Xavier, who was buried here before being moved to his permanent resting spot in Goa, India, where he began his missionary career. The **Church of St. Peter**—built in 1710 and now the church of the Portuguese Mission under the jurisdiction of the bishop of Macau—is interesting for its mix of Occidental and Oriental architecture. It is about a half-mile east of the city center, on Jalan Bendahare. The only surviving part of the Portuguese fortress **A Famosa** is the Porta de Santiago entrance gate, which has become the symbol of the state of Malacca. Near the Porta de Santiago, the **Muzium Budaya,** a museum with collections on Muslim culture and royalty, is housed in a re-creation of a traditional wood palace.

The Dutch influence in Malacca is more prevalent. **Christ Church** was built in 1753 of salmon-pink bricks brought from Zeeland (Netherlands) and faced in red laterite. Across the street from Christ Church is the **Stadthuys,** the oldest remaining Dutch architecture in the Orient. This complex of buildings was erected between 1641 and 1660 and used until recently for government offices. It has now been restored and converted into a museum with artifacts on display from both the Dutch and Portuguese eras. The Stadthuys is good and solid, in true Dutch style: Note the thick masonry walls, the heavy hardwood doors, and the windows with wrought-iron hinges.

Malacca's history, of course, predates the arrival of the Western colonialists. Six centuries ago, a Ming emperor's envoy from China set up the first trade arrangements in this ancient Malay capital; a daughter of the emperor was sent to Malacca as wife to Sultan Mansor Shah. She and her 500 ladies-in-waiting set up housekeeping on **Bukit China** (Chinese Hill). The early Chinese traders and notables who lived and died in Malacca were buried on this hill, and their 17,000 graves remain, making Bukit China the largest Chinese cemetery outside China. Stop off at the **Sultan's Well,** at the foot of Bukit China. Tossing a coin into the well—a custom that dates to the founding of Malacca by Raja Iskandar Shah in the 14th century—is said to ensure your return to Malacca.

On the west side of the Melaka River, the **Chinese quarter**—narrow streets lined with traditional shophouses, ancient temples, and clan houses (note the interesting carved doors)—reflects the long Chinese presence. **Cheng Hoon Teng Temple** is one of the city's oldest Chinese temples. You'll recognize it by its ceremonial masts, which tower over roofs of the surrounding old houses, and by the porcelain and glass animals and flowers that decorate its eaves. Built in the Nanking style, the temple embraces three doctrines: Buddhist, Taoist, and Confucian. You can tell the monks apart by their robes; the Taoists expose their right shoulder. On your way out, you can buy sandalwood (the scent that permeates the temple) as well as papier-mâché houses and cars and symbolic money ("hell money"), used to burn as offerings during funeral ceremonies.

Close by on Temple Street are the papier-mâché doll makers, who fashion legendary figures from Chinese mythology. Wander on, turning right onto Jalan Hang Lekiu and right again onto Jalan Hang Jebat, and you'll find good pork satay at No. 83 and several coffee shops selling wonderful noodles. From Jalan Hang Jebat take a left onto Jalan Kubu, then another left onto **Jalan Tun Tan Cheng Lock.** This street was once called "Millionaires Row" for its glorious mansions, built by the Dutch and then taken over by wealthy Babas in the 19th century.

If you have more time, there is more to do. The ferry from Malacca to **Dumai** on Sumatra (Indonesia) takes four hours, costs M$80, and departs (usually) every day at 10 AM. You'll need a visa to enter Indonesia. You can also spend the day picnicking on the little tropical isle of **Pulau Besar,** about 5 kilometers (3 miles) off the mainland in the Straits of Malacca. A boat service from Umbai Jetty costs M$10 per person; or you can charter a boat for around M$80 (☎ 06/261–0492).

To return to Singapore, get back to the toll road expressway and you'll be crossing the causeway within four hours. Buses take about the same time; Malacca does not have a railway station.

Lodging

$$$ 🏨 **Ramada Renaissance.** This 24-story Ramada operates smoothly for
★   both the business traveler and the tourist. The guest rooms are bright, decorated in pastel colors, and equipped with IDD phones, color TV and video, and refrigerator; those overlooking the gardens and shore

are obviously pleasanter than those at the back. In addition to the Renaissance floor, with concierge services, there are two nonsmoking floors. In the evening there is usually live entertainment in the **Famosa Lounge,** and throughout the year the hotel offers various festivities. Special room packages up to 60% less than the listed room rates are sometimes available. ⊠ *Jalan Bendahara, 75100 Melaka,* ☎ *06/284–8888,* ℻ *06/284– 9269. 295 rooms. 2 restaurants, room service, pool, exercise room, squash, dance club, business services, meeting rooms, travel services. AE, DC, MC, V.*

\$\$ ⊞ **City Bayview.** Opened in 1987, this modern 14-story high-rise stands in contrast to the older buildings of Malacca. The look of the hotel is strictly functional, with no personality, but the rooms, with motel-like furniture and IDD phones, are clean and satisfactory. ⊠ *Jalan Bendahara, 75100 Melaka,* ☎ *06/239–7888,* ℻ *06/236–7699. 181 rooms. 2 restaurants, coffee shop, pool, exercise room, nightclub, laundry service, business services, meeting rooms. AE, DC, MC, V.*

¢ ⊞ **Majestic Hotel.** If you are looking for a local hotel where you can settle in to write *the* novel about colonial Malaya, the Majestic has the right ambience. Across from the Melaka River and situated in its own courtyard, the hotel has large, airy public rooms with slow-turning fans. Guest rooms are spartan, with little more than a bed, a table, and a chair; a few have tired air-conditioning instead of fans. ⊠ *188 Bunga Raya Rd., 75100 Melaka,* ☎ *06/222–7387. 20 rooms, some with bath. Breakfast room. No credit cards.*

Peninsular Malaysia A to Z

Arriving and Departing

BY BUS

Buses connect all towns within peninsular Malaysia with great frequency and very inexpensively. Usually more than one bus company makes the same trip. For example, seven companies run hourly service between Kuala Lumpur and Malacca with fares varying only marginally between companies—from a low of M\$6.50 to a high of M\$7.

From Johore Bahru, peninsular Malaysia is your oyster. You can even take a bus all the way up to the Thai border. Buses leave from Bangunan Mara Terminal. One company is **National Express** (☎ 07/234– 494). Sample fares: to KL, M\$15; to Malacca, M\$10.30. Bus service is fast and efficient; departures are frequent. Both air-conditioned and non-air-conditioned buses are available. To reach Johore Bahru for S\$.80 by bus from Singapore, take Bus 170 from Bukit Timah Road (off Newton Circus). **Majulah Travel & Express** (⊠ #01–38 Golden Mile Tower, 6001 Beach Rd., ☎ 291–6533) makes several trips daily to Malacca; the journey takes 2½ hours and costs S\$18.

BY CAR

A rental car is the most convenient way to see West Malaysia. Roads are well paved and well signposted. But be aware that driving here is more freewheeling than in Singapore. To rent a car you need a valid driver's license, a passport, and a credit card for deposits and charges. One-way drop-offs are permitted, with a small surcharge. Check the brakes before you drive away, and make sure there's an inflated spare tire and a jack. And driving is on the left side of the road.

In Malaysia, typical rental rates are M\$125 a day or M\$700 a week, with unlimited mileage. A collision-damage waiver (CDW) insurance premium of M\$10 a day will cover you for the initial M\$2,000 not covered by the insurance included in the basic charge. Singapore rates are significantly higher because of the surcharge imposed for taking the car out of Singapore. For rental agencies in Singapore, *see* Car Rental *in* Important Contacts A to Z. In Johore Bahru, try **Sintat/Thrifty** (☎ 07/332–313) or **Calio Car Rentals and Tours** (☎ 07/233–325). Wearing seat belts is required (fine is M$200), and remember that traffic gives way to the right on rotaries.

Singapore Airlines (in Singapore, ☎ 223–8888; in KL, ☎ 03/292–3122) and **Malaysia Airlines** (in Singapore, ☎ 336–6777; in KL, ☎ 03/746–3000) have frequent service between Singapore and Kuala Lumpur's Subang Airport; they also serve many other destinations on the peninsula, including Johore Bahru, Kuantan, and Penang. **Pelangi Air** (☎ 03/746–3000) has 45-minute flights from Singapore to Malacca, and **Silk Air** (⊠ SIA Bldg., 77 Robinson Rd., ☎ 322–6881) flies to Tioman Island, Kuantan, and Langkawi. Sample times and prices from Singapore: to Kuala Lumpur, 50 minutes, S$130 (S$90 if you go standby); to Kuantan, 45 minutes, S$120. From Johore Bahru to KL or to Kuantan, the fare is M$77, so you might consider crossing the causeway by bus and flying out of Johore Bahru if you're interested in saving money. To Tioman Island from Singapore on **Silk Air** is S$110.

Malaysian Railways operates four trains a day from Singapore's Keppel Station (☎ 222–5165). These trains go up Malaysia's west coast to Kuala Lumpur. From Singapore, the fare for the 7-hour run to Kuala Lumpur is M$60 first class/M$26 second class (day runs), and M$80 first class/M$40 second class (berth bunks). There is also the mail train (third class), which makes the run twice a day for M$14.80. Malayan Railways also offers a KTM Railpass, which gives unlimited first-class train travel in Malaysia and Singapore: US$55 for 10 days and US$120 for 30 days. There is no train to Malacca nor to Kuantan.

In addition, there is the luxury train, the **Eastern and Orient Express,** which operates a weekly service between Singapore and Bangkok via peninsular Malaysia and Thailand (☎ 227–2068 for reservations). The carriages are opulent, the meals refined, the service courteous—all of which the S$1,840 minimum fare for the three-day-and-two-night run up to Bangkok more than reflects. A Sunday day run from Singapore to Kuala Lumpur costs a more modest S$640.

Currency
At press time, the Malaysian ringgit, also known as a Malay dollar, was M$2.51 to US$1; M$3.98 to £1.

Getting Around
Shared taxis, a popular form of transportation between cities, are usually available at bus stations. Private taxis can cost up to four times more. A private ride from Johore Bahru to Mersing can cost M$10; from Mersing to Kuantan, M$15; from Kuantan to Kuala Lumpur, M$23; from Kuala Lumpur to Malacca, M$15; and from Malacca to Johore Bahru, M$14.

Guided Tours
Scenic Travel (⊠ #01–02, 110 Killiney Rd., ☎ 02/733–8688) is one Singapore company offering excursions into peninsular Malaysia. Among its choices are three-day, two-night excursions to either Kuantan (including a visit to Cherating village, a kampong that sells beautiful pandan and mengjuang mats, hats, baskets, etc.) or Malacca. For other companies, *see* Sightseeing *in* Important Contacts A to Z.

A number of local companies offer sightseeing tours of Kuala Lumpur and excursions into the nearby countryside. The **Tourist Development**

Corporation (✉ 26th floor, Menara Dato Onn, Putra World Trade Centre, Jalan Tun Ismail, ☎ 03/293–5188) has a list of licensed tour operators, and brochures are available in hotel lobbies and at travel agencies.

Passports and Visas

Passports but no visas are required for citizens of Great Britain, Canada, or the United States wishing to enter Malaysia for less than three months.

Visitor Information

Free maps and information are available at the Singapore office of the **Malaysian Tourist Promotion Board** (✉ #01–06 Ocean Bldg., 10 Collyer Quay, ☎ 532–6321). For those heading to Sarawak rather than peninsular Malaysia, there is the **Sarawak Tourism Centre** (✉ #08–07 Yen San Bldg., 268 Orchard Rd., Singapore 0923, ☎ 736–1602), with maps, brochures, and an unhelpful staff. In the United States, contact the **Malaysian Tourist Promotion Board** (✉ 818 W. 7th St., Los Angeles, CA 90017, ☎ 213/689–9702, 212/754–1113, or 800/558–6787).

When to Go

The monsoon months—from November through January on the east coast, from May through August on the west—can be very wet. However, even then the sun pokes through the clouds most days. Temperatures are 70°F–90°F year-round, and the humidity is always high. March and April are the ideal travel times.

9 Portraits of Singapore

From Lion City to Asian Tiger

The Peoples of Singapore

A Nation of Contradictions

FROM LION CITY TO ASIAN TIGER: A BRIEF HISTORY

MODERN SINGAPORE dates its history from the early morning of January 29, 1819, when a representative of the British East India Company, Thomas Stamford Raffles, stepped ashore at the mouth of the Singapore River, beginning the process that would quickly turn a sleepy backwater into one of Asia's main commercial and financial centers. But let us go a bit farther back.

The Early Days

Though little is known of Singapore's early history, it is clear that by the 7th century AD Malays had a settlement here known as Temasek—"sea town." According to legend, a 13th-century prince of Palembang (Sumatra) landed on the island while seeking shelter from a storm and sighted a strange animal, which he believed to be a lion but was more likely a tiger. The prince subsequently fought and defeated the ruler of the settlement and proclaimed himself king, then renamed the island Singa Pura, Sanskrit for "lion city." (More appropriately, Singapore is today referred to as one of the Asian Tigers, in recognition of its economic success.)

The first recorded history of Singapore, from a Chinese chronicler who visited in 1330, describes a thriving Malay settlement. By the 14th century, Singa Pura had become an active trading city important and wealthy enough to build a walled fortress—and to make others covet the island. Drawn into a battle between the Java-based Majapahit empire and the Siamese kingdom for control of the Malay Peninsula, Singa Pura was destroyed and the settlement abandoned to the jungle.

In 1390 or so, Iskandar Shah (or Parameswara, as the Portuguese called him), another Palembang prince, broke from the Majapahit empire and was granted asylum on the island. After killing the local chieftain, he installed himself as ruler but was driven out before long by the Javanese and fled north into the peninsula. Singa Pura became a Thai vassal state until it was claimed by the Malacca Sultanate, which Iskandar Shah had established and brought to great prominence a few years after fleeing the island.

When, in 1511, the Portuguese seized Malacca, the Malay admiral fled to Singa Pura and established a new capital at Johor Lama. Obscurity engulfed Singa Pura in 1613, when the Portuguese reported laying waste to a small Malay settlement at the mouth of the river.

Enter Raffles

With the development of shipping routes to the West around the Cape of Good Hope and the opening of China to trade, the Malay Peninsula became strategically and commercially important to the West. To protect its shipping interests, the British secured Penang in 1786 and threw the Dutch out of Malacca in 1795. (The Dutch had thrown the Portuguese out earlier.) In 1818, to prevent any further northward expansion by the Dutch, who controlled the East Indies (now Indonesia), Lord Hastings, governor-general of India, gave tacit approval to Thomas Stamford Raffles, an employee of the British East India Company, to secure a British trading settlement and harbor on the southern part of the Malay Peninsula.

On January 29, 1819, Raffles made an exploratory visit to Singa Pura, which had come under the dominion of the Sultan of Johore. When Raffles arrived, the two sons of the previous sultan, who had died six years earlier, were in dispute over who would inherit the throne. Raffles backed the claim of the elder brother, Tunku Hussein Mohamed Shah, and proclaimed him sultan.

Offering to support the new sultanate with British military strength, Raffles persuaded the sultan to grant the British a lease allowing them to establish a trading post on the island in return for an annual rent; within a week the negotiations were concluded. (A later treaty ceded the island outright to the British in return for increased pensions and cash payments for the sultan and his island representative.)

Thus began the continual rapid changing and adapting that characterizes Singapore to this day: Within three years, the small fishing village, surrounded by swamps and jungle and populated by only tigers and 200 or so Malays, had become a boomtown of 10,000 immigrants, administered by 74 British employees of the East India Company. In 1826 Singapore joined Penang and Malacca in Malaya to form the British India–controlled Straits Settlements (named for the Strait of Malacca, also called the Straits—the channel between Sumatra and the Malay Peninsula that connects the Indian Ocean with the South China Sea). In 1867 the Straits Settlements became a crown colony.

As colonial administrators and businessmen, the British led a segregated life, maintaining the British lifestyle and shielding themselves from the local population and the climate. In the humid tropical heat, they would promenade along the Padang (cricket green), men in high-collared, buttoned-up white linen suits and women in grand ensembles complete with corsets, petticoats, and long kid gloves. In part, they believed that maintaining a distance and the appearance of invulnerability would help them win the respect and fear of the locals. Indeed, the heavily outnumbered colonials needed all the respect they could muster. But holding on to familiar ways also gave the colonials a sense of security in this foreign land where danger was never far away—in the mid-1850s, for example, five people a week were carried off by tigers.

As Singapore grew, the British erected splendid public buildings, churches (including St. Andrew's Cathedral, built to resemble Netley Abbey in Hampshire, England), and hotels, often using Indian convicts for labor. The Muslim, Hindu, Taoist, and Buddhist communities—swelling rapidly from the influx of fortune-seeking settlers from Malaya, India, and South China—built mosques, temples, and shrines. Magnificent houses for wealthy merchants sprang up, and the harbor became lined with *godowns* (warehouses) to hold all the goods passing through the port.

It was certainly an exotic trade that poured through Singapore. Chinese junks came loaded with tea, porcelain, silks, and artworks; Bugis (Indonesian) schooners carried in cargoes of precious spices, rare tropical hardwoods, camphor, and produce from all parts of Indonesia. These goods, and more like them from Siam (now Thailand), the Philippines, and elsewhere in the region, were traded in Singapore for manufactured textiles, coal, iron, cement, weapons, machinery, and other fruits of Europe's industrial revolution. Another major product traded here by the British was opium, grown in India and sold to the Chinese.

Meanwhile, much of the island was still covered by thick jungle. As late as the 1850s, there were dozens of tigers still to be found here. Early experiments with agriculture (spices, cotton, coffee, and the like) were soon abandoned, as almost nothing except coconuts would grow successfully in the sandy and marshy soil. (Singapore does, however, have the distinction of having introduced the rubber plant to Malaya: In 1877 the first seedlings were successfully grown here by botanist H. N. Ridley, then director of Singapore's Botanic Gardens, from plants brought out of Brazil.)

With the advent of steamships (which found Singapore's deep-water harbor ideal) and the opening of the Suez Canal in 1869, the port thrived as the "Gateway to the East." Its position at the southern end of the Straits made it a vital link in the chain of ports and coaling stations for steamers. Shipyards were established to repair the oceangoing cargo carriers and to build the ever-increasing number of barges and lighters bringing cargo ashore to the godowns. With the development of the rubber industry in Malaya starting in the 1870s, Singapore became the world's top exporter of the commodity.

The 20th Century

By the turn of the century, Singapore had become the entrepôt of the East, a mixture of adventurers and "respectable middle classes." World War I hardly touched the island, although its defenses were strengthened to support the needs of the British navy, for which Singapore was an important base. Until 1921 the Japanese and the British were allies and no need was felt to maintain a large naval presence in the region, but then the United States, anxious about Japan's growing military strength, prevailed on Britain to cancel its treaty with the Japanese, and defense of Singapore became a priority. A massive military expansion took place: Barracks were created for up to 100,000 troops, and Sentosa Island was heavily fortified with huge naval guns.

As the likelihood of war in the Pacific grew, Singapore's garrison was further strengthened, and naval shipyards and airfields were constructed. The British were complacent about the impregnability of Singapore, expecting that any attack would come from the sea and assuming that they were well prepared to meet such an attack. But the Japanese landed to the north, in Malaya. The two British battleships that had been posted to Singapore were sunk, and the Japanese land forces raced down the peninsula on bicycles.

When the Japanese made their first bombing runs on Singapore, all the city's lights were on. The key to turn off the switch was in the governor's pocket, and he was at the movies. The big guns on Sentosa Island sat idle, trained vainly on the quiet sea; they were not designed to fire on land forces. In February 1942 the Japanese captured Singapore.

Huge numbers of Allied civilians and military were sent to Changi Prison; others were marched off to prison camps in Malaya or to work on the notorious "Death Railway" in Thailand. The 3½ years of occupation was a time of privation and fear for the civilian population; up to 100,000 deaths are estimated during this period. The Japanese surrendered on August 21, 1945, and the Allied military forces returned to Singapore. However, the security of the British Empire was never again to be felt, and independence for British Southeast Asia was only a matter of time.

Military control of Singapore ended in 1946. The former Straits Settlements crown colony was dissolved, and the island became a separate crown colony, with a partially elected legislative council representing various elements of the community. The first election was held in 1948. In the 1950s, the degree of autonomy allowed Singapore increased and various political parties were formed. One of these was the People's Action Party (PAP), established in 1954 under the leadership of a young Chinese lawyer, Lee Kuan Yew, who had recently graduated from Oxford.

In 1957 the British government agreed to the establishment of an elected 51-member legislative assembly. General elections in 1959 gave an overwhelming majority—43 of 51 seats—to the PAP, and Lee Kuan Yew became Singapore's first prime minister. In 1963 Singapore became part of the Federation of Malaysia, along with the newly independent state of Malaysia.

Mainly due to the Malays' anxiety over a possible takeover by the ethnic Chinese, the federation did not work. When it broke up two years later, Singapore became an independent sovereign state (its independence day—August 9, called National Day—is celebrated each year in grand style). In 1967 Singapore issued its own currency for the first time, and in the general election of 1968 the PAP won all 58 seats in Parliament.

In 1971 the last of the British military forces left the island. The economic future of the nation seemed unsure: How could it survive without the massive British military expenditure? But Singapore did more than survive—it boomed. The government engaged in programs for rapid modernization of the nation's infrastructure to attract foreign investment and to help its businesses compete in world markets.

The electorate stayed faithful to Lee Kuan Yew and the PAP, returning the party almost unchallenged in one election after another. It was something of a surprise when, at a by-election in 1981, a single opposition member, Indian lawyer J. B. Jeyaretnam, was elected to Parliament, followed by a second non-PAP member in the general election of 1984. Today the PAP's popular majority is the lowest it has ever been. Nevertheless, the party is still sufficiently entrenched to hold all but a few of the parliamentary seats. Lee has stepped down from the all-powerful post of prime minister, but as elder statesman ("senior minister") he still acts as the guiding hand behind the PAP and, hence, the government. In recent years he has encouraged freer expression (to some extent, at least), and consequently more and more citizens have begun voicing their criticism of the government's sometimes heavy-handed dictates.

THE PEOPLES OF SINGAPORE

MODERN SINGAPOREANS are proud of their nation's multiracial heritage. In 1911 the census found 48 races speaking 54 languages, though some of these races have dwindled since then. Once 5,000 strong, the Armenian community, which built the Armenian Apostolic Church of St. Gregory in 1835, numbers fewer than 50 today. The Sephardic Jews, mostly from India and Iran, have moved out of Singapore to Israel, Australia, and elsewhere; just two synagogues, one on Waterloo Street and one on Oxley Rise, survive. The fortunes amassed by Bugis from the Celebes (now Sulawesi) in Indonesia—pirates before Raffles arrived, later turned real-estate investors—have passed into the hands of the few Bugis families who remain.

Still, numerous ethnic communities exist: Filipinos, Japanese, and Thais, Germans, Swiss, and Italians. There are also about 20,000 Eurasians—half British, Dutch, or Portuguese; half Filipino, Chinese, Malay, Indian, Thai, Sri Lankan, or Indonesian. An overwhelming 97% of the population, however, come from among just three ethnic groups: Chinese, Malay, and Indian. It had been Lee's wish to make Singapore multiracial, but increasingly in his later years Lee has spoken of Singapore as a Sinic society and sought immigrants from Hong Kong.

The Chinese

Raffles had one ambition for Singapore—to make it a thriving trading port that would secure British interests in the Orient and undermine the Dutch. To achieve these goals, he made the island a free port. Traders flocked to Singapore, and soon so did thousands of Chinese in search of work. Every year during the northeast monsoon, junks crammed to the gunnels with half-starved Chinese would ride the winds to Singapore. Many arrived intent only on saving money and then returning to their families on mainland China. However, most did not make the return journey.

These immigrants were from many different ethnic groups with different languages, different foods, different clothes, and often different religions. Each group carved out its own section of Chinatown, the part of Singapore that Raffles's master plan (drawn up with the intention of avoiding racial tensions) had allotted the Chinese, and there they lived basically separate lives.

The largest group of immigrants was the **Hokkien,** traders and merchants from southern Fukien Province, who now make up 43% of the Chinese population and still work predominantly as merchants. The early arrivals settled in Amoy Street. One of Singapore's oldest temples, the Temple of Heavenly Happiness, was built in 1841 by Hokkien immigrants in honor of the goddess of the sea, and here they made offerings in thanks for their safe voyage.

On Philip Street in Chinatown is the Wak Hai Cheng Bio Temple, also dedicated to a goddess of the sea. It was built by the **Teochews,** the second-largest immigrant group (constituting 22% of Singapore's Chinese), who came from the Swatow region in Guangdong Province. The temple suggests one of their chosen professions—they dominate the port and maritime labor force—but they also make a strong showing as cooks.

The **Cantonese** are the third-largest group, making up 16.5% of the Chinese population. They are often artisans and craftsmen. Their Fuk Tak Chi Temple on Telok Ayer Street is dedicated to Tua Pek Kong, who can bring prosperity and safety to a voyage. Southern neighbors of the Teochews on the mainland, the Cantonese dedicate enormous amounts of time and energy to eating. Three-fourths of all the Chinese restaurants in Singapore serve Cantonese food.

The **Hakka**—who had lived a nomadic existence in Fukien, Guangdong, and Szechuan provinces—remember old times at the Ying He Hui Guan (Hakka Clan Association Hall), just off Telok Ayer Street, which served as a sort of foster home for immigrants stepping off the junks a century ago. The **Hainanese,** many of whom work in hotel or domestic service, were employed as cooks by the colonials (you'll often see "breaded pork cutlet" on the menus at Hainanese restaurants).

By the 1920s, the number of **Straits Chinese**—those born in Singapore or in Malaya—exceeded the number of mainland-born Chinese in Singapore. Though some continued to consider themselves "overseas Chinese," an increasing number began to recognize Singapore as their home. The Straits Chinese British Association (formed at the turn of the century) served as a forum for exchanging views on Singapore's future and, unofficially, worked alongside the colonial administration in the island's development. Chinese families that had made fortunes in the 19th century began sending their children to British universities. These graduates became businessmen, politicians, and statesmen. Today Chinese constitute 76% of Singapore's total population.

One of Singapore's most interesting aspects is the more than two dozen **festivals** celebrated so colorfully each year, and more than half of these are Chinese, based on traditions brought over from the mainland. Even the keenest Chinese businessman does not discount *joss*—fortune—and festivals are considered important in ensuring good joss, by appeasing ancestral spirits during the Festival of the Hungry Ghosts, celebrating the birthday of the mischievous Monkey God, or ushering in the Chinese New Year.

The Malays

When Raffles landed on the island in 1819, there were perhaps 100 Malay houses in a small fishing village on the banks of the Singapore River. Aside from the Malays, there were about 30 *orang laut* (sea gypsies) living farther upriver in houseboats. (The orang laut, aborigines from Johore, were later decimated by an epidemic of smallpox, but there were still families living in waterborne settlements until after the Second World War. Since then they have come ashore, intermarried with Malays, and become mainstream Singaporean.)

To help develop Singapore as a free port, the East India Company encouraged Malays to migrate from the peninsula. By 1824 their numbers had grown to more than 5,000, and today Malays account for 15% of Singapore's ethnic mix.

Malays, in contrast to the Chinese, did not adapt to the freewheeling entrepreneurial spirit that engulfed Singapore. Overwhelmingly Muslim, they sought fulfillment in serving the community and winning its respect rather than in profit making. Their lives traditionally centered on the *kampong*, or village, where the family houses are built around a central compound and food is grown for communal use. Kampongs have mostly disappeared from Singapore, but one does remain on the island of Pulau Sakeng. If you visit this island, you will immediately feel the pervasive community spirit and the warmth extended to visitors. With luck, you may even get to witness the traditional Malay sport called *sepak tatraw*—similar to badminton, except that the feet, arms, and body are used instead of rackets.

The early Malays chose to be fishermen, woodcutters, or carpenters rather than capitalists, and today they continue to concentrate on the community and their relationship with Allah. (No visitor to Singapore can fail to hear the plaintive call to prayer five times a day from the Sultan Mosque, whose gold-painted domes and minarets tower above the shophouses.) Hence, wealth and power have, for the most part, eluded the Malay community.

Still, the culture has infiltrated all aspects of Singapore life. Though there are four "official" languages—Malay, Mandarin, Tamil, and English—Malay is the national language, used, for example, in the national anthem, "Majulah Singapura" (May Singapore Prosper). Singaporeans have incorporated Malay food into their cooking as well. Nonya (Malay for "woman" or "wife"), or Peranakan, cuisine is one aspect of the blending of Chinese and Malay cultures, featuring Chinese ingredients prepared with local spices.

The Indians

At least seven centuries before Christ, Indian merchants were crossing the Bay of Bengal to trade in Malaya. Some settled in, and their success in trade made them respected members of the community. Hindu words were absorbed into the Malay language; Singapore's name, in fact, derives from the Sanskrit *singa pura* ("lion city").

With success stories floating back to the Indian subcontinent, little encouragement was needed to entice other Indians to seek their fortunes in the new Singapore. Some, however, had no choice. Seeing a way of both ridding Calcutta of its miscreants and building an infrastructure in Singapore, the East India Company sent Indian convicts to the island in chains and put them to work draining marshes and erecting bridges, churches, and other public buildings. For themselves, the Indians built Sri Mariamman, Singapore's oldest and most important Hindu temple, in 1862 (it has since been expanded and repainted).

In fact, serving time in Singapore during the mid-19th century was not so bad. The convicts were encouraged to learn a trade, and often, after their term was served, they opted to stay. Many Tamils from South India went as indentured laborers to work Malaya's rubber plantations and, when their time was up, moved to Singapore.

The majority of Indians in Singapore are, in fact, Hindu Tamils from South India. There are also Muslims from South India and, in smaller numbers, Bengalis, Biharis, Gujaratis, Marathis, Kashmiris, and Punjabis, from the north, west, and east of India. From Sri Lanka come other Hindu Tamils, as well as the Sinhalese (often mistaken for Indians), who are neither Hindu nor Muslim but follow the gentle teachings of Hinayana Buddhism. The Sinhalese traditionally work in jewelry and precious gems; incidentally, they are among Singapore's finest cricket players—witness their domination of the teams playing at the prestigious Singapore Cricket Club.

During the colonial period, the Indians in Singapore regarded India, and more particularly their region, as their true home. They would send money back to their families and dream of returning. Of all the immigrant groups, they were the least committed to the future of Singapore. When the Japanese occupied the island in World War II, some 20,000 Singaporean Indians volunteered for the Japanese Indian National Army, led by Subhas Chandra Bose, which took advantage of local sentiment and Japanese expansionist goals in an attempt to evict the British from India. This collaboration left Singapore's Chinese and Malay communities—both of which had suffered greatly at the hands of the Japanese—distrustful of the Indians. However, India, after independence, actively discouraged expatriates from returning.

Today, Indians, who account for 7% of Singapore's population, increasingly see themselves as Singaporean. Their respect for education has taken them into the influential professions of law, medicine, and government. Nevertheless, the Tamil-language newspaper gives more space to events in South India than to local events, and Indians remain deeply tied to their community and traditional customs. Hinduism remains a powerful force—Singapore has more than 20 major temples devoted to Hindu gods—and some of the Tamil Hindu festivals (such as Thaipusam) are expressed with more feverish ritualism than in India. Indian food, too, remains true to its roots; it has been said that one can eat better curries in Singapore than in India.

A NATION OF CONTRADICTIONS

FROM ECONOMICS TO FOOD, Singapore is a nation of contradictions. Except for Japan, it has the best-educated, most knowledgeable, and most worldly-wise society in Asia, but the government still tries in many ways to regulate its citizens' lives. Although Singapore has no enemies—Communism no longer poses a threat, and the island's relations with its immediate neighbors, Malaysia and Indonesia, are vastly improved—it continues to maintain one of the largest armies in the world proportionate to population and has a ruthlessly efficient and intrusive intelligence agency, the Internal Security Department, or ISD, which is tireless in its pursuit of dissent. Despite the fact that Singapore is a bastion of capitalism, the government owns many of the largest local companies and frequently interferes with economic decisions. The government is so prudish that it bans *Cosmopolitan* as well as *Playboy,* yet the national airline promotes itself with slogans on the order of "Singapore Girl you're a great way to fly." And although Singapore has many "hawker centers," each with an ethnic mélange of food stalls, which offer some of the best street food in the world, young Singaporeans flock to American fast-food restaurants. . . .

For any Westerner accustomed to Asian cities choked by pollution, traffic jams, and snarled communications, Singapore is an oasis. The airport is so efficient, the taxis are so numerous, and the roads are so good that a visitor arriving at Changi Airport, on the eastern tip of the island, twelve miles from downtown, can reach his hotel room there 30 minutes after stepping off the plane. That visitor can drink water from the tap; get business cards, eyeglasses, or a tailor-made suit the day after placing an order; and ride a modern subway system whose underground stations as well as its trains are air-conditioned. An international phone call can be directdialed as quickly in Singapore as in the United States. Business can be conducted in English, because it is the language that all the schools use. (Only one out of five

Singaporeans speaks English at home, though.) While the dreary high-rise buildings convey no atmosphere, Singapore has retained enough greenery to make it a pleasant city for walking. Every block has trees and flowers; the island's entire east coast, facing the South China Sea, is a string of parks and beaches, and only half an hour from downtown are a nature preserve and some semirural areas with farms. No litter mars a walk through Singapore's streets, because a litterbug must pay a fine of up to US$700 and undergo counseling. (Cigarette butts count as litter, and many of Singapore's litter baskets—there are 45,000 of them—are equipped with ashtrays.) Everything in Singapore is clean; everything in Singapore works.

In a nation known for efficiency, the government is most efficient of all. In other parts of Asia, government services can take an eternity to arrive and then come bound in red tape, the instrument for cutting the tape being a bribe. But in Singapore when someone calls to report a pothole, the Public Works Department fills it within 48 hours. The Telecommunication Authority will install a new phone the day after the order is received. Secretaries are so conscientious that a journalist gets unsolicited wakeup calls to make sure he'll be on time for early-morning interviews with their bosses. A bribe, whether a little tip to an employee or a large payoff to a high-ranking minister, represents a ticket to jail. A postman was once arrested for accepting a gift of one Singapore dollar—equal [at the time] to 62 American cents. A civil servant who receives a present in the mail must send it to a government agency, which puts a price tag on it and then offers to sell it back to the recipient. If the employee doesn't want to buy it, the gift is sold at an auction. Such is the shame attached to corruption that in 1986, when the minister of national development was accused of accepting a bribe to save private land from government acquisition, he committed suicide.

The government of Singapore, ever fearful of snakes in its capitalist Garden of Eden, loves to make rules. The walls of buildings are plastered with rules, telling people what they can't do and how much they have to pay if they dare to try it. The fines represent considerably more than a slap on the wrist, and they're enforced often enough to make most potential miscreants think twice. . . . Few proscribed activities are left to the imagination, as opposed to being posted; for example, in the Botanical Gardens, where "Prohibited" signs threaten to outnumber plant-identification markers, a pictograph warns against shooting at birds with slingshots. Nor do violations always depend for discovery on a passing policeman. Trucks and commercial vans are required to install a yellow roof light that flashes when the vehicle exceeds the speed limit. When a taxi exceed the maximum speed on freeways of 48 miles an hour, loud chimes go off inside; the chimes are so annoying that the driver is likely to slow down. At some intersections, cameras photograph the license plates of cars that pass through as the light is changing to red; the drivers receive bills for that offense in the mail.

TODAY, SINGAPORE is a city with almost no poverty. Hong Kong may have grown as rapidly, but in Hong Kong the gap between rich and poor is visible everywhere. By contrast, I never saw anyone in Singapore shabbily dressed, and everyone appeared to have at least a passable place to live. Food is cheap and plentiful. Even low-income Singaporeans have access to high-quality medical care; doctors at public hospitals in the United States might look enviously at the public wards of Singapore General Hospital.

But Singapore was not always so prosperous or so tidy. When Lee Kuan Yew [who was prime minister from 1959 until he stepped behind the scenes in 1990] took power, he found himself governing a mosquito-infested swamp dotted with pig and chicken farms, fishing villages, and squatter colonies of

tin-roofed shacks. The streets of the central city were lined with shophouses—mostly two-story buildings with ornate façades. A family would operate a business on the ground floor and live on the second floor. Often without plumbing and electricity, and housing as many as 10 people to a room, the shophouses may have presented a picturesque sight for tourists, but they were far less agreeable for their occupants. "The Chinese, who constitute the main current of the city, live in utter filth and poverty," *Asia Scene,* a travel magazine, reported in 1960. "Their poverty is phenomenal. One must see with his own eyes to believe it." Compounding the problem of poverty were racial and political tensions, coming both from the Malay minority and from young Chinese infused with the ideals of the Maoist revolution; these tensions frequently spilled out into the streets.

In not much more than a decade, Singaporeans were passing from poverty to affluence, and the nation's economy from a basket case to the powerhouse of southern Asia. The explanation for this transformation, as for nearly everything else that happens in Singapore, rests with Lee Kuan Yew. Lee has put his stamp on Singapore to an extent that few political leaders anywhere in the world have ever matched. Tough and authoritarian although operating under a pretense of democracy, uninterested in personal wealth among a people who devote their lives to financial gain, often rude and contemptuous in a country that runs annual campaigns promoting the virtues of courtesy, Lee embodies as many contradictions as does Singapore itself.

— Stan Sesser

Stan Sesser has written extensively about Southeast Asia. While researching the article from which this essay is excerpted, he interviewed Lee Kuan Yew twice. The article, which originally appeared in *The New Yorker,* is reprinted in Sesser's *The Lands of Charm and Cruelty: Travels in Southeast Asia.*

NOTES

NOTES

NOTES

NOTES

NOTES

NOTES

NOTES

Fodor's Travel Publications

Available at bookstores everywhere, or call 1–800–533–6478, 24 hours a day.

Gold Guides

U.S.

Alaska

Arizona

Boston

California

Cape Cod, Martha's
Vineyard, Nantucket

The Carolinas & the
Georgia Coast

Chicago

Colorado

Florida

Hawai'i

Las Vegas,
Reno, Tahoe

Los Angeles

Maine, Vermont,
New Hampshire

Maui & Lāna'i

Miami & the Keys

New England

New Orleans

New York City

Pacific North Coast

Philadelphia &
the Pennsylvania
Dutch Country

The Rockies

San Diego

San Francisco

Santa Fe, Taos,
Albuquerque

Seattle & Vancouver

The South

U.S. & British
Virgin Islands

USA

Virginia & Maryland

Washington, D.C.

Foreign

Australia

Austria

The Bahamas

Belize & Guatemala

Bermuda

Canada

Cancún, Cozumel,
Yucatán Peninsula

Caribbean

China

Costa Rica

Cuba

The Czech Republic
& Slovakia

Eastern &
Central Europe

Europe

Florence, Tuscany
& Umbria

France

Germany

Great Britain

Greece

Hong Kong

India

Ireland

Israel

Italy

Japan

London

Madrid & Barcelona

Mexico

Montréal &
Québec City

Moscow, St.
Petersburg, Kiev

The Netherlands,
Belgium &
Luxembourg

New Zealand

Norway

Nova Scotia, New
Brunswick, Prince
Edward Island

Paris

Portugal

Provence &
the Riviera

Scandinavia

Scotland

Singapore

South Africa

South America

Southeast Asia

Spain

Sweden

Switzerland

Thailand

Tokyo

Toronto

Turkey

Vienna & the Danube

Fodor's Special-Interest Guides

Alaska Ports of Call

Caribbean Ports
of Call

The Complete Guide
to America's
National Parks

Disney Like a Pro

Family Adventures

Fodor's Gay Guide
to the USA

Halliday's New
England Food
Explorer

Halliday's New
Orleans Food
Explorer

Healthy Escapes

Kodak Guide to
Shooting Great Travel
Pictures

Nights to Imagine

Rock & Roll
Traveler USA

Sunday in New York

Sunday in
San Francisco

Walt Disney World for
Adults

Walt Disney World,
Universal Studios
and Orlando

Wendy Perrin's Secrets
Every Smart Traveler
Should Know

Where Should We
Take the Kids?
California

Where Should We
Take the Kids?
Northeast

Worldwide Cruises
and Ports of Call

Special Series

Affordables

Caribbean
Europe
Florida
France
Germany
Great Britain
Italy
London
Paris

Fodor's Bed & Breakfasts and Country Inns

America
California
The Mid-Atlantic
New England
The Pacific Northwest
The South
The Southwest
The Upper Great Lakes

The Berkeley Guides

California
Central America
Eastern Europe
Europe
France
Germany & Austria
Great Britain & Ireland
Italy
London
Mexico
New York City
Pacific Northwest & Alaska
Paris
San Francisco

Compass American Guides

Arizona
Canada
Chicago
Colorado
Hawaii
Idaho
Hollywood
Las Vegas

Maine
Manhattan
Montana
New Mexico
New Orleans
Oregon
San Francisco
Santa Fe
South Carolina
South Dakota
Southwest
Texas
Utah
Virginia
Washington
Wine Country
Wisconsin
Wyoming

Fodor's Citypacks

Atlanta
Hong Kong
London
New York City
Paris
Rome
San Francisco
Washington, D.C.

Fodor's Español

California
Caribe Occidental
Caribe Oriental
Gran Bretaña
Londres
Mexico
Nueva York
Paris

Fodor's Exploring Guides

Australia
Boston & New England
Britain
California
Caribbean
China
Egypt
Florence & Tuscany
Florida

France
Germany
Ireland
Israel
Italy
Japan
London
Mexico
Moscow & St. Petersburg
New York City
Paris
Prague
Provence
Rome
San Francisco
Scotland
Singapore & Malaysia
Spain
Thailand
Turkey
Venice

Fodor's Flashmaps

Boston
New York
San Francisco
Washington, D.C.

Fodor's Pocket Guides

Acapulco
Atlanta
Barbados
Jamaica
London
New York City
Paris
Prague
Puerto Rico
Rome
San Francisco
Washington, D.C.

Mobil Travel Guides

America's Best Hotels & Restaurants
California & the West
Frequent Traveler's Guide to Major Cities
Great Lakes
Mid-Atlantic

Northeast
Northwest & Great Plains
Southeast
Southwest & South Central

Rivages Guides

Bed and Breakfasts of Character and Charm in France
Hotels and Country Inns of Character and Charm in France
Hotels and Country Inns of Character and Charm in Italy
Hotels and Country Inns of Character and Charm in Paris
Hotels and Country Inns of Character and Charm in Portugal
Hotels and Country Inns of Character and Charm in Spain

Short Escapes

Britain
France
New England
Near New York City

Fodor's Sports

Golf Digest's Best Places to Play
Skiing USA
USA Today
The Complete Four Sport Stadium Guide

Fodor's Vacation Planners

Great American Learning Vacations
Great American Sports & Adventure Vacations
Great American Vacations
Great American Vacations for Travelers with Disabilities
National Parks and Seashores of the East
National Parks of the West

WHEREVER YOU TRAVEL, *H*ELP IS NEVER FAR AWAY.

From planning your trip to providing travel assistance along the way, American Express® Travel Service Offices are always there to help.

Singapore

American Express Travel Service
#01-04/05, Winsland House
3 Killiney Road
Singapore
235-5788

Travel

http://www.americanexpress.com/travel